David Cunningham

Conditions of Social Well-Being

Or, inquiries into the material and moral postition of the populations of Europe and

America, with particular reference to those of Great Britain and Ireland

David Cunningham

Conditions of Social Well-Being
Or, inquiries into the material and moral postition of the populations of Europe and America, with particular reference to those of Great Britain and Ireland

ISBN/EAN: 9783337322960

Printed in Europe, USA, Canada, Australia, Japan

Cover: Foto ©Suzi / pixelio.de

More available books at **www.hansebooks.com**

CONDITIONS

OF

SOCIAL WELL-BEING

OR

INQUIRIES INTO THE MATERIAL AND MORAL POSITION
OF THE POPULATIONS OF EUROPE AND AMERICA,
WITH PARTICULAR REFERENCE TO THOSE
OF GREAT BRITAIN AND IRELAND

BY

DAVID CUNNINGHAM, F.S.S., M. Inst. C.E.

AUTHOR OF 'TABLES FOR FACILITATING THE CALCULATION OF EARTHWORK IN THE
CONSTRUCTION OF RAILWAYS, ROADS, ETC.'

LONDON

LONGMANS, GREEN, AND CO.

1878

PREFACE.

IT is my endeavour in the following work to describe some of the principal influences that have affected, and now affect, the position and prospects of the populations of Europe and America, with particular reference to those of Great Britain and Ireland, and to indicate the nature of those social conditions which appear to be the most healthy.

The numerous facts brought forward have been carefully selected from a vast mass of materials; and, though it is possible some of them may be found to be inaccurate, the principles propounded, which necessarily are based on larger considerations, will not, I hope, be invalidated thereby.

It is necessary to acknowledge my great and especial indebtedness to various series of Government Blue Books, particularly to the extremely valuable and interesting Reports upon the Tenure of Land in the several countries of Europe, and to those respecting the condition of the Industrial Classes in Foreign Countries. I have also made considerable use of M. Maurice Block's admirable works, 'L'Europe, Politique et Sociale,' and 'Statistique de la France comparée avec les divers pays de l'Europe.'

I have not wished to distract the reader's attention with too many references, and I have therefore frequently supplied the facts and opinions given in the shape of quotations in the text, which I trust will often be found most appropriate and satisfactory.

Newport, Fifeshire:
April, 1878.

CONTENTS.

—◦◦◦—

CHAPTER I.

THE HISTORICAL DEVELOPMENT OF SOCIAL WELL-BEING.

CHAPTER II.

POLITICAL ABSOLUTISM ANTAGONISTIC TO SOCIAL WELL-BEING.

CHAPTER III.

POPULAR MOVEMENTS TOWARDS THE ATTAINMENT OF THE POLITICAL CONDITIONS OF SOCIAL WELL-BEING.

CHAPTER IV.

OBSTACLES TO SOCIAL WELL-BEING IN GREAT BRITAIN AND IRELAND.

CHAPTER V.

LANDHOLDING AND AGRICULTURAL CONDITIONS OF SOCIAL WELL-BEING IN EUROPE AND AMERICA.

CHAPTER VI.

WHAT ARE THE BEST LANDHOLDING AND AGRICULTURAL CONDITIONS OF SOCIAL WELL-BEING?

xii CONTENTS.

CHAPTER VII.

THE SUSTENANCE AND ABILITY OF THE INDIVIDUAL WORKMAN.

CONTENTS. xiii

CHAPTER VIII.

WHAT ARE THE BEST ECONOMICAL CONDITIONS OF SOCIAL WELL-BEING ?

CHAPTER IX.

WHAT ARE THE BEST COMMERCIAL CONDITIONS OF SOCIAL WELL-BEING.

CHAPTER X.

THE MASSES SHOULD BE INSTRUCTED REGARDING THE BEST CONDITIONS OF SOCIAL WELL-BEING.

CONDITIONS

OF

SOCIAL WELL-BEING.

————◦◦———

CHAPTER I.

THE HISTORICAL DEVELOPMENT OF SOCIAL WELL-BEING.

THE most striking difference between ancient and modern civilizations undoubtedly consists in the degree
in which freedom and well-being are disseminated amongst
the population. In the former the magnificence of the
ruling classes hid beneath it an immense mass of oppression and misery ; in the latter the people are free to labour
and to reap the fruit of their labour, and they are even
free to assist in the government of their community or
nation. Formerly, as regards power, the masses were
cyphers, mere instruments of it, who could be applied by
the ruler in any way he might desire, whether his objects
were warlike or peaceful. Hence the colossal results in
architectural structures that even now survive.

There was a condition of absolute service required
from the whole people, and it depended upon the produce
of the earth, season by season, what the amount of that
service should be. The surplus product of a good year
was generally consumed in the greater exertions of an
enforced service for some kingly scheme of peace or war,

while the deficiency of a bad year caused widespread misery, destitution, and death.

The manner of the transformation that has taken place must always afford the most significant lessons, and without a knowledge of the principles involved in a revolution so profound, we shall be unable to comprehend the nature of the present active social and political movements. It is, therefore, of essential importance that the extremely different conditions in which the ancient and modern civilizations were placed be understood, and we shall, therefore, proceed succinctly to describe them.

Whilst in the ancient civilizations—and we refer particularly to the eastern, or semi-tropical, division of them —there was no adequate security against governmental rapacity, men hid their treasures. As, therefore, there could be little or no display of wealth, there was no powerful inducement toward its realization, and no habit of saving was practised.

But why was the government tyrannical and rapacious, why was wealth insecure, and why were the people pillaged?

The more ancient civilizations existed in countries possessing prolific soil and hot climates. The consequences of these conditions manifested themselves on the one hand in an almost spontaneous harvest, and on the other in there being scarcely any felt necessity for clothing. There could be, therefore, comparatively little inducement to active exertion, and the natural result was an hereditary indolence. In a prevailing hot temperature the body loses little of the natural heat generated internally by contact with the atmosphere, and in this way that great division of food which consists of the carbonaceous or heat-producing materials is not required by inhabitants of tropical countries in any considerable degree. It is also not the less true that an indolent

people requires not nearly the same amount of nitro-
genous or tissue-forming substance of food as one that is
active and laborious.   When these two circumstances are
kept in view it is easily understood how a large and
dense population may be maintained on a comparatively
small extent of country, and they explain how the tropical countries of Asia contain such vast multitudes.
Thus we find that the agricultural population of the
valley of the Ganges is more dense than that of any part
of Europe—even denser than that of Belgium, which
exists so largely in virtue of mining and manufacturing
industries. 'A fertile soil and a warm climate, with a consequent facility in obtaining food, and contentment with
the most easily obtained vegetable diet, have covered the
teeming plains of northern and central India with a dense
throng of inhabitants, packed together far too closely to
allow them to do more than barely to support life.'[1]

On the other hand, colder climates, for the opposite
reasons, produce populations that are relatively laborious
and energetic.   The individual of the north requires
more to sustain him, and what he requires must be
wrung from a more reluctant soil and protected from a
more treacherous climate.   Constant exertion will breed ·
the habit of labour.   The taskmaster now is not human
tyranny, but natural necessity.   The labour which is now
greater demands a greater sustenance, and produces a
more powerful frame and a spirit active and free.

The people of northern or temperate climates, therefore, must necessarily be of a stronger and bolder type
than those inhabiting tropical regions.   The former, on
discovering the beauty and richness of the south, and the
indolent life led by the inhabitants, would naturally be
filled with the desire to take possession of the land, and
would coalesce in numbers sufficient to effect their object

[1] *Times,* Oct. 21, 1875.

by invasion. Each individual of the northern invaders being more powerful and more active than his opponent of the south would overcome him in battle, and the result would be an occupation of southern territory and an enslavement of its puny and indolent inhabitants.

Such has been the actual history of both Asia and Europe. India has been repeatedly occupied by northern hordes, and the few tribes of the original inhabitants are reckoned to number now not more than one-tenth of the whole population, if indeed these be the original inhabitants.

The extensive, though enervated, dominion of Rome, extending from Britain to Persia, was likewise overrun by barbaric hordes till the whole of the countries, formerly under the Imperial sway, passed into the dominion of peoples who had issued from the impenetrable and unknown regions of the north.

The consequences of these repeated invasions of a more warlike northern people on the countries occupied by the feeble inhabitants of the south, was to keep the latter constantly in a condition of slavery. Thus the ruling people, and more particularly the small section of them which constituted the ruling family, or head, kept under despotic subjection extensive countries. Multitudes were governed according to the caprices of an individual. No opportunity remained for enterprise, for the fruits of that enterprise would have been at the mercy of one who had become enamoured of those luxuriant and expensive pleasures which a warm climate and an irresponsible situation can so abundantly confer. The whole necessarily became the subservient slaves of one absolute personal will, that ruled not altogether for the efficient government and defence of the country, but also for selfish personal gratification—a vice most natural to those who transfer their residence from the

comparatively bleak and sterile north to the sunny plains
of the south, where more particularly the means of
unlimited indulgence are easily and inexpensively obtained.

Such then was the lot of the great mass of mankind
under the ancient civilizations. There were, however,
exceptions to this condition; and in the more recent
times the exceptions increased in number, so that, at any
rate in Europe, they ultimately became under the Roman
Empire the rule. What were the circumstances and
characteristics of these exceptions?

The peoples who were situated on the sea-coast were
not in every case altogether dependent upon the fruits of
the neighbouring country. They might surround their
habitations with walls on the land side, and possess
natural or artificial havens on the sea side. They could
in this way isolate themselves from the general community
of their own country, and they could preserve communication by sea with the inhabitants, and supply themselves
with the produce, of other countries. Thence arose
another and a completely distinct source of power from
that of Conquest, namely, the power of Commerce. Thus
the Mediterranean—that sea in the middle of the earth,
as its name indicates—became surrounded by countries
engaged in commerce with each other, those so occupied
being at first situated within large enwalled sea-port
towns. Hence arose Tyre and Sidon, the great cities of
Phœnicia, Athens of Greece, Rome of Italy, Smyrna of
Asia, Syracuse of Sicily, Carthage of Africa, and Marseilles
of Gaul. In course of centuries these and the other innumerable towns situated on that sea and on the Euxine
became powerful in their influence over the adjoining ter-
ritories, and thus gradually but completely transformed
the character and condition of the adjoining peoples
and governments. Thus the character of Rome became

stamped on Italy, which, from the immense advantages
presented to its rural inhabitants, from their comparative
proximity to sea-ports trading with other countries,
and their consequent ability to exchange the produce of
their fields for the riches of foreign countries, became
ultimately cultivated in every part. Indeed, it is true
that wars had been waged between the representatives
of the principles of Conquest and Commerce in Italy in
the time of the Etruscans, hundreds of years before
Rome itself had emerged from obscurity, and probably
the result was that the country was somewhat settled
before Rome rose into importance. The area of Etruria
was occupied by twelve sovereign cities, which often
joined together to promote their common interests and
to resist the incursions of those who invaded the peninsula
from the north.

The strength of ancient united Italy was great and
elastic. From Rome, the centre of that first greatest
commercial civilization, there sprang an indomitable
spirit of law and government, which ultimately impressed
itself over the length and breadth of the ancient world,
linking the populations together by the firmness and
impartiality of its rule, and the material benefits it conferred. It was, however, impossible that such a rapidly
agglomerated empire could have maintained itself for
long. The prosperity created was for the most part a
superinduced one. The colonised countries had not had
time to grow naturally to a condition of strength : their
life was in some degree forced and artificial, and they
were for the most part altogether differently situated
from those whence they had derived their civilization.
They had comparatively few physical facilities for commerce, and that which could thrive must have been too
insignificant to entirely restrain the people by the promise of rewards. And besides, the people as a whole

were still in shackles, and therefore comparatively heed-
less of the welfare of the State.

On the other hand, the wealthy and powerful became
careless, then immoral, then weak. The barbarians at
last broke the lines of mercenaries placed to oppose their
progress, and wave succeeded wave till, first the colonies,
and ultimately the centre of the empire, were submerged
by their constantly increasing power. The principle of
Conquest had triumphed over that of Commerce, but
not before the virtues of the latter—weak as it had
always been from the presence of slavery—had become
clouded.

There remained, however, in the general collapse, a
few old Roman towns which preserved a feeble flicker
of their primal life. To these in course of the gradual
settlement of the new state of things were added other
towns situated in positions on the coast or on navigable
rivers. These grew very slowly into centres of commerce. When the cities were still embryonic, they could
scarcely be distinguished from the country except by the
fact that their inhabitants drew together for the advantage
of asylum and defence. The defence was imperfect, for
even the lord of the domain wherein the town was situated would gratify his avarice by attempting its pillage.
Thus, in the words of Guizot, ' The merchants, after having made their journeys, were not permitted to enter
their towns in peace ; the roads and approaches were
incessantly beset by the lord and his followers. The time
at which industry was recommencing was exactly that in
which security was most wanting. Nothing can irritate
a man more than being interfered with in his work and
despoiled of the fruits which he had promised himself
from it. . . . There is in the progressive movement towards
fortune of a man or a population, a principle of resistance against injustice and violence far more energetic

than in any other situation.'[1]   Thus the necessity for a more perfect defence arose. Fortifications were built and manned by the men who had acquired and were acquiring wealth. The acquisition of this wealth was the cause of settled order within the towns that were thus defended against external attack. These then gained a strength superior in many cases to that of the lords. But the struggle for freedom was a long one, and in many cases the lives as well as the goods of the citizens of the towns were sacrificed. Even when peace had been apparently attained, and the burgh charter had been sworn to by either party, it was frequently violated, and the war renewed with increased bitterness and waste.

But ultimately the enfranchisement of the burghs was completely established. The perpetual loss and danger that had been submitted to and risked in the course of these struggles can never be known; history is not eloquent regarding these first popular struggles for liberty. The principle of commerce, however, eventually triumphed, and merchant guilds were firmly established in many towns. The profit upon the exchange of commodities produced in different countries was the greatest and easiest inducement to the establishment of these guilds, and to their mutual defence. Afterwards the craft guilds arose and secured a footing alongside and in co-operation with the merchant guilds, thereby binding the two classes of merchants and traders together intimately for common interests. In the twelfth century the inhabitants of the towns ' consisted almost entirely of merchants, traders carrying on a petty commerce, and of small proprietors either of land or houses, who had taken up their residence in the town. Three centuries after, the bourgeoisie comprehended besides advocates, physicians, learned men of all sorts, and all the local magistrates.'[2]   The state of the

---

[1] *History of Civilization*, by F. Guizot.   [2] *Ibid.*

towns during these three centuries had been one of gradual, unmarked improvement in the most part of Western
Europe. Settled order was felt to be the first necessity
of trade, without which the towns could not have existed,
and when this had been only partially established, other
interests grew up side by side to consolidate that order.

But the source and spring of all this settled order,
and the free life and action which it permitted, was undoubtedly the desire for material improvement on the part
of the inhabitants. The serfs of the country, too, were
not long in seeking to realise the advantages of the freemen. They sought the protection of the town whenever
possible. They became freemen, instead of slaves. The
lord, it was said in France, ' shuts up his clowns, as under
gates and hinges, from heaven to earth. . . . All is his,
hoary forest, fowl of the air, fish in the water, beast in
the bush, running stream, far-sounding bell.' The escape
from such a felt and oppressive servitude was everywhere
desirable.

Having been schooled in the fields by the necessity of
existence to the exercise of labour, the serfs were prepared by their exertions in the towns from sunrise to
curfew to value and maintain their freedom. It was a
transference from a condition of compulsory service to
one of independent labour ; from one of exposure to the
fluctuations of a lord's temper, and the uncertainties of
war and climate, to another of security and protection.
This important change was rendered possible by the existence of the surplus wealth which enabled the burgesses
to employ and sustain them. This wealth had been acquired painfully in great labour and peril. The existence
of realised capital permitted a competition for free labour
whereby the labourer was incalculably benefited. And
he has now the opportunity in most civilized countries of
transferring his efforts to any sphere in which he supposes

he can secure to himself the greatest advantages. In every quarter there is the most eager outlook on the part of those who possess wealth for opportunities of investing it most advantageously. Without stability of government, however, no wealth would be secure ; and what is so essential to the capitalist is likewise as essential to the labourer ; what the one imperiously calls for the other cannot exist without.

While the freedom of the urban population was thus gradually acquired, that of the rural population was still far from being accomplished. Those countries which possessed the greatest natural facilities for trade and commerce—such, for instance, as possessed a relatively extensive range of sea-coast—were those which had the greatest number of towns in a position to trade freely at an early period with other countries similarly situated. Until within the last century or two during which superior means of inland communication have altered the old conditions of things, the countries bordering the Mediterranean, and those within sailing distance of it, enjoyed not only the greatest advantages in regard to the amount of sea-coast they possessed, but the greatest opportunities from their relatively short distances apart of communicating by sea with each other. We therefore find all the more powerful nations of antiquity occupying the countries upon that sea, and even in modern times, before the arts of ship-building and navigation had been sufficiently well developed, maintaining their predominance in the trade, navigation, freedom, and civilization of the world. When, however, vessels were found to navigate the Atlantic Ocean for days and weeks together safely, the position of things was rapidly changed. While the nations bordering the Mediterranean Sea were subject to attack from the land side, and required to maintain fortifications and forces to resist those attacks, the position which they held

while strong in affording immense advantages in the prosecution of naval commerce, was comparatively weak in
the opportunities of adequate internal defence, for the
interior was filled by multitudes of warlike peoples.
Their cities could not always contain sufficient force to
resist the attacks made upon them from the land side.
They then either colonised the adjoining districts, sharing
the advantages of their wealth and freedom with the
inhabitants who were thus enrolled for the common defence, or they employed mercenary troops, who might at
any time prove a great danger.   The interior of such
countries was even at a late period unaffected by the
beneficent influences which commerce was producing on
the maritime towns.   France, for instance, ' throughout its
length and breadth remained (in the middle of the fourteenth century) almost impenetrable to commerce.   The
roads were too dangerous ; the tolls too numerous.   The
barons did not pillage to the same extent as formerly, but
the king's agents plundered in their stead.   Robbed like
a merchant, became a proverb.   The royal hand reached
over all ; but it was seldom felt save as represented by
the paw of the treasury.   When the order came, it was
for universal seizure ; salt, water, air, rivers, forests, fords,
defiles, nothing escaped fiscal ubiquity.' [1]

These serious disadvantages were not felt in the island
of Britain.   Its progress was uninterrupted for the most
part by perils from the land side, and the influence of the
prosperity of the large towns situated on or near the coast
more rapidly spread itself over the narrow intervening
districts of the country within.   A measure of security
was thus enjoyed by Britain which had an immense influence in fostering her progress.   She traded with other
countries without the fear of internal attacks despoiling

[1] *History of France*, by M. Michelet, book 6, chap. i., transl. by G. H.
Smith, F.G.S.

her of the fruits of commerce that she had laboriously gathered. The merchants and traders of the sea-port towns became wealthy, and in employing their accumulated riches the interior population was largely benefited. The people, therefore, became at an early period bound together in one commonwealth. The comparatively short distances lying between the nearest towns that traded by sea with other countries and the inmost recesses of the island permitted a great traffic to be carried on even at unsettled times between the urban and rural districts. Nothing could more effectually tend to break up the great institutions of the feudal system than the fact of wealth being so near at hand. The productions of foreign countries were to be had by the great lords at a price equivalent to the subsistence of some of their vassals. The vassals, on the other hand, often preferred, when they could exercise the preference, to escape to the towns. The effect on both lord and vassal was therefore in the same direction. Thus Adam Smith says,[1] 'What all the violence of the feudal institutions could never have effected, the silent and insensible operations of foreign commerce and manufactures gradually brought about. These gradually furnished the great proprietors with something for which they could exchange the whole surplus produce of their lands, and which they could consume themselves, without sharing it either with tenants or retainers. . . . In a country where there is no foreign commerce, nor any of the finer manufactures, a man of 10,000*l.* a year cannot well employ his revenue in any other way than in maintaining perhaps a thousand families who are all of them necessarily at his command. In the present state of Europe a man of 10,000*l.* a year can spend his whole revenue, and he generally does so without directly maintaining twenty people, or being able

[1] *The Wealth of Nations,* book 3, chap. iv.

to command ten footmen not worth the commanding. Indirectly, perhaps, he maintains as great or even a greater number of people than he could have done by the ancient method of expense. . . . Though he contributes to the maintenance of them all, they are all more or less independent of him, because generally they can all be maintained without him. . . . The personal expenses of the great proprietors having in this manner gradually increased, it was impossible that the number of their retainers should not as gradually diminish, till they were at last dismissed altogether. . . . It was thus that through the greater part of Europe the commerce and manufactures of cities, instead of being the effect have been the cause and occasion of the improvement and cultivation of the country.' But this revolution in the condition of the country was effected only very slowly, except when it was as in England accelerated by legislation. ' It was not until after a long period, when manufacturing industry had heaped up men and money in some strong cities, that the overflowing population could create suburbs, burghs, hamlets, or change hamlets into towns. In this manner, generally speaking, the country was created by the town, the soil by man. Agriculture was the last manufacture born of the success of the others.' [1]

Upon the continent of Europe, indeed, many towns that had been at one period in a flourishing condition were unable to resist the as yet wild and unreformed forces of the country. There were pirates, too, who infested the seas which were frequented by the richly laden argosies from distant lands. Thus it was that obstacles to the growth of these centres of industry and wealth were continually presented by the outer populations, who were ultimately to be the richest gainers by their prosperity. The want of a settled order outside of the towns prevented the

---

[1] *History of France*, by M. Michelet, book 12, chap. i.

establishment of those relations between the municipalities and the country which would have otherwise taken place. There was too great a force outside, too large an area of wild unsettled country to leaven at the first, and its impulses often could not be withstood in the early stages of existence. Hence arose the necessity for individual towns combining together for mutual protection. An independent power in the north of Europe was thus formed. It was named the Hanseatic League, and embraced at one time as many as eighty-five towns. At a period two centuries anterior to the effective political unification of France the League affected a greater extent of country than is measured by that kingdom. Thus the enterprise of individuals, associated together in towns favourably situated on the sea-coast or on the great rivers, was effective in building up a government for the protection of their own interests, and ultimately in securely binding together the whole regions wherein these towns existed in one common welfare. It was a natural development which gradually affected all the countries within the range of its influence, establishing the opportunity of material independence in every household, and furnishing inducements to exertion which were the necessary antecedents to an immense amelioration in the condition of the people. Yet this development was seriously retarded by other influences. Where war and violence were still to be dreaded, the great lords could not let go the hold which they had upon the multitude of people who lived upon their domains as serfs. While the numbers of personal followers, and the expenses of the household of the lord were therefore so far as possible reduced, a certain hold was maintained upon the rural populations, by which they could at any time be called upon to supply the necessary means of defence. And even, as we shall see, after the period at which

standing armies had been organised, the power and distinction of the great proprietor, depending as it did upon
the amount of land he possessed that was cultivated by
serfs, lent another influence in maintaining the old state
of things.

Yet notwithstanding these counteracting influences,
the influence of the towns was clearly distinctive, and
there now exists the most comfort and wealth as well as
settled prosperity amongst the people of those countries
which can reckon the greater number of towns. At the
present day the towns in the principal European States
which possess populations of 40,000 inhabitants and
above are in number as follows[1] :—Great Britain and
Ireland contain fifty-five such towns ; France twenty-eight;
Italy twenty-four ; Prussia twenty-one ; Russia fourteen ;
and Austria six. There is no country in Europe which
can excel Britain either in the number of her towns, in
the period during which they have flourished, in the uniformity of their progress, or in the height of prosperity
acquired ; and neither is there any other country in which
the peasantry have been so long free, and wherein they
have had opportunities, from the uniform development of
manufactures and commerce, of improving their condition.
From the latter half of the fourteenth century to the time
of Elizabeth, the peasantry of the country as a whole
changed their condition from one of servitude to one of
freedom.

The influence of the towns in France was not altogether dissimilar from that of the towns in Britain, but it
did not result so happily either for the urban or rural
population. For there were other influences at work in
France which unfortunately largely interfered with the
free action of commerce and manufactures in either en-

---

[1] Brachelli's *Staaten Europas*, quoted in the *Journal of the Statistical
Society*, vol. 38, p. 379.

riching the towns or enfranchising the country. One of these proceeded from the disastrous effects of the wars with England and the consequent spoliation of French territory. The continual want of security that resulted from the overrunning of the country produced the most pernicious effects on the strength of the towns. Already from the position that they held on relatively widely separated coast lines, they were not in a fortunate condition to confederate for common defence, nor even were they always able to maintain internal peace. The consequent diminution of municipal strength was great. But the same causes aggrandised the monarchy. The lords were supplanted by the astute policy of the successive monarchs, so that in course of time the general effect came to be that they were too weak to resist the encroachments which were continually made by the central government. The necessity for the arbitrary predominance of a central power to gather the forces of the nation and keep them united for the purpose of common defence existed scarcely at all when the English had at last been driven from French soil. But the mischief of a powerful and unchecked monarchy controlling all the other forces of the kingdom became during peace the inevitable result of the preceding situation. The lords and commons had been perpetually weakened in the long continued wars, but the king had been strengthened. The advantage of despotism in the camp was followed by the disadvantage of despotism in the civil government. The will of the king became the law. The lords were stripped of their important feudal functions, and reduced to the condition of being only the principal inhabitants of the country. The few duties of which they had not been stripped had now become uninteresting and irksome to them. It therefore happened that they found their pleasure in attending upon the Court, where the ambition to outvie each other

in splendour produced an undue expenditure. Their
fortunes were too lavishly spent in the drawing-rooms of
Paris. Thus the necessities of their position sometimes
compelled the sale of their lands. The townsmen and
the peasantry in many parts of France had therefore become proprietors of a large part of the country long before
the first Revolution. The celebrated traveller, Arthur
Young, was astonished at the great subdivision of the
land in France, and he gave it as his opinion that probably
one-third of the country was held in fee by the peasantry.
While the political duties of the lords had almost wholly
disappeared, their peculiar emoluments were for the most
part retained. They became as a caste still more divided
in their position and interests from the mass of the people.
The spiritual lords occupied a similar position. Both of
these retained their feudal rights over the people. The
exercise of these was severely felt, the more so that the
correlative duties had been transferred to the deputies of
the Crown, the intendant of the province, and the parochial officers. These rights still retained by the lords,
lay and clerical, consisted in the levying of dues on fairs
and markets; the monopoly of sporting, the power to
compel the peasants to have their corn ground only at the
lord's mill, and the pressing of their grapes at the lord's
wine-press. They also embraced taxes on the transfer of
land, and dues on the land of all kinds, which were in-
commutable, tolls on the roads and the enforcement of
labour-rents. It was a complaint that the whole country
was loaded with rent-charges, which were experienced as
a peculiar hardship, since there were no correlative duties
performed by the lords.

Again the expenses of government bore heavily on
the poorer portion of the community—that portion which
was not able successfully to resist the imposition and augmentation of the State taxes. The king's necessities were

alone the law upon the subject; and as it happened that the privileged classes were exempted from the chief burden of taxation, the maintenance of the grandeur of the State and of its military campaigns fell to be paid chiefly by the poor. The king required money always. Louis XIV. stripped the towns of their municipal liberties for no other purpose than that they might be bought back again for sums of money. He compelled the purchasers of letters of nobility to purchase them over again, on the allegation that all of them, the most having been conferred during his own reign, had been obtained by surprise! There were taxes on the owners of non-noble land from which the nobility were exempt. Trading companies were established, and individuals compelled to become members of them with the sole view of extracting money in the process. Those holding offices under the State could obtain them only by purchase, and the number of offices created depended, not upon the requirements of administration, but upon the king's necessities. The middle classes were always eagerly upon the search for such distinctions as would confer privileges that would set them above the common people, and relieve them from taxation. A rich farmer would send his son to the town and purchase for him a government office, for there was no distinction or advancement to be gained in the rural districts. Thus the funds which should have been destined for the improvement of agriculture went into the State purse. The administration of the country was therefore lodged in the hands of a multitude of place-holders, who having purchased their situations could not readily be displaced, though the necessity of affairs might demand it. Thus the nation was divided by artificial means into three distinct classes, or two castes and one class. The former were privileged and favoured in every way; the latter, which formed the poorer portion of the community, was required to bear a continually increasing burden of the general and local taxation.

Thus in every way the central power, that had, from the advantage of its situation, gradually acquired the whole force of government, nourished the representatives of the old principle of Conquest, and depressed those of Commerce. The one were the companions and favourites of the king; the other were kept down at a distance, and only tolerated with the view of supporting from their resources the despotism which repressed them. While the natural advantages of the situation were considerable, the artificial disadvantages of a tyrannical government had hitherto counterbalanced them. The towns that had to a certain extent, during two centuries or more, been the means of freeing a large portion of the soil, were deprived of the needful security of progress, for the management of their affairs had been taken out of the hands of the citizens.

Thus, in almost all parts of France, the country had come under a yoke of a more harassing kind than had been felt even during the full vigour of the feudal period. The burdens had been greatly increased, while the corresponding benefits had been diminished or reduced to something merely nominal. A period at last arrived, however, when modern interests became too powerful to be treated any longer in this manner, and the ancient régime was felt to be all the more oppressive. The material progression of the country demanded urgently a greater opportunity of development, and the obstruction of a despotic government, whose every movement was characterised by oppression, extortion, and caprice, was at last unbearable, and came to be violently met and destroyed.

In Italy, again, the cities, which at an early period were

numerous and powerful, and which gave birth to a high civilization, became the prey ultimately of their own violence. They incorporated the feudal baron, who, though turbulent and sometimes expelled, was still a citizen. The retainers of the great lords naturally became dependent on the city also, and the whole country in the neighbourhood of these centres of commerce and manufactures was permeated with freedom. It is supposed that the cessation of predial servitude took place in the thirteenth century; but as in France, the free peasant was afterwards, when the Italian governments had become corrupt, ground down by the most intolerable exactions. The result of this misgovernment was that property was attacked, and society was perpetually endangered. The country was impoverished, the peasants were driven from their fields and scoured the country, subsisting by robbing whomsoever they could.

The cities, which at first could confederate together to expel the Emperor Frederick Barbarossa from Italy, became — from the absence of a central restraining power — divided against each other. The immediate proximity of high mountains and deep valleys resulted, first, in the interests of various cities becoming diverse, for their natural boundaries were difficult to traverse; and, second, in the intermingling of the fierce, untamed inhabitants of such a country with the milder inhabitants of the towns. The money of the latter was employed in calling in the arms of the former to defend each city from the aggression of its neighbours, and the very means of defence was the cause often of further aggression and warfare without, and of strife and bloodshed within. The governments of the various republics into which Italy was thus divided, became ultimately so oppressive and tyrannical, that political freedom was extinguished; and when Charles VIII. of France invaded and overran the peninsula, towards the end of the fifteenth century, there was neither a national force nor a free spirit to oppose him. The country thereafter became the prey in turn of every nation whose soldiers could find their way into it; it was frequently ravaged from one end to the other, and from having enjoyed a condition of the highest prosperity, it sank to one of utter misery and destitution, being perfectly despoiled of any riches of which it could at any time repossess itself. The various portions of the country that had formerly been divided into separate republics, were from time to time combined together under the government of the most powerful foreign force; but the dominion of Italy was the object of ambition to every neighbour, and its soil was for centuries the battlefield of Europe. From this condition it arose when the French, in the beginning of the nineteenth century, invaded Italy, this time, however, to bestow the blessing of freedom which they themselves had acquired at the Revolution; and it has since become one united nation, whose position is being wisely consolidated by the rapid construction of numerous roads and railways, that will in the future practically reduce the physical barriers which divided in the middle ages the fortunes and interests of its various States.

The Great Revolution in France has had, without doubt, the most powerful influence in the emancipation of the peasantry of central and eastern Europe. The degree of violence which accompanied that radical social and political transformation, alarmed the ruling classes in the other countries. Their attention was drawn to the necessity of change, and their minds were agitated by the consideration of the importance and urgency of the emancipation of the peasantry. In Prussia it became apparent, at the beginning of the present century, that the peasantry who had risen in revolt three centuries previously, were suffering from an oppression which contributed to the weakness of the country. The statesmen, Stein and Hardenberg, when invited to report upon the best means of invigora‑ ting the State, agreed in placing the liberation of the peasantry in the foreground. The edict of October 9, 1807, was then issued as applicable to the whole kingdom. In the words of the king, the underlying principle of this edict was ' to remove whatever has hitherto hindered the individual from obtaining that degree of well-being which he was capable of reaching, by exertions according to the best of his ability.' In the year 1810, the liberation of the peasantry from servitude was completed, and the result on the condition of the country became speedily apparent. The increase to the national welfare during the following years was unprecedented. The peasants being free to improve their condition indefinitely, a great stimulus to exertion was created, in consequence of which, in the course of a few years, the estates of the gentry that had been previously mortgaged to over fifty per cent., were to a large extent bought up by their former serfs. This transference has taken place to the largest extent in Upper Silesia, where the former estates of the gentry have in great measure gone into the hands of the peasantry, who, from the position of serfs, have in a few years risen to that of substantial yeomen.

The basis of the arrangement upon which the edict was framed, by which the relations between the lords of the manor and peasants were adjusted, consisted in a mu‑ tual compromise of rights; and as the land hereditarily held was to become, as far as possible, the absolute pro‑ perty of the peasant, the lord was to receive one-third of it, or an equivalent compensation in money or kind, in exchange for the relinquishment of all his feudal rights and obligations. Only the house and garden remained without division in the possession of the peasant.

In Germany, also, a similar arrangement for the commutation of services was carried out. In the year 1836, the Grand Duchy of Hesse led the way, the State undertaking to advance to the great lords a sum equivalent to eighteen years' purchase of the rent-charge of the lands in occupation, a precedent which was afterwards followed by almost every State throughout Germany.

Again, so recently as the year 1847, the Austrian peasantry were serfs, and by their forced labour the estates of the great lords were cultivated. By the land laws of 1848-49, they were emancipated, and from serfs they became proprietors. This was accomplished in the following manner :—A valuation of the whole properties which were occupied by the peasantry in name of feudal service was made by the State, one-third of the value was declared to be cancelled, another third formed a tax upon each province, and the remaining third was provided for by a tax levied exclusively upon the peasant proprietors, which was regarded as the price payable by them to the State, for the free and unrestricted ownership of the land that had been formerly held under imposed services. There was thus a great revolution effected, which produced direct and indirect results of immense importance. One of the direct results was the comparative impoverishment of the landlords, who to escape ruin were compelled to adopt a more scientific method of agriculture, and a more extended employment of machinery ; while the indirect results have been recognised in the creation of a class of thriving peasant proprietors, and an increase in the value of land to the extent of over one hundred per cent.

But the most remarkable instance of definite legal emancipation proceeds from Russia. In that country, natural causes have operated neither in the enslavement nor in the liberation of the peasantry. The condition of serfdom in Russia was not created by a necessity for

the existence of feudalism, with its correlative rights and
duties, as was the case in other countries. Serfdom was
introduced in Russia Proper by the sovereigns of Moscow,
who conferred upon the lord the right of property in the
cultivator of the soil. The peasantry were prohibited
from their customary migrations on the day of the festival
of St. George, in the year 1592. From that date the
mass of the people of Russia was composed of villeins
bound to the soil, and owned by the landed aristocracy
and gentry, by the Crown, and by the Imperial Family.
In Little Russia and Lithuania, again, serfdom was introduced in the reign of the Empress Catherine, who distributed serfs among the nobility. It was thus that as
many as 30,000 male serfs became the property of some
favourites.[1]

In the reign of the Emperor Nicholas, the subject of
emancipation began to occupy the attention of the government of Russia ; and in 1826 a secret committee was
appointed to inquire into the entire organisation of the
empire. It was not, however, till the year 1861 that the
Act of Emancipation was passed into law. This act had
the effect of conferring freedom on 22,000,000 of individuals, who formed the serf population of Russia Proper.
It also affected indirectly the peasantry of the Crown,
numbering 23,000,000, and of the appanages, numbering
3,000,000. To understand what was the full effect of
this act, it is necessary to consider first what the previous
condition of the serf actually was. Each male serf, of
whatever age, enjoyed the usufruct on an average of from
eight to ten acres of land. The rent levied by the lord
varied greatly. The necessities of the proprietor caused
him not unfrequently to mortgage his land and serfs in

[1] *Reports on the Tenure of Land in the several Countries of Europe.* See
Report by Mr. Michell on the System of Land Tenure in Russia, part ii. pp.
22, 23.

order to obtain a loan from the government, and it generally happened that the interest on the loan had to be
added to the amount of the quit-rent. In this way the serf
was taxed not so much according to the value of the land,
as according to his lord's necessities. It was impossible
for the serf to resist any claim that might be made upon
him, for the law heard no complaint, and it gave no redress. He might be flogged with impunity, enrolled in
the army, sent off to Siberia, or stripped of all his possessions, just according to his lord's good pleasure. The
condition of the peasantry belonging to the Crown and
the appanages was, however, in some degree different
from this; for though they were not at liberty to leave the
soil, they were free from the more grievous kinds of
oppression. Most of the lands—about three-fourths—
were held for service only, which service was bestowed
upon an equivalent extent of lands occupied by the lord.
In the industrial provinces, however, where there were
other sources of income than that from land, the holdings
of the serf were increased, so as to increase the amount of
the quit-rent. Besides payment to the lord in money and
service the serf was bound at all times to supply horses
and carts to transport his produce, to supply poultry and
other contributions in kind, and in giving numerous other
services.

The Emancipation Act, as regards the serf, decreed
the right to commutation of personal services, the right
to the homestead on terms fixed mutually or by law; the
right to purchase the lands under his cultivation at eighty
per cent. of their estimated value, or at the lord's option,
the free gift of one-fourth of such lands with the homestead; also the privilege of communal and cantonal self-
government.[1] But what the Emancipation Act did not
provide for was the individual right to freedom of locomo-

[1] *System of Land Tenure in Russia*, p. 29.

tion, for since the government held the village communes as corporate bodies, responsible for the payment of the quit-rents, taxes, and 'redemption dues,' the communes were in a manner placed in the position which the lords had formerly occupied as landlords. They accordingly, becoming responsible to the State, were compelled to make their individual members responsible to them, and there was generally no more practicable way of securing that responsibility, than by keeping the peasant chained to the soil and to his commune.

In this cursory survey of the circumstances in which the emancipation of the masses of the people in Europe has taken place, we may discern clearly the preponderating influence which the towns have exerted. In Britain, where the towns were most numerous and prosperous, the rural population became free at an early date. In France, the emancipation of the masses of the peasantry was undoubtedly effected at an early period, but their well-being was retarded, and ultimately destroyed, through the enslavement of the towns by the despotic central power. In Italy, again, the towns were the centre of European civilization and freedom, when other countries adjoining had scarcely emerged from barbarism, but unfortunately while their commercial interests were severed by lofty physical barriers, their military interests, if we may so say, were in the hands of the inhabitants of these barriers—the lords and their followers. The consequence was a mutual weakening to such a degree, that the various independent republics became the prey for centuries of foreign powers. In the eastern parts of Europe, again, the States which border upon the natural highway —the sea—have possessed the greatest natural advantages for commerce, and they have preceded the more landward States in the freedom of their peoples, and progress in civilization. Russia, above every other country, the most dependent upon its own resources, from the absence of facilities of intercommunication, has only a few years since, by authoritative decree, proclaimed freedom to the serfs; but unfortunately conditioned in such a way as to render the boon, if it is one, of an entirely problematical character.

Generalising, therefore, from the more prominent facts, we may conclude that whatever influence the presence of a peculiar government may have on the immediate future condition of a people emerging from barbarism, the over and ever ruling influence consists in those physical circumstances which admit of a ready interchange of goods and ideas with the remainder of the world. Indeed, the process of development cannot be forced on from above, cannot be superinduced by the artificial means of legislation. What legislation alone can accomplish is the removal of all the obstacles to natural growth, which the selfish interests, or the blinded prejudices, of others may have imposed. The establishment and maintenance of an enlightened self-interest, as the actuating and freely-acting power, among the masses, ought surely to be one of the first objects of government, and that object will be best accomplished by affording the most ample field for the unrestricted operation of natural law, by the unshackling of all fetters, and the abolition of all privileges.

We shall in the next chapter consider more attentively the evils of political absolutism, and its attendant, over-legislation.

CHAPTER II.

POLITICAL ABSOLUTISM ANTAGONISTIC TO SOCIAL WELL-BEING.

THERE are, therefore, two principles at work in the government of States, the one or the other of which may be clearly predominant. The one is the principle of repression, which is the result of conquest; the other, the principle of freedom, which is the result of commerce. In the States where the first is predominant, it may be said to shut out largely, often unnecessarily and harshly, the possibility of the existence of the other, for freedom is not allowed where the people are regarded by the government with fear or suspicion, the main object of the government, which has established itself by force, being to keep order by force, even though that order is the order of stagnation. The principle of liberty, indeed, is one which grows up gradually, not from the establishment of States, but from the increase in the material interests of individuals, which become united together for the prosecution of commerce. Liberty is a necessity to the growth of wealth, comfort, and refinement, and it must be invariably associated with commerce. Repression is a necessity to the maintenance of force and arbitrary government on the one hand, and necessitates serfdom or slavery on the other, wherein the lives and interests of the masses are sacrificed to the convenience and enjoyment of a few.

In this and the succeeding chapter, we shall devote some consideration to the characteristics of the working of the two principles as exhibited in Europe, during the eighteenth and nineteenth centuries, so that we may clearly apprehend the nature and tendency of the changes that have occurred, and discern also the character of the present movements.

There can be no doubt that the emancipation of the peasantry of Europe, which has taken place within the last one hundred years, has placed the masses, as a whole, in a better position as regards opportunities for individual exertion and improvement than formerly. But the method of the emancipation has greatly affected that position, and in the degree in which the process has been due to natural causes rather than to autocratic legislation, will be the amount of solid security, and the resulting well-being.

But there is a necessary antagonism between political absolutism and social well-being. Wherein, then, does that antagonism consist?

In replying to that question, we shall refer to the two best known instances of modern times. There is a remarkable similarity between the condition of Russia of to-day, and of France before the Revolution of 1789. In both there is a great centralised autocratic power, administering throughout the country by means of a widespread ramification of place-seeking and venal bureaucratic officials. According to the personal character of the autocrat, will be, for the time, the character of the administration. It will be either hard and relentless, as under the military régime of Louis XIV., or the iron Czar Nicholas; or it will be humane and full of reforms, as under the mild rule of Louis XVI., or the present Emperor of Russia, Alexander II. When it is severe, the spirit of repression will weigh heavily upon the people, and the privileged classes will prove that they are, as is said, ' well-intentioned ' towards the government, by favouring all its plans, and glorifying the wisdom of the ruler. The result of this behaviour will be to intensify the character

of the administration. While generally the tendency of
a despotic government is towards military aggression,
rather than commercial extension, is to favour the arts
and increase the instruments of war, rather than to foster
peaceful internal development—that tendency is intensified when a sovereign, whose character is competent to
carry out a repressive system, finds his every wish gratified, and it only receives a check when the results of
foreign war are disastrous.

The whole of Russia was held by Nicholas in the
sternest bonds of absolutism. Men were forbidden everywhere to deal with any matters of a social or political
kind. If they possessed active minds, should they desire
to extend their energies beyond the immediate sphere of
their everyday business, they must find employment for
them in the arts or belles-lettres. Thus an intellectual
lethargy, a perfect indifference to political and social
measures, laid hold of the educated minds of Russia
during the reign of Nicholas. It was only when the
disasters of the Crimean war proved to everyone the
rottenness of the whole system, which had been so rigidly
adhered to, that an intellectual awakening took place;
and many who had never before dreamt of criticising,
vigorously denounced, though in secret, the governmental
measures that had been the means of procuring such a
catastrophe. Everything, indeed, had been sacrificed to
the military power and grandeur of the State, and it could
not fail to be galling to awakening patriotic feeling to
find that the sacrifice had been made in vain.

Thus a natural revulsion took possession of the mind
of the nation, and the new Emperor shared it along with
his people. The reign of Alexander II. has been characterised by the mildness of the individual ruler. It has
been one of humane reforms, dictated by compassion for
the miseries of the people, and considerations for the

necessity of internal development. The emancipation of the serfs has immemorably signalised the present reign, and that step has been followed by the institution of a new and a higher kind of administration to supplement that of the commune, as well as a complete reform of the law courts. While, however, the character of the government has changed for the better, and the harassing and narrow restrictions placed upon the lives and energies of the people have been largely removed, there is no letting down of the Imperial authority. Local administration must in no case trench upon the position occupied by the central government. Though the bureaucracy may be, in some measure, a reformed one, and less amenable to gross bribery, and less given to glaring injustice, it is there still, equally necessary to dispense the will of the government. Though the gendarmerie may be less cruel and capricious in its actions than heretofore, yet it is there still to spy upon the behaviour of individuals whom the government may regard with suspicion. The machinery is still in active exercise, the intimate connection that existed between the numerous officials and the central bureaucratic office exists unchanged; and the manifold reports and documents that flow from the extremities to St. Petersburg, and the ukases, regulations, and circulars that flow back again from St. Petersburg to the extremities, have not ceased : there is, indeed, no more approach in Russia of to-day towards an extension of political power amongst the people, than there was in the days of the repressive rule of Nicholas.

In thus describing the course of feeling and of action that has taken place in Russia, we describe at the same time the history of France under the old régime. It is true that there are some notable differences that might be recorded between the positions of the two countries under the rule of absolutism. Thus while in Russia the masses

of the agriculturists were serfs, in France they were, for
the most part, free men, and the free peasantry had, to a
large extent, become owners of the ruined estates of the
nobility. But the actual condition of the people scarcely
differed on that account; indeed if there was a difference, it
was in favour of the Russian serf, who, when under a humane
master, which was not unseldom the case, was able to lead
a comfortable and easy life. The French peasantry, upon
the other hand, were one and all ground down to the
dust by the exorbitant and ruinous pressure of taxation, so
that it was scarcely profitable to cultivate the land; much
of it lay waste, and the people died of misery and starvation.

Under Louis XIV., the country was exhausted by the
extravagant expenses of the government, chiefly incurred
in foreign wars. Everything was sacrificed to military
glory and drawing-room display, and a reign of hard and
unscrupulous repression prostrated the energies and the
spirit of the people. When the tide of fortune in war,
however, turned, a public opinion began to manifest itself
against the continuance of a system that was at last found
to lead to ruin, and that opinion ultimately took possession of the court. No one could have proclaimed more
loudly and clearly against the monstrous cruelty of his
predecessors and the system that had been handed down
to him than did the amiable and unfortunate Louis XVI.;
indeed his expressions were only too well fitted to rouse
the spirit of the nation against the continuance of such a
system any longer. But it was not easy to change everything at once, for men had been long accustomed to
certain modes of life, certain ways of action, and certain
means of living. A great part of the better classes were
intimately connected with the government, and derived
their incomes from it. The military officers, the clergy,
and bureaucratic officials, whose numbers included almost
everyone of any position, could not be stripped of their

emoluments without raising up a hostility that could not be encountered. It therefore happened that while everyone lamented the miserable fate of the great body of the common people, no one was willing to sacrifice much towards its alleviation. The whole system, indeed, had become so rotten that no mere alleviatory measures could touch it, and nothing but a complete regeneration could meet the case. The nobility, who still retained their feudal privileges without performing the correlative duties, often yielded charitably so much for the relief of the abounding misery, but they would not consent to part with any portion of those special class privileges which had so much to do with the ruin of the lower classes. While a spirit of humanitarianism took possession of everyone, it was impossible to give effect to that spirit by instituting a radical change in the government of the country.

Thus we find that there is a wonderful parallelism between the history of French and Russian absolutism. There is one great central power, supported by classes which are privileged, and whose interests, therefore, lie in supporting the government against the people as a whole, which is taxed to support an administration that is all-powerful and irresponsible. There is, indeed, no check to the most wanton extravagance except the actual ruin of the country. The possession of such a power, therefore, must lead at length to such an increase of taxation as will be too heavy to be borne.

But in the very every-day administration of such a government there lies radical evil. We have seen that the tendency after a period of repression, when there is any opportunity of a public opinion being formed and expressing itself, is towards humane reforms. These, however, do not spring naturally out of the wants of the people as an organic growth: they are imposed from

above. But it would be impossible for the most enlightened and well-intentioned ruler to know fully the
circumstances in which reforms are to be applied, and it
is the more difficult for a central bureaucratic office to be
possessed of . the information necessary to guide it in the
creation of institutions that shall everywhere exactly fit
the wants of the people. Indeed, however, scarcely a
serious attempt is made to frame such well-fitting institutions, and therefore we find that in France the establishment of provincial administrative bodies and municipal
elective councils by Louis XVI. was the immediate cause
of the great Revolution. These bodies came immediately
into collision with each other, and with the former
functionaries whose position was thereby undermined,
though their office was not cancelled. The consequence
of this Revolution, which it indeed was, was a state
of the greatest confusion and irritation, for the condition
of every man in France was perniciously affected by it.
' This first Revolution exercised a prodigious influence
on the Revolution that was about to succeed it, and
caused the latter to be an event different from all the
events of the same kind that had ever till then happened
in the world and from those which have happened since.'[1]

In Russia, again, the Emancipation Act was framed to
apply equally to the whole country, no cognisance having
been taken of the very various circumstances in which it
would operate. But not alone the Emancipation Act
but the whole measures of government are framed without regard to the circumstances in which the people are
placed. Indeed it may be said that these circumstances
have never been reckoned as essential factors in the consideration of the problems under discussion, and the
measures contemplated to be adopted. For, as in France,

[1] On the State of Society in France before the Revolution of 1789, by
Alexis de Tocqueville, p. 368.

every new scheme proceeds from the desire of the sovereign to improve the State according to his own conceptions, without any strict reference to the wants of the people. 'Every young energetic sovereign has attempted to inaugurate a new epoch by thoroughly remodelling the administration according to the most approved foreign political philosophy. Institutions have not been allowed to grow spontaneously out of popular wants, but have been invented by bureaucratic theorists to satisfy wants of which the people were unconscious.'[1]

There can be no healthy social life where the relations of the people are perpetually liable to change. The circumstances in which individuals find themselves cannot, then, be taken as likely to remain constant, and cannot, therefore, be safely calculated upon with reference to action, the results of which lie in the future. There must, therefore, spring up a feeling of dissatisfaction and irritation, particularly when public opinion begins to be enlightened, for there will then be a comparison made between what is and what might be. The greater the opportunity presented by natural circumstances and the general situation of the country for the acquirement of a certain measure of material well-being, the more will irritation be felt at the interposition of artificial and arbitrary changes, with whatsoever intention they be superimposed. And at the very period at which these arbitrary changes are made, there is probably a natural revival of commercial action and social intercourse; for the period is one of internal reform, and restrictions which bore hardly upon exertion have been at least partially removed. Everything, therefore, conspires in raising up a fierce spirit of discontent that threatens the existence of the government. It is thus that 'experience has shown that the most dangerous moment for a bad government is usually that when it

[1] *Russia*, by D. Mackenzie Wallace, M.A., vol. i. p. 344.

enters upon the work of reform. . . . . The evils which
were endured with patience so long as they were inevitable, seem intolerable as soon as a hope can be
entertained of escaping from them.'[1]

It would appear, from one point of view, that of all
the various kinds of reforms upon which any government
could embark, there is none more likely to affect the
masses of the people beneficially than the abolition of
serfage, particularly when the serfs to be emancipated
enjoy neither civil rights nor domestic independence.
But then, from another point of view, the very depth and
extent of the reform make it dangerous ; for a great proportion of the people are to be placed in a position of
independence and responsibility to which they have never
been accustomed, and for which the vices inseparable
from their former condition unfit them.   A large step is
to be made, ' a gigantic experiment in social science ' is
undertaken.   ' The necessary ingredients have been put
together, but *natura naturans* has not yet played her
part in the operation.'[2]

But will Nature play her part at all in the operation so
as to produce the desired results? or will the new conditions of human existence in Russia defy the soluble
powers of natural operation ?

These questions are of immense importance to Russia ;
and, so far as she has answered them, the answers appear
to be, upon the whole, disappointing.   Let us inquire
what the new conditions are, and what has already been
their effect upon proprietors and serfs.   First, then, the
landed proprietors have been stirred up suddenly from a
life of apathetic ease to exert themselves to procure
a revenue independently of the labour of their serfs, upon

---

[1] *On the State of Society in France before the Revolution of* 1789, by
Alexis de Tocqueville, pp. 323, 324.
[2] *Russia*, by D. Mackenzie Wallace, M.A., vol. ii. p. 312.

which till hitherto they had always exclusively relied.
Second, the serfs themselves, having been relieved from
forced labour, devote their time as much as possible to
the cultivation of their own land, unless necessity compels them to labour additionally upon the lands of their
former masters.   Third, the serf, being also relieved from
the government of the patriarch of the family, has set up
a home of his own.   And, fourth, the peasant shares
now in the administration of the affairs of his commune,
in which the proprietor has no voice.

What has been already the effects of these new
conditions?   These effects appear to be very various
according to the very various circumstances in which the
proprietors and serfs had formerly been placed.   All over
Russia it is now the complaint of the proprietors that it is
impossible to induce their former serfs to work so as to
produce a fair return, and they are, it is alleged, too
often inclined to show their independence in much the
same way as tradesmen of more favoured countries not
unfrequently do—namely, in choosing the most urgent
period of work as that in which they shall cease their
labours.   Thus the harvests which are upon the point of
being saved are sometimes seriously imperilled by the
action of the free labourer ; and the former master, while
exerting himself in a way he has never been accustomed
to, is thereby threatened with ruin.   The landed proprietors
of the northern and of some of the central provinces
have suffered most heavily.   The reason of this partly
lay in the fact that in these portions the rural population
was most injured by the Emancipation.   There the soil
was chiefly worn out, and not worth the dues put upon
it.   The proprietor had formerly received a tax from his
serfs, which they paid while being allowed to work at some
other occupation than agriculture.   The individual serf
might dwell in a town at a great distance off, or he might

enrol himself as a member of one of the *artels*, or travelling companies of workmen who band themselves together, and engage in different kinds of industrial occupation. When, however, the Emancipation Act became law, this tax was payable to the government in another form through the commune. The commune was and is in many cases a harder master than the proprietor, and could not or did not allow the same degree of liberty to its subjects. This partly arose from the fact that the more worthless members of it frequently had a good deal of voice in the amount of liberty granted, and it would not be to their advantage to confer too much freedom on the more industrious members. 'The misery of the peasantry who were tied by the redemption process and the communal system to unproductive tracts of land, affected the circumstances of the landed proprietors. This peasantry sold much of their stock for rent and taxes, and consequently did not require the lease of pastures and meadows. A want of enlightenment, combined with careless management, favoured the spread of murrain among their cattle. From the village the rinderpest spread to the manors. Penury led to want of seed, and want of seed to short crops, and, in many provinces, to famine. The seasons were unfavourable, and there was no provision against such an emergency. The communal reserves of corn placed under the special care of the peasant self-government were in too many cases found empty. Province after province was called upon to feed the hungry. The charges on land consequently increased in the very provinces in which agriculture was pursued least advantageously. The inevitable emigration of the peasantry from those provinces in large numbers—not in 1870, for they are yet too firmly attached to the soil, but as soon as the government shall have become convinced of the necessity of allowing them to employ their labour more productively elsewhere—will finally accomplish the ruin of a great proportion of the proprietors of the northern and central provinces.'[1]

Many of the proprietors, indeed, have abandoned the country and betaken themselves to official life in the towns, or have engaged in industrial or commercial pursuits. Thus, particularly in the northern agricultural zone, 'the houses in which the proprietors lived—many of them as *grand seigneurs*—are for the most part deserted, and left exposed to the ravages of time.'[2] In this way, therefore, the restraining influence of the proprietor over his former serf, as regards whatever moral force his presence might exercise, has been so far lost, and the two great classes of the nation are more effectually separated from each other in position and sympathies than before.

But what have been the results of the new conditions so far as they affect the peasantry? In the northern agricultural provinces we have seen that they are in a miserable condition, and that there appears to be no relief from impending ruin. The peasantry are compulsorily attached to the soil that is taxed at a rate above its value, so that the Imperial taxes, which amount to about 3*l*. per peasant family, are only a portion of the burden of taxation to be borne by those peasants who belong to the most unproductive districts, and who possess the fewest resources.

But the misfortunes of a declining condition are seriously aggravated by the fact that the members of the commune are jointly responsible for the payment of the taxes. Although the most industrious individuals may have paid their proportion for the year, yet their stock may be seized to pay the debts of their less fortunate or

---

[1] *Report by Mr. Michell on the System of Land Tenure in Russia*, p. 58.
[2] *Russia*, vol. ii. p. 328.

more worthless neighbours.   It thus follows that, if there
be any marked tendency to decline, there is a positive
danger that every industrious peasant shall cease his toil,
for there is no certainty that the fruits of it shall be secure
from the demands of the tax-gatherer.   The consequences
of such conditions must often be disastrous.   Thus where
a member of a commune, perhaps after a life of toil
in a distant part of the country, has amassed riches, his
wealth is not secure, for he may be called upon to pay at
any moment for those members of his commune who
are defaulters, mayhap to subsidise the whole commune.   The uncertainty of such a position is also aggravated by the fact that it is no uncommon occurrence to
see the most vicious man at the head of the village
community.   'He is generally a greater drunkard than
the rest—a quality which admits of his being pro-
pitiated. . . . . It cannot be denied that, as a rule, the
despotism of such an utterly uncivilized democracy
exercises a most baneful influence on the moral and
material development of the people, and that that development is at present subservient to the paramount
interests of the Exchequer and the War Department.' [1]

'The journals are full of cases in which the industrious members of the communes are ruined for the
benefit of their brethren.   One day, it is a rich peasant
whose brickworks are seized and sold for a tenth of their
value, in order to make good the communal arrears ; the
next, it is a peasant woman in despair at seeing her
cottage sacked, the distraining officer leaving her but one
garment—her gown.' [2]

It therefore appears that, at any rate in large portions
of Russia, the condition of both proprietors and peasantry
has been very seriously and prejudicially affected by
the Emancipation Act.   But has there been any general

[1] *Report by Mr. Michell*, p. 52.   [2] *Ibid.*, see note, p. 51.

effect produced upon the peasantry as a whole by the change? Surely, at least in the most productive regions, the influence of freedom must have been, as was fully expected, most beneficial? There has been a certain general effect produced which does not, however, appear to be in the direction of improvement. Contingent upon the acquisition of liberty, the price of vodka was reduced, so that it acquired the new name of 'deshofka,' or 'cheap stuff,' thereby presenting increased temptation to the liberated serf. All appear now to agree that the peasant is very badly off, and, indeed, is in such a condition that the political writers are only divided upon the question as to what new legislation is required to place him on his legs again. He is treated by everyone as a chattel that may and must be constantly experimented with, although the results of the numerous experiments already made appear to have created within him a certain 'moral laxity and limpness.'[1] What is now the condition of the peasantry with regard to religion and morals? The Imperial Commission appointed in 1872 under the presidency of M. Walouieff, Minister of Domains, reported as follows in the following year:—'All the information and evidence obtained by the commission point to a considerable development in the observance by the peasantry of holidays which are not established by the Church, and which reduce, to the prejudice of the productiveness of the country and the moral interests of the people, the sum total of working days available for agriculture. It is supposed that the clergy not only fail to hinder an increase in the number of holidays, but that they even promote that increase. In addition to the waste of time that would otherwise be available for labour, those holidays are accompanied by another evil—namely, by an augmentation of the frequency of cases in which the

[1] *Russia*, vol. ii. p. 364.

use of alcoholic drinks is abused. As regards the statements made to the commission on the subject of the development of a baneful passion for drink among the agricultural classes, and with respect to the injurious influence of idleness and drunkenness on peasant life, and generally on the peasant economy, the commission must first of all direct attention to the fact that the complaints on the subject of drunkenness refer principally to the provinces of Great Russia, considerably less to those of Little Russia, and scarcely at all to the western and Baltic provinces. In the provinces of Great Russia drunkenness prevails not only in an individual but also in a public form. The incentive to such drunkenness is to be found not only in the numerous "family" and "Church" holidays, but also in the forms of rural self-government. Few village (communal) meetings terminate without scenes of drunkenness. Business is settled at those meetings under the influence of "treating with vodka" (corn brandy). Fines are imposed in the form of vodka. Such facts, even if desultory in their occurrence, prove that the passion for drink has taken deep root in the national character, and that the people look upon drunkenness from a peculiar point of view, without in the least recognising its moral indecency.' And, again, they proceed :—' Unfortunately a falling off in morals is very apparent, and proceeds from an increased use of spirits. The peasants (of Simbirsk and Kasan) only respect the property of others when it is impossible for them to enjoy it with immunity from punishment. In the Volokohama district of the province of Moscow the people have given themselves up entirely to drink, and are morally corrupted, so that no confidence can be placed in them. There is no respect for the rights of property; robbery is daily on the increase; horse-stealing has assumed frightful proportions.'

Again, Mr. Wallace says:—'The Volost Court is very often accessible to the influence of vodka and other kinds of bribery, so that in many districts it has fallen into utter discredit, and the peasants say that anyone who becomes a judge "takes a sin on his soul." The village assemblies, too, have become worse than they were in the days of serfage. At that time the heads of households—who, it must be remembered, have alone a voice in the decisions—were few in number, laborious, and well-to-do, and they kept the lazy, unruly members under strict control; now that the large families have been broken up, and almost every adult peasant is head of a household, the communal affairs are often decided by a noisy majority; and almost any communal decision may be obtained by "treating the Mir"—that is to say, by supplying a certain amount of vodka. Often I have heard old peasants speak of these things, and finish their recital by some such remark as this : " There is no order now ; the people have been spoiled ; it was better in the time of the masters." '[1]

Again, since the promulgation of emancipation, the serf has separated himself from the patriarchal family and set up a house of his own. The consequences of such a step having been taken are that the expenses of existence are greater, and that the head of the household cannot now so freely leave his commune to work at a distance, for in that case his wife only would remain for the most part to cultivate the communal land. There are, therefore, a greater number of peasants engaged in cultivating the communal lands than before ; and, as the Emancipation Act did not confer upon the cultivators a sufficiency of it, it becomes necessary for them to lease arable land adjoining the commune, which they find necessary to do at rack-rents. These results are of the most serious import in the future, and even now many of the peasantry have fallen a prey to greedy usurers.

From such evidence, then, we may conclude that, while in some parts of Russia matters are now much worse than before, in general the peasantry have largely made use of their freedom in an immoral self-indulgence, from which alone the hand of the master had previously preserved them. It could scarcely be otherwise. All such sudden reforms must be dangerous, for they proceed upon the assumption that men are all equally well fitted to make good use of the opportunities they possess, whether they have been accustomed for generations to slavery or to freedom. Nature moves by slow steps—by a gradual evolution along ' the lines of least resistance,' her operations being always insensible to the unaided senses. When, therefore, masses of men who have been for ages held in tutelage, and forced to work by the lash or other physical punishment, find themselves free to do as they may, it is not surprising, particularly when the guiding and restraining hand is suddenly withdrawn, that they fall down from the moral or at least decent and useful position at which they have been artificially maintained. The stimulus of self-interest ought, then, to be present in the highest degree to tutor such men to look to the future. Owing to the financial necessities of the Russian government, however, the communistic institutions were drawn tighter upon the people than before, so that, as we have seen, they now often regard the commune as ' their ruin.' While it is necessary, above all things, that the masses of the population should be free to emigrate to any part of the empire they may find most advantageous, an additional tie, which is arbitrarily regulated, binds them to their commune more closely than before. Again, when we consider that the policy of the Imperial government is strenuously exercised in developing the natural resources of the country and in establishing manufactures—towards opening mines, starting ironworks, factories, and mills, through the operation of which the demands of the country may be supplied by home productions—the evil of the new communal restrictions becomes the more apparent. A considerable proportion of the inhabitants of the villages of Russia had ceased to be agriculturalists, yet the domestic industries are not fitted to contend in any successful degree with the new industrial works of the towns, and the natural course of events demands their presence in these manufacturing centres. While a prohibitive tariff—which, as Mr. Bezobrazoff, a distinguished political economist of Russia, says, 'is one of the greatest acts of injustice that a legislature can possibly commit against the interests of agriculture '—is maintained against the introduction of good and cheap foreign goods, thereby enhancing the price and reducing the quality of all manufactured articles required by the great masses of the people being agriculturalists, those masses are still held down, at least in large districts, to the soil as agriculturalists. It is thus that the policy of the government fosters with one hand and destroys with the other.

While, indeed, the infinite number of relations of which society is made up is being constantly changed by the frequent introduction of new reforms, it is impossible that it can exist in a healthy condition. While organic functions are ignored or regarded as useless, its parts are taken to pieces and set together again artificially—often, it may be, with the best intentions, but with little likelihood of ever coming within any reasonable distance of the positions in which the operations of natural growth and development would place it.

There can, indeed, be no reform more reasonable and urgent than the liberation of the slave ; and the Russian serf was in many respects a slave. Such a condition must always be pernicious in its effects upon human well-being. It tends to degrade the human nature of the serf to the lowest level, and to influence the remainder of the people—including the master of the serf—in the same direction. The perpetuation of such a condition, then, cannot but be inimical to the general welfare. But the means by which a change in such a condition is to be effected is all-important. The relations of society must not be rudely shaken or broken asunder. Everything should be changed by natural means, and as gradually as is necessary to prevent a pernicious shock. Indeed, all obstacles to a process of emancipation by the individual serfs themselves are simply to be withdrawn. In this way the stimulus of self-interest would be enlisted, and the serf enabled to purchase his freedom upon a practicable basis.

The pre-eminent characteristic of slavery is utter indifference to the master's interest, and, therefore, perfect carelessness as regards the work done for him. Upon the other hand, self-interest induces strenuous exertions. The difference between perfect carelessness and strenuous exertions will be, as regards the value of the work done, very large. Such a difference in value will be sufficient to enable the serf to purchase his own liberty within a moderate period. But, while the necessary fund is being formed, the natural operation of emancipation must induce new habits of labour and prudence that will fit the serf to be a freeman. The process may be a tedious one, but it is also a safe one. It will not be so gratifying to the vanity of a great ruler as a large scheme of emancipation to be carried out at once by authority. But then it will proceed upon natural principles, and in a course regardful of existing relations and established interests.

The principle or method of absolutism, however, is that of arranging everything for the people, even to interfering with their private affairs. The autocratic mind cannot conceive that the interests of the country would not be endangered were the regulating bureaucratic hand to be withdrawn. There is, therefore, frequent intermeddling, and a chronic state of irritation is engendered which, when severe, threatens to develop into action. But the power of absolutism adopts measures of repression; and, to enable it to do so with safety, the upper classes of the country are drawn to the side of the government by the establishment of peculiar favours and the maintenance of special privileges. The country is therefore divided into two great divisions—the privileged few, and the repressed and oppressed many. In Russia, the many were kept down by granting them as serfs to the few, of which there are some extraordinary historical instances; while in France they were equally kept down by loading them with an unbearable taxation.

The intellectual tendencies of Russia and of France before 1789 are strikingly similar. While the philosophical writers of France descanted upon the rights of man from an abstract point of view, the educated Russians, when any question arises, 'launch into a sea of philosophical principles.'[1] In both, while the masses are oppressed, the political and social writers are divided between abstract theories in guessing without experience what may be the true medicine for the State. The mind of each nation is largely imbued with a notion that certain methods of treatment have only to be applied by the central power to cure or at least to palliate the present evils. The cry of artificial remedies is constantly heard from those who witness the suffering; but the people themselves will have none of these, which serve to produce only irritation. The last reform in France contributed, as we have seen, to hasten the climax. The very changes that are thought

[1] *Russia,* vol. ii. p. 284.

necessary to the salvation of the State are those that produce the most frightful disaster. The State dies, the parts
suffer complete disintegration, but a new life arises that
develops naturally and healthily. Every improvement
that now takes place is a real step in advance. Liberty
is now the genius of the country. The government is now
the servant of the people, not the instrument of a privileged
order. The liberty of Commerce has now triumphed over
the repression of Conquest.

France has made enormous progress since the Revolution. At that period the people had to bear the burden
of the country's defence against foreign foes, and that
defence was converted into triumphant and overwhelming
attack. It was only unfortunate that the general, through
his insatiable ambition, weakened the resources of the
country by an unnecessary extension of his military operations. Notwithstanding, however, this excess, the cultivators generally, having become, upon the expulsion of the
privileged orders, the proprietors of the soil, occupied the
most advantageous position, and bore easily the heaviest
burdens. But the taxes were light in comparison with what
they had been. Formerly, the taxation amounted from two-
thirds to eleven-twelfths of the produce, when in England
it was reckoned to be only one-fourth. It was calculated
that the condition of the labouring poor in France was
such that the necessaries of life which they could procure
were only one-fourth of that of the corresponding class in
England. The soil was in many places lying uncultivated,
for the ruinous and unequal taxation wrenched the fruits
of toil from the grasp of the labourer. When, however,
the Revolution changed all this, the hope of retaining
the fruits of labour stimulated everyone to unwonted
exertions. The greater part of the produce was now the
property of the cultivator. The result was a general improvement. The produce of France was doubled in twenty

years. From a condition of unlettered ignorance, when not one in fifty of the peasantry could read, they rapidly improved. The influence of a wide distribution of property has continued to produce the same results, so that now the agricultural produce of France has again nearly doubled. The commerce of the country has also taken enormous strides, and there are now few restrictions to the national and individual increase of wealth and prosperity.

Russia has not yet commenced this course of progress. She must first give birth, it may be with much pain and labour, to the new life that is within her, which now is constantly extinguished as it begins to breathe; and, in order to attain this, the present system of absolutism, and all the blind veneration it inspires, must pass away, and give place to another system by which the well-being of the whole people will be secure to evolve naturally from the unrestricted, and unaided, and self-regulating exertions of each and all.

CHAPTER III.

POPULAR MOVEMENTS TOWARDS THE ATTAINMENT OF THE
POLITICAL CONDITIONS OF SOCIAL WELL-BEING.

EUROPE since the period of the first French Revolution
has been for the most part in a condition of political as
well as of social transition.

The ideas of the French philosophical writers, originally derived from the democratic thought of England and
the republican action of America, spread rapidly abroad
throughout the Continent. The effect of their views, thus
widely disseminated at a time when the various States were
struggling against the power of the French arms, was
great. They were spread abroad everywhere in secret.
Secret societies were organised to assist in their promulgation. These consisted of members pledged to each other
to exert themselves to the utmost in the cause of freedom.

One of the most extensive of these societies, named
the Tugendbund of Germany, was originated by Stein, the
Prime Minister of Prussia.[1] He conceived the possibility
of inspiring the whole of Germany with the idea of parliamentary institutions, free speech, and a free press, holding
these forward as a proposed reward for the delivery of
their country from the French yoke. The League spread
rapidly, and soon numbered amongst its members the
principal inhabitants of North Germany. Later on, in

---

[1] A considerable proportion of the information contained in the first half
of this chapter has been derived from Mr. Thomas Frost's work ' *The
Secret Societies of the European Revolution,* 1776–1876, 1876.'

1808, the whole length and breadth of Germany was inspired by the idea, and the utmost exertions were ready to be made when the first opportunity for contesting the possession of the country should present itself.   This moment at length arrived.   The early and exceptionally severe winter which met the army of Napoleon in the centre of Russia suddenly reduced the strength which the imperial arms had heretofore possessed.   That disastrous campaign, therefore, became the first signal for the coming struggle.   The unity and concert which had been ensured induced the King of Prussia, mean and timorous though he was, to join Alexander of Russia in declaring war against Napoleon.   The secret organisation of the Tugendbund was now the means by which numerous corps of volunteers were at once forthcoming, as well as sums of money for their maintenance in the field.   The result of the combined operations was, therefore, that in the space of eight months the last of the French armies had crossed the Rhine.

The people, however, did not receive the expected reward of their patriotism, for the kings and princes of Germany, as soon as re-established, forgot or denied the rights of their people to political freedom.

In Spain, again, a constitution had been established by the Cortes in 1812.   Ten years thereafter that body was elected with a strong democratic majority.   The nation desired still more liberty, and the Communeros, a secret society which fostered the idea of popular sovereignty, had largely influenced the elections.   The ministry found themselves in a decided minority, and the king, possessing strong tendencies towards absolutism, was inflexible.   At this juncture Austria and Russia proposed to land a joint army on the shores of Spain, but the remonstrances of Britain prevented that means of solving the difficulty being carried out.   Ultimately a French army poured

E 2

through the passes of the Pyrenees and in less than three months overran Spain, and established Ferdinand in the full possession of an absolute sovereignty. On the one side of this struggle we find the first men in Spain, headed by Riego, the president of the Cortes; on the other the king and the ecclesiastical leaders, the former being a mere puppet in the hands of the latter.

In Italy, again, Maghella, the Neapolitan Minister of Police under Murat, entertained the idea of inspiring his countrymen with the prospect of national independence and constitutional government. With this object he introduced the secret system of the Carbonari, which early embraced in its list of members the names of the first families of the country. It spread through all classes of society, and in some of the southern towns of Italy it reckoned all the adult male population as members. Soon afterwards, in 1817, the Guelphs and the Roman Carbonari, two other secret societies, were instituted with views somewhat similar, particularly directing their attacks against the temporal power of the Pope, whose government had always been of the most despotic character. Other societies existed here and there throughout the peninsula, some consisting of desperate characters whom the misgovernment of Naples and other States had partly the credit of creating. By the year 1820 lodges of the Carbonari were established throughout all the principal States of Italy. · These contributed in uniting the greater part of the inhabitants together in the same ideas of freedom and unity. In the summer of 1820 the standard of revolt was raised, and Naples declared for the constitution. Ferdinand, however, had pledged himself to Austria to maintain the despotic character of his rule, and he therefore abdicated in favour of his son, who accepted the constitution. This success, however, exasperated the Austrian emperor, who, like the Pope, denounced Carbonarism, threatening with death and confiscation of goods all those who might be found to be members of the society.

At this time the King of Prussia was equally alarmed by the Tugendbund, and both these monarchs concerted together and with the Emperor of Russia as to a plan of mutual support. They met and formed a ' Holy Alliance' for the defence of the principle of Legitimacy against that of Revolution which was created by the growing desire of the people for liberty and popular government. On the other hand the most influential members of the secret societies of Italy met together, and made provisional arrangements for the unity of the north of Italy, and the establishment of a federative bond with the remainder so soon as the Austrian troops should be driven out.

The existence of the constitution in Naples, and particularly the occurrence of some rioting, led the leaders of the Carbonari to throw off the secret character of their association which they had hitherto maintained there. The forces of the Holy Alliance now invaded Italy. Their power was too great to be withstood with a reasonable prospect of success until they reached the confines of the Neapolitan territory. Here the revolutionary forces had been intended to meet them, but the treachery of the King of Naples spoiled the chances of effectual opposition, and the general commanding the troops found them dispersing almost without a combat. Thus the freedom of the government of Naples was destroyed, and those who had occupied the leading positions in its administration were executed, the Austrian drums meanwhile beating so as to drown the dying utterances of the victims.

The Carbonari in the north of Italy were at this time by no means inactive. A constitution was demanded by the people and the military from Victor Emmanuel in Piedmont. The same objection to the sacrifice of the principle of Legitimacy that had actuated Ferdinand of Naples caused this king likewise to abdicate. His son, who was a member of the revolutionary society, was meanwhile appointed regent, the brother upon whom the crown devolved being at some distance. The Prince of Carignano, however, was vain, fickle, and treacherous. He marched to the frontiers, but, instead of engaging the Austrians, he invited them to invade his country and to effect a counter-revolution. The result was that the successor to the throne was established thereon by the intervention of the troops of the Holy Alliance, the patriots retreating to Genoa, from whence they expatriated themselves. Thus the aspirations of the populations of Italy after the liberty and the unity of their country proved, in their first attempts at realisation, abortive. The nearness of the prize for which they had risked so much, however, induced them, notwithstanding the melancholy fate of their most illustrious leaders, to maintain the hope of its eventual acquisition.

A year or two after the collapse of these revolutionary movements, Joseph Mazzini, a young man of eighteen, took the oath of the order of the Carbonari in a garret of a house in Genoa. Shortly afterwards he became suspected by the government, and, without anything being laid to his charge, he was imprisoned for six months in the fortress of Savona. On his release he was ordered to leave Italy. Having taken up his residence in Marseilles, he united himself with others in the same situation, and originated a new society upon improved principles, which he named 'Young Italy.' From his new position as a centre he strove to reinspire his countrymen with the same ideas as had formerly been cultivated by the various associations, of which that of the Carbonari was the principal one. But, in addition, he promulgated the belief in a law of progress and duty, and in the conception of a United Italy, established under a republican government. He printed and distributed his views in a journal which was produced by the united gratuitous labours of a small colony of exiles. By means of sailors and private individuals favourable to the new society, the journal was conveyed into Italy in a clandestine manner, where its sale provided funds which assisted in printing the succeeding copies. The new association spread rapidly throughout the country, especially in Lombardy, Tuscany, and the Papal States. Private presses were employed in some of the cities to reproduce the journal, and print other matters for the service of the society. It is said that in twelve months from its origination the new association became the dominant one throughout Italy. But, while Mazzini and his compatriots were thus engaged, the attention of the French government was drawn upon them, and sentence of expulsion from France was pronounced. The work, however, necessitated the continued presence of the head of the society in Marseilles, which was in every way the most excellent situation for the seat of the apostolate.

It was therefore at perpetual imminent risk of discovery that Mazzini continued for more than a year busily employed, confined all the time within the same small room, editing and superintending the printing of the journal, and managing the other details of the society. At length, it being impossible to defeat the efforts of the police longer, Mazzini removed to Geneva, from which city he continued to inspire the members, and to organise and regulate the efforts of those of them who were from time to time bound together for common enterprises. Through the indiscretions of some, and the treachery of others, the police of Piedmont discovered the names of several of the members, who were immediately imprisoned in large numbers. Many of them were executed; others were compelled to leave the country, among the latter being Garibaldi.

An expedition, under the guidance of Ramorino, a general who had distinguished himself in the last Polish insurrection, proved abortive on account of his treachery. At this time Mazzini's labours in the cause of his country were incessant. The governments of Austria, Russia, and Prussia complained to the federal government of Switzerland because of the asylum which they afforded to one whom they regarded as an arch-plotter, and the result was an order from the Swiss government for him to quit the country. Having no other place of retreat more promising, he betook himself to London, where occasionally pawning his articles of clothing, and sometimes, when better off, distributing them among his fellow exiles, if anything worse off than himself, he persevered heroically in the prosecution of the object of his life.

A new attempt to attack the position of Legitimacy in Italy was prepared in 1846, and matured into action two years later. Nothing but the view of imminent danger to the thrones of kings and princes appears to have any effect in inducing them to relax the hardness of despotic rule. On this occasion, after much excitement manifested throughout Italy, in which the popular force was ostensibly encroaching in various States upon the hereditary prerogatives of the Crown, the instinct of self-preservation dictated to the rulers the necessity for granting various privileges. In some of the northern States, however, the Austrian troops, being not far distant, were called in as the least of two evils, and the rights of Legitimacy were saved at the expense of an occupation. This measure, which was carried out in the summer of 1847, served only to increase the popular excitement over the remainder of Italy. The King of the Sicilies and the Grand Duke of Tuscany granted a

constitution, and the Pope took the matter of representative government into consideration.   In this state of
affairs the French revolution of 1848 cast its influence
suddenly into the popular scale.   The Pope quickly
called into council a body of laymen.   Venice was
evacuated by Austrian soldiers, and it appointed a provisional government of its own.   Milan ran the same
course, and the most part of the intervening country
was in the hands of the insurgents.   Contingent on
this condition of affairs in Lombardy, Piedmont broke
with Austria ; but the war which followed, being conducted by the Piedmontese army for the most part, was
trammelled by the selfish policy of Charles Albert, the
King of Piedmont.

Mazzini, then at Milan, impressed on the provisional
government there the necessity of acting only with volun-
teer forces, who would be commanded by experienced
officers, political exiles from other countries.   This wise
advice was ignored, and the result was that the lively
spirit of patriotism which abounded everywhere was
curbed, checked, and defeated in its contest with Austria
from its association with the forces of the king.   The
same error took place in the south of Italy.   The
Neapolitan army was restrained in its action by its
reluctant king and the collusion of the Pope, through
whose dominions it had to pass.   The discovery of the
king's treachery caused a tumult in which the popular
cause was defeated through the organisation of the Swiss
Guards, and this afforded a pretext for the giving over the
property of the liberals to pillage.

Notwithstanding, therefore, the numbers of volunteers who attacked the Austrians, and the success of their
measures, the complete failure of the various armies of
Italy to fulfil the trust placed in their cooperation caused
the war to terminate ingloriously.

Shortly after this the Pope, being hard pressed, fled to Gaeta, from which retreat he launched his thunders against the revolution. Garibaldi now reached Rome with a few thousand volunteers, and, a republican government being instituted, the constituent assembly voted almost unanimously for its confirmation, and for the extinction of the sovereign power of the Pope. No dissentient voice came from the municipalities of the provinces ; all was accord in favour of the new condition of things.

In other parts of Italy the progress of events was chequered. In Genoa the popular party was triumphant. In Brescia the insurrection was suppressed after the partial destruction of the city by bombardment. In Venice the defence was still actively maintained. During the months of April and May, however, the Austrian armies had subjugated Lombardy, occupied Piedmont, and entered Tuscany and the Romagna, so that Rome and Venice alone remained in the hands of the people. In Rome the triumvirs, with Mazzini at their head, governed with a success that had never before been known, while admitting at the same time a liberty that had never before been experienced.

The French now came to the assistance of the Austrians. They entered Rome upon July 3, when Mazzini and Garibaldi immediately fled. Venice also had capitulated, and the efforts of the popular forces throughout Italy in the cause of freedom and unity were frustrated. Schemes of revolt were thereafter perennially planned, but their execution was as continually marred. In 1859 Napoleon III., as the ally of Victor Emmanuel, assisted in driving the Austrians from Lombardy, and that province was united to Piedmont, in exchange for which service Savoy and Nice were added to France. This programme of acquiring Lombardy was the old one of Charles Albert, not the fulfilment of any aspiration of

the people.   This is proved by the continued occupation
of Rome on the one hand, and the toleration of the
Austrian possession of Venetia upon the other.   The
designs of Young Italy, however, were not to be over-
thrown, and after Austria had been driven from Lombardy the unity of Italy was rendered the more easy of
accomplishment.   The whole people were of one mind ;
they were resolute in a desire for unity, even though
it were through an extension of the Piedmontese kingdom.

Mazzini, a thorough republican, was temporarily
brought over to this view, and the amalgamation of the
various States under one government became only a question of time.   This was soon accomplished.   Cavour, the
Piedmontese minister, guided the forces of his country so
well that the fruits of the revolutionary agitation were
plucked to enrich the rule of Victor Emmanuel at the
moment they became ripe.

Thus Italy became united and independent ; and, however much the idea of freedom had been associated with
the republican form of government, the expectations of
the people were not disappointed by the introduction of
a government, though monarchical, that had prescription
and experience in its favour.   The degree of freedom
might not have been so great as that hoped for ; but the
lack was amply supplied by the amount of security that a
settled government, whose machinery was already in full
working order, at once introduced.   The Italian revolution thus accomplished was distinctively a political one.
In other parts of Europe, however, the general popular
movement partook somewhat of a religious character.

The countries that were thus agitated were those
which had advanced well politically.   It is the natural
order of progression in the regeneration of all States.
First, the material effects of political despotism are felt

and struggled with; afterwards, when a measure of freedom has been attained, the conservative character of ecclesiastical despotism is all the more keenly felt; the political despotism having been got rid of, the other, occupying the whole field, becomes, though weaker, relatively more prominent than before. It is true that the influence of freedom of thought that is consequent on freedom of speech and of the press will ultimately dispose of this tyrannical element in ecclesiastical organisation. But at first, and so long as large classes of men are bound up either by the effects of their early education or their inability to see and contest the influences of superstition, the ancient ideas of paternal domination will still float about, and so long will there exist two parties in the State, one of which will perpetually endeavour to gain a domination over the other. The influence of the ecclesiastical party may not be powerful enough to dominate the government, but it may be sufficient to excite frequent strife, the manifestation of which will often be the excuse with a new government for the restriction of liberty.

No more pernicious association has ever existed in Europe than that of the Jesuits. They have, with a transcendently powerful belief in the importance of their own mission, disregarded every idea of honour and virtue in order to compass their designs, and no foe has ever with more persistence attacked the liberties of mankind. Switzerland was constantly in trouble from the standing disagreement between the Roman Catholics and the Protestants, or Dissidents. The Jesuits were at the root of the distraction which divided the country, and it was found to be essential to its freedom that the power and influence of the Roman hierarchy should be effectually curbed. In 1844 and 1845 Lucerne was repeatedly attacked, but unsuccessfully, by volunteers.

Thereupon the Catholic cantons, in defiance of the constitution, formed a league for their mutual defence. The strength of the federal government was, however, amply sufficient to repel this attack, and the Diet resolved by large majorities that the Catholic League and the Society of Jesus were illegal associations. The result was that the League was dissolved, and the Jesuits were expelled from Switzerland. Monastic establishments were suppressed all over the country, and the cantons that had attacked the constitution were put on the same footing as the others, the privileges of the ruling conservative minorities being taken away.

Political freedom has been followed in Italy by a reduction of ecclesiastical privileges, and by a suppression of the monastic houses. In Germany, at the present day, the contest between liberalism and the claims of the clergy proceeds, and the apparently firm determination of the government to reduce the clerical pretensions indicates their appreciation of the danger to the internal peace of the country which now exists in this direction. In Spain the influence of the clergy has always been too powerful for the existence of liberal government ; and at the present time the power of an undue centralisation seeks to deprive the towns of self-government, and, instead of allowing the civilization of the towns to manifest itself freely, it is now placed under the espionage of mayors who are nominated by the central government—a step which is as inimical to liberty as it is priestly in its origin. Till Spain understands more clearly what it is that freedom springs from, her government will verge more and more towards absolutism, and the germs of revolution will grow to maturity, and freedom will be temporarily obtained at the price of civil war. There seem to be the elements of constant disturbance in a country one part of whose people are influenced by the growth of commerce, but another part live on the soil and breathe the atmosphere of long past generations, whose whole ideas are those of paternal government. In France the clergy exercise a baneful influence, and that influence does not appear materially to diminish. The reason of this may arise largely from the retrograde movement which has taken place in the national education. The numbers of monks and nuns that are now occupied in teaching the young has largely increased. In 1869 more than half the girls were educated by nuns, and a large proportion of boys were educated either by monks or nuns; and a German writer[1] therefore concludes that, 'as all public instruction is by degrees being confided to the various ecclesiastical societies, the nation will become more and more weaned from independent thinking, and in consequence a more docile and powerless tool of the Roman Church.'

Whatever form the struggle for freedom has taken, the desire for its existence has been manifested, more or less openly and violently, in every European State during the last eighty years. Greece has become free from the dominion of Turkey; Poland has struggled bravely, and might have, but for her intestine divisions and conflicts, proclaimed her independence; and Russia, even, has not been free from the enthusiasm which has exhibited itself everywhere for popular freedom. Alexander I. travelled through his extensive dominions, and found it lifting its head everywhere. At his death, a revolutionary insurrection took place, which, but for the indecision of its leaders, most probably would have upset the government of the Czar. Its suppression revealed the extent of the conspiracy. The leaders occupied high positions in

---

[1] A. Freiherr von Fircks. See *Journal of the Statistical Society* for March, 1875.

society, and were brave, able, and upright men. The army was permeated to a large extent by the spirit of rebellion. At the present time Russia is full of discontent, and tracts relating stories descriptive of the miserable condition of the country are spread abroad and read with avidity everywhere. The secret society of the Nihilists numbers among its members numerous government officials; and hundreds of persons, including youths of both sexes, have been prosecuted and drafted off to Siberia, as having been found to be, or suspected of, entertaining revolutionary designs.

The general tendency, therefore, which has been manifested throughout Europe since the period of the first French Revolution, has been towards the assertion of popular rights; and there has been, in consequence, a universal conspiracy against the ancient, organised, and combined forces of absolutism. It could not be that such a tendency, though manifesting itself everywhere, would be successful in its operations, without the most violent struggles and the most unfortunate losses. The impossibility of organising any extensive movement with efficiency in secret, has prevented in general a success equivalent to the popular desire for, and expectation of, it. Yet success has not been altogether wanting; and the map of Europe is now formed to a large extent as the result of the new expressions of the popular will, and partly with the exhibition and the action of popular force.

But those who have come forward to influence the political life of their country by their words or actions, thereby inspiring their fellows, have been chiefly men of education, and often men of position, sometimes of the highest. These individuals have proceeded for the most part from the towns, and they have risen not by the favour of the Crown, but by the exercise of their own faculties. With them the inducements to exertion, which a sense of property, an extended sphere of action, and an increased knowledge produce, are now felt to be sufficient to restrain those who were formerly restrained by the hand of physical force. The time of repression and of slavery is looked back upon as having for ever passed, and that of liberty and spontaneity as having arrived, but the laws remain unaltered, and free action is forbidden ; the faculties and the opportunities that have developed thus far are prohibited from proceeding farther, and the strength of nature chafes and exerts itself to break the ties which bind it.

The new condition of things has mainly arisen in Europe within the last century. The progress of knowledge that had been fostered by the establishment of settled governments, after the period of violence and anarchy which characterised the middle ages, led to a further development of the arts. The arts of navigation and of roadmaking profited like the others ; and the increase of commerce, and consequently of material benefit which followed thereon, led the way to moral and intellectual progress. Every further step in the direction of uniting mankind together by improvements in these arts, particularly in the introduction of railways, has had its effect in promoting the development of the mental faculties of mankind, and of creating a desire for further means of advancement. We thus trace the origin of the extensive symptoms of dissatisfaction with the reign of absolutism in Europe, which have continued to manifest themselves more particularly within the last few decades, to the extraordinarily rapid extension of the means of communication, which have bound the people and their interests together more closely, and have conferred upon each section thus united, more abundantly than ever before, the most extensive material, intellectual, and moral benefits.

The extension of the means of civilization, which has of late become so rapid, has broken powerfully upon the heretofore quiescent reign of the few, and the breach has been the more sudden and violent in proportion as modern ideas and modern facts have laid hold of the people. The result has been, where legislators have not taken warning by the course of events in other countries, and relaxed the reins of government as they saw the desire of the people for a more ample freedom, that the collision of the old and the new principles has been a violent one, and blood has been extensively shed. Where, upon the other hand, enlightened statesmanship has counselled the extension of new rights and privileges suitable to the new conditions, a progressive freedom has established itself as the normal condition of the State, and liberalism and individualism are gradually supplanting restriction and despotism. In the words of Lord Palmerston, there are revolutionists, ' blind-minded men, who, animated by antiquated prejudices and daunted by ignorant apprehensions, dam up the current of human improvement until the irresistible pressure of accumulated discontent breaks down the opposing barriers, and overthrows and levels to the earth those very institutions which a timely application of renovating means would have rendered strong and lasting.' But, as Lord Palmerston also has it, there are rulers who are ' mere men of straw and Guy Faux,' like the Emperor of Austria, when Metternich ruled with cruel repression, and could ' draw on, by his personal influence, various other governments, despotic like his own, to pursue the same policy, to prevent all improvement, to stifle all symptoms of life among nations, and to enforce the stillness of death, and to boast that such a state of tranquillity is a proof of contentment and a guarantee for happiness.' But the system of progression has never been willingly acted upon by sovereigns who

F

have been accustomed to despotic rule ; and, when the
tide of popular enthusiasm has become strong enough and
has provided itself with the means, a battle of the most
bloody kind must needs be fought, in which, the popular
side being successful, an anarchy of freedom is too likely
to result.   All authority is apt at first to be cast aside,
as the accustomed exhibition of it has been found to be
galling and oppressive.   Thus, then, there is likely to be
a sad and painful oscillation, such as we have witnessed
in France and Spain, and may peradventure see in Russia.
It is essential, in the liberalisation of political institutions,
that some sort of authority shall be preserved.   None can
be worse than that which relies alone on physical force—
that is the last step available on the road from order to anarchy.   There can be none better than that which is based
on the sanction of tradition, its sternness being relaxed as
the masses of the people become fitted for representative
institutions.   But with despots such as Nicholas of Russia,
Philip II. of Spain, Ferdinand VII. of Naples, and the
Austrian minister Metternich, who can see no gradation
between absolutism and anarchy, the difficulty of an
amendment of the situation becomes formidable.   The
views of such rulers stand in entire antagonism with those
of their most enlightened subjects, and there appears to
be no method available by which that difference can
be reduced which may ostensibly preserve the sanction of
authority.

   In England we are accustomed to regard political
institutions as being of an essentially developmental character, changing their bearing according to the changes
which take place among the people.   The precious advantage of free commerce in bringing wealth, or at least
comparative comfort, to everyone engaged in it, has become the most secure guarantee of the maintenance of
a peaceful progress.   Internal tranquillity has become in

Britain such an accustomed condition of existence that no fears are entertained in the enlargement of popular liberties. It has unfortunately, however, been otherwise in many parts of the European continent, and, but for the terror inspired in the minds of rulers and statesmen by the first French Revolution, repression and oppression might have been still dominant. That system of progressive improvement which Lord Palmerston, in the name of the government of this country, persisted in recommending to foreign monarchs and statesmen, appears to have been little appreciated by them. The masses of the people in the continental States were feared by those above them, a kind of incipient anarchy existing which threatened at any moment to break out anywhere. Freedom has, in fact, prospered not so much as unification of late years in Europe. Commerce could not exist at all in its modern proportions, without the creation of a greater unity than has existed heretofore. Men were often content with that amount of freedom which would enable them to prosecute with fair success their individual interests, and they could dispense with that full amount of it which is felt to be indispensable when they desire to govern themselves, and when each one becomes more accustomed to independence.

Italy and Germany have within a very few years past become united into great countries. The petty harassments of separate petty States, having their own customs unions, and their own restrictions on personal movements, had become intolerable, and the first necessity was that of unity, and these States now await the extension of a further degree of liberty. The social democratic party of Germany, it is true, are not inclined to wait; but the small proportion of their representatives, when compared with the loudness and apparent extension of their doctrines, may indicate fairly their real power in the country.

The two greatest statesmen of modern Europe—namely, Count Cavour and Prince Bismarck—are the two who have been the most successful; for they have courted fortune for the glory and the solid advantage of their respective countries to a large extent, by forgetting the old traditions of monarchy, and by bending to meet the popular view and to satisfy the popular aspiration.

The present position of Europe is one of political transition. Those States which have recognised the advantages the extension of commercial transactions creates, are those which will gravitate most rapidly towards free institutions; while, upon the other hand, where the prevalent ideas are those of territorial aggrandisement or commercial exclusiveness, the political condition may be one of incertitude. The first class of States are those which produce citizens capable of self-reliant vigour of mind and of action—men who will traverse the world and subdue it; the other class will produce a slavish, inactive people, dreading unknown evils, and impressed by nothing so much as the mysterious strength of their own government.

The spirit of free institutions, however, may prevail while the form which ought to have perished is still retained—so slavish are mankind in their regard and veneration for the past.

The representatives of the old ideas of lordly domination and privilege, temporal and spiritual, in Great Britain, still maintain a position and sit in a house distinct from the representatives of the people. In the two oldest republican governments the Senate is composed of the representatives of the several States of which the countries—Switzerland and the United States—are composed; so that the representatives of the people and those of the State governments are separated, and, so far as their interests are different, the harmony of governmental institutions may be disturbed; and, as the Senate is the house of chiefest authority, in every case of collision the interests of the people are apt to suffer. The influence of the slaveholding States of America before the Civil War was powerful enough to create unjust and pernicious wars and quarrels, and ultimately it brought on the country the disaster of that great war itself, all of which would have been, as inimical to the interests of the people, avoided had not the popular vote been embarrassed and nullified by the preponderance of the States. In the European States the system of two representative houses has been maintained. Even in republican France, the representatives are separated into two classes sitting in two chambers, although the difference existing between the qualifications of the individuals sitting in each chamber is essentially one of age; for the deputies must be at least twenty-five years of age, whereas the members of the Senate must be forty. Thus, whatever advantage results to the upper house from this difference of age must be in the nature of additional experience, though it does not follow that the representatives of the people in the lower house will be inexperienced; and in this country, and probably to some extent in France, the younger men would be often chosen for their recognised position and ability, and therefore they would be as likely as men of inferior acquirements, though of more experience, to legislate and administrate rightly.

The chief arguments in favour of the retention of the two houses have been well stated by Baron Stockmar as follows :—'A first chamber is to form a solid counter-weight to the demagogic element. Everything depends on this, that the first chamber should not continue to be an exclusive aristocratic caste institution. It must be as popular as the second chamber; but it must at the same time, in opposition to that, contain conservative elements, and thus promise a greater security for stability, quiet, and moderation.

'This, it appears to me, can be effected as follows :—On the one hand, the first chamber should be as popular as the second. This is only possible if it have the same origin as the latter, and springs by election immediately from the people as does the latter. Not birth, but election must make a man a member of the first chamber. And his election is not to be for life, but, as with the second chamber, only for a certain time. Whoever elects for the second chamber should elect for the first. . . . . Every gleam of prerogative, of aristocracy, of exclusiveness, must be extinguished in it. . . . . Both chambers must be numerically alike. It is only in this way that the rejection of the decisions of the second chamber by the first can avoid having an invidious, an offensive, and caste-like character, which might appear as an arbitrary, and therefore illegitimate, impediment to the progress aimed at. . . . . Conformably with its more conservative nature, the first chamber must be grounded on a conservative law of election. The conservative element in this State is and remains two-fold—wealth and intellect.'

When it became the duty of Lord Grey to shape the constitution of some of the British colonies, he found that when he extracted all the men of wealth, intellect, or honesty for a first chamber, the number left to form legislators of a second were few and ill-qualified. In America, the members of the second chamber have never been recognised in that country as singularly able ; and Horace Greeley even affirmed, as the result of his experience, that the chamber was no place for a gentleman. The effect, therefore, of the institution of two chambers is frequently, if not always, to consign the most important and active duties of legislation to the one which is composed of men

who are not remarkably well qualified for the execution of
such functions, the first chamber having naturally attracted
all those of superior character. Mr. John Stuart Mill
has shown that if the second chamber possess a revolutionary character, the safety of the first is imperilled; for,
as the representatives of the people are dissatisfied, they
will brook the interference of those above them the less,
until peradventure the passion of popular fury should
seize them, and the obstacles in their path will be violently
swept aside.   In this way, at the very time in which the
first or conservative chamber is supposed to afford a check,
its influence is found to be unavailable in stemming the
current.   All countries may be subject at intervals to the
clamours of popular discontent; for if, from whatever
reason, multitudes of workpeople are thrown out of work,
there arises an instinctive clamour against the government.
' A hungry man is an angry man,' and violence takes the
place of reason.   Where the popular representatives are
readily influenced by the mob, where they are inclined to
join the cry of discontent, the safety of the government
will be to some extent threatened.

When, however, the whole wealth of intellect, position,
and experience are concentrated in one chamber only, the
interaction of the various forces within it must continually
tend to correct the extreme tendencies of the few.   An
amount of stability is thereby acquired which could not
be otherwise secured; the reign of reason is established
within the one chamber, instead of the action of force between the two.   The objections of the previous first
chamber may now be replied to by the members of the
combined chambers; discussion of each measure now takes
the place of arbitrary stoppage, and probably of legislative conflict.   Conciliation is substituted for persistent
opposition.   There would therefore arise from such a
progress manifest advantages to the government of the

people : for, first, the best men would be selected for the one chamber ; and, second, those so selected would be in the best position to discuss and deal with the various measures proposed ; the government would be in the maximum degree representative, respectable, and stable. In Great Britain such a change would affect the interests of the country probably not so much as the interests of the members of the Upper House, who instead of being, as at present, relegated to a sphere of inactive serenity, would continue—as many of them commence—to occupy a position of high influence in the counsels of the country. The outlets that certainly exist for the activity of the members of the House of Lords are at present amply recognised ; but those outlets would continue the same though the members, or those of them who should become representatives, were to condescend now to form with the Commons a great national assembly, which would then probably become the 'greatest legislative assembly' in the world.

The principal administrators of the government of a country must, in the interests of the nation, be made responsible for their actions directly to the nation. Although, therefore, they may be set up by the representatives of the people, they will not be at every turn of policy at the mercy of those representatives, but of those who, upon any particular question at issue, will be appointed by the people. The chief magistrate or minister would therefore possess the power of dissolving the assembly, so that the country should have the opportunity of deciding at any time upon any question of policy that might arise. In such a manner would the interests of a free people be preserved from encroachment ; in such a way would their voice be heard upon every important issue ; no unnecessary step would then intervene between their actual power and the manifestation of it. Government would then exist for the people; it would form an engine capable of adaptation to purposes multifariously social as well as political. The chief function of government would then become engrossed with peaceful internal development. Commerce would demand successfully more attention to the conditions of its safe and successful prosecution, and the more recondite facts of its secure development would form a science to be eagerly prosecuted not merely by scattered and unqualified individuals, but by the people's representatives with the public funds and for the general good. The more commerce binds the people of a country together, and joins the inhabitants of the world in one family, the individual interests of each of whose members is recognised to the utmost extent, so much the more will the establishment of free representative institutions be desired.

CHAPTER IV.

OBSTACLES TO SOCIAL WELL-BEING IN GREAT BRITAIN AND IRELAND.

IN a previous chapter we have described the effect which the presence of towns has had upon the emancipation and prosperity of the inhabitants of the country ; and we shall endeavour to point out in this and in the following chapter some of the influences which the position of a country as a whole, including the existence and growth of towns within it, has had in defining the kind of the emancipation, and the subsequent results of it.

While the rural population in commercial England was attracted to the towns at an early period in considerable proportions, those who dwelt in the country did not ultimately become, as a whole, the possessors of those rights in the soil which their fellows upon the continent of Europe, and more particularly in France, were fortunate enough to acquire. The facts were really against the masses of the English agricultural population. While, as we have already seen, the serf ultimately became or is now becoming over the length and breadth of the continent the possessor of the land whereon he had lived and which he and his ancestors had for long cultivated, in England he was dissociated from the soil by the laws enacted in the reigns of Henry VII. and his predecessors. These laws though on the one hand curtailing the power of the barons, who turbulently threatened the monarchy, on the other compensated them for the loss at

the expense of their dependents who were living on and
drawing their subsistence from the soil.   The retainers
who were accustomed only to military and personal service formed a large proportion of these, and, being unacquainted with agricultural labour, they were manifestly
unable to occupy a farm or to pay rent for it, and they
could scarcely be prepared to descend to menial labours
under those whom they had hitherto regarded as
their inferiors.   But in addition to that class, which the
enactment of the new laws rendered useless, there must
have been large numbers who, already occupied on the
soil, were deprived of employment; for the effect of the
laws, when rigidly enforced, was seen in the pulling down
of houses, and the throwing of arable land into grass.
The lot of the remaining portion of the rural population
was somewhat more tolerable—they became tenants
under the landlords, or labourers for the tenants.   The
consequence of such an extensive displacement of population was unexpected and unparalleled.   The country
was filled with sturdy beggars who, necessarily being
desperate, preyed upon their more fortunate fellow-
countrymen.   The consequent evils of this legislation
soon became tangible enough, and as early as the fourth
year of the reign of Henry VII. it became the earnest
object of further legislation to counteract the mischief
already created.   Numerous enactments were promulgated in his and the succeeding reigns.   Nothing, however,
could undo the evil that had so easily been accomplished ;
for the landlords, recognising immediately the immense
advantage of a money rent, and the relief which the
reduction of the numbers of their retainers afforded them,
were strongly affected towards the new order of things.
The king had virtually surrendered his lordship over the
soil to the lords, who had originally obtained it in gift
mediately or immediately, and held it on feudal service.

The land was now freed from the maintenance of a large population which, though oftentimes in the hands of quarrelsome and imperious lords a source of intestine disquiet, had nevertheless acted as the defence of the kingdom. It was now decreed that houses should not be pulled down, that those which had should be rebuilt, and that land thrown out of tillage should be restored thereto. It was enacted in the reign of Henry VIII. that no one should possess more than 2,000 sheep on lands not his own, and that no-one should have more than one farm ; both of which, it may be noted, are ordinances that would prejudicially affect the large tenant rather than the proprietor.

Notwithstanding, however, all the statutes that were enacted, the country was filled with vagrants who, having been made vagrants by iniquitous laws, wandered about, supporting themselves ruthlessly as necessity compelled them. Other laws, namely those protecting property, being constantly violated, the punishments legally attachable to their infringement became as a consequence gradually more severe ; so that we find in England, up till a very recent period, heavier and more disproportionate sentences executed against thieves than probably any other country was ever acquainted with. The result was that during the reign of Henry VIII.—a period of thirty-six years—seventy-two thousand persons were hanged for vagrancy, while in that of his daughter Elizabeth the number of executions still averaged from three to four hundred yearly.

At an early period poor laws were made with the view of relieving the destitute, and a system of taxation for the support of the poor was established ; for voluntary charity at the first had been found insufficient, although the special attention of the clergy was directed to encourage the people to almsgiving.

On the one hand, the people, as a whole, were now
called upon to maintain a paid army for the defence of the
kingdom; on the other, to support the poor dispossessed
vagrants who had formerly been the army, supporting
themselves from the cultivation of the land that was now
in unrestricted possession of the great proprietors; and from
that time to this the people, as a whole, have borne the
burdens which the land of the country should have continued to support. But from the large numbers of poor
to be sustained, and the reduction in the wealth of the
country consequent on the subtraction of such a quantity
of useful labour from the soil, it is obvious that the inhabitants generally would be ill-prepared for the support of
such a tax, and the poor laws would necessarily be directed
too much at first with an exclusive view to provide funds
to sustain the poor, and the important consideration of
means by which their number should be reduced would
be lost sight of.

The position attained may be well expressed in the
eloquent words of Mr. Joseph Fisher:—'The British
poor law is a slur upon its boasted civilization. The
unequal distribution of land and of wealth leads to great
riches and great poverty. Intense light produces deep
shade. Nowhere else but in wealthy England do God's
creatures die of starvation, wanting food, while others are
rich beyond comparison. The soil which affords sustenance
for the people is rightly charged with the cost of feeding
those who lack the necessaries of life, but the same object
would be better achieved in a different way. Poor rates
are now a charge upon a man's entire estate, and it would
be much better for society if land to an amount equivalent
to the charge were taken from the estate and assigned to
the poor. If a man is charged 100l. a year poor rate, it
would make no real difference to him, while it would make
a vast difference to the poor, to take land to that value,

put the poor to work tilling it, allowing them to enjoy the produce. Any expense should be paid direct by the landlord, which should leave the charge upon the land, and exempt the improvements of the tenant which represent his labour, free.

'The evil has intensified in magnitude, and a permanent army of paupers numbering at the minimum 829,281 persons, but increasing at some periods to upwards of 1,000,000, has to be provided for. The cost, about 8,000,000l. a year, is paid not by landlords but by tenants, in addition to the various charities founded by benevolent persons.'

'. . . . The owner of land is the people as represented by the Crown, and the charges thereon next in succession to the claims of the State are the Church and the poor.'[1]

Large holdings have continued to grow in size, for the transfer of land in this country has always been difficult, tedious, uncertain, and costly, so that whatever small freeholds existed have in course of time been absorbed by the large estates. Additionally to this cause of their growth, the extensive commons which existed have for the most part been divided amongst the landowners; indeed it is reckoned that no less than 7,600,000 acres, equal to one-fifth of the whole area of England and Wales, have been enclosed between the beginning of the eighteenth century and the present time, a very considerable proportion of which was land whereon the poor had the right to graze a cow and keep pigs or poultry.

Indeed before the commencement of this century there was no legislative recognition of the rights of the peasantry to the commons, and during the whole of the eighteenth century a systematic robbery of this property from the

---

[1] *The History of Landholding in England*, by Joseph Fisher, F.R.H.S., 1876, pp. 80, 81.

peasants, whose it had been from time immemorial, was carried out by the political interest of the great landowners for their own private advantage. Mr. T. E. Kebbel refers to this subject as follows:—' The fact is, that the right of the peasant to compensation for the loss inflicted on him by enclosure is just as clear as any other right which rests on usage and prescription. Allotment grounds, wherever such rights have been extinguished, are not a question of benevolence but of simple justice. A hundred years ago this seems to have been wholly overlooked. Everybody was compensated but those who stood in need of it most ; and the rapid rise in poor rates which followed this policy, though it sometimes punished those who were the chief gainers by it, was but cold comfort to those who were the chief losers. And even now, we repeat, but little has been done, compared with what it seems reasonable to suppose might have been done, towards carrying out the intentions of the legislature and preventing such mistakes in future. The Act of 1845 provided that out of every enclosed waste a proportion of land should be set aside for the use of cottagers in lieu of their rights of common, subject, however, to the discretion of the Enclosure Commissioners, of which these gentlemen seemed to have availed themselves very largely. The land was to be vested in trustees, to be called the " allotment wardens," who should receive the rents and devote them to parochial purposes. But out of nearly 500,000 acres which have been enclosed since the date of that Act, only about 2,000 acres have been so assigned. And the point is one of great practical interest, as several millions of acres of waste land still exist in England capable of cultivation, and doubtless destined to the plough.' [1]

The result is that now two-thirds of the lands of England and Wales are in the hands of 10,207 persons,

[1] *The Agricultural Labourer*, by T. E. Kebbel, Esq., 1870, pp. 64-66.

and, if we include Scotland, four-fifths of the island are held by 12,791 persons. If, however, we deduct from the figures given in the new Domesday Book the proportion due to names counted repeatedly, we could probably discover that four-fifths of the whole British soil is held by something like 5,000 owners,[1] or that nearly one-half of it is held by less than 1,000. These owners are, however, to a large and preponderating extent only life-renters, the estates being entailed. ' By legal devices which are not advantageous to the personal interests of the nominal proprietors, nor to those of the people at large, these lands (40,000,000 acres in Great Britain) are, with insignificant exceptions, placed under permanent disabilities; they are the preserves of entail, fenced with strict settlement ; they belong to no man, and to a certain extent they are doomed to infertility, because they are ever in waiting for the unborn hand of the next generation.'[2]

In consequence of the land, therefore, not being fully at the disposal of its present proprietors, for their own benefit and for the general benefit of the community, its value increases only very slowly; for while the annual value of the lands of England and Wales was 36,2'0,000l. in 1814–15, it was no more than 48,947,879l. in 1873–74, an increase at the rate of 35 per cent. On the other hand, the other real property has increased three or four times in value, and the profits of trades and professions have increased six-fold.[3]

It appears, then, that while the wealth of England has increased from industry and commerce enormously, the value of lands, and consequently their produce, has been very immaterially affected. The very greatly in-

    [1] See Paper on *The Abuses of a Landed Gentry*, by Arthur Arnold, in *The Nineteenth Century* for May, 1877.   [2] *Ibid.*
    [3] See *Journal of the Statistical Society of London* for September, 1869, pp. 316–318 ; and *Statistical Abstract for the United Kingdom*, from 1860 to 1874, p. 17.

creased demand for the produce of the soil, caused by
the existence of a much larger and much more wealthy
population, has had a very inadequate influence upon the
value of the soil ; and it would seem, therefore, that, considering the increased prices, the land must be upon the
whole not much more productive than formerly.   Mr.
James Caird, in his ' English Agriculture,' affirms that
farms producing meat, wool, and butter, although supposed to have undergone no improvement in the preceding eighty years, would yield in 1852, when he wrote,
200*l.* instead of 100*l.* at the earlier period.   If we adopt
this statement as a criterion of the rise in nominal values
on meat-producing farms, we must arrive at the conclusion that the real values cannot have increased to any
appreciable extent.

Professor Fawcett describes the effect of the present
system of land tenure as follows :—' The English system
of land tenure directly tends to divorce capital from the
soil ; and this evil, instead of being cured, is each year
assuming increased proportions since the area of land
cultivated by those who own it is gradually becoming
smaller. . . . But the farmer, who is tenant-at-will, has
no security whatever. . . . It is impossible to suggest
any arrangement which, by discouraging individual energy,
can be more antagonistic to good husbandry.   Some idea
may be formed of the injury thus inflicted on the community when it is remarked that a great part of the cultivated land of the country is occupied by tenants-at-will.'[1]

And this condition of agricultural stagnation has
continued to exist, while the food supplies of the population have been largely and increasingly drawn from
abroad.   Thus there is now about 100 million cwts. of
corn, four million cwts. of meat, and 680 millions of eggs,
not to enumerate cheese, rice, &c., imported annually

[1] *Pauperism, its Causes and Remedies,* by Professor Fawcett, p. 219.

into the United Kingdom ; so that, on the basis of Mr. Caird's estimate of the agricultural food produce of the country, it now results that about two-fifths of the whole food required by the population must be regularly imported from other countries.[1]

The internal agricultural policy of England having thus been regulated for centuries, the masses of the people have been compelled to direct their attention and energies almost exclusively to trade, manufactures, and commerce for support and advancement.

But the treatment of the Irish people by the government of England has been still more evil than that of the English, and the policy carried out until lately towards that unfortunate island may be characterised as having been one of perpetual spoliation. Rebellion against the most unjust tyranny has been continually the excuse for, and the occasion of, renewed oppression and spoliation. Ireland had for long been the prey of English adventurers ; and it mattered not what government was in power, the policy was unchanged. Until within a few decades the people of that island have been treated by the government, and sometimes by the people, of England as a conquered and an inferior race, and the effects have been disastrous to Ireland and unfortunate for England. It is true, indeed, that the Irish, in the hands of their native princes and chieftains, could not very well have emerged from barbarism ; for their internecine quarrellings were chronic, and a strong external

---

[1] The estimate which Mr. Caird formed of the agricultural food produce of the United Kingdom for the year 1867 (see *Journal of the Statistical Society of London* for June, 1868, p. 139) was 180,000,000l. ; and if we allow an addition of 10,000,000l. as the increase of the nine intervening years, we shall probably be above the truth. But the declared value of the food supplies (excluding spirits, wines, tobacco, and spices) imported from abroad in 1876 was 136,000,000l. ; so that the supplies imported stand in relation to the home produce as 136 to 190, the former being therefore fully two-fifths of the whole.

power was necessary to maintain order, and to implant
a firm and just rule. Instead of justice, however,
being predominant, whether a Charles I. or a Crom-
well occupied the throne, the course of seizure, rapine,
and murder was unchecked. It could scarcely be expected that, while the lands of Ireland were frequently changing hands, the poor agriculturalists would
have any opportunity of thriving. We find, in fact, that
the unsettled state of the country, and the condition of
chronic rebellion and spoliation that existed, was entirely
against the material well-being of the poorer classes
which have always formed the great mass of the
population. It was always found most convenient
to deal only with the head of the sept, as if he were
the sole proprietor of the soil, not with its members;
for when the former was incriminated, his lands were
at the disposal of the Crown. The rights of the people
to the soil were ignored; it often followed that the people
themselves were found to be incumbrances on the land,
and they were driven not unfrequently therefrom wholesale.

Thus, on the division of forfeited lands after the suc-
cesses of the Protector, the people, in order to make way
for the settlement of the disbanded soldiers, were driven
across the Shannon into Connaught and Clare, and
were kept there by a chain of garrisons. Whoever
remained behind was liable to be murdered. What
followed was necessarily of the most disastrous kind.
The people died everywhere either of violence or starvation, so that Sir William Petty, the commissioned sur-
veyor of the English government, estimated the loss of
population between 1641 and 1682 at 504,000 persons,
a number approaching one-half of the whole inhabitants
existing in the year 1672.

One hundred years later we find that the landholders

G 2

were clearing their lands of 'great numbers of labouring peasants,'[1] and penal laws were enacted against the population on account of their religion, which had the most pernicious effect. The famous Arthur Young visited Ireland in 1778, and describes the condition of the common people as that of the utmost material and moral wretchedness. They were treated as slaves by their landlords, to whom they cringed with the meanest servility.[2] William Pitt thus described the legislative policy of England towards Ireland previous to 1782 : —' The system has been that of debarring Ireland from the enjoyment and use of her resources, to make that kingdom completely subservient to the interest and opulence of this country (England) without suffering her to share in the bounties of nature and the industry of her citizens, or making them to contribute to the general interests and strength of the empire. This system of cruel and abominable restraint has been exploded.' The penal laws against Roman Catholics were shortly afterwards relaxed, but the vacillations of policy produced great sufferings amongst the people. As in England, the common people were everywhere dispossessed. The proprietors, who for the most part could have little sympathy with their miserable tenants, drew out of them what rack-rents they could; and the people, shut out from the absence of equitable conditions of leaseholding, saw no door open by which they could improve their circumstances. The Act of Union created also indirectly great mischief, for absenteeism became common in consequence of the great landowners preferring to reside in London rather than upon their estates.

The resources which the population of England pos-

---

[1] Gordon's *History of Ireland*.
[2] See *History of Landholding in Ireland*, by Joseph Fisher, F.R.H.S., 1877, p. 103.

sessed in the extension of industrial occupations were cut off
almost altogether from that of Ireland; for, in the first place,
the soil of Ireland was not productive of those minerals
which that of England possessed in such abundance ; and,
in the second place, the jealousy of the English perpetually insisted upon an embargo being laid on the
exportation of Irish goods, and up till the end of last
century the exportation of woollen goods—the most
important of native manufactures—was altogether prohibited.   From these causes, therefore, as well as from
the constant intestine divisions of the country, Ireland
could not thrive ; and the great mass of her population
depending upon agriculture alone, and being dissociated
from those rewards which spring from an earnest and
successful cultivation of the soil, progressed from one
kind of misery—that of perpetual conflict, to another
kind—that of over-population and its consequent chronic
and occasional acute starvation.   There has scarcely ever
occurred in the lifetime of a nation such a wretched
transition as this.   Professor Fawcett describes the condition thus :—' The   economic   condition   of   no   other
country has ever been so unsatisfactory as was the
condition of Ireland under the cottier tenancy ; for the
cottiers, having taken the land at a rent which it was
impossible for them to pay, had no motive whatever to
be industrious ; if by skill and labour the land was
rendered more productive, the increased produce was
absorbed in the rent of the landlord.   The rents were,
in fact, fixed so high that whether the seasons were
favourable or not, whether the land was well or badly
cultivated, the cottier tenants could never expect to
obtain for themselves any more than a bare subsistence ;
hence it has been aptly remarked that the Irish cottiers
were the only people in the world whose condition was
so deplorable that they gained nothing by being indus-

trious. No scheme could possibly be devised which would act more effectually to impoverish the people, and throw the land into the most wretched state of cultivation. The progress of Ireland cannot be marked by a surer sign than by the gradual abolition of the cottier tenure.' [1]

Every influence appeared to be disastrous ; but the two special influences of habitual early and productive marriages, which the general imprudence of the population, as well as its diminution by war, produce, and the severing of the connection between labour and profit by the universality of tenancy-at-will and rack-renting, were those which constantly tended, and unfortunately still do tend, to plunge the inhabitants deeper and deeper into material wretchedness. Mr. Joseph Fisher describes the later period of Irish history in its true colours, when he says :—' The boasted civilization of the nineteenth century and the mild rule of the last of the Hanoverian sovereigns have not done much to alleviate the condition of Ireland, or to place the ownership of the soil upon a sounder basis. Social changes have been effected. The poor, who heretofore wandered about and were supported by alms, have been immured in workhouses, and been supported by compulsory taxation. Vast numbers perished from famine, and still greater multitudes have been forced to seek in another country the employment or sustenance which was denied them in their own land.' [2]

On examining into the present condition of things, we find that the same tree is still unfortunately bearing the same poisonous fruit as heretofore. Thus the cost of maintaining the poor in Ireland has about doubled

---

[1] *Manual of Political Economy*, by Henry Fawcett, 4th edition, 1874, pp. 214, 215.

[2] *History of Landholding in Ireland*, 1877, p. 115.

between 1859 and 1874, and this while the country has been rapidly depopulated, and the progress of the world generally has been unprecedented. Between the years 1851 and 1875, 2,406,277 of the population have emigrated. Of the four provinces Ulster and Leinster have parted with a number each more than one-third of their present populations, while Connaught has parted with one-sixth, and Munster with about two-thirds, and these without reckoning the numbers which have come over to Britain. For the last two years, however, the average numbers of persons emigrating, owing apparently to the depressed condition of trade and the want of employment in America, has very much decreased.

Again, it is a striking fact that the natural increase of the population of Ireland, as marked by the ratio of births to deaths (if, indeed, the registers are to be relied upon), is the greatest in the purely agricultural districts, and the least in the towns. In Munster and Connaught the total proportions of Roman Catholic marriages are respectively 91 and 95 per cent. of the whole ; and of those marrying there is a greater proportion of persons not of full age than in the other two provinces, the percentages being respectively 7·8 and 9 per cent. of such. There can be little doubt that the priests, whose reputation for virtue stands very high, foster early marriages and virtuous living without regard to economic considerations ; for we find that in the western district of Ireland the percentage of illegitimate children born to the whole number births is only 0·8 per cent, while it is 2·3 per cent. for the whole country, and 4·6 per cent. for the north-eastern Protestant division of it. But, on the other hand, of those who marry nearly one-half (46 per cent. in 1874) did not and, we may very well suppose, could not sign their names at marriage—a condition of illiteracy which, indeed, cannot but be highly prejudicial to the material advancement of the people, to whatever sphere they make betake themselves. Again, in Connaught there are only 4½ persons to one acre of potatoes; whereas in Scotland the proportion is 21 persons, and in England 70 persons, to one acre of potatoes; in France it is 13 persons, and in Prussia 6 persons to one acre. In Prussia, however, it must be noted that the root is used to a large extent industrially—in the manufacture of brandy, for instance, which is for the most part exported, the refuse being utilised as cattle-feeding stuff. We may therefore safely say that, as regards the dependence upon this highly fluctuating crop, the Irish at the present day—for the proportion of persons to an acre throughout the country does not differ materially from that stated for its western province—are in a position just as dangerous as that which they occupied before the famine, and that the situation is one very materially lower than that of any other civilized people. The average daily wage of a labourer in Connaught, as reported by the inspector of the unions which lie in portions of that province in 1870, was stated to have doubled since 1849; but it was still only from tenpence to a shilling, rising somewhat above that meagre pittance in the hurried times of spring and autumn, and from the increase in the prices of all kinds of provisions the money rate of five shillings per week in the latter period represents no very material advance on the starvation wages of the period immediately succeeding the famine.

When we come to examine into the causes for such an exceptionally impoverished condition as that which exhibits itself generally throughout Ireland, there can be no doubt that amongst and at the head of these must stand the fact that, although the people are almost entirely dependent upon the successful cultivation of the land, almost all inducement to such is taken away when nearly five-sixths

of the agricultural holdings—527,000 out of 682,000 in
1870—are tenancies-at-will, and, as a fitting corollary,
512,000 out of the same total are (1870) of less value
than 15*l.* a year each.

'The percentages of tenancies-at-will under 15*l.* to the
total number of holdings at the same value is 84 ; at 15*l.*
and under 30*l.*, it is 67 ; at 30*l.* and under 50*l.*, it is 55 ;
at 50*l.* and under 100*l.*, it is 41 ; and at 100*l.* and upwards, it is 24 only. Here, then, it is manifest that the
poorer class of tenants is in a greater degree dependent
upon the landlords than the more opulent class.'[1] Since
that time there has been little change in the nature and
extent of the holdings, save that tenants-at-will can now
claim, under the Land Act of 1871, compensation, on leaving their farms, for agricultural improvements. The extent
to which compensation has already been made is apparently
insignificant, being at the rate of only 25,000*l.* per annum
for the five years from 1871 to 1876. Now what has
been the change effected in the produce of the country since
the famine years? It has been chiefly a substitution of cattle
for people.   The probable diminution of the population
between 1846 and 1876, has been according to the estimate of Mr. Jonathan Pim, president of the Statistical
Society of Ireland, no less than 3,000,000 of persons ;
while cattle have increased from 1,863,116 in 1841, to
4,115,288 in 1875 ; and sheep from 2,106,189 in 1841,
to 4,254,027 in 1875. This change no doubt was largely
induced by the abolition of the corn laws ; and it seems to
be regarded as one upon the whole not detrimental to the
interests of Ireland, for it is supposed that green crops
and cattle are more suitable to the soil and climate than
cereals. The improvement in the condition of the inhabitants of Great Britain during the period referred to has

[1] *Journal of the Statistical Society of London* for March, 1870, pp.
152, 153.

enabled them to live more fully upon meat than formerly,
and there has therefore been a relatively increased advantage to the Irish cultivator arising from the increase of
cattle. But it is extremely questionable whether the
enormous transformation in the character of the cultivation has not been owing in some measure to the undue
emigration of the population. Mr. Jonathan Pim says
upon this subject in a valuable address delivered at the
opening of the thirtieth session of the Statistical Society
in 1876 :—' It is to be regretted that the tillage of the
country should have so much decreased. The climate is
certainly better suited for the rearing of cattle than for
the growth of corn ; but it seems to me that, even if the
rearing and feeding of live stock be the principal object
of the farmer, this object will be obtained more profitably
by the mixed system of agriculture, in which there will
be sufficient tillage to supply him with winter food for
house feeding ; and this will, I have little doubt, require
a greater extent of tillage than at present exists in Ireland.
. . . . The experience of Scotland fortifies me in
this opinion, as I find that while the tillage of Ireland was
decreasing, the reverse was taking place in Scotland—the
tillage there having increased from 1,996,000 to 2,085,853
acres between 1855 and 1876 ; and this increase of tillage
has been accompanied by an increase of cattle from
974,728 to 1,132,587, and of sheep from 5,694,735 to
6,989,719. . . . . There are many thousand acres
of waste land in Ireland which, though now of very
little value, might become a great source of future wealth
if planted ; and this is especially the case in the wilder
parts of the west where two or three hundred years ago
there were extensive forests, though now you may travel
for miles without seeing a tree. Trees would not only
become a valuable property, but the shelter they afford
would improve the adjacent land ; and if the pasture and

CH. IV.   CULTIVATION OF CROPS IN IRELAND.   91

tillage lands of the west of Ireland were properly drained and the barren and rocky parts planted, it would, I have no doubt, have an important effect in ameliorating the climate. Under the present defective state of the law there is no inducement to a tenant to plant trees, as has been on various occasions pointed out by members of the Statistical Society; even as respects landlords who are limited owners there are many legal difficulties which greatly lessen the inducements to plant, and which certainly ought in the public interest to be removed.'

If there has been, as we have seen, little or no agricultural advance in England, there has been retrogression in Ireland. Thus there has been a diminution between the years 1851 and 1875 in the cultivation of the various crops as follows :—Wheat has decreased by 345,253 acres, namely from 504,248 to 158,995 acres; oats have decreased by 687,908 acres, namely from 2,189,775 to 1,501,867 acres; barley by 48,714 acres, from 282,617 to 233,903; bere by 52,634 acres, from 53,347 to 713 acres; rye by 10,080, from 19,697 to 9,617 acres; turnips by 51,010 acres, from 383,548 to 332,538 acres; and flax by 39,362 acres, from 140,536 to 101,174 acres. On the other hand four crops have increased in breadth of cultivation as follows :—Potatoes by 32,085, namely from 868,501 to 900,586 acres; mangel wurzel by 17,294, from 25,847 to 43,141; cabbage by 5,984, from 28,962 to 34,946 acres; and hay by 698,268, from 1,246,408 to 1,944,676. Thus the diminution in the cultivation of cereals amounts to a breadth of 1,144,589 acres (which is equal to about 22 per cent. of the present cultivated area of the country); and the diminution in turnips and flax to an additional 90,372 acres; while potatoes, mangel wurzel, and cabbage are increased by 55,363 acres, and hay by 698,268. It therefore results that while hay now occupies three-fifths of the land formerly employed for the cultivation of cereals, 481,330 acres have actually been altogether thrown out of cultivation (probably into permanent pasture), an extent equalling about 9 per cent. of the total cultivated area of the country. But it may be supposed that the energies of the agriculturalists are now concentrated with more success upon the reduced acreage of land which is cultivated; and the doubling of the numbers of cattle and sheep would entitle us to expect, from the doubling of the manure derivable from them, a greater produce per acre than before. We shall therefore examine whether or not this be so. For this purpose we shall consult the 'estimated average produce per statute acre' [1] of the various crops for the decenniads terminating 1858 and 1875 respectively. The average produce of wheat per acre in the two periods was 13·3 and 12·6 cwts. respectively, showing a decrease at the rate of 5·3 per cent; for oats the figures are 13·6 and 12·7 cwts., showing a decrease of 6·6 per cent.; for barley 17·0 and 16·2, a decrease of 4·7 per cent.; bere 16·1 and 15·7, a decrease of 2·5 per cent.; rye 17·9 and 10·8, a decrease of 40 per cent.; potatoes 4·93 to 3·24 tons, a decrease of 34 per cent.; turnips 15·1 to 12·7, a decrease of 15·8 per cent.; mangel wurzel 16·6 to 13·2, a decrease of 20 per cent.; cabbage 13·1 to 10·2, a decrease of 22 per cent.; flax 35·8 to 23·5 stones, a decrease of 34 per cent.; and hay 1·97 to 1·86 tons, a decrease of 5·8 per cent. The only crop which shows an increased produce per acre is that of beans and peas, which has increased from 13·6 to 17·2 cwts., being at the rate of 26½ per cent.

If in summarising these results we regard the weights of the respective crops, the result will be that during the last twenty-two years there has been a reduction in the produce of cereals per acre of about 6 per cent., and of root crops

[1] See *Agricultural Statistics, Ireland,* for the year 1875.

of 23·3 per cent. It may be remarked, however, that no portion of this change can be said to have taken place within the last period of ten years referred to ; for when we compare the average of the earlier portion of this period with the latter, a certain increase of productiveness may be found, though the differences in the characters of the seasons may account for this ; for unless a comparison is made of a considerable group of years with another considerable group, it is manifest there can be no secure information gained with regard to the nature of the cultivation. It would therefore appear that, so far as the cultivation of land in Ireland is concerned, the gross amount of the crops, and their rate of produce as well, have fallen off during the last quarter of a century in a most serious degree, probably in a proportion not far short of the relative diminution in the numbers of the inhabitants. To be sure, the ten and a half millions of acres which are devoted to grass or pasture may be in no way deteriorated ; indeed, the large increase in the number of cattle and sheep we may suppose ought to add to their productiveness, though, if we judge from the result of such an increase upon the produce of the crops cultivated, that addition may be by no means assured. In spite, therefore, of everything that has been already attempted and executed with the view of improving the condition and productiveness of Irish agriculture and the state of the Irish people, there is no doubt a very palpable retrogression indeed. The main resource of that agriculture —namely, its cattle—seems now very likely to be taken away from it, for the enterprise of America has discovered a method by which the cattle of that and of other regions of the world may be as readily imported into Great Britain as wheat is, and the partial monopoly which the sister isle has possessed of the meat supply will be effectually taken away, and the condition of the country, so far as agricultural products are concerned, will be rendered as precarious as it was in the earlier decades of the century. But in fact of late years, even without such competition, the stock of Ireland has been decreasing in a manner not altogether satisfactory. Thus while the cattle have decreased in numbers steadily from 1873, the sheep are now (1877) 20 per cent. fewer than they were nine years ago, the numbers being respectively in 1866 and 1877, 4,905,000 and 3,989,000.

As a fitting corollary to these facts, we find that whereas one person in every 15 is a savings bank depositor in England, there is only one in every 100 in Ireland, and the amount of savings invested in government stocks and savings banks in the latter is less in 1877 than it was in 1876.

Before the famine, namely in 1845, the exportation of grain from Ireland was upwards of two million quarters, and of oatmeal and flour two and a half millions of cwts. ; in 1875 these quantities were diminished by nearly one-half and one-third respectively. Whereas, however, in the former year there was no importation of these, in the latter the imports of grain amounted to four million quarters, besides 400,000 cwts. of meal and flour. So that Ireland has become a grain importing instead of an exporting country as formerly. I think there can be little question, when the whole of these facts are passed fairly in review, that the nature of the change in the style of agriculture is one of an unhealthy description, and must proceed to a large extent from a want of the necessary exertion to labour on the part of the cultivators who remain, or in the diminution of their numbers which has taken place by emigration. 'Deficiency in the supply of labour has lessened the culture of the soil and the supply of food. The mode of farming has become more and more barbarous ; the land which used to be tilled is converted into pasture ; the production of cereals has diminished ;

the insufficient supply of winter food for cattle has lessened the production of meat and butter, and in their stead an exhaustive method, the rearing and shipment of young stock, has taken its place.'[1]

In the return of the numbers of owners, the area of their estates and their value, made in 1870, it is a re-markable fact that the values of the estates diminish regularly from the smallest size up to the largest.

'The smallest ownerships are about 12 acres each; and if the whole of Ireland were as productive as these estates the valuation would be upwards of 30,000,000*l*.,'[2] and it is only (1870) 10,182,681*l*.

The interest of the great landowners is still for political reasons on the side of retaining their tenants as tenants-at-will, and since the Irish Land Act of 1871 was passed the Irish tenant finds himself less secure in his holding. 'Evictions have increased since the Act was passed, and the feeling of insecurity instead of diminishing has in-creased. The landlords find that they have to pay less than the value both for disturbance and improvements, and instead of the Act imposing a penalty on them it gives them a bonus. They can either in money or increased rent get a larger sum from the incoming tenant than they paid the outgoing one, and in some cases the conduct of the landlords has been arbitrary, cruel, and unjust.'[3] Under the present state of the law the tendency will undoubtedly continue, so soon as emigration has received a check, as indeed it already has, to incline towards further division (though the opinion generally held in Ireland is that a family cannot properly support itself in a farm under from 15 to 20 acres)[4] and also towards further dependence and impoverishment. At the present time the average

[1] *The History of Landholding in Ireland*, by Joseph Fisher, F.R.H.S., 1877, p. 128.   [2] *Ibid.*   [3] *Ibid.* pp. 133-134.
[4] See *Journal of the Statistical Society* for March, 1869, p. 74.

estimated rental is only 13s. 4d. per acre (being half as
much in the province of Connaught), which is about one-
third that of England. 'The laws relating to land tenure
have prevented improvement, and kept the people in a
barbarous and uncivilized state which is disgraceful to free
institutions. A standing condemnation of these laws is
found in the continuous exodus of its people. Ireland
possesses great resources—a genial climate, a fertile soil,
capacious harbours, navigable rivers, a good position in
the map of Europe ; these advantages ought to make her
rich and prosperous, and her people happy and contented ;
she is, however, poor and non-progressive, her people are
restless and dissatisfied, and she will continue so until her
laws are more equitable, and her land system is renovated
by returning to the equitable system of the Brehon code.' [1]

But it may be asserted that the radical evil lies in the
nature of the people themselves, which is considered to
be lazy, unenterprising, and satisfied with the simplest
necessaries of life and the rudest style of existence. It
has even been maliciously whispered that the true cure for
Irish ills would be, were it possible, to sink the island for
a space beneath the level of the ocean—so little are some
persons aware of the true nature of the evils that afflict
Ireland; and, as Mr. Herbert Spencer says:—'Equity utters
dictates to which we have not yet listened ; and men may
learn, that to deprive others of their rights to the use of the
earth, is to commit a crime inferior only in wickedness to
the crime of taking away their lives or personal liberties.' [2]

Now it may be confidently asserted that whenever the
Irish have had a fair field, they have distinguished themselves. They have earned laurels in war and they have
exhibited the assiduity of their labour in peace, even
within Ireland itself. The most conspicuous exertions

[1] *The History of Landholding in Ireland*, p. 135.
[2] *Social Statics*, p. 143.

which a people will put forth will be when their efforts lead them, by the rewards which they offer, to a near prospect of comfort, plenty, and prosperity. In no two countries does there exist a greater contrast between the rewards of labour in the field than in Ireland on the one hand and the United States on the other. But a population which in the former is never secure of the reward of its labour—nay, instead, is sure that that reward will be reaped by another—will not and can never reasonably be expected to exert itself. When, then, it does not, there will be a poor out-turn of work, and what is done will be performed in a slovenly manner. The soil will only be half tilled, and weeds will encumber the ground, and withdraw the sustenance of the crops. Thus the Registrar-General for Ireland reporting in 1876 says:—'There can be no doubt that if due attention were bestowed on the destruction of weeds, the lands of Ireland would afford a largely increased yield; but, unfortunately, *luxuriant crops of weeds*, which are to be seen in almost every part of the country during summer and autumn, not only rob the farmer himself, but often inflict a vast amount of injury on his neighbour. It has been *estimated* that the money loss to this country from the above cause *exceeds a million and a half* sterling.' The produce being thus diminished, the sustenance of the labourer is diminished also, and he does not possess that capability to work steadily and well that he would do if well nourished. The power of labour, in fact, is continually being reduced towards that limit which is necessary to the maintenance of the vegetative functions of life only. The vicious circle of poor production, poor living, and then again poor production, will continue constantly to give rise to the same evils, till mayhap the sudden failure of the potato crop will create a second time the miseries of famine. No one can be benefited by the perpetuation of such a system as the present; and probably, of all others, the proprietor of the land himself loses the most heavily, for there can be no doubt that, were the energies of the people awakened by the prospect of gaining a sure reward for their labour, the land would soon produce greatly increased crops, and it would, therefore, become consequently much more valuable. So far, indeed, as tenants have bought their holdings under the Church and Land Acts, great benefit has already resulted. Mr. Shaw Lefevre, M.P., who has examined into the condition of some of the new owners, has reported that they are full of energy and hope, and that the fact of the land having become their own has been ' a spur to industry and thrift.'

In the United States the Irishman is known to work hard, steadily, and successfully. Mr. Ford, reporting from the British Legation, Washington, in 1869, describes the way in which Irishmen work when they know that the natural reward of work—property—will follow :— ' A. B. was a young Irishman who came to America in 1848. He was first employed in a foundry at 75 cents (3s. 1d.) a day, which were then the wages of a day labourer. As he became a more skilled workman his pay was increased. In 1859, he owned, free from debt, a house and lot worth 3,000 dollars (620l.), and was an alderman of a rising city, and clerk of the county at a salary averaging with fees from 1,500 to 2,500 dollars (310l. to 516l.) a year.'

Again :—' In the year 1862, a gentleman, having become possessed of 7,000 acres of wild land in the State of New York, parcelled them out into lots of from 20 to 60 acres each.

' The larger proportion of them he disposed of to Irishmen (who had little or no money) on contracts for six years, with one-sixth payable of the cost of the land at the end of each year.

' These Irishmen constructed for themselves huts of log, cut on the spot, made a clearing for a garden, sold the wood at the nearest village, and, by hard work and stimulated by the certainty of owning a home at the end of six years, managed to meet their payments. . . .

'The first year was the hardest; and the first winter, which was the hardest of all, an agent on the property was instructed to lend a helping hand and supply provisions whenever there was actual necessity.

'At the expiration of the six years, out of several hundred contracts there have been only two failures.

'The men, from wild, turbulent fellows, have become quiet, sober, and law-abiding citizens. . . .

'Many indeed are the examples that could be cited of Irishmen who from small beginnings have become land-holders in this country.

'All the instances present the same features.

'May not some of the discontent that has been ripening in the minds of Irishmen (since the great exodus in 1848) towards British institutions and the system of land tenure in Ireland be partially traced to the easy acquisition of real estate in the United States?'

Again, Mr. Dennis Donoghue, reporting in 1872, describes another interesting case :—'The son of a tenant of four acres upon the estate of a nobleman in Ireland emigrated to the United States about the year 1848. At first he worked as a labourer in an iron foundry. In 1852 he was a working gardener on wages of 6l. per month. In 1870 he transmitted to Ireland enough money to purchase his landlord's castle, then for sale, and at the same time owned in the United States a sugar plantation upon which he had spent about 40,000l.; also a very fine farm and valuable fancy stock, as well as a handsome town residence. He came very nearly being elected United States Senator.'

The population of Ireland, notwithstanding a natural increase as reckoned by the excess of births over deaths, of about 49,000 per annum, has been declining during the last thirty years. The emigration, however, of the people during the last two years has, probably owing to the depressed condition of trade in America, rapidly diminished, so that, for the first time during that period, the surplus population will probably add to the numbers in Ireland, instead of adding to the numbers in America ; and that this addition to the native population will not tend to reduce the natural increase materially may be judged of from the fact (if we can rely to that extent upon the registers) that the proportion of births to deaths is higher in the poorest agricultural districts of the west and south than in those of the east or north, or of the towns, the ratios being 167 per cent. of births to deaths in Connaught and Munster, 138 per cent. in Leinster and Ulster (together), and on an average only 127 per cent. in the eleven larger towns of the country.

It is still more unfortunate that the condition of the Irish emigrating is so poor that they appear not to possess sufficient ability to move westwards when they arrive at the port of debarkation in America, to which country they almost wholly resort. If, for instance, we take the eight States of the Union which are in close proximity to New York, we shall find that the people of no other country stop their journey so soon on arrival across the Atlantic as do the Irish ; and this in spite of the fact that of all other European peoples they are more accustomed to agricultural than to industrial pursuits, and therefore as a whole they are more fitted for the occupation and cultivation of the vast fields of the Great West than the people of any other State. Thus we find that in the eight States referred to—namely, Connecticut, Delaware, Maryland, Massachusetts, New Jersey, New York, Pennsylvania, and Rhode Island—there were, at the time of the ninth census (1870), no fewer than 1,199,161 native-born Irish, out of a

total of 1,855,779, being in the proportion of 64·5 per
cent.; whereas of Germans (including Prussians) there
were only 605,926 out of a total of 1,690,410, being in
the proportion of 36 per cent.; of Dutch, only 23½ per
cent. of the whole were found in those States; of Swiss,
only 22 per cent.; of Swedes, only 10½ per cent.; and of
Norwegians, only 1⅓ per cent. Again, in the eight chief
towns of those States—namely, New York, Philadelphia,
Brooklyn, Baltimore, Boston, Buffalo, Washington, and
Jersey City—there were 480,682 native-born Irish,
whereas there were only 313,131 natives of the whole of
Germany and Prussia. Further, in the fifty chief towns of
the United States there were, at the period of the census,
1870, 826,388 native Irish; whereas there were only
664,687 from the whole of Germany and Prussia.
Moreover, there were, at the same period, considerably
more native Irish than native Germans and Prussians in the
United States, the figures being, respectively, 1,855,779
and 1,690,410; and it may also be noted that the
natives of the United Kingdom of Great Britain and
Ireland found in the United States, in 1870, were very
considerably in excess of the natives of the whole of the
remainder of Europe put together, the figures being,
respectively, 2,625,923 and 2,308,647.

In the case of the people emigrating from this country,
they are, to a large extent, indebted to their friends in
America for the means whereby they are enabled to
leave their native land; and notably is this the case with
the Irish, to whom remittances, in the twenty-one years
from 1848 to 1868 inclusive, amounted to 14,967,568*l*.
at the least; for the Emigration Commissioners state that
this return is unavoidably imperfect, and that the sums
actually sent home are probably much larger. No one
in this country has, therefore, any right to congratulate
us upon the fact that the world is being, to such an
extent, populated by the British stock; for when we

regard the circumstances, being those of poverty and
destitution, in which, for the most part, the people leave
their native shores, it is apparent enough that the country
receiving such crowds cannot be benefited in any degree
comparable to what it might be were the emigrants not
so miserably necessitous.   The evil of such a state of
things is recognised and lamented; but it may be satisfactory to think that the Government of the United States
has at least as yet made no movement towards placing
any obstacle in the way of unlimited immigration.

Mr. Edward Thornton, the British Ambassador to the
United States, writes, under date Washington, November
26, 1869, thus :—' With regard to the Irish who arrive in
this country, it is the result of every-day observation that
the majority remain in the larger towns, where, with
rare exceptions, they do little good for themselves, are
unthrifty, quarrelsome, and intemperate; but where
single families devote themselves to agriculture, and are
able to purchase the land which they cultivate, they at
once take so great an interest in what they can call
their own, that their character is entirely changed, and
they become thrifty, orderly, and useful citizens, and
acquire a great respect for the rights of property.'   And,
again, Consul-General Archibald reports from New York,
in 1873 :—'As to the destination of the immigrants recently arriving, it is ascertained that where one German
goes to the eastern or manufacturing region, there go
thirteen Irish; but where one Irishman goes to the agricultural regions of the middle, western, and West Mississippi States, he is accompanied by three Germans.'

We must now turn our attention to Scotland, whose
history has been highly chequered, where, at an early
period, civilization and progress were, as in Italy, well advanced; and, later on, the constant desolation of war produced retrogression, misery, and comparative barbarism.

The same dissociation of the people from the soil has proceeded in Scotland as in England and Ireland, though this operation has taken place at very different periods and in very various ways.

Probably, the great proportion of the agricultural population in the southern lowlands became free labourers at an early period, before the destructive wars with England had driven the country back from its former condition of wealth and enlightenment. In the north, however, the majority were probably emancipated only on the settlement of the country in the middle of last century, when men of wealth and enterprise purchased many of the estates, and introduced capital and agricultural machinery and improvements. Until that period, the miners and salt-workers in the middle of the country were also serfs. In the Highlands, however, the transformation was effected with the greatest amount of hardship; for, as in England, and to a greater degree, in all likelihood, the retainers of the chiefs were unaccustomed to labour. They despised every occupation of a non-military character, and could not, therefore, at once become tillers of the ground. The result was, that the supernumerary population was driven off the soil with great hardships, the remaining numbers becoming tenants or labourers.

In no country in the world has the phenomenon of mighty landed properties become so striking, and in none has the amount of suffering experienced by the poorer classes of labourers been greater. It has, however, been a happy thing for them, and for their country, that so many have been able to emigrate to lands where the boldness, hardihood, and self-reliance of the mountaineer have been amply rewarded by better fields for the exercise of these characteristics. Had there been no such outlet for the dispossessed population, the result would have probably been quite as deplorable to the people and country as we have seen it to have been in England.

It appears, from the returns of landed property in Scotland, lately published, that there is more than one-fourth of the whole country in the hands of only 21 individuals; that nearly one-half is the property of 49 individuals; and that more than three-fourths is owned by 583 persons. And, as Mr. John Bright, speaking at Birmingham, in January, 1876, points out, one proprietor in Scotland holds nearly as much land as three millions of its population. In the same address, Mr. Bright characterises the power exercised by the interest of the great proprietors of the United Kingdom as 'the greatest political power in this country, which is enormous now, and which, whenever it chooses to act together in Parliament, spite of your household suffrage in boroughs, bears down all opposition, and carries everything which it thinks necessary for its own interest.' The influence which this interest has insensibly exercised has divorced the people from the soil; and we cannot doubt that the evil would have been greatly intensified had it not been for the natural advantages which the country possessed in other respects; so that the people thus disinherited were able to open out those channels of trade and commerce by which the nation has attained to a high position of material prosperity.

While upon the continent of Europe the great proprietors have found their interest in parting with a portion of their estates in favour of the cultivating serfs, in Britain the same class has retained its hold on the government through its organisation, and their power could not be so readily threatened by the intervention of foreign force. The proprietors now are not, however, the proprietors who saw the serfs living on their land dispossessed; they are men who have generally given the fruits of labour for

the lands they now possess ; and were the present system
of large ownership, and the laws and usages which sustain
that system, perfectly unobjectionable, nothing could be
more unjust than to expect the proprietors not to reap
the benefits of their investments.   Why should land not
be dealt with on commercial principles ? why debar the
landowner from the enjoyment of the fullest revenue he
can obtain ?   These questions are asked every day, and it
is thought a monstrous thing to suggest any change upon
the present system.   We shall first look at some of the
results which flow from the land being in possession of so
few hands, or rather from its not being in possession of
many ; and then we shall seek to discover the direction
in which these results are leading us.

The number of Scotch who emigrate from their native
land to find a livelihood in other parts of the world has
lately averaged about 17,500 persons per annum.   There
is, besides, an annual emigration from the rural parts of
the country to the ' large and principal ' towns of 10,100
persons.[1]

There are thus 27,600 persons who annually find it
necessary to leave their homes to seek a livelihood elsewhere—a number nearly two-thirds of the total natural
increase of the population.   Yet the natural increase of
the population is, as we have seen it to be in Ireland,
somewhat higher in the rural parts than in the towns, and,
if we regard the ratio between the births and deaths in
either relatively the one to the other, the difference is
very marked.   Thus, in the portions of the country from
which the emigrants come—namely, from the rural districts and the small towns—the births are (for 1873) 68
per cent. above the deaths, while in the towns which

---

[1] This number is obtained by deducting the increase due to the difference
between the births and deaths from the actual increase in the towns having
upwards of 10,000 inhabitants.

absorb so much of the surplus population the excess is
only 44·7 per cent.   It must be noted, however, that these
ratios are affected on the one hand by the country having
a low rate of mortality, and by the towns having their
populations swelled by immigrants as well as by births.

But when we look to the outlying and more completely rural parts of the country, the natural rate of
increase of the population becomes more striking.   The
Orkney and Shetland Islands are remarkable for the vast
numbers which they constantly hive off to the mainland
and to other countries.   In the first group of islands there
are fifteen divisions out of the total number of thirty, in
the Registrar-General's returns, where the births are to
the deaths (in 1873) on the average as 2 to 1, yet the
population of these divisions had decreased between 1861
and 1871 by 524 persons.   Taking, however, all the
islands of Orkney into account, we have a ratio of births
to deaths of 156·2 per cent., or a rate of excess of births
over deaths to the population of 0·9 per cent. per annum,
which is almost the same as the ratio of the principal
towns of Scotland, although in the Orkneys there is a
disproportion between the numbers of the sexes which
ought to reduce the ratio, all other things being equal,
considerably below the latter, for the females number 118
to every 100 males.   Instead, however, of there being an
increase of population, in consequence of this excess of
births over deaths, there is a decrease, the numbers in
1861 having been 32,395, while in 1871 they were only
31,274.

In the Shetland Islands, again, in 16 out of the 27 divisions, the births averaged 222 per cent. of the deaths, yet
the population of these divisions had decreased between
1861 and 1871 by 534 persons   But, reckoning all the islands, we have a ratio of births to deaths of 165·5 per cent.,
which is higher than that of the Orkneys; and this although

there is a disproportion between the numbers of the sexes
that ought to reduce the ratio below that of the neighbouring group, for the females number 142 to every 100 males.
Yet, notwithstanding, the numbers of the population being
in 1861 and 1871 respectively 31,670 and 31,608, show
a decrease of 62 persons in the ten years.   It is true that
the death rate is, as in the west and south of Ireland, in
these islands a low one, averaging 1·49 per cent. per
annum of the population, while in the towns it is 2·80 per
cent. ; for where individuals have little inducement to
exertion, they exert themselves little, and where healthful
natural influences generally abound, life appears to wear
well, and the rate of mortality is low.   On the other
hand, the want of the prospect of improving their condition keeps thrift at a discount, leads the people to marry
improvidently and to produce families, throwing them
upon the world without having any assurance as to what
their future is to be.   The condition of Shetland, the
poorest group of the two, is, therefore, with regard to the
question of population, in the most unfavourable position.

It will be noted, that the inhabitants continue
regularly to increase and to emigrate, in a great degree
allowing the females to remain behind.

The report on the census of Scotland for 1871 con-
tains the following just remarks with reference to the
fact and probable consequences of the disproportion of
the sexes which exists in the country :—' So far as known,
there is no country in the globe where the disproportion
of the sexes and excess of females is to be found at all
approaching that of Scotland.   No population can be in a
sound and healthy state with a disproportion of 114 females above 15 years of age to every 100 males.   Scotland could spare from her population 130,685 females
above 15 years of age, being the excess of females above
the males between 15 and 60 years of age.'   And the

reporter goes on to speak of the philanthropy of any
scheme which would undertake to transport those women
to the colonies, where they are undoubtedly wanted.
The disproportion in the Orkney and Shetland Islands is
very much greater than this, probably averaging 150
women for every 100 men above 15 years of age. If,
therefore, the condition of Scotland generally be unhealthy, the condition of these northern groups must be
much more so.

The question for solution, then, is, how such an unhealthy condition arises; where is the origin of the evil?

In glancing at the past history of these islands, we
find it to be in many respects similar to that of Ireland;
indeed, a long tale of misgovernment, oppression, and
spoliation, so that the people cried out that ' they were
heavily troublit, percit, and oppressit.' Colonel Balfour,
the largest proprietor in Orkney, writes in 1860, of the
history of Orkney, that ' every change was to the islanders
only a change of tyrant, and their complaints served only
to warn the new donatory [of the Crown] of the rocks
and shoals on which his predecessor had made shipwreck
of the thriving trade of robbery. The Crown might do
justice on the oppressor, but it invariably appropriated his
plunder, and adopted his profitable exactions as prescribed
rights and precedents for further claims.' . . . ' The very
enormity of such anomalies makes it hard to believe them
possible at a time and place so near our own, and harder
still to persuade the nineteenth century, and its self-com-
placent admiration of the just and enlightened rule of
Britain, that much of the evil still exists uncorrected and
unredressed in this the 23rd year of Queen Victoria.'

The evils perpetrated have left a bitter feeling in the
breasts particularly of the people of Shetland, which is not
so advanced in agricultural improvement as are some of
the Orkneys. Capital, which is much required, is very

scarce, and the people have been thirled to the landlords and the tacksmen, and enslaved by the truck system.

'It thus happens that a Shetland family may be industrious in all its branches—farming, and fishing, and knitting to the best of their ability—and yet it will be constantly behindhand, dependent upon their superior, and never perhaps handling a pound note from year's end to year's end. . . . It has been said that the very boys, when they begin to work for wages, get no money, but are supplied with clothes, including specially a coat to go to church in ; and thus they get very early into the mer·· chant's books, so that perhaps it is not much of an exaggeration to say that a Shetlander is under truck from his cradle to his coffin.'[1]

The prevailing methods of cultivation have, consequently, been of a hand-to-mouth character. In many places the soil has been stripped off, leaving the rock bare and the land permanently barren. The 'run-rig' system, which has not yet disappeared, still characterises the style of agriculture. Yet the soil is of a variable and often improvable quality, and the climate is mild. There is only one-tenth, however, of the total area cultivated ; so that the farmer of thirteen acres of arable land, which is the average size of farms, possesses, or possessed till lately, nearly ten times that area of ' scathold,' or waste land, upon which his domestic, or rather wild, animals range at large during the most part of the year.[2]

The Orkney Islands possess a better soil, often a rich clay land ; and within the last twenty-five years a great improvement has been effected in the condition of these islands from the introduction of new proprietors with

[1] *Opening Address of the President of Section F (Economic Science and Statistics) of the British Association for the Advancement of Science,* August, 1871, by Lord Neaves, one of the Lords of Session.

[2] See a paper *On the Agriculture of the Islands of Shetland,* by Henry Evershed, in the *Highland and Agricultural Society's Journal,* vol. vi. 1874.

capital, some of whom occupy and farm their own estates. The great majority (2,360 out of 3,668) of the farmers are, or were till very lately, tenants-at-will, holding their farms from year to year at a rental under 10l. ; and among the various hindrances to the progress of agriculture, Mr. Thomas Farral mentions six—three of which are want of capital, want of leases and insecurity of tenure, and lack of compensation for unexhausted improvements. That opportunity of improvement which the possession or the secure tenure of the soil would give to the inhabitants, therefore, has never been created, and is very far indeed from being realised, and the most improvident systems still hold their ground. Nineteen years' leases, indeed, have been, within a few years back, introduced into Orkney by Colonel Balfour, which may possibly in time create a greater desire for agricultural improvement amongst the people ; but, as yet, these leases appear to be confined to the larger farmers. Where, however, the time of the men is necessarily passed more or less at sea, the labours of agriculture must be entrusted in some measure to the women ; and what appears to be required is the institution of small landed properties, by which the trade of fishing would contribute to assist that of agriculture by supplying funds, while the land would form a secure and most trusted bank ; a conjunction similar in character to many which exist, and which, we shall see further on, have produced populations the most industrious, thrifty, and well-doing in the world.

But we shall revert to our examination of the condition of the population of the outlying districts of Scotland. In the insular portions of Ross and Cromarty, the births were to the deaths, in 1873, as 2·312 to 1, and the rate of excess of births over deaths to the population was 1·84 per cent., while the population had increased only from 21,056 to 23,483 in the years between the latter two censuses—a rate little more than half as great as that due to the natural increase.

In the insular part of Inverness, again, eight out of nineteen islands could boast of a birth rate exceeding the death rate as 2 to 1, yet the population had decreased from 1861 to 1871 respectively from 14,335 to 13,586; and the total population of the nineteen islands had decreased, in the same period, from 36,068 to 34,646.

Upon the mainland we find that the northern counties are constantly losing numbers, notwithstanding a large natural rate of increase, and in the five northern counties there are 113 females to every 100 males.

In the midland counties, and more particularly in the iron and coal districts, the numbers of inhabitants have rapidly increased, and the disproportion between the numbers of the sexes is less than it is for the whole of England. Thus in Renfrew and Lanark there were found to be, in 1871, respectively only 68¼ and 69¼ per cent. of the Scotchmen native born.

The result of such an extraordinary increase to the wealth and population of the central districts of Scotland, is manifested in the condition of agriculture in these regions. Farmers having nineteen years' leases partake, during a period of extraordinary manufacturing, mining, or mercantile prosperity, of the benefits which are always possessed by proprietary cultivators, for they then find that portion of the increased value of the land, derived through the increased prices of its productions, is reaped by them during the currency of their leases. The consequence is that they do not, at any rate during the early part of their leases, stint their farms. They supply to the utmost extent of their resources those constituents to the fields and to the live stock, and even sometimes to those permanent improvements of the property from which they can hope to derive nothing after the termination of their leases, abundant capital, and the result of greatly increased crops and much improved cattle necessarily follows. This improvement and increased supply is a mutual benefit, for the community gains by the increased supply of abundant and cheap food, and the farmer profits by his improvements, in having for a defined term an increased produce to dispose of, which is gained at a relatively less cost where the rent of land and buildings is a sum common to any amount, and the manure and feeding stuffs are greatly less costly than the surplus produce they afford.

We therefore find that in the Lothians and in Fife, for example, the produce of the land has increased in a considerably greater ratio than it has in England during the last twenty-five years. In East Lothian the produce of wheat now is estimated to be from 35 to 40 bushels per acre, of barley from 48 to 56, and of oats from 56 to 64. In Fife, again, the average yield of wheat per acre is estimated to be from 28 to 52 bushels, that of barley from 32 to 64, and that of oats from 36 to 72, the heavier crops being produced on the richer lands which border on the sea. These rates, when compared with those estimated officially in 1854–55, show an increase respectively on the average of from 20 to 30 per cent. for the first county, and from 30 to 50 per cent. for the second.[1] During the period referred to the soil has been drained, and scientific farming has become general.

A complete contrast to the social and material condition of Britain generally, and more particularly of the rural parts of it, exists in the Channel Islands. In Jersey and Guernsey we find that the cultivators are generally the proprietors of the soil, and everyone who has visited

---

[1] Compare results given in papers on the Agriculture of East Lothian, in *Transactions of the Highland and Agricultural Society of Scotland* for 1873, and on the Agriculture of Fife in the same Journal for 1876, with the results of official estimate given in the *Journal of Agriculture* for January, 1856.

these thriving and luxuriant islands can testify to the gratifying aspect of solid comfort which everywhere meets the eye. Of the latter island, Mr. Wm. Thomas Thornton says :—' In thirty-nine years population had increased fifty-eight per cent., while wealth had increased one hundred and seventeen per cent. It should be added that the largest augmentation of property had taken place in the country parishes, while two-thirds of the increased number of inhabitants belonged to the town ; and it, moreover, seems probable that the increase of population, both in town and country, was produced principally by immigration, for at the census of 1841 the number of inhabitants not natives was not less than 6,517, equal to the whole addition made to the population since the year 1818, when settlers from Great Britain first began to resort to the Channel Islands. If no other example could be given, this alone might be accepted as a decisive proof that peasant proprietorship has no tendency to create a redundant and poor agrarian population, but is rather calculated to make each succeeding generation wealthier than that which immediately preceded it.'[1]

Since the above was written, if further decisive proof were required, it is afforded by the returns of the Registrar-General, for we find that the ratio of births to deaths in Guernsey has declined from 130·5 per cent. in the five years ending 1865 to 100 per cent., or equality, in the four years ending 1874. In Jersey the ratio of births to deaths is also diminishing, and it is at present 121·7 per cent. The value of the diminutions in the ratio of births to deaths becomes the more apparent when we take into account the very important fact that during the last twenty-five years the death rate has declined six per cent. in both islands.

[1] *A Plea for Peasant Proprietors*, by William Thomas Thornton, C.B., New Edition, London, 1874, pp. 101–2.

It is often, however, objected that population is still
wanted for the British Islands, and that should the surplus
population emigrate, it emigrates to populate the world
with the British stock.   Now the actual rate of increase
of population in the United Kingdom is greatly below the
natural rate of increase, for in the prosperous years
1872–3 some 200,000 natives emigrated per annum.
This gives a proportion of 16 per cent. (it was in England
25 per cent. from 1851 to 1870) of those who are born
emigrating, and if we regard it with relation to the increase of the population in another country such as
Switzerland, we shall find that as many permanently
leave the shores of Great Britain and Ireland every year
as forms the addition to the number of the inhabitants of
the former country during fifteen years.   Any check,
therefore, which may arise to such a vast volume of
emigration, from the decline of trade in other countries,
will tend as it is now doing at once to increase the population of this country beyond its normal rate.   This
increase would occur while the rest of the world was
presumably not able to purchase the usual quantity of
goods from the manufacturers and miners of Britain, and
when as a result there would be a want of employment
for working people.   Thus at every period of commercial
depression the people who emigrate, as we have seen they
do by the hundred thousand from these shores in prosperous years, would be thrust upon the labour market of
this country, not only therefore impoverishing themselves,
but dividing the bread of those who had been customarily
in the receipt of good wages and in the enjoyment of
constant employment.   Three or four years of stagnation
would thus add to the population of the United Kingdom
some six or eight hundred thousand additional mouths,
the hands not being required.   But the worst of the evil
has not been stated.   The addition of such a number, if
spread over the total population in periods of depression,

would indeed be a considerable source of poverty and
misery to multitudes; but when that addition must be
divided amongst the most prosperous parts of the country
only, for Ireland and the north of Scotland cannot at any
time support any proportion of their natural increase, the
evil must become one of great magnitude and of imminent
peril to the country. In ordinary times, as Professor
Jevons has proved,[1] the towns which possess the greater
proportion of Irish are those wherein the death-rate is
the highest. Thus, dividing the eighteen principal towns
of England into three classes of six each, the percentages
of Irish population and of average mortality are as
follows :—1st class, population 21·9 per cent., mortality
29·8 per 1,000; 2nd class, population 7 per cent., mortality 26·0 per 1,000; and, 3rd class, population 5·6 per
cent., mortality 22·9 per 1,000. In Scotland, again,
Professor Jevons, dividing the towns into two classes,
finds the relative proportions of Irish population and of
mortality to be as follows :—1st, for the towns of large
Irish population, being Dundee, Glasgow, Greenock, and
Paisley, the Irish rate is 21·7 per cent., the mortality 28·7
per 1,000; and, 2nd, for the towns of small Irish populations, the rates were respectively 5·5 and 23·8.

Whether these results proceed from an excessive
mortality amongst the Irish residents solely, or amongst
the population generally, there are no statistics to determine; but there can be little doubt that to some extent,
even in ordinarily prosperous times, the poverty, misery,
and death of the lower orders in those towns possessing a
large Irish population, must be increased by such a competition for employment as the immigration of undue
numbers from the sister island must cause.

The Report accompanying the Census of Scotland,
1871, vol. i., speaks regarding this subject thus :—' Till

---

[1] See *Journal of the Statistical Society* for September, 1870, p. 324.

the year 1820, these (Anglo-Saxons, Celts, and Norsemen) were the three races of men in Scotland, but during that year an invasion or immigration of the Irish race began, which slowly increased till it attained enormous dimensions after 1840, when the railways began to be constructed over the country. This invasion of Irish is likely to produce far more serious effects on the population of Scotland, than even the invasion of the warlike hordes of Saxons, Danes, or Norsemen. Already in many of our towns do the persons born in Ireland constitute from five to fifteen per cent. of the population ; and if we include their children born in this country, from ten to thirty per cent. of the population of these towns consist of the Irish Celtic race. The immigration of such a body of labourers of the lowest class, with scarcely any education, cannot but have most prejudicial effects on the population. As yet the great body of these Irish do not seem to have improved by their residence among us ; and it is quite certain that the native Scot, who has associated with them, has most certainly deteriorated. It is painful to contemplate what may be the ultimate effect of this Irish immigration on the morals and habits of the people, and on the future prospects of the country.'

In 1871, there was one in every sixteen of the inhabitants of Scotland, and one in every forty of the inhabitants of England, born in Ireland, and these proportions must now, since emigration to America has been so greatly checked, be rapidly increasing. There can, therefore, be no question of more importance to the inhabitants of Great Britain than that of the influence which these immigrants exert when they have come across the Channel. We have been furnished by Lord Aberdare, in his inaugural address to the Social Science Congress in 1875, with interesting and valuable information on this subject. He points out that while the Irish immigrant population

of England is one-fortieth of the whole, the amount of
crime committed by them is one-seventh of the whole.
But he institutes a comparison between the Irish born
and the native population of the counties of Lancashire
and Cheshire above twenty years of age, as affording
juster data, the result being that while the Irish number
nearly one-ninth of the whole population, the committals
to prison among them number about two-ninths of the
total committals. Again, he points out that while the
crime of Irishmen in Ireland—excepting the Dublin district—is very low, their crime, when transplanted to
Scotland and England, is very high. ' Whence does
this arise? Why do Irishmen, comparatively free from
crime at home, fall so readily victims to its seductions in
England, Scotland, and America? The only explanation
I can offer is that, even more than the migrating Englishman or Scotchman, the Irishman suffers from being removed from his home, and the many safeguards—social
and religious—which there environ him. There is much
to be said for a system under which the more ignorant
submit themselves, their consciences, and their actions, to
the guidance of those whom they believe to be wiser and
more virtuous than themselves. Only the guidance must
be continual ; for, once withdrawn, its objects fall a helpless and easy prey to temptation or bad example.' May
we not, however, say that the unwonted command of
money and of opportunities of spending it on personal
indulgences, have quite as much to do with the degrada-
tion of the Irishman's morals, as his withdrawal from the
influence of the priest, who indeed is to be met with in
Britain as well as Ireland? With no other nationality
immigrating to America is there so much unfitness, from
previous poverty, unthriftiness, and the want of education,
to occupy their new sphere successfully and profitably, as
there is with the Irish, and there can be no question that

a continued and increasing immigration of Irish to Great Britain is a matter of the most serious import to the material and moral position of its native inhabitants.

But the same thing will hold good of the influx of the poorer inhabitants from the outlying districts, who do not enjoy at present suitable opportunities of improvement. As these, then, together crowd to the centres of industry in this country more fully at periods when trade is dull, and emigration has received a check, what shall we expect?

There must undoubtedly follow in such circumstances a lowering of the general rate of wages, and this reduction will take place when it is least easily supported, when the limitation of foreign demand for articles of British manufacture has caused the manufacturers to reduce output, and therefore also to reduce the numbers of their workmen.

The inevitable result will be an addition to the number of paupers and an increase in the poor-rates, and we find that at the present time the number of paupers in Lancashire and Cheshire—the districts most easily accessible to the Irish—has increased more considerably between 1876 and 1877 than in any other portion of Britain.

But in ordinarily prosperous times, notwithstanding the organised efforts made recently by the more stringent application of what is called the workhouse test, it cannot be said that the number of paupers, or the cost of their relief, materially diminish. If we take the decade 1861–70, we find the sums expended for the relief of the poor in England and Wales to be increased from 5,778,943*l.* to 7,644,307*l.*, being at the rate of 32 per cent., and this notwithstanding that wheat had fallen in price from 55*s.* 10*d.* to 46*s.* 3*d.* per quarter. In Scotland the increase in the expenditure on ordinary paupers between

1860 and 1869 was at the rate of 25 per cent., and in Ireland it was between 1861 and 1870 at the rate of 29 per cent. In 1870 the rates for poor relief per head of the population were for England 7s. 2¼d., for Scotland 5s. 4¼d., and for Ireland 3s. 7½d. While, however, the annual expenditure is increasing at a not unequal rate in the three divisions of the kingdom, the pressure is felt more severely in Ireland, where the population has now been long on the decrease, and therefore the rate per head is more rapidly on the increase than the rate of expenditure, while in the other two divisions it is not far from stationary.

It thus appears that even in prosperous times, when the extension of mining and manufacturing enterprise is rapid, when commerce increases by leaps and bounds, and when the labouring population is relieved by an annual exodus of some 200,000 of their number to other lands, the cost of maintaining the poor, and the burden that is felt, increases.

What, then, may we expect when America and our colonies begin to supply their own wants by manufactures, and when they become so fairly inhabited that there shall be no further space for the accommodation of our surplus population? There appears to be only one reply to that question, if we can judge at all from the obvious facts, namely, that over-population will lead to poverty and pauperisation, then to sudden, it may be, and disastrous increase to the present burdens on property, while those verging on destitution will form a growing mass, discontented and rebellious, ready to adopt measures, however violent and anarchical, by which their material necessities shall be supplied.

The great want which the labouring classes of the population of the United Kingdom exhibit to every observer is the want of thrift. Almost everywhere on the Continent of Europe the people are characterised by this virtuous quality; but in Britain the masses save little, and it is the complaint of every observer that, notwithstanding the high rate of wages earned in times of prosperity, there is the same melancholy misery to be seen so soon as that rate ceases. Nothing has been saved against the dull times, and the short period of extravagant expenditure changes into the pinched supplies which necessity compels. This is, of course, not the case with every family, but, as a rule, the description applies to the British workman. The agricultural labourer is in general too poor to be able to save, and the townsman has prospects of improving his position, which the other has not. Though the latter may not be able to own land, for the disproportionate percentage of legal costs, and the entire uncertainty as to their amount, preclude him from that form of ambition, of comfort, or of enjoyment, he may become an employer, and it has been said by one who knew the district and the trade intimately, that almost the whole of the employers in the iron-works of the Cleveland district had risen from the ranks, and scarcely one of them had at that time (1875) heads of grey, so rapid had been the rise of their prosperity. Such opportunities produce exceptional thrift. Working men as a rule, however, are too heartless to look far ahead for rewards. They must see encouragement constantly, and as they go, within arms' reach; the steps of the ladder of their ascent must not be far between each other. And, indeed, in these days, when large capital is required to carry on works profitably, few can be masters, and where trade unions prescribe a uniform rate of wages as receivable by all, there is the less chance of able workmen reaching that position. Still the opportunities which a workman possesses in a town to raise himself are more frequent than they can be in the country, and the result is that thrift is to be found chiefly amongst workmen in the former. Indeed, the agricultural labourer has for long been in a state of semi-pauperisation. 'The English poor-law and the English poor-house have no counterpart in any other society or country. They belong to a mechanism designed to support, or to help in supporting, a very large part of the working classes in certain circumstances out of the common funds of the community. The principle pushed a little further is precisely that of communism. It is not too much to say that some of the applications of this principle are the principal subject of the agricultural labourer's thoughts. His father and mother are in the " house ; " it is for that reason he does not support them. He has a legal right to go there himself in old age or extreme penury ; it is for that reason he does not save. His children must be taken care of, and, if necessary, educated by the guardians—this is why he marries early and freely multiplies his kind. . . . . The class in the cities and towns which live by wages may have many heresies in its stock of social and political ideas ; but it knows little of the poor-law, and the expedients on which it relies to secure its interests are to a certain extent healthy. . . . The agricultural labourer, on the other hand, has heard of no contrivance for bettering himself, except an extension of the principle of poor-law relief.'[1] And Mr. Goschen, when speaking in the House of Commons on the County Franchise in June, 1877, described the condition of the agricultural labourer in England thus :—' Wages had been very low in the rural districts for years, and, as a rule, the agricultural labourers were in a dependent position. It was, in fact, their ordinary future to end their days in the workhouse, and both in respect of their want of training, and their dependence upon the poor-laws, their position was widely different from that of the voters in towns.'

It is therefore apparent that what amount of thrift

[1] *Pall Mall Budget*, July 20, 1877.

there exists in this country is fostered by the great opportunities of advancement which workmen enjoy from the
immense strides manufactures and commerce have made
within a few decades.   But should a period approach
when these strides shall become more measured—and
that period cannot be far distant—then this source of
opportunity, which is in its nature an exceptional one, shall
be lost, and the people of England, having additionally
the surplus population of Ireland to support, will relapse
into that hopeless condition which has for so long
characterised the more completely agricultural portions
of the kingdom.

It may indeed be said that the condition of the lower
classes in England differs from that of their fellows in
Ireland almost altogether, upon account of their non-
dependence upon agriculture, and this difference has
occurred chiefly through the mineral wealth of England
enabling cheap manufactures to be carried on, which,
supplying the most part of the world, produce those
harvests of foreign imports, of which working-men may
either, as ordinary workers, or by advancing in the social
scale, reap their full share.   So soon then as this wealth
decreases, or is more difficult to realise, so much more
will the manufacturers of other countries be in a position
to compete successfully with the manufacturers of Britain ;
the markets then of this country will be curtailed, and the
amount of work available will consequently diminish.
This means then clearly enough that the vantage ground
which British workmen have hitherto enjoyed depends on
the easy realisation of profits drawn through the consumption of the mineral wealth of the country, and that
as that mineral wealth is gradually being consumed,
these profits will diminish, and the capital of Great
Britain will seek investments in the manufactures of other

countries, such as the United States, where the mineral wealth is enormous, valuable, and easy of realisation.

Now, at the present time, it is unfortunately too true that the labouring classes are not the saving classes, and the reason undoubtedly is, that their wages being only in general a small way in advance of their necessities, and there being no very profitable, secure, or pleasant means of investment for their savings, the small balance is spent instead of being saved. If, however, instead of savings banks, which yield less interest upon the capital, land were easily obtainable in the market by everyone, there can be no doubt as to what the result would be. Eager endeavours to save would take the place of squandering, thrift would restrain the expenditure and improve the man. Land is, as we shall see in the next chapter, the property which of all others most calls out the virtues of prudence; the desire to realise it increases the will to work, and augments the endeavours of every workman in every trade, even in that of farming another's land. 'But here, partly in consequence of their extrusion from landowner-ship, the largest class is not a saving class. Outside this kingdom the savings of the multitude is invested in the land and in public funds. The debt of France is held by 4,000,000, that of England by 250,000 persons; and a like proportion holds in regard to the land. The first demand of the small investor is never high interest; that form of folly belongs to the upper classes. His want is security, and the consequence is that at this moment an amount nearly equal to one year's revenue of the United Kingdom is held by savings banks for a return less than the average received by the landowners of this country. . . . . Say that a man, by years of self-denial and careful thrift, has saved 500l., and the idea, so delightful to the minds of most men, of purchasing a small property upon which to spend his loving labour and the remainder of his life presents itself to his imagination. In this country, and in this country only, the thought is chilled and checked because he has no assurance that the cost of purchase may not amount to a fourth, or even a third, of his store ; and if the purchase money exceed his possessions, and he wishes to raise a further sum by way of mortgage, that process, to be repeated perhaps at the end of three years, may involve him in a lifelong charge for legal costs equal to the amount of the mortgagee's interest. He abandons, with a shudder, the coveted land to the men of ten and twenty thousand acres.'[1] . . . .

There can be no doubt, therefore, that the artificial hindrances which exist in this country to free trade in land are serious evils. They may appear to be slight, but they are effectual in shutting out the people from the use of the country, in keeping them divorced from the soil. Capital is diverted too much away from the land, and it is also not created in consequence of the impossibility of investing it freely in this way.

A free competition for land would, the English Law Reform Association declared, produce an increase generally in its price of from four to five years' purchase. That would arise from the additional numbers which would, with increased capital, compete for its possession. Till, however, a simple, expeditious, and costless system of registration is devised and carried out this will not be attained.

Upon this subject it may be instructive to quote the opinion of Mr. Harriss-Gastrell, contained in his able and elaborate report on land tenure in Prussia, dated Berlin, 1869. He says :—' I venture, also, looking to Prussian agricultural economy past and present, to draw a few

[1] *The Abuses of a Landed Gentry*, by Arthur Arnold, in *The Nineteenth Century* for May, 1877.

inferences of general application to Great Britain. The
title to land should be simplified, and its transfer rendered
as easy and as cheap as possible. The freest exchange in
land, although it may not bring more land into the market,
is desirable as being beneficial. Laws of settlement and
entail should be at any rate so modified as to enable a
life tenant to improve estates without the outlay being
swallowed up for ever by them, and the children being
deprived of their portion in his fortune separate from the
estates, and as to lessen the probability of so much land
being kept in fetters, as appears to be now the case.
Children's rights should be recognised in law to about
the same extent as, but with less complexity than, in
Prussia. The law of intestacy should prescribe equal
division amongst next of kin for real as well as personal
property. But otherwise full liberty, subject to children's
rights, should be allowed in the disposal of property by
appointment or bequeathal. Lastly, all remaining rights
of common should be commuted. . . . . It will perhaps
be considered that these inferences point to more or less
various defects in our land system ; and if they be defects,
as Prussian experience teaches, it is well to know them
even if they be more numerous than we like to acknowledge. The man who has many defects and knows them
is better than he who has fewer defects and does not
know them. But the best man is he who has few defects
and knows them. This is likewise true of nations. The
best nation is the nation which has few defects and knows
them. Let it, then, be the glory of England to have as
few defects as possible and to know them. The remedy
is usually easy when defects are known. Our statesmen
can always be trusted to apply practical remedies or to
judiciously remove defects. The wisdom of another
century of the governed, and the experience of another
century of the governing, will prevent the presentation

of measures which shall share the fate of too many of
the admirable measures of a Turgot.   But if with minor
defects the greater defects affecting land require removal,
and if a great evil, arising mainly from these, demands
urgently the most careful attention, our statesmen will be
earnestly called upon to deal effectually with it and with
them.   That great evil is the lack of capital from which
British agriculture suffers.   It is in no small measure
owing to the present land system with its obstructive-
ness of freedom.   The maintenance of agriculture at a
maximum of prosperity must ever be the solicitude of
the statesmen of even an industrial country like England.
Moreover, there are not wanting signs, looming, it may
be, on the far horizon, that two great dangers are
menacing England.   The one is the disproportionate
unlanded or unpropertied class.   The statesman who
shall pass measures for removing that disproportion will
indeed deserve well of his country.   The other is a
possible decline of manufacturing industry.   If the
possibility should assume the portentous shape of a
probability, the statesman who shall pass measures to
facilitate and provide for the transfer to agriculture of
any capital which may be liberated from manufacture
will indeed deserve well of his country.   The names of
such statesmen, and of him too who shall content the
discontented cultivators of Ireland, will be handed down
to posterity as household words, and will be passed from
generation to generation with, if it be possible, a yet
greater renown and yet greater national gratitude than the
renown and gratitude with which the names of Stein and
Hardenberg are being passed from generation to generation as household words of the great Prussian people.'

Can there be a subject, then, which should engage
the attention and the active interest of the constituencies
of this country more anxiously than that of the reform

of the land laws?   And should it not be the first political object of every elector to promote a system of free trade in land by which capital shall be bestowed upon its improvement in the highest practicable degree, and the maximum inducement be presented to everyone, however poor, to labour and save to the utmost, so that he may perchance possess some of it?

No reform appears to promise fruits richer alike to the agriculture and to the people of the country; for while the one would be rendered more productive, the other would become more thrifty and well-doing, and more zealous conservators than they can be at present of the best interests of society.

We shall see in the next chapter what influence the ownership of land by the people of the European countries has had upon their character and position.

CHAPTER V.

LANDHOLDING AND AGRICULTURAL CONDITIONS OF SOCIAL WELL-BEING IN EUROPE AND AMERICA.

WE shall now turn our attention to France, in which country social and political action has been of an extremely radical character. In a previous chapter, the bearing of the great Revolution upon the tenure of the land has been indicated.

The result of that great movement was, as regards the proprietorship of the land, that the nobles were displaced, the common people, who lived on the soil, falling heir to it at a cheap rate, the assignats, which were issued by the French Assembly, being bought for the most part by the resident agricultural population when they were heavily depreciated. Additionally, however, the enormous burdens which had lain upon the shoulders of the masses of the people were suddenly removed. Not only was the land obtained by those who were ready to cultivate it, but it was obtained free from those ruinous restrictions which had hitherto rendered it infertile, and impeded and burdened the cultivator.

Arthur Young, in his 'Travels in France,'[1] writes that 'the effect of the Revolution to the small proprietors of the kingdom must, according to the common nature of events, be, *in the end*, remarkably happy.' And, after showing the wealth which must have fallen to them, he says:—'Their agriculture must be invigorated by such

[1] *Travels in France* in 1787-8-9, vol. i. pp. 609-610.

wealth; by the freedom enjoyed by its possessors; by
the destruction of its innumerable shackles; and even by
the distresses of other employments, occasioning new and
great investments of capital in land: and these leading facts will appear in a clearer light when the prodigious division of landed property in France is well
considered; probably half, perhaps two-thirds, of the
kingdom are in the possession of little proprietors, who
paid quit-rents and feudal duties for the spots they
farmed. Such men are placed, at once, in comparative
affluence; and as ease is thus acquired by, at least, half
the kingdom, it must not be set down as a point of
trifling importance. Should France escape a civil war,
she will, in the prosperity of these men, find a resource
which politicians at a distance do not calculate.' These
words proved to be remarkably true. The people, set
free from their former shackles, displayed in the future
wars a power and endurance which astonished Europe,
and, as we shall see, they are now steadily advancing, so
far, at least, as they are owners of the soil, in comfort and
prosperity. At the present day, or rather, in 1862, the
last period of which we have information, there were
3,799,759 agricultural proprietors, of whom there were
only 57,639 who did not cultivate the land with their
own hands. One-half of the whole number farmed their
own lands, nearly a million were farmers of their own
and of other lands, and métayers, and more than a
million were day labourers. In 1851, the total number
of landed proprietors amounted to 7,846,000; that is,
more than a fifth of the number of inhabitants in the
country. Of this number, however, there were, as cer-
tified by the municipal authorities, 3,000,000 who did
not pay any personal tax on account of their poverty.
The property of these consisted, generally, of an extremely

K

small spot of land, or a cottage.[1]   More than one-half of
the country is the property of individuals who possess an
average of about six acres each, and almost the whole
extent consists of properties under 60 acres each.

The condition of France, then, in this respect, is a
complete contrast to the condition of the United Kingdom,
for even the poorest persons are proprietors of land.   In
addition to this important consideration, we have to
remember, when we regard the rate of improvement
that may characterise the agriculture and the agriculturalists of France, that the rate of progress of manufactures
and commerce, owing to the paucity of mineral wealth,
neither has nor could have been anything approaching
to that of Britain; and, as a result of this, we find that
the agricultural population of France is about one-half of
the whole, while in England it is reckoned to be only
one-seventh or one-eighth.   And the agricultural population is not relieved, as it is in Ireland and Scotland,
by an enormous rate of emigration, for the whole emigrants from France number no more than 6,000 or 7,000
per annum.   Whatever reduction there is in the numbers
of the agricultural population, is due to the superior
attraction of the towns; and the country as a whole
provides, from decade to decade, for the wants of its
population.   There appears, too, to be little absolute
destitution to compel the inhabitants to leave their native
country, for a large portion of the comparatively insignificant number of emigrants find their way across the
Mediterranean to the French colony of Algeria, where
they can scarcely consider themselves to be permanently
expatriated.

Now, we find the population of France to increase in
a different manner from that of the United Kingdom.

---

[1] *Statistique de la France comparée avec les divers pays de l'Europe*, par
Maurice Block, 1875, vol. ii. pp. 23-28.

Amongst the rural population, which is fully two-thirds of the whole, the natural rate of increase is only 1-405th, the births being to the deaths as 10 to 9, and the deaths to the population, per annum, as 1 to 45.[1]

The produce of the crops of the country, and the quality of the live-stock, have, since the early part of the century, improved greatly; but the improvement has been most noteworthy during the last 25 or 30 years.

Thus, if we take wheat, one of the most important crops of France, occupying full one-fourth of the whole arable land, and full one-eighth of the total area of the country, we find the crop to have progressed as follows :—In the period of ten years, 1820–29, the average production of this crop over France was at the rate of 13 bushels per acre; in the years immediately preceding 1840, it was $13\frac{1}{2}$ bushels, the price being, at each period, about 16s. 6d. per bushel. The quantities and prices continued the same for six years more, after which the first rose till it averaged, in the ten years preceding 1875, 16 bushels per acre, and the second, 20s. per bushel, the quantity having increased by about 23 per cent., and the price by about 25 per cent.[2] Now, during the period in which these improvements have occurred, it is a noteworthy fact, that the agricultural population of France has decreased about 11 per cent. (the figures are 21,992,000 in 1851, and 19,598,000 for 1866),[3] numbers having, from time to time, resorted to the towns. Thus, it is quite apparent that the lot of the agriculturalists, who are almost wholly proprietors of the soil, must, with respect at least to this important crop, have improved considerably.

But the evidence of agricultural progress and ameli-

[1] *Annuaire de l'Economie Politique et de la Statistique,* 1876, par M. Maurice Block, pp. 7-13.
[2] *Ibid.* pp. 141, 142 ; also *Statistique de la France,* pp. 42-44.
[3] *L'Europe Politique et Sociale,* par Maurice Block, Paris, 1869.

K 2

oration is all in the same direction, and we shall proceed, further, to adduce that evidence. Whereas, from time immemorial, the systems of cultivation in the centre and eastern districts of the country have been those of the biennial and triennial rotations, wherein the soil neces- sarily lies fallow in the largest degree, now these are being displaced largely in favour of a more ample rota- tion. This is more particularly the case in the north, where capital applied to the soil has produced the most beneficial effects, not only in enabling the cultivator to spare the fallow, but to reduce the net cost of working the soil at the same time that the produce is more abun- dant than formerly.

The greater culture of wheat, which has taken the place of inferior grains, has been one of the effects of such an improvement, and it may be said that whenever such a change happens, it is an indication that the condi- tion of the people is improved. And, again, the increased physical strength derivable from the substitution of a superior for an inferior grain, enables the cultivator to perform his duties the more energetically, and, in con- sequence, to reap the more valuable and abundant crops. Not only, as has already been said, has the productiveness of this important cereal been increased—and in half-a- century the relation of crop to seed has risen from 5·50 to 7·30,—and not only has its price increased, but the extent of the land appropriated to it has increased from 11,360,000 acres, in 1815, to 17,290,000 in 1869, being at the rate of more than 50 per cent., and that increase has taken place more from a displacement in the cultivation of inferior cereals than from the appropriation of lands that were formerly waste.

But the progression in the productiveness of wheat characterises other crops as well. Thus, the crop that is formed by a mixture of wheat and rye, though not much

more than half as extensive as 60 years ago, has increased
in its produce from $13\frac{1}{3}$ to 17 bushels per acre. Rye,
which has fallen off in cultivation to the extent of one
quarter in the last 30 years, has increased from 11 to $14\frac{1}{3}$
bushels per acre in productiveness in the last 50 years.
Barley, again, has allotted to it about the same extent of
land as formerly, but its productiveness has increased in
a remarkable manner, namely, from $14\frac{1}{3}$ bushels per acre
in 1815-20 to 18 in 1852-57 ; and to $21\frac{1}{2}$ bushels per
acre in 1871. Maize, or Indian corn, now occupies nearly
one-third more of the soil of France than it did in 1815 ;
but the produce per acre has increased from 11 to $18\frac{1}{2}$
bushels in that time, equal to 68 per cent. Lastly, of
cereals, oats have increased in cultivation, between 1815
and 1873, to the extent of 29 per cent., and the increase
per acre has been from $16\frac{2}{3}$ bushels in 1815-20, to $27\frac{1}{4}$
bushels in 1862, equal to 60 per cent.

Potatoes have increased in quantity from about
59,000,000 of bushels, in 1815, to 354,000,000 in 1873 ;
seven-twelfths, however, only are employed directly as
food, the remainder being partly used for seed, and
partly for industrial purposes. The year 1843 was
marked by even a greater produce than the present rate,
but the disease, in the second year thereafter, having
reduced this quantity to less than one-half, the crop was,
for several years following, a comparatively poor one.
At the present time, however, about $2\frac{1}{2}$ times as much
land is at the disposal of this crop as in 1817. France
now produces twice as many potatoes as Austria, and
four times as many as Great Britain and Ireland.

The produce of the gardens of France, whether for
sale or for consumption by the proprietary cultivators, is
now estimated to be double that of 1842. Again, the
extent of the natural and sown meadow lands of France
have notably increased within 20 years, the official

figures for 1862 showing, for the first, an increase of 20, and for the second, of 80 per cent. over those for 1842. The total annual production of hay derived from natural meadows, in those 20 years, has increased 52 per cent., and the value has considerably more than doubled. The productiveness of clover has increased from 1842 to 1862 as much as 35 per cent.; the gross produce has risen as much as 120 per cent., and the price, in the same period, has increased about 30 per cent.

The culture of the vine in France has increased considerably from the period of the first Revolution. In 1788, about 3,850,000 acres (Arthur Young's estimate was 5,000,000 acres) [1] were appropriated to that crop; in 1849 the average rose to 5,410,000, since which it has not varied much. The crop of the vine, however, has greatly improved in productiveness. It was 23½ bushels per acre in 1788, forty years thereafter it averaged 30¼ bushels, and in 1850 it was 36 bushels. Disease, how-ever, thereafter immensely reduced the crop, and pro-duced great privations amongst the cultivators. From a gross production of nearly 45,000,000 of hectolitres in the last-named year, the crop fell to less than one-fourth four years thereafter. It rose again to the first figure in 1858, and in 1865 it was half as much again as the crop of 1850. This plant, like the potato, is extremely liable to the ravages of disease, and cannot, therefore, be considered as the most appropriate for the cultivation of peasant proprietors who depend on its produce solely; nor is it one to be regarded as typical of the growing agricultural prosperity of France. This is shown the more clearly as, since 1870, when the pro-duce reached 70,000,000 of hectolitres, the crop again declined to the year 1873, when the gross produce was only about half as much.

[1] See *Travels in France* in 1787-8-9, vol. i. p. 471.

If we turn now to examine into the numbers and
condition of the domestic animals of France, we shall
find abundant confirmation of the previous evidence of
the gradually-increasing prosperity of the agriculturalists. There can be no better test of the degree of agricultural prosperity than the fact of improved live-stock;
for while improvement in the productivity of land may
be the result of hard work in tilling it, the improvement
in cattle can result only from a proportionately higher
expenditure of capital, and the husbandman, on the
other hand, receives a better food to nourish him, and
his family are supplied with that precious nutriment—
milk—in a greater abundance and of an improved quality.
The numbers of cattle increased as follows :—In 1812,
they were 6,681,952 ; in 1829, 9,130,632 ; in 1839,
9,936,538 ; in 1852, 10,093,737; and in 1866, 12,733,188;
after which, owing to the depression of the country consequent on the war with Germany, and the separation of
Alsace and Lorraine, the numbers fell to 11,284,414 in
1872. It may be said that the numbers of cattle doubled
in sixty years, though in a slight measure this increase
was attributable to the annexation of Savoy. But the
numbers form only one and the least part in the consideration of the amount of improvement which has taken
place. The condition in which the animals exist probably affords a better criterion of the state of agriculture
and the value of improvement to the agriculturalists ; for
while cattle are poorly fed, the proportion of offal in the
carcase to the total weight, and consequently to the
portion adapted for human food, is greater than when
they are well fed, and good feeding means an improvement of the quality as well as increase in the quantity of
the butchers' meat.[1]

[1] This has been proved experimentally, as may be seen from a paper by
Mr. Alfred Harwood, Suffolk, in the *Transactions of the Highland and Agri-*

We find, therefore, that the average weight of oxen according to the official report of 1858 for the year 1852, was, for common beasts, 858 lbs., the net weight of the food (four quarters) being 506 lbs., while for fed beasts the weights were respectively 1,058 lbs. and 858 lbs., the net weight of the food in the latter case being equal to the gross weight of the animal in the former ; but, further, while in the former case the relation of the net available food to the gross weight was only 59 per cent., in the latter it was 81 per cent. If, again, we compare the mean of these two net weights with the mean of the net weight of the flesh available for food on the oxen of ten years previous, namely 1842, according to the statistics we shall find they stand thus :—For the first, 682 lbs., for the second, 546, showing an average increase of flesh in oxen during ten years, of 136 lbs. weight, equal to 25 per cent.

If we proceed to examine the results with regard to cows and calves, we shall find them to be equally satisfactory. They are tabulated as follows :—

	Weight of live animals			Weight of the four quarters		
	1839 lbs. avoirdupois.	1852 lbs. av.	1862 lbs. av.	1839 lbs. av.	1852 lbs. av.	1862 lbs. av.
Cows	528	576	713	317	343	403
Calves	105	109	136	64	77	86

The increase in the mean weight of the butchers' meat is more strikingly shown, however, in the following table, which is derived from official documents published in 1856, from the records of the slaughter-houses of the chief towns :—

cultural *Society of Scotland* for 1874, pp. 312-23, in which he says, ' It appears that the digestive organs of animals increase according to the amount of indigestible fibre that passes through them.'

Year	Oxen lbs. av.	Cows lbs. av.	Calves lbs. av.	Year	Oxen lbs. av.	Cows lbs. av.	Calves lbs. av.
1816	633	396	79	1844	689	435	83
1820	644	383	79	1849	689	460	90
1833	629	398	77	1854	699	482	90
1839	649	420	83	1862	695	460	94

And if we analyse the results of this table we shall find that the ratios of increase in weight per annum of butchers' meat of oxen, cows, and calves have been during the forty-six years respectively, two-ninths, one-third, and two-fifths per cent.

Again, the produce of milk from such improved cows has greatly increased and become more valuable, for we find that while in 1862 the mean gross produce of a cow had been valued at 6*l.* 15*s.* per annum, in 1842 the official statistics represent it as not so much as one-fourth of that sum, thus indicating that during these twenty years of improvement not only had the lactiferous qualities of the cows been increased by an improvement in the breed, but by at least an equally great improvement in their aliment. Since 1862, the price of milk has increased considerably, and doubtless also the quantity, though there appears to be as yet no further particulars obtained upon this head.

Horses and sheep have not increased in France in the same way as cattle for various reasons which it is scarcely necessary to refer to, but which are not of a nature to invalidate the indications of continuous prosperity which we have been describing. Indeed, however, it may be said, parenthetically, that a decrease in sheep is sometimes a good sign of agricultural prosperity, inasmuch as it indicates an increase in cultivation and a diminution of waste lands; and this feature of improvement is even more marked in Prussia than in France, for in the former country the decrease of sheep between 1867 and 1873 amounted to more than 10 per cent. This kind of stock is liable, however, to great annual fluctuations, and no important inference can, therefore, be based upon it, or indeed upon any but the sure and gradual improvements which occupy considerable periods of years.

In France, however, the gross and net weights of sheep have increased between the years 1842 and 1862, in a ratio that would indicate a satisfactory improvement in the individual animal, and the prices per head in that period have on the average, like those of cattle, doubled, or nearly so. The weight of swine has also on the average increased. In 1839, the live weight of this animal averaged 200 lbs.; in 1852, 229 lbs.; and in 1862, 260 lbs.; the weights of butchers' meat in those three years being respectively 161 lbs., 180 lbs., and 193 lbs., and the increase of price per head has been in the twenty years, from 1842 to 1862, at the rate of 50 per cent.

If, then, we place all these facts in juxtaposition, we cannot but regard the increase in the prosperity of the agricultural population of France as one of the most remarkable character; for, while we have seen that numbers, weights, and prices all have risen together exceedingly, as well as upon the whole uniformly, we cannot omit the consideration that the greater amount of wealth and of income thereby derived falls to be divided amongst a number of individuals not increased, but for many years diminishing.

Such a consideration indicates, first, the great labour and prudence which are practised by the French; and, second, the remarkable salutariness of the system of peasant proprietorship under which they live and prosper. We are, therefore, quite prepared to receive the testimony of Mr. L. J. Sackville West, when he reports that 'the prevalent opinion as to the advantages or the disadvantages of the tenure of land by small proprietors is, decidedly, that it has been advantageous to the production of the soil, and has tended to the improvement of the material condition of the agricultural population.'[1] In the report which accompanies the 'Enquête Agricole,' it is stated that ' au point de vue de la production il est hors de doute que la diffusion de la propriété a été favorable. Le cultivateur qui cultive pour lui-même cultive mieux que le salarié pour celui qui le paye, et des soins plus assidus assurent des produits plus abondants;' and with respect to the condition of the cultivator:—'Il résulte des recherches faits par les Commissions d'Enquête qu'aucun signe extérieur n'accuse de gêne plus grand que jadis chez les cultivateurs. Loin de là l'immense majorité des déposants a reconnu que toutes les conditions de la vie du cultivateur s'étaient améliorées universellement et dans une proportion notable. Logement, nourriture, vêtements, tout dans ses habitudes démontre un bien-être inconnu il y a trente ans.'

What can be more conducive to the prosperity of any people than the knowledge that that which they sow they shall also reap ; that what they place in the soil to-day may be securely extracted from it next season, nay, even 20 or 30 years afterwards ? Of this nature, farmyard dung, which Mr. Lawes, of Rothamsted, informs us, comes up still to fructify the crops after many years, preeminently consists. But the agricultural capabilities of the soil are dependent upon the constant and ungrudging supply to it of manures of all kinds, organic and inorganic, artificial and natural, which cannot be extracted from it at once. These advantages are possessed by the French in the greatest measure. It results that capital—which is, relatively to this country, scarce in France—can be

<hr/>

[1] *Report on the Tenure of Land in France.* Paris, Nov. 19, 1869.

securely committed to the soil. It is the best bank that can be had, because it is the most secure, because it is the most productive, and because the percentage of return depends upon the individual investor himself.

When we seek to test the condition of the rural population of France by the standard of natural increase—that is, the relation between the birth rate and the death rate— we find that there is a material difference between it and the rural parts of the United Kingdom. The normal birth rate in the rural parts of France is about 2·5 per hundred inhabitants, and the normal death rate 2·21 per hundred inhabitants, the difference being 0·29 per hundred inhabitants. In Ireland, the birth rate, for a series of late years has been 2·75 per hundred, but approaches 3·00 in the western and southern districts; the death rate is under that of France. In Scotland, the birth rate is 3·15, and the death rate 2·01. In England, the birth rate is 3·60, and the death rate 2·23. The difference between the natural rate of increase in the rural parts of France and the United Kingdom is, therefore, a very great one. Now the total births in the rural parts of France are at the rate of nine-tenths those of the towns, but the rate of illegitimate births in the former is only two-fifths that of the latter. On the other hand, the rate of mortality amongst the rural population is from 15 to 20 per cent. beneath that of the towns population.[1] It is, therefore, apparent that the rural population is the more moral and also the more healthy of the two. It is interesting to note what Mr. Prévost-Paradol has said on this subject.[2] 'General prudence and the desire not so much of wealth as of a quiet and sure competency is the main feature of French temper. The children are loved in France with a tenderness often excessive, and

[1] *Annuaire de l'Economie Politique et de la Statistique*, 1876, pp. 8–13.
[2] *France*, by M. Prévost-Paradol, 1869.

the law of equal inheritance, which has become a part of
our national character, renders the Frenchman still more
prudent from the perpetual anxiety which he feels about
the future of his family.   Now, if you bear in mind that
all French inheritance, real or personal estate, is constantly divided in equal proportions amongst the children,
that they have no India or Australia to go to, and that
emigration is generally considered as a kind of penalty
or desperate remedy for great faults, you will at once
understand the cause of the two facts which separate
most deeply the French family from the British one, to
wit, the small number of children, and our peculiar way
of contracting marriages.   On the small number of
children, I won't dwell here; but a curious fact is, that
the apprehension about bringing up children keeps pace
among us with the acquisition and increase of property.
Our peasant, as a landowner, does not like to see its lot
dwindling to nothing after him, and dreads a large
family, and the same feeling pervades all classes.'

But how is it that the French do not colonise? That
question has been generally answered by the assertion
that their country is so beautiful and so fertile that the
inhabitants have no desire to leave it.   It cannot be
said, however, that emigrants leave their native soil on
account of the want of these qualities, but rather either
because they find life too hard for them or they are
assured it will be much easier in the land to which they
are going.   Now, while it is certainly true that the
greater proportion of French agriculturalists have prospered well and regularly, there are considerable numbers
of them who, possessing only small patches of land,
cannot gain a sufficient livelihood thereby ; and, indeed,
many are too apt to lead a life of great poverty upon
their patch of patrimonial estate.   Thus there are numerous instances of extraordinary *morcellement* which are

truly regarded as deplorable. The individual owners are
not situated advantageously to engage in industrial occupation of a remunerative kind. There can be little
doubt that it would be better for those individuals, for
the land, and for the community, that they should remove to positions where their toil would be more successful. But the necessity of employing a notary, and the
high rate and uncertainty of the cost of sale and transfer
of their land virtually often prohibits such removal. It
appears that the whole expenses of such a process, including registration fees, seldom fall below 10 per cent.
of the whole value, and they are frequently considerably
more. In Norway and Sweden, upon the other hand,
the exchange of landed property is performed without
judicial aid, is extremely simple, and its costs are strictly
defined and very low; namely, little above 1 per cent.
upon the whole value. The result is that the small proprietors, and sometimes whole groups of them, emigrate
freely, furnishing themselves, however, with prudent fore-
thought, with every possible requisite for comfortable
subsistence in the land of their choice,—very differently
from the Irish and some of the English, who possess often,
unfortunately, little more than what they stand in.

Again, in Belgium, from which country, though most
densely populated, there is extremely little emigration,
the land is extremely divided, and the charges and taxes
upon land transfer compare with those of France;
whereas in Bavaria, the Grand-Duchy of Hesse, Saxe-
Coburg Gotha, and other German States, in and from all
of which there is an appreciable movement of population, and where the soil is held in larger breadths than
in Belgium, the costs of transfer are very small, and the
process is simple and easy.

Indeed, it must be apparent that heavy charges upon
the transfer and sale of land must restrain the population

from either migrating to the industrial centres of their
own country, or from emigrating to another, and thus
when coupled, as it is in France, with a law of inheritance
enforcing an equal division of real estate among the
children, the tendency towards a minute division of the
soil, and a separation of properties into small fragments
divided from each other, is inevitable. While the law of
inheritance in France compels division, the law of transfer virtually forbids the requisite consolidation of landed
properties.

It is interesting to compare the results of these laws
in France with the results of the corresponding laws in
Great Britain. While in the former country the people
own the soil, and derive their subsistence in a great
degree directly from it, scarcely increasing in number or
emigrating at all; in the latter, the people are virtually
precluded from ownership, and, therefore, having no interest in the soil, they migrate, emigrate, and multiply
freely. The extraordinary influence which the existence
of such laws exercises is, therefore, easily discerned;
indeed, it may be said they are competent to cause the
reduction or the augmentation of the numbers of a particular nationality; so that while the individuals of one
country are seldom to be met with outside of it, those
of another extend over the whole world, often being
driven from their native shores in utter poverty; the
influence in France and Belgium being towards the
formation of opinions and habits opposed to emigration,
while in other countries, particularly in the United Kingdom, such tendency is not felt or even understood.

We shall now turn to Prussia. In that country, the
proportion of the inhabitants engaged in agriculture is 45
per cent., being somewhat less than it is in France, the
difference being amply accounted for by the superior

stores of mineral wealth which the former enjoys, which
enable manufacturers to work at greater advantage. The
greater part of Prussia is now held by small proprietors. In 1859 there were upwards of 600,000 small
holdings, averaging rather more than six acres each, and
344,000 averaging ten times that area, which, when
added together, equalled in extent the amount of land
held by the larger class of proprietors.[1]

There is no sort of restriction over the disposal of
four-fifths of the land ; the remainder, however, equalling
about fifteen and a half millions of acres, is in a measure
tied up, so that its free exchange is prevented. The steps
in the progress of this change in the condition of the
agricultural classes of Prussia, as well as those of other
European countries, have characterised the nature of the
revolution effected. We have already adverted to the
fact that the statesmen of Europe were alarmed and
spurred into action by the outbreak of the first French
Revolution. Hence, the ample legislation, affecting agricultural interests and the agricultural population, undertaken shortly after that period. But the absence of the
prospect of foreign danger, or of internal disquietude,
which followed the period of general war and political
perturbation at the beginning of the century, allowed the
political mind to reassure itself and, as it were, to go asleep,
so that in Prussia the agricultural legislation took a retrograde direction, and the operation of the previous enactments was much restricted. The French revolution of
1848, however, again awoke slumbering statesmanship ;
and not only were the former regulations confirmed, but
new ones of a more revolutionary character were set
in motion. The instinct of self-preservation was, undoubtedly, the acting agent, throughout the most part of

[1] *Report on the Tenure of Land in Prussia*, by Mr. Harris-Gastrell,
dated Oct. 27, 1869.

Europe, in promoting in the minds of statesmen, and the upper classes generally, those movements towards legislation in favour of the labouring agricultural classes, which we have already seen to have been so generally instituted since the commencement of the century. The first French Revolution manifested the tremendous power which lay unsuspected in classes that had hitherto been despised and downtrodden ; and after the terrific punishment it had dealt upon the upper classes of France— particularly upon the old nobility, who were at that time permanently expatriated—there could be no mistaking the direction and force of the lesson which was inculcated for all the future.

The progress in agriculture, which has taken place in Prussia since the emancipation of the serfs, is becoming more and more decided. It is assisted in the industrial portions of the kingdom, and particularly in Silesia, by the demand for a greater amount of produce, by a population increasing in wealth more rapidly than it is in numbers. The Report of the Agricultural Board for 1868 states that ' agriculture has been improving in Prussia, and the advantages of deep ploughing, irrigation, drainage, improved implements, introduction of high-bred cattle, scientific feeding and rearing of cattle, more careful attention to manures, and use of artificial manures, are receiving more and more recognition by small as well as large proprietors ; and in some provinces, such as Silesia, Saxony, and Pomerania, more than in others.' The parts of the kingdom where the greatest strides have been made in the improvement of agriculture are also those where the greatest strides have been made in industrial progress ; the one reacts beneficially upon the other, and many who would have been competing by hard agricultural labour on their little properties with their neighbours in the sale of their marketable produce, find a certain relief and a

L

great improvement in their position by disposing of so
much land, retaining only a comparatively small plot, in
order that they may bestow their labour more profitably
on manufactures or mining. That is one considerable
source of relief, and the other source arises from the
increased demand by the non-agricultural labourers for
the produce of the agriculturalists thus reduced in numbers. Without such a resource as this, no country has as
yet been able to maintain all its inhabitants, where those
inhabitants are not either reduced in number by war or
pestilence, or where they do not emigrate to other
countries. In France there is a natural increase in the
rural portions though that increase is a small one, and the
increasing numbers find an outlet for their labours in the
manufacturing and mercantile operations of the towns,
from whence, in consequence of their presence there as
non-agricultural labourers, there is—so far as the country
itself is concerned—a relatively greater demand than
before for the productions of the agriculturalist. In Norway and Sweden the surplus population finds additional
outlets to those of towns occupations which are not extended in their opportunities, in the rapid extension of
fishing and shipping enterprise; and the knowledge which
the smaller proprietors of those countries possess of the
superior ease and profits of agriculture in America, induce
many of them to emigrate to that country. In Prussia,
however, not only has the soil not been until lately cultivated so assiduously as in the Scandinavian Peninsula, so
that there is ample margin for improvement, but there are
more ample fields for industrial enterprise and labour.
In Silesia the peasant properties largely predominate in
number over the estates of the gentry, some of which
latter are of the largest size in Prussia, and more than
half the soil is in the hands of peasant proprietors, though
these are to a large extent industrial proprietors. The

division of the land among such properties is as follows :—
4,320 properties are under 3$\frac{1}{2}$ acres (5 morgen); 3,921
between 3$\frac{1}{2}$ and 19 acres (5 to 30 morgen), 1,759 between
19 and 190 acres, and 1,084 are above 190 acres (300
morgen). A large number are under one acre in extent,
and this is accounted for by the fact that the holdings are
held subsidiarily to an auxiliary occupation—such as
weaving, mining, or working in the paper or flour mills,
—or rather it may be said that these latter are the principal occupations, and that of agriculture or garden cultivation is the auxiliary one. Where agriculture is carried
on without other occupation, it is reckoned that the
peasant proprietor cannot be well off unless his holding is
above twenty acres. It therefore results that about four-
fifths of the whole number of proprietors must be engaged
in industrial occupations or as agricultural labourers.

The prosperity of the proprietors of ordinary-sized
farms has been of late years very marked, so that several
of the estates formerly belonging to the gentry have been
bought up by them. The increase of cattle in Silesia has
been of late years considerable. Between 1861 and 1867,
the number of cows increased from 684,882 to 793,770,
being at the rate of 15 per cent. ; the number of goats
increased in the same period from 72,801 to 126,037,
being at the rate of 73 per cent. ; of swine, the increase
was from 231,195 to 445,563, or at the rate of 93 per
cent.[1] The condition of the labouring population of
Silesia generally has of late years greatly improved, and
the improvement appears to be largely due to the change
in the character of the people ; for whereas in the earlier
period of the century they had no inducement to labour
beyond a certain limited degree prescribed by the hereditary indifference of serfdom, in the later period their

---

[1] *Report on the Tenure of Land in Silesia*, by Consul White. Dantzig,
December 21, 1869.

energies have been awakened, and their resolution to labour has been animated by the continual hope of improving their condition and of becoming landowners.

Thus Consul White reports :—' The traditions of the Silesian people, as well as their tastes, lead them to ask for the acquisition of land as owners, and not as tenants. If they can obtain enough to make them independent, so much the better; but, even as labourers or artisans, they desire to own some, even though it be not sufficient to provide for their modicum of wants, increasing the quantity as their means or opportunities enable them to do so; hence arise those changes of ownership which are reported in every locality, and which tend to reduce some holdings and to increase others, and are and must be inseparable from free trade in land.

' The desire, however, of preserving their holdings to their posterity, which is naturally to be found in a people attaching so high a value to ownership, produces, as it would be likely to do, a remedy against a too rapid division of inheritance, which would otherwise be sure to follow where the laws of the country entitle each child to an equal share of every kind of intestate property, and impose on the parents the obligation of leaving their offspring a certain minimum share of their substance.' And again he says :—' This class (the peasant proprietors) has preserved the economical habits for which the peasantry are generally known, and their standard of living is, therefore, still very simple ; the fare I saw on their table was, however, substantial and abundant, and their whole arrangements such as to confirm what I heard on trustworthy authority in these localities—that most of them had arrived at that stage at which they were accumulating capital, and becoming quite able to afford out of their savings marriage portions for their sons and daughters.'

The people of Prussia are now generally fully aware

of the advantages of practical knowledge in agriculture, and they associate themselves, therefore, together, and employ trained instructors, who travel about the country and deliver lectures to the peasantry on the most advanced principles and practice of agriculture. The principles upon which the great statesmen of Prussian agricultural legislation carried through the division of properties had full consideration of the necessity of the farms allotted being sufficient to support the cultivators, and the result is that these can, in average times, keep poverty at a great distance, and are able by great thrift to increase the ease of their position. 'The small proprietor is usually exceedingly thrifty.' . . . 'As a rule, it may be affirmed of the agricultural population that, although rudimentary instruction is remarkably wide-spread and almost universal, yet there is much work for education, as distinguished from instruction, to accomplish. The peasants, however, lose nothing, so far as I am acquainted with them, by being compared with the corresponding classes in England. The middle proprietors are distinguished for their liberality in religion, their conservatism in politics, their careful economy in money matters, their praiseworthy sobriety in morals, their conduct in social relations, and their practical knowledge of agriculture ; but they are not distinguished as they might be for curiosity in knowledge, out of their own immediate sphere of labour. The want of this kind of curiosity may not be natural, but may be artificial. It may be merely the result of the too paternal government, which till lately kept the peasant in the state of an infant citizen ; and, in a generation, indolence in knowledge may be as completely shaken off, as indolence in agriculture has been since the accomplishment of the objects of the Stein-Hardenberg legislation.'[1] Among the purely rural parts of Prussia there

[1] *Report* by Mr. Harriss-Gastrell.

are now no beggars, and pauperism is very rare, a condition of things extremely happy—as happy as the condition of the purely rural parts of the United Kingdom is
undoubtedly the reverse ; for in England the vastest
proportion of pauperism exists in the purely agricultural
districts of the south, and in Scotland amongst the crof-
ters of the Highlands and Islands. As to the farming in
Prussia, the same reporter says :—' Medium farming seems
to be better and more careful than the medium farming
of England. This, at any rate, can be noticed, that the
average farming of the less-acred middle proprietor is
more careful than the average farming of the corresponding tenant farmer in England. This applies in the
main to the small proprietor also, who has a cow, or a
couple of cows, or a team of oxen, or a horse, for farm
work.'

The gardening cultivation is renowned for its care
and intelligence. Consul White also testifies of the
Silesian peasant in the same way :—' As regards the
cultivation of the farms owned by this class of freeholders
(peasant proprietors), it has been constantly improving
during the last twenty years. . . . On inspecting the
premises occupied by their farm buildings, and inquiring
about the dates of the various additions, as also of the
more recent constructions, the owner will point out what
has been done by himself, and will, of course, establish
a comparison with their condition at the time of the
previous occupants, possibly his own father or grand-
father ; and it becomes easy to come to the conclusion
that all these arrangements must have undergone gradual
improvements as the capital of the proprietor was increasing.' And, again, Mr. Harriss-Gastrell speaks of the
condition of the agricultural labourer, and the change
effected by his acquired ability to purchase land, thus :—
' The agricultural labourer lives and dies a mere day

labourer. He knows he cannot change his lot. How different all would be if he saw even before his eyes the opportunity of acquiring a plot of land by the exercise of economy! The proof of this is repeated in the numberless examples which in this respect are offered by the Rhine province and other districts with minutely subdivided land. Thousands of agricultural labourers, who formerly had not a single inch of soil, have, by a period of economy, purchased house and a plot of tillage.' It may be therefore well understood that the condition of the agricultural part of Prussia is approximating gradually to that of France, by slow stages undoubtedly, but still surely, every step gained being not only a step of improvement, but a step towards rendering further improvement more easy. The same reporter observes that the annual rate of increase in population has been lately diminishing, but there are no data upon which the particular increase among peasant proprietors can be ascertained in Prussia or probably in any other country. The principle of recognising the inexpediency of investing a peasant with absolute ownership of land, unless it were sufficient for his maintenance, and acting upon it, has enabled the pure agriculturalist in Prussia to thrive, and he has thriven all the more that while the population as a whole during the fifteen years from 1846 to 1861 had increased only 13 per cent., the increase of those engaged in manufactures, mining and other industries, has, in the same period, been 29 per cent. ; and doubtless this kind of progress still continues. There is, therefore, so far as it can be ascertained, a real basis of progress now established throughout Prussia ; a vantage ground for the exercise of thrift and prudence has been gained, and is being more fully made use of, so that a people who formerly had no inducement to individual exertion because no prospect of individual reward, are now im-

proving from year to year upon the secure basis of an
enlightened self-interest, which indeed it may be said is in
human affairs the only secure basis. It may be added,
in conclusion, that the law of succession to land in case
of intestacy is the same as for movable property, and
that there is therefore a tendency to its dispersion ; and,
again, that the right of the disposition of property is
restricted, so that in the case of a family of one or two
children their share must be at least one-third, for three or
four one-half, and for more than four two-thirds of the
property, whether that property be real or movable, so
that the tendency again is to dispersion, and therefore in
favour of the public interest as against the private interest
of the favoured individual, mayhap the eldest son of the
family. Not only therefore does the statical basis of Prussian agricultural legislation, but its dynamical force also,
tend towards a perfect freedom of the soil, and therefore
towards a universal mobility and interchange in its proprietorship. The ownership is again ultimately determined
by the degree in which the individual proprietors are most
capable for its successful acquisition and cultivation—a
condition which, while dealing justice towards the competitors, benefits the public indirectly but most materially
from the beneficial effects flowing from the best kinds of
cultivation being generally practised. Indeed it is the
case of freedom begetting that selection of the fittest from
which alone the greatest good can be secured to the
greatest number.

We will now glance at the condition of the agricultural population with respect to their tenure of the land
and their prospects of improvement in four of the principal
German States—namely, Bavaria, Würtemberg, Baden,
and Saxony.

In Bavaria the rural population has during the last two

or three decades prospered greatly. The increase in the
number of live-stock has been per thousand of the population as follows :—For the years 1833 and 1861, namely,
horses from 21 to 81; cattle from 525 to 679; sheep
from 413 to 439; swine from 303 to 198; and goats
from 31 to 33.[1] The agricultural population has been
almost stationary as regards numbers between the years
1840–67 (the increase is at the rate of 0·17 per cent. per
annum),[2] and in consequence the results of the increase
which has taken place in every kind of live-stock except
swine must have been, other things equal, an increase of
wealth to the proprietors. Mr Fenton reports in regard
to the system of peasant proprietorship thus :—' Judging
from all the information I have been able to obtain, both
from official and private sources, I should say that the
general feeling in this country is decidedly favourable to
the system so widely spread over the whole kingdom—
that of land cultivation by peasant proprietors, this system
being in accordance with the traditions and habits of the
population, and its result upon the whole satisfactory ;
for, as I have already stated, the general condition of this
class of proprietors is acknowledged to be in the main
prosperous, and one with which they have reason to be
well satisfied.' Throughout this State—the largest in
point of area in Germany—the mass of the land is held
by the peasantry, and is farmed by them almost without
exception, the general average area of each property being
estimated at from 35 to 45 English acres. Some peasants,
however, possess from 200 to 300 acres, though as an
exception to the average. The total lands in the hands of
private proprietors is reckoned at about thirteen millions
of acres, which is owned by some half a million of

---

[1] *L'Europe Politique et Sociale*, by Maurice Block, 1869, p. 391.
[2] *Report on the Tenure of Land in Bavaria*, by Mr. H. P. Fenton.
Munich, January 20, 1870.

peasantry, there being not more than one hundred estates above 850 acres in extent.

The law as regards succession to property in Bavaria decrees that from one-half to one-third (according to the number of children in a family) of the property must be divided, whether it be movable or immovable. In the case, however, of the property being—as when it consists of a small farm—indivisible, the widow or eldest son pays to the remainder of the family the proportionate legal amount of its value as their share. Large estates, however, of which, as already stated, there are but few, are not subject to this law, being frequently entailed and maintained in the hands of noble families.

In Würtemberg the increase of cattle (unfortunately there appear to be no statistics in Prussia or Germany as to the produce of the land) in the twenty-two years from 1843 to 1865 was from 688,029 to 974,917, or at the rate of 42 per cent., while the population in the districts of small proprietors had increased at the rate of only 0·64 per cent. per annum, and in those where large farms were predominant the rate was considerably lower, while in the towns the rate of increase was 1·9 per cent. In this State there is not an adequate opportunity of relief to the agricultural population from the paucity of industrial occupations, which are in general the resource of an increasing population, and the result is that the land is too much subdivided, and there is too great a struggle for a livelihood. There is, however, another and an additional reason for the extreme subdivision which exists, and that consists in the too great a dependence of the small cultivators upon the produce of the vine, which is a crop, like the potato, too subject to violent fluctuations in annual produce, and to attacks of disease, to be one on which a proprietary farmer, devoid of capital or other land to cultivate with arable crops, could depend upon successfully.

In this State, therefore, the peasantry must depend upon the land for support, and often a very doubtful support. 'Yet the Würtemberg peasants, who are a careful, thrifty race, and who do not cultivate the land in a slovenly manner, but make it, by careful though primitive labour, produce as much as it is capable of producing,'[1] though living in a poverty bordering on that of the Irish peasantry, yet owing to their being owners of the land, and therefore feeling sure that its return can be theirs alone, they altogether differ in character from the cultivators of Ireland, who possess, unfortunately, no such material advantage. The position of the day labourer in Würtemberg, too, is considered to be superior to his fellow in England, for 'most of them possess a part of a house and a patch of land, if but one-fifth of an acre.'[1]

In Baden the rural population is diminishing, which may probably be in a considerable measure attributable to the conscription laws, which are very stringent. The towns, however, are increasing in population faster than the country districts are diminishing. In this State the legal limit of subdivision of the land on inheritance is rather more than one thousand square yards, beneath which it cannot diminish in extent—a regulation which would appear to meet neither agricultural nor industrial requirements; for it cannot be doubted that such a patch is quite inadequate to support the smallest family if regarded only as an agricultural subject, whereas as an auxiliary property it is doubtless also unnecessarily large for the majority of labourers. Whether the application of law in restricting the division of land upon inheritance be beneficial is very much to be doubted, and in any case the practical difficulty of forming a rule applicable

---

[1] *Report on the Tenure of Land in Würtemberg*, by Mr. Phipps. Stuttgardt, November 20, 1869.

to a whole country where the character of the land will probably vary greatly, and the circumstances of the people may be even more different, will be readily recognised.

In Baden the poor grains largely predominate, but the condition of the peasant proprietors is not stationary but progressive, and since the revolution of 1848 a great improvement has been effected in the mode of cultivation and in the clothing, feeding, and housing of the cultivators; and 'the prevalent public opinion is that the system of small freeholds tends to promote the greater economical and moral prosperity of the people, to raise the average standard of education, and to increase the national powers of defence and taxation.'[1]

In Saxony, again, the agricultural population is probably on the decrease. In 1849 34¼ per cent. of the whole population were engaged in land and forest culture; this percentage fell in 1861 to 26¾ per cent., a rate of decrease higher than that of increase for the whole population. More lately, however, the inhabitants of the rural districts have been increasing, though probably on account of the extension of industrial occupations. In this State nearly one-half of the proprietors of the land hold less than three acres, and of the remainder more than one-third hold properties under ten acres, and 61 per cent. hold properties between ten and a hundred acres.[2] As a rule the owners of the land cultivate their own estates, and the smaller owners work with their own hands, and are also aided by their families. The price of land is high, which may truly be regarded as a sign of increasing wealth among the possessors of it; for unless there is accumulated capital, the passion for land, however strong,

---

[1] *Report on the Tenure of Land in the Grand Duchy of Baden*, by Mr. Evans P. M. Baillie. Carlsruhe, December 9, 1869.

[2] *Report on the Tenure of Land in Saxony*, by Mr. J. Hume Burnley. Dresden, May 6, 1870.

cannot be gratified.   In a certain degree, therefore, the
price of land is a measure of the prosperity of its proprietors, and of the State as a whole.   But the prosperity
of all in Saxony has largely proceeded from the rapid
development of industry in that State.   Probably no
other European State has been more completely revo-
lutionised economically and socially by the introduction
of the steam engine ; and it would not be too much to say
that its agency has broken down the strict system of
guilds, enfranchised the labourer, and augmented his resources when no other force could have produced much
movement toward such results.   The multitude of small
masters and independent establishments which characterised the former condition of industry have given way
to the factories, where everyone is benefited by the cheap
labour of the steam engine.

The industrial advantages which Saxony has reaped
during the last thirty years have been great, and these
have powerfully affected the position of the peasant proprietors.   In this State industry and agriculture proceed
on a healthy basis, and their steps of progress are sure
and solid.   Opposite to the direction as stated in Great
Britain, the course of pauperism in Saxony has been
diminishing, for between the years 1858 and 1864 the
numbers of individuals in the poor-houses fell from one
per cent. to two-thirds per cent. nearly.   In these States
generally the population which overflows in the country
finds its way into the towns, and they are therefore able to
sustain the native population without, at any rate, any
considerable degree of emigration, and what emigration
there is appears to be owing in some measure to the
severity of the military conscription.

In the other German States for the most part the
same thrift and labour, sobriety and satisfactory progress

exist, but it would probably be tedious to the reader to
describe in detail facts which are of the same nature in
each, and which tend to show that unless in exceptional
circumstances, such as when there are no industrial occupations to which any surplus population may resort—a
condition that with a United Germany can scarcely be
said now to exist—as well as when the cultivator should
depend too much on the produce of a fluctuating crop
such as the potato or the vine, the progress in comfort
and wealth is both real and solid.   It may be, however,
not altogether useless just to glance at the testimony of
the reporters on land tenure in regard to the condition of
the peasantry in some of the other smaller States. Thus as
to Saxe-Coburg Gotha Mr. Barnard writes in 1869: —'This
frugal and economical way of living (of the peasant proprietors) has done much good, and to it must be ascribed
the very evident amelioration of the peasantry. Their
debts have been reduced, and many have even saved
small fortunes.' . . . 'The small proprietors of the middle
class of agriculturalists are greatly respected.   A number
of substantial landowners cannot fail to be a great advantage to a country where they purchase many articles for
their own use and consumption, and thereby further
trade and industry. The public revenue is a gainer by
them, as the taxes they pay are sure and considerable.
They are altogether respectable and very industrious
people, and not disposed to take any part in acts of
opposition.'   Again, as to Sleswig-Holstein, Mr. Ward
reports in the same year:—'There is little or no emigration from the peasants' properties. Their dwelling-
houses are mostly on their own lands; they are well fed
and clothed, and live on the whole very comfortably.'
In the Grand Duchy of Hesse, where two-thirds of the
land cultivated is owned by peasants, an able-bodied
pauper is probably altogether unknown. The emigration

which takes place to the United States is relatively not much above one-third that of the United Kingdom, and consists chiefly of peasant proprietors who prefer to transplant themselves to regions where their little capital and their great labour will afford a richer opportunity of progress and prosperity.

The evidence as regards the general character which peasant proprietors possess, and the influence of their presence upon the prosperity of a country, may be, from its importance, adduced still further. Thus, as regards Sweden, Mr. Audley Gostling reports in 1870 :—'As a class they (the peasant proprietors) are decidedly above poverty, and a large proportion are in comfortable circumstances. Some are rich for their station, and possess property to the value of from 1,000*l.* to 10,000*l.*' Consul Colnaghi reports on the peasant proprietors of North Italy (Piedmont) in 1870 thus:—' The condition of the small proprietors may on the whole be considered a happy one, when their properties are not too deeply mortgaged. Moreover, the system is reported to be an excellent barrier against communistic doctrines. The small proprietor feels that he has a stake in the country, and that he may hope to advance in prosperity.' And with reference to the peasant proprietors of Lombardy:— ' From a social point of view, and looking to the wellbeing of the peasant, there is no doubt but that his position is improved whenever he shares in the produce of the soil, and that he is more independent in spirit as a small proprietor unless his freehold be too small to enable him to make a living from the land.' With regard, again, to the same class in Greece, which is one of the most backward of countries, and where agriculture is still carried on in its most primitive style, Mr. Gould reports in 1869 :—' They are both warmly and comfortably clad for the climate, and generally appear to be in comparatively easy circumstances. Whatever may be the amount of money they possess, it does not in any way cause them to alter their mode of living; they either bury it for the sake of security, or lay it out in the purchase of additional land. Recent instances have occurred of extensive estates having been purchased by the peasants in the adjacent villages without any apparent difficulty on their part in finding the requisite amounts, which have generally been paid off before the stipulated term;' and Consul Ongley also reports similarly as to the financial means of the peasants, their properties being rarely mortgaged, though those owned by persons in the towns are frequently heavily burdened. Now, two-fifths of the labouring community in Greece are peasant proprietors, and such palpable indications of their prosperous condition are not without significance in the future of that country, which has yet so much to learn.

But probably Holland, Belgium, and Switzerland, which are as well known and as interesting to the average Englishman as either of the countries already referred to, are quite as remarkable for the characteristics of thrift, contentment, and gradual improvement in their agricultural populations as any of the others. In Holland the peasantry are reputed for their economical and indefatigably industrious character. Their land, which for the most part is naturally poor, has to a large extent to be maintained against the constantly threatened inroads of the sea. Notwithstanding, however, that they possess a situation so disadvantageous, their lands where cultivated are comparatively productive, and their condition is one of assured prosperity. Indeed the head-dress of the female Dutch peasant is probably more valuable than all the possessions of many of her fellows in England. Comfort and case seem to mark the whole character of the country, for beggars are not known, and there is a happy absence of anything approaching to squalor. In Holland the same law of inheritance applies to land as to movables, as is indeed the case almost without exception throughout Europe, and the tendency is therefore towards dispersion, particularly since entail is neither recognised nor allowed. Yet the average quantity of land held by each proprietary farmer is considerable, varying probably from 50 to 100 acres, but it is in some districts considerably more ; also this land is generally compact, and not parcelled out in many fragments, as is to a large degree the case in France.

The situation of Belgium is a peculiar one. In centuries gone by the condition was relatively with other countries highly prosperous, for the inhabitants, like those of Venice, made use of the waters of the sea to protect themselves against their enemies. At an early period, then, industry sprang up because capital was comparatively secure, and there were ample facilities, from the proximity to the ocean, for the extension of commercial relations with neighbouring countries. Thus, Bruges and Ghent thrived securely when the neighbouring towns of France had a precarious and fitful existence. More lately, however, rivals arose, and the prosperity of Belgian trade declined, the decline being accelerated by the fierce democratic violence of the industrial classes and the wars with Spain. A larger population, therefore, was thrown upon the land than it could fairly support ; and when steam was introduced in the adjoining countries, the domestic industry of the small proprietors was undermined, and a degree of wretchedness and pauperism arose which has probably not been exceeded in any other country, so that Sir Henry Barron describes Belgium as ' the classic land of pauperism.' As Mr. William

M

Thomas Thornton points out, the cause of the stagnation and poverty in Belgium was one of inability to compete with the productions of steam. Those who suffered, suffered because their spinning and weaving could not continue to produce the same returns after as before the introduction of the factory, and, therefore, whereas before, their little property was ·simply an auxiliary to their trade, after, it was their sole resort; and, as it was insufficient to provide a maintenance, the people, in spite of being small peasant proprietors, were, from the failure of their industrial occupation on which they chiefly relied, plunged into beggary. The natural cure of such a condition was undoubtedly the introduction of steam; but this could not be so easily done in the low-lying parts of Belgium, where there are no mineral resources, and it may be said that the force of the change could not be appreciated fully before it was fully felt, and before, therefore, the people impoverished were reduced to such a degree that enterprise and capital had been extinguished.

Since that period, however, the mineral resources of the higher parts of the country have been developed to a great degree, centres of industry possessing comparatively dense populations have arisen, and that part of the population which cultivates the soil had decreased between the census years 1846 and 1856 (reckoning individuals above 12 years of age) from 1,083,601 to 1,062,115, and it now appears that pauperism has decreased to a large extent, or entirely disappeared in the purely rural communes.[1] Yet Belgium, which is the most densely-populated country in Europe, retains and provides for all her inhabitants, there being no appreciable emigration. The natural rate of increase of the population is still augmenting; for whereas the rate was

---

[1] See *A Plea for Peasant Proprietors*, by Wm. Thomas Thornton, C.B., 1874, p. 157, *note.*

0·443 per cent., per annum, between 1846 and 1856, it was 0·658 between 1856 and 1866, and it is reckoned that it has again increased since 1866; and, notwithstanding such increase in the rate of multiplication, the people seem to be not worse off than before, or rather we should say, considerably better, for we find that the number of households, though increased 10 per cent. between 1856 and 1866, accommodate each fewer members, the average numbers having decreased from 4·84 persons in the former year, to 4·65 persons in the latter. It may, therefore, be concluded that the increase in the population of Belgium has arisen on account of the increasing manufacturing and mining wealth of the country. Notwithstanding, however, that the cultivators of the soil are decreasing, their wealth must be increasing, for the land is now better cultivated and, therefore, more productive than formerly, and from 1846 to 1860 170,000 acres of waste lands have been reclaimed and added to the arable and pasture lands, great quantities of agricultural produce are being exported, and, besides, a larger industrial population is fed. As in France, therefore, so in Belgium, the quantity and the price must have risen during the last two or three decades in a very important degree; and as the number of cultivators, who are mostly proprietors, has somewhat diminished, the proportion of income falling on the average to each of them must have increased very materially. Mr. John Stuart Mill was doubtful of the effect of property in land as regards Belgium, supposing, from the evidences of poverty which at one period were only too apparent, that there might not be in that country the same restraining influences exerted on the people from their possessing the land which appeared to be the case so clearly in other countries with a peasant proprietorship. He says[1] :—'I

[1] *Principles of Political Economy*, vol. i. p. 358.

M 2

am not aware of a single authentic instance which supports the assertion that rapid multiplication is promoted by peasant properties. Instances may undoubtedly be cited of its not being prevented by them, and one of the principal of these is Belgium, the prospects of which, in respect to population, are at present a matter of considerable uncertainty. . . . As yet, it must be remembered that the indefatigable industry and great agricultural skill of the people have rendered the existing rapidity of increase practically innocuous ; the great number of large estates still undivided affording, by their gradual dismemberment, a resource for the necessary augmentation of the gross produce ; and there are, besides, many large manufacturing towns, and mining and coal districts, which attract and employ a considerable portion of the annual increase of population.'

It is worthy of notice that in Belgium, though the land is chiefly owned by peasants, it is not to the same extent as in other countries cultivated by the owners, for in 1866 only one-half the land was in the hands of the proprietors.[1] The peasant proprietors, however, are for the most part still cultivators, for they hold land as tenants. There were about 270,000 proprietors, who, in 1856, cultivated less than 12 acres each ; the remainder, 65,673, cultivated more than 12 acres.

The subdivision of land in Belgium is very great; for of the whole number of farms there were only $15\frac{1}{2}$ per cent. which exceeded 12 acres in extent, the average size of holdings being about $7\frac{3}{4}$ acres.

M. de Laveleye says with regard to the effects of subdivision that it 'is not quite an ideal to propose to modern society, for it demands of man redoubled exertion and labour but little compatible with the develop-

---

[1] See *Belgium. Statistical and Commercial Report*, by Sir H. Barron. Brussels, March 5, 1875.

ment of his intellectual faculties; but it can be affirmed that up to this time the results in Flanders have proved advantageous, at least as far as production and rents are concerned.' The fact is, that though the tenants in Belgium, holding as they do about two-thirds of the cultivated land, have leases of three, six, or nine years, and sometimes of only one year, yet they work with all their strength, and save with all their might, for they are themselves generally proprietors of the soil, and they continually hope to be able to become larger proprietors. The produce, therefore, of land which in Ireland would be waste and looked on as uncultivable, consisting as it does almost entirely of pure silica, is very great, equal almost to the produce of the best lands of Ireland. Thus the average produce per acre of the wheat crop in Belgium is reckoned to be about 21 bushels, and in Ireland it is 24 bushels; but in the Pays de Waes, in the former country, where the *petit culture* prevails, the produce is 27 bushels per acre. The average produce of barley is the same in both countries, being 32 bushels per acre. Of oats, the produce is 40 bushels in Belgium; it is about 34 in Ireland. Of rye, it is 23 in Belgium and 19 in Ireland. But in the same district, about St. Nicholas, where the spade culture prevails, the crops of barley and rye average respectively 38 and 29 bushels per acre, being largely beyond the figures for Ireland, although the land is very poor. Respecting the state of public opinion in regard to the holding and cultivation of land in Flanders, M. de Laveleye says:—'So convinced are people in Flanders of the advantages of small holdings, that large farms are frequently divided and converted into small ones;' and Sir Henry Barron reports in 1875 that 'land, which is already dearer here than anywhere else, continues to increase in value in every province. There are few, if any, countries where

land will fetch on an average 63*l.* an acre. In East
Flanders the average value is set down at 97*l.* per acre,
which, at the letting price of 2*l.* per acre, represents 48½
years' purchase. . . . Yet, few of these soils are the
deep black loam constituting wheat land of the best
quality.' Notwithstanding these prices, which we would
consider to be exorbitant, there is no unwholesome
trading in land, for it is soundly held, and it is little mortgaged. As a contrast to this we find the average estimated rental per acre in Ireland to be only 13*s.* 4*d.*, and
the proportion of owners to population 1 in 79, whereof
more than one-half are proprietors of less than one acre ;
so that the agricultural proprietors number certainly not
more than 1 in 158 of the population, a proportion the
reverse of that of Belgium. What is to be chiefly
observed is that the two systems, being entirely different
in character, produce entirely different results, in the one
case the people being laborious and frugal beyond
measure, in the other being idle and wasteful beyond
measure. Yet we must not leave out of sight the important fact that the struggle for existence in Belgium is too
hard, and that there is too little opportunity gained from
toil for the cultivation of the man, so that about two-
fifths of the inhabitants above 7 years of age cannot
read and write. The explanation of such a condition,
however, consists in the restricted nature of the sphere in
which the people work ; not only is there little capital
comparatively, but what there is, is not employed to
produce the most considerable effect. The people cultivating the soil, who number nearly half the inhabitants,
labour with their hands in a primitive way on land
which naturally is often very inferior in character. The
result can, therefore, only be comparative failure. The
system of landholding in Belgium is no doubt, except as regards the cost of transfer, generally favourable to the people

and the produce; but the circumstances in which the system operates are unfavourable, and it is, therefore, apparent enough that the total result cannot be favourable.

There is no country in Europe which is more disadvantageously situated for the extension of manufactures and commerce than Switzerland, and she is covered with mountains, so that her cultivable land is small. Yet no other country shows a people more industrious and thrifty, more free and contented. She has no shores and no navy, her outlet is through other countries which to her may be enemies, and even in times of peace her roads are through gorges and over mountains where the traffic cannot be carried on except at heavy cost. One might have supposed that a country embarrassed by such formidable natural disadvantages must be oppressed by stagnation and poverty. But the very opposite is the case. Mr. G. F. Gould thus writes of Switzerland in 1872 :—' Without being a rich country, Switzerland is in every sense of the word a highly prosperous one, this prosperity being due, not to any exceptional advantages offered by its geographical position, the fertility of the soil, or its mineral wealth, but to the gradually and laboriously accumulated wealth of the patient, indomitable energy and industry of its inhabitants.' And how are such inhabitants so different in character from those of Ireland and the agricultural districts of Great Britain? Simply because of their extremely different circumstances. The same reporter in another and previous report describes the situation of the working man thus :—' The working man not unfrequently resides in his own cottage ; cultivates with the assistance of his family the small patch of ground belonging to him ; is the possessor of a cow or two or three goats, which at times find pasturage on the communal lands, and can draw from the same

sources the supply of wood required for household purposes.' . . . Again :—'The working man in Switzerland is described, by those best able to form a correct
opinion, as being in general laborious, intelligent, honest,
sensible, and above all conscientious in the performance
of the task assigned to him. He fully appreciates that
the interests of employers are identical with those of
the employed, and that Swiss industry can only compete
successfully with that of other countries on two essential
conditions : moderate profits for the former, and low
wages for the latter. This will seem the less strange,
for elsewhere, unfortunately, the fallacy is but too common among working men that the interests of their employers are antagonistic to theirs, when it is known how
intimate are the relations between masters and men in
this country. . . . The frugal habits of all classes
tend to deaden the sting of the privations to which the
working man has to submit in consequence of the
smallness of his wages. They cannot be considered
insufficient, since he not only manages to live on them,
but even in many cases to lay by money, as the Returns
of the Savings Banks conclusively prove.' . . . 'Nowhere are the products of the soil more evenly balanced
with the fruits of industry. When one fails, the other
secures the population from the danger of being in want.
As the operative tills the land when not employed at his
usual avocations, which, in many districts, he is allowed
to carry on under his own roof, so the agriculturalist
in his leisure moments, and particularly during the long
winter months, when field labour becomes impossible,
adds to his resources by working at some trade.' . . .
'Thus by turns the operative is engaged in agriculture
and the husbandman in manufactures, and the happy
combination of both, here so frequently met with, has
tended as much as anything else to make of Switzerland

one of the most prosperous countries in Europe. Another equally powerful element of success is to be found in that industry and perseverance, that spirit of self-restraint and economy, that practical sound sense which pervade all the ranks of the community.'

Everyone in Switzerland is educated, and there are lectures, reading-rooms, choral societies, and libraries to be found amongst the working men in almost every village. Everyone is improved by means of those agencies, and idle time is not allowed to pass listlessly or be spent, as it is very generally in this country, recklessly. 'The question naturally arises, how it is that the working classes can dispose of so much leisure time. The answer is already at hand. Besides the evenings when their work is generally over, they can here turn to good account the Sundays and holidays (the latter are, of course, much more numerous in the Catholic cantons than in the Protestant), instead of being driven, as often happens elsewhere, by the want of rational amusements, to ramble about listlessly, making an occasional halt at a public-house, or to sit at home decorously drunk.'

Now what is the reason why the Swiss should be so eminently prosperous? We shall in reply again quote from the report by Mr. Gould:—'In no other country is property so equally divided among the mass of the people. For instance, in the Canton of Berne, which has about 500,000 inhabitants at the present time, the real property holders numbered, in 1868, no less than 88,670. There were besides 22,856 individuals paying taxes on an average capital of 10,680 francs (427l. 4s.), and 24,301 on incomes averaging 739 francs 60 centimes (31l. 11s. 8½d.). Taking the number of individuals in a family to be $4\frac{7}{10}$, which is the calculation generally accepted in Switzerland, it would thus appear that nearly five-sixths of the whole population of this canton either hold or have a direct interest in real property alone, and there is no reason to suppose that as regards the rest of the country the same relative proportions would not be found to exist.'[1]

The length of these extracts will be excused when it is considered that they so clearly bear upon the point under discussion; namely, the effect which the possession of the soil has upon the inhabitants who possess it.

There is one difference between the appearance of the country in Switzerland and that here, which is very striking. In the former there is a total absence of high fences or walls; whereas in this country everywhere these are to be seen, and in villages and the suburban districts the gardens are almost entirely shut out from view by these erections.

This difference is singularly indicative of the difference which exists in the distribution of property in land; for as everyone is vulnerable in Switzerland, there is no pillaging, but as the rich only are vulnerable in Britain, pillaging; is so inveterate that even high walls will not always save the produce of a garden from spoliation. In the one case, the people are everywhere proprietors or intimately associated with them; in the other, they are dissociated altogether from proprietors and proprietorship, and, therefore, regard those so situated with feelings of envious jealousy.

In Switzerland, as in France and Belgium, the inhabitants are, being landowners, extremely attached to their country; and there is only, therefore, a very inconsiderable amount of emigration. Everyone, however poor, lives in the continual hope of being able at some time or other to improve his position and to possess some land and a house on it, and he who has already

---

[1] *Reports on the Condition of the Industrial Classes in Foreign Countries,* 1871.

acquired that position expects to be able by a constant exercise of thrift and prudence to consolidate and improve his property, or even to extend it. In these circumstances, where exertion is surely rewarded by the acquirement of property, it is not wonderful that it is excessive and much beyond an Englishman's carefully-meted standard. In the one country the manner of the reward is everything, and in the other the amount of the reward is everything: that is to say, that the acquisition of land in the one case is regarded as greatly more valuable than a mere money payment, whereas in the other case the money payment is all that is obtained and is never felt to be enough; in the one case, the reward tends to induce a greater economy, and, therefore, to give a greater value to everything acquired; in the other, the acquisition of high wages tends to induce a greater lavishness and wastefulness, and whatever is gained is considered to be only a part of that to which the individual was entitled, and he is still dissatisfied, and if possible the acquisition of higher wages tends to make him more reckless than before. In Switzerland a natural outlet is provided for the savings of the working classes, for everyone can purchase and possess land. In Britain and Ireland few can do so, and the earnings that may be in excess of those necessary to provide the mere necessaries of existence are too apt, in want of such a natural outlet, to be squandered, for there is no prospect of ordinary workmen ever being able to acquire property in land.

We have in a previous chapter discussed the present condition of the people in Russia, and we have seen that, with reference to the cultivation of the soil in that country, the commune owns the land, and the result is that there is no adequate development of individual energy, and, therefore, no improvement in agricultural

practice, resources, or production. But in course of
time the peasantry will have paid off the redemption
dues; the State will then no longer bind its people
together communistically, for its present object in maintaining such a tie, namely, guaranteeing the payment of
these dues, will have been by that time accomplished.
The principle of the healthiness and success of individual
freedom of action will then be recognised, the communes
will no longer maintain their authority, and a progress
based on a free and unrestricted trade in land will be
the result. Even now by special arrangements made
by the communes themselves, where some of the principal
individuals composing them feel the advantage of freedom
of labour, there is occasionally a foothold whereby the
energy of the peasantry is gaining some advantage over
the indolence of their old masters ; but everywhere at present that portion of the Commune, which consists of the
laziest and most dissolute, has the power to call in any too
enterprising members whether at home or abroad. There
is thus nothing to prevent the selfishness of the majority
of the Commune interfering with the rewards of individual freedom and success. And this selfishness may
be and is frequently exercised ignorantly and viciously ;
and when the primary difficulty of one member sepa-
rating himself from his commune and advancing along
a path of his own is considered, it is apparent enough
that the amount of progress possible at the present time
is small, and that amount when realised is all the
more likely, when it is exercised under such restraint,
to breed dissatisfaction and discontent. The amount of
liberty to be gained by strong exertion is just enough
to incline the individual to feel that it is, after all, too
little to repay him, and, therefore, it is not likely that
there will be, with even a considerable desire after it,
any great development and experience of it ; the dull

and stagnant round of communistic life and labour will be preferred by the great masses who have always been accustomed to it.

There is just one other country which may engage our attention in this connection, but it is a great one, namely, the United States of America, and we may reckon that the countries newly populated by Europeans, such as Australia and New Zealand, have adopted similar principles with regard to the disposition of the land. In the United States there are no land laws established by which the soil is made to fall gradually into the hands of a few great families as in Great Britain; there are generally no restrictions upon its sale, its inheritance, or its application. The system of occupation is generally that of small proprietors. The proprietors are thriving, and their numbers are increasing, while that of tenants is decreasing. The idea which permeates the people is that of the advisability of universal proprietorship, and the feeling against anything approaching to landlordism is pronounced. There is as yet plenty of cheap land, and it is expected that every provident man will possess some of it. Those in towns may have their own plot if nothing else. The plot may be small, but it will possess a comfortable house on it. This may be only a step towards a larger ownership. Those who immigrate to the towns instead of to the country from Europe, depend on town work for employment and success, and we have seen that of all countries Ireland supplies by much the greater proportion of such immigrants. But towns depend on capital for their prosperity, and capital in the United States is still very dear because it is very scarce. The source of it is largely British. In the country land is cheap, and where a good market exists within a reasonable distance, it soon becomes valuable. The produce then bears a value relatively much greater to the fee simple of the land than it does in other countries. The cultivator gains every year a greater and greater advantage as the population round him increases in numbers and in wealth. Now when the cultivator is the proprietor, the increase in the value of the produce goes to enrich the proprietor, and the result is that capital soon begins to be held largely by the cultivators. The great inducement to exertion which arises from the knowledge that the road to wealth is thus not difficult, enables the country to thrive under circumstances which might be otherwise disadvantageous. No doubt a great amount of discontent exists, and some workmen have emigrated lately from New York to New South Wales; but, without entering upon the reasons for such an unfortunate condition of affairs as exists at present, it may be pointed out that there are two great evils that undoubtedly go far to produce such mischief; the one being the disproportionate rate at which circulating capital or money in hand is expended on permanent works, whereby the capital is fixed or the money is sunk, which is doubtless a principal cause why the whole people have become temporarily impoverished; the other evil referred to being the artificial restriction of commerce and diversion of industry which flow from the maintenance of the system of prohibitory duties levied upon the importation of goods from foreign countries.

Now, it is not intended to enlarge upon the operation of these causes in this chapter, which is devoted to ascertaining the condition of the population with respect to the occupation and cultivation of the land. It is probably necessary, however, to indicate here that the appearances of dissatisfaction and even the manifestations of disorder and violence that have lately been noticed in America may proceed from far other causes than those belonging to the rural economy of the country, and it may even be said that the general dispersion of property which is the result of its being so easily obtained and so successfully held is the best safeguard against these manifestations proceeding beyond a certain limited area, or attacking in any serious way the fabric of the State.

What may be the policy which induces the government of the State of Maryland to restrict the right to property in land within their boundary to native-born Americans and to exclude aliens, it is difficult to say, but certain it is that the price of the land would undoubtedly be raised were that restriction removed, for the 5,500,000 that are natives of other countries, being about one-seventh of the whole population, are necessarily excluded from being competitors in its purchase. The result is (or was in 1873) that there are plenty of good farms and land in the market that have no purchasers, and yet Englishmen who land at Baltimore (in the State) every year with money looking for farms, being aliens, pass on to Virginia, where they are free to possess them. This appears indeed to be a restriction on free trade in land of the most unfortunate kind, which it would be difficult to justify upon ordinary grounds. In this State of Maryland the produce of a well-cultivated farm may be more valuable in one year than the land itself, and the profit may approach very nearly to that value. Thus a case in point is mentioned by Consul Donohoe reporting from Baltimore, in January, 1874. Dr. Thomas H. Crane, about 1867, purchased a farm of 60 acres, at a cost of 50 dollars per acre. The land was all arable, but run down or exhausted. He cultivated it with fruit, namely, peaches, grapes, strawberries, pears, and some cereals. The produce in 1873 brought 3,198 dollars 50 cents, the expenses were 303 dollars, and the net proceeds, therefore, amounted to 2,895 dollars 50 cents, being within 105 dollars of the original cost of the farm. With fruit, however, which is a very fluctuating crop, it may be well to note that the average produce may be considerably under the figures stated.

The native-born population in the State of Maryland is naturally, owing to this restrictive land law, higher than it is for the whole country.

In the first the foreign-born are to the native-born as 1 to 9½, and in the second as 1 to 7, and if we were to deduct the Southern States from the calculation—for there is little immigration to them—the disproportion would be still more apparent. Such restrictions upon free trade in land are the more worthy of notice when it is possible to put the finger so plainly upon the consequences, and this can only be done when the remainder of an extensive country is in other respects similarly situated. 'The range of price for small improved farms is from 2*l.* to 25*l.* per acre; at the latter price houses and buildings are usually very good. . . . Unimproved land throughout the State varies from 15*s.* to 6*l.* Most of this land has been at some time under cultivation, but has been allowed to run to waste upon the abolition of slavery. The practice of renting farms prevails very generally throughout this State. The usual method is renting on shares,—that is to say, the owner accepts in lieu of rent from one-third to one-half the crop, the tenant in most cases providing everything necessary for the working of the farm. In a few cases the owner furnishes seeds, implements, and stock, and receives two-thirds of the crop.'[1] Whatever tends to dissociate capital from the soil is pernicious, and the restriction of free trade in the State under consideration has, therefore,

[1] *Report on the Condition of the Industrial Classes in the United States,* by Consul Donohoe. Baltimore, February 27, 1872.

caused a disproportionate increase in the number of
tenants who, whatever be the period or terms of lease,
other things being equal, cannot cultivate with the same
advantage either to themselves or to the community as
do proprietors; and it appears, from the fact of the
metayer system being adopted, that the tenants are individuals not possessed of resources to meet the expenses
of an ample cultivation.

In the Southern States the produce of the ground
when assiduously cultivated is, relatively to the price of
the land, very high.   Thus in Georgia, one of the most
poorly cultivated States, a great deal can be done by the
small proprietor.   According to Messrs. Loring and Atkinson's ' Cotton Culture in the South : ' [1]—' A Mr. H—— told
me that with the aid of two little negro boys he made 21
bales on 27 acres, with the aid of manure.   These he
sold at 27 cents. per lb. (the bale weighing 460 lbs.),
realising nearly 2,000 dollars net profit on the year's
work, after paying for manure and labour, and yet this
land can be purchased for from 8 to 10 dollars per acre.'
' Another instance quoted from Georgia, in which three-
fourths of an acre was cultivated with cotton, the whole
expenses were, including rent at 5 dollars, 25 dollars, the
gross receipts 622 dollars, net ditto 597, or at the rate of
about 800 dollars per acre ; ' and the writer thus exclaims :
—' What a future looms up for the Southern people, if they
will only be wise and industrious in the use of the splendid
advantages which nature has given them ! '   The inveterate
repulsion, however, which the ex-slaves conceive for
work, leads them to squat, and occasionally to pillage ;
and the insecurity which prevails over the South is a
great obstacle to the commencement of that progression
which depends on individual enterprise.   A government,

---

[1] Quoted in *Report on Factories in the United States*, by Mr. J. P. Harriss-
Gastrell, Washington, 1873.

which distributes its political power broadcast amongst
the masses without respect to their fitness to use that
power, undoubtedly contributes to perpetuate that insecurity. It is impossible to expect that creatures, who
have for generations been driven to work by the lash,
will, upon their emancipation, suddenly conceive that love
of work, which is so instinctive with Northern and
European peoples. Although generally 'two acres of
land well farmed, with the usual appendages of pigs and
poultry, and the products of the rivers and forests which
are generally (in South Carolina) within the reach of all,
might keep a family of negroes in great comfort,'[1] yet
there is no settled agricultural industry among them of
any kind. The negro in the State of Louisiana earns
sufficient for his maintenance in five days in the week,
the remainder being given up to idleness and amusement.
'With his earnings in that limited space he has enough
to spend in worthless gewgaws and trumpery; such as
an old soft shot-gun; a galvanised imitation gold watch;
a cheap broken-down worn-out old horse, or the just
movable wreck of a gig or buggy, together with a fear-
ful amount of bad whisky, and to lead generally a pur-
poseless existence.'[2] The result of the sudden emancipation is, that he has become demoralised, and has gone
from bad to worse, so that 'he is no longer the object of
interest and solicitude that he was in his former state
of slavery, when unquestionably he was more useful to
himself and others than he is now.' He has the best
chance in the world to get on, but he does not; and the
excessive rate of mortality, coupled with the reduced
number of births, renders it probable that the greater

[1] *Report on the Tenure of Land in South Carolina*, by Consul Walker,
1869.
[2] *Report on the Condition of the Industrial Classes in Louisiana*, by
Consul Briggs, 1871.

proportion of the negroes, will in time disappear, and that 'the residue will not become of greater use to civilization than they are at present.' The women now stay at home in the cabins, refusing to work in the fields, and they exhibit an aversion to the care and responsibilities of bringing up children.

The hope of the South lies in a change from the old plantation system, where the greater proportion of the cultivators had no interest in the product of the cultivation, to new methods, where the cultivators, if not owners of the land, share its products with those who are. Thus in time, as the country becomes settled, and the white man more largely supplants the negro, the organisation of labour in the fields will be broadly based upon the independent self-interest of the actual cultivator, whether he be labourer, 'metayer,' or proprietor. The 'share' system, by which the labourer shares his proportion of the crop with the owner, is being established upon the farms that are taking the place of the old plantations. Its success no doubt is ensured. As yet, however, the production of the South is a mere fraction of what it is undoubtedly destined to be, for the land will be acquired in process of time by energetic and industrious immigrants from the North, who are greatly required. Meantime, though we have seen from the examples adduced that the possibilities are great, the movement toward prosperity is measured. It is worthy of note that the cows in the States of North and South Carolina and Georgia, where the yield of wheat is only from six to eight bushels per acre, are valued at from 3*l.* to 3*l.* 12*s.* each, the oxen from 1*l.* 15*s.* to 3*l.*, and sheep from 6*s.* to 7*s.* a head.

An intelligent and experienced agricultural correspondent of the *Scotsman* writes, with reference to cultivation in the States, thus:—'The great drawback to farming in Texas, as in all the new States of America, is the want of market or proper outlet for the produce of the soil. The home consumption is limited ; and then Texas is so far removed from the large centres of population that its farmers are severely handicapped in the race with the farmers in the older States, and have their returns continually crushed down to a minimum— occasionally, in fact, squeezed to the wrong side. A long time must elapse before this obstacle can be overcome. If cultivation in the States I passed through on my way South was bad, it is ten times worse here, if indeed that were possible. What a Texas farmer calls ploughing is simply scratching the surface to the depth of two or three inches; and the harrowing, grubbing, cross-ploughing, clod-breaking, rolling, and weed-gathering of Scotland are to him utterly unknown. One could scarcely help feeling grieved at seeing such fine land so shamefully ill-treated. The average yield of grain is miserably small, considering the richness of the soil ; but, indeed, no one need wonder that wheat sometimes does not exceed fifteen bushels per acre. . . . It is to be hoped that the Texas farmers will see their error, and spend some little effort to avail themselves of the rich advantages bestowed on them by nature. In fact, if one might judge from the thousands of new and improved farm implements that have come into the State this season (1877), they have indeed already resolved to behave better towards their land.'

In the cultivation of the States generally, the most prominent characteristic is the sparing amount of labour and capital that is bestowed upon the soil. Of the three principal elements required in farming, the land is the least regarded, because its extent is practically unlimited and its price is cheap. Labour generally is costly, and capital cannot be had at much under double the rate at which it can be obtained in Great Britain, and in the West and South it is still more difficult of acquisition. Of the two, however, labour is the most costly—hence the universal employment of machinery; and the cost of labour is largely enhanced by the case with which the labourer may become possessed of land himself.

The farms generally in the Eastern States are small, those in the Western, large; for in the first the population is comparatively dense, and the land is in consequence comparatively dear; additionally, the amount of wealth held by each person in the Eastern States is greatly less than it is in the Western, for there is a greater struggle for a livelihood on account of the natural advantages being in the former relatively few. The readiest means of acquiring wealth rapidly in the West have been fully made use of; whereas in the Eastern States of the Union, there is a preponderating population engaged in non-agricultural occupations, the proportions engaged in agriculture and mining in the Western States are the most numerous, and the natural wealth that is rapidly extracted from the soil is chiefly exported to Europe and the Eastern States. The proportion of the Industrial population throughout the States is, notwithstanding the artificial system adopted of promoting manufactures by the maintenance of prohibitive duties on foreign goods, insufficient to supply a market for agricultural produce that could justify the farmer in the adoption of a more thorough kind of cultivation than he at present practises. The most advantageous policy would therefore appear to lie in facilitating the means of export, by which the raw produce of the country may reach the markets of the Old World with the least cost and delay. Of such a kind are the works that have recently been successfully undertaken towards removing the bar of the Mississippi, by which means the transport of produce is rendered less difficult and costly. By such means are the material interests of the Old and New Worlds knit more closely together, and the respective populations become mutual benefactors.

In San Francisco, the numbers of depositors in the Savings Banks and Loan Societies increased, between 1869 and 1873, from 35,000 to 52,000, and their average deposits from 153*l.* to 181*l.*; and in this State (California) the numbers of depositors increased in the same period from 5,200 to 22,000, and their deposits in a still greater ratio. In California wheat is grown to the largest extent, nearly 2,000,000 acres having been under this crop in 1873. The cost of labour in this State is relatively high, owing to the proximity of rich mines which employ many labourers; so that machinery is indispensable in cultivation, the fields are large, and the labourers are few—about one to every seventy acres. It is noteworthy that the farms are very various in size, but that many are extremely large. The distribution of the land in 1872 into farms was as follows :—23,315, from 100 to 500 acres; 3,419, from 500 to 2,000; 892, from 2,000 to 10,000; 158, from 10,000 to 20,000; and 122, above 20,000 acres. These latter extraordinary dimensions are explained doubtless by the enormous fortunes which are made in mining, for the strides of this State in the possession of wealth are probably greater than those of any other State in the Union. These immense properties are not, however, held ' by persons who wish to be regarded as large proprietors, but simply as a matter of business or speculation,' and there is no obstacle presented by their existence to the acquirement of land by the working population. The produce per acre has steadily declined, for the continual cropping of wheat upon the same land has reduced the growth from 35 to 40 bushels per acre, which were at first obtained, to probably little more than one-third of that amount now. This gradual depreciation by continual cropping indeed characterises the agriculture everywhere. The average size of farms, however, throughout the States is not very different from that of the representative agricultural counties of England, namely, 154 acres. In spite, however, of the vast amount of land now occupied, the proportion of the value produced, at least in 1865, by agriculture appears to be strikingly small ; for Mr. Wells, the Special Commissioner of the Revenue, stated it to have been 656,590,000*l.*, whereas the values created by manufacturing and mining amounted to upwards of 700,000,000*l.* ; so that if we assume the proportion to be still the same—a likely enough supposition—we find that the United States are probably not so fully agricultural as some European countries are.

The landowner in the United States has entire freedom in the disposal of his property ; but, should he die intestate, the law decrees that his real estate shall be equally divided amongst his children, irrespective of sex, though burdened, in the case of there being a widow, with a widow's dower. As regards the transfer of land, the expense is not such as to act restrictively, though indeed it is higher than in some European States. There cannot be any doubt that the effect of the law will be similar to that which exists in the continental European countries—namely, towards a frequent though gradual distribution and redistribution of the land into many different-sized parcels. Everyone in the country may then hope that the reward of his labours will be the possession of land, whereon he may build and settle. He may have any description of it, and, as his labours add to his resources, he may increase his holding indefinitely. Even now there must be many who possess land which they farm auxiliarily to another occupation, for in 1860 there were no less than

52,642 farms of from 3 to 10 acres only—a size considerably less than is required to maintain a family. The result of free trade in land is therefore already apparent, and the people are influenced to labour and to economise in the New World as much as they are influenced to arduous exertions and the practice of self-denial in the continental countries of the Old; and, as we have seen, the only exception to this happy condition exists in Great Britain and Ireland, and its effects are most severely felt, on account of there being a paucity of industrial occupation in the latter.

CHAPTER VI.

WHAT ARE THE BEST LANDHOLDING AND AGRICULTURAL CONDITIONS OF SOCIAL WELL-BEING?

IN the two previous chapters we have endeavoured to describe generally the leading characteristics of land tenure in the various countries of Europe and in America, and their effects. In the greater number of countries land is practically as free and descends to the next generation according to the same law as movable property. But in Great Britain and Ireland there are certain restrictions upon its inheritance and transfer which operate to prevent its being free,—it is, in effect, generally shut up in the hands of rich landowning families, and specially it is so shut up that the nominal are frequently not real or full owners. The results flowing from such different systems have been fully indicated, and they have been shown to be, where the people generally may possess land—and that is almost everywhere—most beneficial to the material and moral condition of the country ; and where the people generally may not possess land—and that is in Great Britain and Ireland—they have been shown to be unfortunate, and likely to be disastrous.

But it may be objected that the system adopted in this country must be, as regards the cultivation of the soil, a most beneficial one; for the crops of the United Kingdom are immensely heavier than those of any other country, and the existence of large proprietorships tends towards the maintenance of large farms where machinery may be profitably employed; so that not only are heavy crops grown, but they are grown cheaply. And, additionally, the tenant—not having his capital shut up in the soil, which would be the case were he the proprietor of his farm—is the more able to utilise it profitably in cultivating the land. And then, upon the other hand, it is asserted that the influence of the system of small proprietorships must necessarily be pernicious ; for, as for instance in Norway, which is not very far away from Britain, the proprietors have become common labourers, being all reduced to one dead level, no men of wealth existing anywhere among the farming proprietors of that country.

Now it may be premised that in such a comparison as is instituted when we compare systems of land tenure prevailing in countries differently situated, there are a vast number of different considerations to be taken into account and carefully weighed before we can hope to arrive at any satisfactory conclusion, and it is, therefore, very easy to draw false inferences. In comparing in any respect the condition of Great Britain with that of other countries, there are two large considerations to be taken into account. The first is, that capital in the United Kingdom is more secure, and, therefore, more abundant and cheaper, than it is in any other country ; it is indeed, so far as the danger of foreign war or interference is concerned, at home, dwelling in perfect peace, multiplying without restriction, possessing thus a very singular advantage. The second consideration consists in the fact that the mineral wealth of Great Britain is enormous, so that in many parts the land is valuable to an immensely greater degree on account of its mineral rather than of its agricultural capabilities. In these two respects this country possesses a decided superiority over any other country in the world ; and this advantage cannot fail to be reflected powerfully on the cultivation of the land and upon the condition of the cultivators, so that any defect in the economical system under which land is owned or cultivated is not easily seen or felt, the bright light proceeding from the firmament of industrial prosperity preventing the ordinary vision from perceiving the dark clouds that may be floating about. In other countries, such as Switzerland, Wurtemberg, Norway, Sweden, and the greater part of France, there can be no such optical deception, for there are none of the same causes of industrial prosperity existing—at least, in anything like the same degree.

It is, therefore, unlikely that any comparison instituted between the agricultural condition of Great Britain and that of these other countries can be instructive, without taking into account the two mighty factors of industrial wealth and prosperity which exist here. Even in the other countries of Europe—and there are few, it may be said only two (Prussia and Belgium)—the rise of industrial occupation has been so very recent, that there has not yet been time wherein the progress and the wealth attained can have very materially affected the position of the masses of the population or the condition of agriculture. There is also another consideration which is applicable to the most part of Europe, and particularly to Russia ; namely, that the people have only within one or two decades escaped from the condition of serfdom, wherein their labours were unspirited, and the fruit of them belonged to others, wherein the stimulus of self-interest was not known, and the ignorance of listlessness and the apathy of monotony characterised the masses of the people. It would be indeed wonderful if, with all their singular disadvantages, the people or the cultivation of the most part of Europe were other than they are. But if the reader have bestowed some attention upon the narration of the condition of the agricultural populations of Europe contained in the last chapter, he will not have failed to perceive that there is now a regular movement of advance, and that regularity is, so far as the movement proceeds on the basis of the enlightened self-interest of proprietorship, perfectly ensured. It is gratifying, moreover, to reflect that that movement occurs at the time in which it does; namely, when the introduction and extension of steam power produces such facilities for the extension of industrial enterprise, so that those who find difficulty in the transition from the old condition of serfdom and dependence to the new condition of action and independence, where there is naturally an enhanced struggle between the individuals composing the masses, have that difficulty resolved into facility. The surplus population which flows from the agricultural districts to the industrial districts everywhere, find, in engaging in the new kind of labour, a rate of remuneration to which, under the old condition of things, they had not been accustomed; and the more capital is realised and the mineral resources of a country or district are developed, the more the individual labourer has the difficulty of adapting himself to the new condition of things reduced. Still, the greater proportion of the masses of the European populations are probably destined to labour as agriculturalists, deriving their living from the produce of the fields. On the other hand, the normal and general occupation of the greater mass of the people in Britain is that of manufactures or mining, where the existence of abounding capital and the rapid development of minerals rewards the labourer much more lavishly than if he had been merely a tiller of the soil.

In the first case, where the population is upon the

whole an agricultural one, the general average of wages and of living is low ; and in the second case, where it is chiefly an industrial one, and the industry is largely carried on by the application of steam power, the rate of remuneration is necessarily high ; and as in Britain, where millions of tons of minerals are procured every year at a cheap rate of expenditure, the average rate of remuneration is much above what it would otherwise be—indeed, it is in its character exceptional. It is not easy, however, for us to convince ourselves of this. What we are so accustomed to see day after day, and year after year, is what we regard as normal ; anything else would appear exceptional. But when we begin to consider that mineral resources dug out of the earth are so much value realised once for all, and that the supply does not grow but is becoming constantly less and less, so that a day will come when the last ton may be dug up, we feel that we are living upon the capital of the country, and a capital which, though indefinite in one sense, is, nevertheless, strictly limited in another. But those countries which live chiefly by the cultivation of the soil do not live upon their capital, but upon their interest ; and, of necessity, the annual amount receivable by all and, therefore, by each, must be considerably under what it would be otherwise. If, then, we bear in mind this fundamental distinction, we shall perceive that the chief reason why Great Britain has become so prosperous is because its inhabitants are, during this nineteenth century, living in an appreciable degree on the capital of the country, not solely on its interest. When this capital approaches exhaustion, or even approaches a perceptibly-increased difficulty of realisation, the tide of fortune will turn and must then permanently ebb.

It may be a disagreeable reflection, but it is a true and therefore a salutary one, that we are living hastily on our capital, and that there is a widespread comfort and enjoyment amongst a large and prosperous population that cannot last for ever, or even for more than a century or two. This condition, then, is not one of permanence, and we cannot, therefore, compare it with one of permanence. Now, to a large extent the various countries of Europe enjoy a position of permanent and growing prosperity, and no other country is so much distinguished above others in this respect as that of France. We cannot, therefore, compare together on terms of equality the condition of Britain with that of France; for the one country lives largely on its capital, and the other does so to no appreciable extent. What prosperity, therefore, exists in the first is of a transient character; what exists in the second is of a permanent character. But in the meantime this transient prosperity is very great, and reflects itself upon the cultivation of the soil. There is an extreme demand for its products, and there is, therefore, relatively a strong effort developed to till the soil and to produce heavy crops, and high farming is the rule. Immense quantities of artificial manures are employed; expensive machinery is used; and capital is drawn from industry and applied to agriculture largely. The result is, notwithstanding unfavourable systems of ownership and of tenancy, that the soil is cultivated in Britain more successfully, though not more carefully, than in most other countries. The population is dense and prosperous, and, therefore, the agriculture is fruitful.

We have seen in the last chapter that in the Western States of America the population is thinly scattered, and the result is there is little demand for agricultural products; there is no sufficient market, and sometimes indeed the corn is in winter time—so little demand is there for it—used for fuel. France occupies, as regards population, an intermediate position between that of Britain and the

United States ; but with this disadvantage—that she possesses no wealth of minerals comparable with that of either
of the others. It will, therefore, be naturally expected that
her agriculture will be less productive and less expensive
than that of Britain, and more careful and laborious than
that of the States.   The same considerations, when
applied to other countries, produce the same results in
our conclusions.   The condition of Norway, of Switzerland, and of some parts of Germany, Prussia, Austria,
and Italy, is similar to that of France, and, therefore,
different from that of Great Britain.   These countries, or
districts of countries, referred to, place their dependence
to a very large extent upon the cultivation of the soil
and the practice of domestic industries, but also more
lately in some measure upon the conduct of manufacturing industries that derive their motive power from the
steam engine, and, therefore, from the combustion of
coal.   Where the latter movement has taken place, the
processes of agriculture have been so far benefited. They
have received benefit by the increase of the numbers
and wealth of the industrial part of the population,
which has produced a better market for agricultural
produce ; and they have also received benefit by the
pressure of the population in the direction of agricultural
pursuits being relieved, so that a lesser number of more
competent individuals share the income derivable from
agriculture.   But these benefits will take place in a
ratio corresponding to the introduction of steam, which
depends on the advantage which capital possesses in
introducing it ; and in those districts where mineral
wealth is found to be easy of realisation, the relief of
the agriculturalist will be the greatest. Also, the measure
of security there may be in the safe expenditure of
capital in any particular district or country will be one
of the most important factors in originating the con-

ditions wherein this superior benefit to agriculture arises.

Upon a full consideration of these points, we shall understand that the advantages which capital and the presence of extensive mineral resources, that are so remarkable in Great Britain, present to industry, will produce everywhere, in spite of false systems, the greatest benefits to agriculture and the agriculturalist. This reasoning is borne out by the actual facts; and the following table will afford a view of the average crops produced over a series of years in the various countries named. It is necessary, however, to caution the reader against supposing that these figures supply any other than a rough estimate, except it may be as regards France, the United States, and Ireland, where the statistics of produce have received the most attention.

Name of Country	Wheat. Bushels per acre	Barley. Bushels per acre	Oats. Bushels per acre	Rye. Bushels per acre	Maize. Bushels per acre	Potatoes per acre	Turnips. Tons per acre	Hay. Cwts. per acre
England . .	29	—	—	—	—	— tons	—	—
Ireland . .	24	32	34	19	—	3·3	13	40
Scotland (1854 & 55)	28	34½	34⅝	—	—	4·6	14½₂₀	—
Ditto at present .	34	41¾	44¼	—	—	6·9	20	—
France . . .	16	18	21	13	—	—	—	—
United States .	13	24	29	14	26	— bushels	—	35
Prussia . . .	20	25	28	18	—	125	10	27
Bavaria . .	16	20	23	16	—	103	—	—
Wurtemberg .	35	—	—	—	—	—	—	—
Saxony . . .	23	—	—	—	—	— bushels	—	—
Austria, Cisleithan	16	24	32	19	—	158	—	—
Do. Transleithan	17	18	23	18	—	—	—	—
Russia in Europe	16	—	12	14	—	— tons	—	—
Italy . . .	13	27	27	—	28	7	11¾	—
Spain . . .	23	24	—	9	—	—	—	—
Portugal . .	9	11	19	7	20	—	—	—
Sweden . .	21	—	—	—	—	—	—	—
Denmark . .	28	—	—	—	—	—	tons 23½	44
Holland . .	23	41	43	21	—	—	—	—
Belgium . .	21	32	40	23	—	—	—	—
Do. St. Nicholas	27	38	—	29	—	—	—	—
Switzerland . .	11	—	—	—	—	—	—	—

This table has been compiled and reduced from various
sources, all more or less authoritative and reliable. One
of these sources consists in the Reports on the Tenure of
Land in the several countries of Europe by H. M.'s
representatives, who have obtained their information on
the spot, or derived it from the more reliable native
works published on the subject. As regards Ireland, the
official statistics convey exact and satisfactory information.
As regards Scotland, the statistics obtained by the Highland and Agricultural Society for the Board of Trade, in
the years 1854 and 1855, give complete returns of the
produce for every county and district; and to ascertain
the probable produce at the present day, I have added to
that for the several crops of the former period, percentages
estimated from the reports on the agriculture of about
one-third of the Scotch counties, contained in the 'Transactions' of the Highland and Agricultural Society for the
years 1873–77 inclusive. A concurrence of testimony
appears to state the average produce of wheat in England
at 29 bushels per acre, but there is no very clear evidence
that this is correct. As regards the produce of the other
crops in England, there is no certainty, and any statement
made would probably be unreliable. The official Reports
of the state of agriculture in the United States of America,
supply satisfactory information on all points of interest
and importance to the farmer: the results in the table
are obtained from the returns of some recent years. M.
Maurice Block supplies extensive and very complete information with regard to the produce of crops in France,
and I have made extensive use of his works, not only in
the table but in the text. The English agricultural returns for 1866–67 supply also information with regard to
the produce of crops in some foreign countries. Notwithstanding the comparative reliability of these and
other sources of information employed in the compilation

o

of this table, for the most part the figures must be considered in the light only of an approximate estimate; indeed, in some cases I have met with figures apparently equally reliable, but considerably different. In such cases it has appeared best to strike an average, in consequence of which the rate of error is minimised, but may still remain considerable. Still, after all has been said, the information tabulated will probably be found to be of considerable interest.

We find, therefore, that the produce of the crops in Scotland at present stands high—higher, indeed, than that for any other country; and if we compare the rates for Scotland and Ireland together, a large difference in favour of the former will be observed. This is strikingly the case with potatoes, the rate for the former country being more than double that for the latter, though undoubtedly this crop is a more vital one for Ireland—one, as we have already seen, which the people depend upon more fully by far than in any other country. Again, the district of St. Nicholas, in Belgium, where the *petit culture* prevails, produces heavier crops than Ireland does, though the land is naturally pure sand, and consequently demands continued and heavy exertion on the part of the cultivator.

It is important to consider the effect of war upon the condition of agriculture and the agriculturalist.

The insecurity of capital, which is consequent on either internal disorder or external disquiet and alarm, will undoubtedly cut the strings of prosperity in agriculture as in manufactures and commerce; for, first, capital will be hoarded and not properly utilised; and, second, as the inducement to acquiring it will be thereby lessened, less will be laid past, and the amount of exertion to realise it will be reduced. Thus a less produce will be obtained, and a relatively dearer price will fall to be paid for what comes to market. The people, then, generally, not being able to provide above a certain minimum rate of sustenance for themselves and their families, will be unable to exercise that energy and enterprise which they otherwise would; in other words, such a people will be less strong, energetic, and progressive than other peoples enjoying these advantages; so that a condition where capital is normally unsafe, or is even periodically threatened, is one wherein the people will be less able to till the soil, so as to produce the most satisfactory results. This is, indeed, the case with the continental countries of Europe generally, when compared with the condition of the United Kingdom. In the former there are frequent internal disturbances or external wars.

Thus, Spain, Italy, and France have had their frequent revolutions, not unaccompanied by bloodshed and violence, and these with other countries have suffered from international wars of frequent occurrence and long duration. The only continental country excepted from these afflictions has been Scandinavia, whose isolation is practically as great as that of the United Kingdom. The result is, independently of other causes, that the people of the continent of Europe are physically inferior to those of Great Britain. But other causes operate so powerfully that it is impossible to compare the position of Britain with that of continental States; for the people of the former derive such benefits from their superior situation, that the security which agriculture enjoys is a very small influence, and it is probably more than counterbalanced by the effects of the vicious system of landholding that prevails. But, other influences apart, where agriculture possesses directly and indirectly the support and assistance of unstinted capital, it must be most successful and most prolific, and must be able to supply the wants of a population in the most full and satisfactory manner, the result being a corresponding augmentation of corporeal strength in the race.

But, again, the difference in climate must produce a great difference in the rate of the produce of agriculture. In the earlier part of this work, we have described how climate affects human *physique*, and there is no difficulty in apprehending the result of such a comparatively power-less *physique*, as belongs to the South, in the cultivation of the fields.   English agricultural instruments are fre-quently sent out to southern continental countries, but are found too cumbrous for the inhabitants to employ success-fully, and the experiment of their introduction fails. Thus those people, who from the heat of their climate demand little more than a vegetable diet, are not competent to employ the same labour-saving machines which are now so extensively used in agriculture by the people of the North, and hence they are not so able, other things being equal, to produce the same heavy crops as are common in lands otherwise not so favourably situated.   And, again, the fact that the southern populations do not rely so much upon butcher meat is the cause of what we should regard as a preponderating cultivation of cereals.   Thus in France the cereals are largely predominant ; for while in England the grass or green crops are as two to one of the corn, the case of France is exactly the reverse, the corn crops preponderating in that ratio.   It therefore follows that the soil is exhausted more rapidly in France and in southern countries than it is in England, for corn crops are in their nature exhaustive, while green crops are in their nature restorative.   It is on this principle that M. de Lavergne and Mr. James Caird account for the extra-ordinary difference in the yield of crops which exists between England and France. As has, however, been indicated, there may be various causes all tending in the same direction, though without doubt this last is a powerful one.

Then, further, there is the whole question of division of the soil, its manner of ownership or occupancy, which may have a very great influence upon its productiveness. Where the land is wholly or very largely owned by the common people, the soil may be so much divided as to preclude the possibility of large farming. When, however, it is found that agricultural operations can be conducted most economically only where farming operations are carried on on a large scale, it is clear that the constant division of the land must be injurious. It therefore becomes necessary to discuss the question of large *versus* small farms, before we can discuss the question of the most advantageous system of proprietorship from an economical point of view.

There have been two schools of economists who have fought that battle, but it is not yet clearly decided. The celebrated Arthur Young favoured large farms though writing before the termination of last century, since which so many vast and important improvements in agricultural machinery have taken place. And the equally renowned John Stuart Mill has favoured small farms, so long as they are cultivated by their owners. Mr. William Thomas Thornton possesses also the same views, maintaining that small farming proprietors are competent to produce a greater actual surplus of farm products, and, therefore, that they are more successful than large farmers.[1] Mr. T. E. Kebbel again comes to the conclusion that 'the weight of evidence seems decidedly against the policy of resuscitating the system of small farming, though it is not unfavourable to a larger admixture of small farmers.'[2]

[1] *A Plea for Peasant Proprietors*, new edition, 1876, pp. 37-41.
[2] *The Agricultural Labourer*, 1870, p. 215.

Now there is an essential difference between the position of small farmers as proprietors and as tenants. When proprietors, if possessing sufficient cultivable land, they will gradually accumulate capital, which they will expend largely on the improvement of their property, tending, thereby, continually towards an enhanced productiveness. When tenants, they start almost invariably with too little capital to do their farms justice ; they will, like the proprietors, labour excessively if they have the hope of improving their position materially by doing so ; but they cannot labour so successfully, or successfully enough, because they are labouring at a considerable—perhaps an overwhelming — disadvantage, against those who have generally abundance of capital, and as a rule a sufficiency of it. From this point of view regarding it, the position of Arthur Young is impregnable. He says [1] :—' Let me demand of the advocates of small farms where the little farmer is to be found who will cover his whole farm with marl, at the rate of 100 to 150 tons per acre ; who will drain all his land, at the expense of 2*l.* or 3*l.* an acre ; who will pay a heavy price for the manure of towns, and convey it thirty miles by land carriage ; who will float his meadows, at the expense of 5*l.* per acre ; who, to improve the breed of his sheep, will give 1,000 guineas for the use of a single ram for a single season ; who will give 25 guineas per cow for being covered by a fine bull ; who will send across the kingdom to distant provinces for new implements, and for men to use them ; who will employ and pay men for residing in provinces where practices are found which they want to introduce on their farms? At the very mention of such exertions, common in England, what mind can be so perversely framed as to imagine, for a single moment, that *such things* are to be effected by little farmers? Deduct from agriculture all the practices

---

[1] *Travels in France*, 1787-89, vol. i. p. 410.

that have made it flourishing in this island, and you have precisely the management of small farms.' Now, since this was written, remarkable progress has been made in the utilisation of new manures, and in the introduction of multitudes of new and expensive machines; and what was true with regard to the superior powers and qualifications of large farmers and large farms at the beginning of the century is more true now; for whereas the application of capital to agriculture may be said to have been then comparatively new, it is now extensively developed and entirely essential, and nothing but high farming will, where a good market exists, survive the struggle of competition. It is, therefore, what we might expect, when we find the Commissioners on the employment of children and women in agriculture, in their third report, dated 1870, state that 'there can be no doubt that in Wales as in England, according to the evidence in our previous Reports, the small farmer lives harder, employs his children earlier, and gives them less education than the ordinary agricultural labourer.' And in regard to the result of small farms on the produce of the lands, the evidence entirely confirms the opinion expressed by Mr. Culley in a former Report, that 'it is impossible for agriculture to make any decided advance in a district where the holdings are so small as to make it unprofitable for the occupier to employ the ordinary mechanical aids, which increase the produce of a farm at the same time that they lessen the cost of production.'

There can be no doubt of the fact that farms of minute dimensions, particularly when parcelled out into fragments, cannot be cultivated to any advantage compared with those which are large and consolidated. It is urged, however, strongly in favour of the system of *petit culture* that there is such an earnest persistency displayed by the cultivators when proprietors as to compensate for

all deficiencies, and to be sufficient to make up the lee-
way caused by the inability to employ the usual appliances. But from the evidence given before the Commission on the employment of children and women in
agriculture, we find that the small farmers, though not
proprietors, ' are unquestionably a very industrious race,
and they impart their industrious habits to their children,'
so that it is unnecessary to go to peasant proprietors to
witness exertions of the most persevering and unremitting description. Now Mr. John Stuart Mill sets
forward this feature of constant industry as one peculiar
to peasant proprietors. He says :—'Those who have
seen only one country of peasant proprietors always
think the inhabitants of that country the most industrious
in the world. There is as little doubt among observers
with what feature in the condition of the peasantry this
pre-eminent industry is connected. It is the " magic of
property " which, in the words of Arthur Young, "turns
sand into gold."' It is scarcely necessary to say, however, that this feature of proprietorship is not altogether
a distinctive one, and that there are others besides who
will work equally hard ; namely those who, proprietors or
not, are looking forward to the hope of earning a competency or more than that, whether it be in agriculture
or industry. It is true this virtue of proprietorship, being
hereditary, is likely to be a fixed, constant, and persistent
one, for the circumstance of working for a competency is
always in that case presumed to exist. But it is presumed in the particular cases of tenant farming that the
land has been let on reasonable terms—that is, on terms
which are likely, with proper work, attention, and
management on the part of the farmer, to lead to a
competency ; and it is rather striking that, with such
preponderating disadvantages as he labours under from
the want of suitable appliances, he still labours assiduously

along with the members of his household, straining every nerve and sinew if it be—so fond is he of his independence—only to make ends meet.

It must therefore be said that the small farmer is at such a serious disadvantage that he cannot, notwithstanding the characteristic hard labour of himself and his family, cope at all successfully with the disadvantages of his position. It is essentially one that can never be economical; it is the contention of muscles with machinery; and as that battle has been clearly won by the latter in manufacturing industry, so will it also be as clearly won in agriculture. Indeed in the improvement of the machinery which exists, in the introduction of new machinery, in the discovery of a new artificial manure, in the introduction of a new feeding stuff, or in some other way, an additional reason is added from time to time to those which have previously existed why large farms, with their capacity for the economical application of large capital, must now be relatively the most economically productive, and therefore the most profitable for all concerned. In former times this may not have been the case. When everyone worked with his arms, whether at the loom, the bench, or the plough, there would be no great difference between the profitableness of small and large farms, and he who was cultivating proprietor of either would probably possess that advantage which flows from the prosecution of his work with an unremitting industry; he then might have been in the capacity of a small proprietary farmer able to compete with the tenant of a much larger farm. But in countries where the agricultural population for the most part own the land and cultivate it as farmers, a considerable proportion of the whole number of farms are frequently of such a small size as to be comparatively unprofitable to work—that is to say, when compared with those farms whereon every modern agricultural improvement can be economically carried into effect. In the continental countries of Europe the people generally own the soil to a large extent, and cultivate it as farmers of their own properties; and where large estates exist, the introduction of new appliances proceeds from the large to the small, and proceeds slowly. Why this is so must be soon evident; for the land was already cultivated by resident proprietors before the introduction of these new appliances, and their use upon the smaller farms could not save labour already there, until after that labour had time to draft itself off to the industrial centres, and its only effect at first if introduced might be to assist the family to cultivate with more ease, and leave time disposable for the prosecution of domestic industries. These latter, however, except in few instances, have been supplanted by the factory, and there could therefore be little inducement to the small peasant proprietor to introduce those appliances which were to save a labour that could not otherwise be very readily utilised. It follows therefore that, as in the slow extinction of the hand-loom and other manual occupations, the slow extinction of a laborious manual cultivation of the soil will the less readily take place where the whole surface of a country is divided into fields and properties too minute for the proper application of expensive machines and new processes, where the resident population has been accustomed to do all the labour required, and do not therefore feel the need for new appliances.

The result is that there is an immense amount of labour performed by peasant proprietors, and a comparatively small amount of capital expended. In course of time those who are most successfully laborious will have been able from their hidden stores to purchase more and more land until their properties become larger than

they were, and at present indeed the realised capital of
small proprietors appears generally to be more willingly
expended in adding to their present lands than in improving them. There seems to be no limit to the amount
of labour bestowed, but a strict limit to the amount of
capital expended on small properties; and this is not
surprising, since the capital is realised with much more
difficulty, much more slowly, and with many more re-
verses in agriculture than it is in industrial undertakings,
particularly in Britain, where, as already pointed out, the
rapid and economical possession of abundant minerals
gives the miner, the manufacturer, and the merchant an
immense superiority in the realisation of property.

The circumstances, however, of different countries are
extremely different; and though no doubt the existence of
large farms must confer great advantages in the cultivation of the soil, there are other considerations that cannot
be neglected in considering the fitness of a particular
system for any particular country or district. In France,
for instance, there are decidedly fewer opportunities for
the rural population betaking themselves to industrial
centres than there are in this country, and as a consequence there is relatively a larger agricultural population
and a lesser industrial one, and the same is the case with
Prussia and generally with the other continental European countries. That being so, a proportionately less
agricultural produce is demanded for the support of the
industrial portion of the population. It happens, also, in
France, and in some at any rate of these other countries,
that the greater part of the soil is cultivated, and there
fore there is for any defined area a less call for high
farming than there is in Great Britain, where only a
certain limited amount of the country is cultivated, and
large tracts, as in Scotland and Ireland, remain moorland
and waste. It is therefore evident that to satisfy the

wants of the European populations generally there is not much call for that high farming which is alone found to be fully remunerative in this country ; and in proportion as the introduction of machinery and the extension of capital in industrial undertakings tends to augment the industrial population and reduce the agricultural, there is afforded the opportunity for supplying the place of the labourers who have left the fields by an adequate introduction of new machinery. Indeed the growth of the industrial population and the reduction of the agricultural will proceed from the introduction of new industrial appliances, and be the forerunner of new agricultural appliances. But this movement can only take place where minerals are being more readily obtained than formerly, or the progress of invention enables their being more fully utilised ; and it is no proof of defect in any agricultural system that this process takes place more slowly in one country than in another—in France, for instance, than in Great Britain—but merely a circumstance altogether independent of agricultural systems, though sufficient in the long run to affect them.

But, upon the other hand, let us suppose that a country such as Great Britain has exhausted her mineral resources—which probably enough she will do as regards coal at the present increasing rate of consumption, to the depth of four thousand feet, in from two to three centuries—then it is apparent that a considerable proportion of the population presently engaged in mining and its allied occupations will necessarily be engaged otherwise, and in all probability they will fall back upon agriculture, for it is inconceivable that industrial employments will continue equally active and important when the great source of them—an abundant supply of the raw materials—disappears. In course of centuries, if the world continues to act with regard to the mineral resources of the earth in the way that Great Britain is doing at present—working upon them without any restraint—a time must come when the present amount of output will considerably diminish, and ultimately approach a termination. That period doubtless is one very far distant, and may not require present consideration. Still, when that time approaches—and it may do so practically for several countries much sooner than for others—a great source of comfort and wealth and also of occupation will no longer exist, and mankind may find it necessary to resort largely to the cultivation of the land, instead of shifting from the land to industrial centres as at present.

It therefore appears that the various systems of agriculture are greatly the creation of the circumstances of particular countries in which they respectively exist, and arise through the relative abundance and remunerativeness of other occupations, or conversely through the absence of such. In whatever condition a country may exist, whether circumstances favour the cultivation of the land by small farms or by large, there can be no doubt that the most advantageous method of farming is that which holds out the greatest inducement to the farmer to cultivate his land thoroughly and to lay out upon it abundant capital. It is not to be supposed, however, that peasant cultivating proprietors will not ultimately devote sufficient capital to the cultivation of their lands. It is only, except in France and some districts of the other southern European countries, a very few decades since the peasant proprietary cultivator was a serf, with no property of his own, and when enfranchised he was only possessor of such as would enable him after many years of heavy toil to clear himself from debt, and to commence laying up capital. That process once begun is a sure one; for the habits of labour and of prudence have become a second nature, and every addition to the capital gained represents so much of an addition to the permanent improvement of, or increase to, the property. Thus a greater crop is produced, and produced with less toil; for the appliances which capital enlists are utilised, and manual labour is economised. But as there will be a general improvement among peasant proprietors, each one will compete with his neighbour for any new land to be purchased, and in consequence the price of land, as we have seen, will gradually increase. When there is a comparatively equal distribution of good fortune and of land, the proprietary cultivators will co-operate to carry out those improvements, introduce those new machines, or utilise those appliances which demand mutual assistance. Mutual self-interest will gradually bind the agricultural society together in such a manner that the largest improvements that may be profitably adopted can be carried out; and indeed we find this to be in some cases the description of the process which is taking place at the present day.

For the future, then, granted a salutary political rule —which is the necessary atmosphere for all progress— the gradual prosperity of a system of small farms that are cultivated by the proprietors is ensured. These farms may not be—although they are notably so in some cases, as in Jersey and Guernsey—so productive as large farms; that is to say, their produce may not stand in such a high proportion to the number of cultivators as in the case of large farms employing extensive and expensive machinery and using every modern appliance; but they serve the necessary function of maintaining in profitable employment a large number of persons for whom there is no other employment to be had, and they maintain them in such a way as to induce them to labour assiduously and practise extreme prudence, both of which tend directly to benefit themselves, and indirectly to enrich the community. Upon the other hand, when farms, whether large or small, are held by tenants, especially tenants-at-will, and where the landlords regard the letting of the land purely as a commercial transaction, the produce of the land will not attain, *cæteris paribus*, to the same amount as when it is cultivated by its proprietor. For in the best of cases, that is, when the lease is long and is assured to the farmer, he cannot continually be engaged in improving his farm ; for towards the end of his lease there is no time in which to reap the benefits which the expenditure upon considerable improvements must produce in order to justify it. The practice therefore is with a farmer who has rented a farm, as in Scotland, for a period of nineteen years, to execute whatever improvements he contemplates carrying out within the first four or five years of his lease. The consequence is that the land is not uniformly improved, and indeed is probably in general comparatively depreciated towards the end of the lease. The farmer who leases a farm expects to reap a fair return upon the capital expended in its improvement, otherwise he would not so employ it. He may lease a comparatively unimproved tract of country at a low rent ; and then the possibilities of improved cultivation may so present themselves to him that he may employ a large amount of capital to the draining of new soil and the erection of new buildings ; and he then probably finds that in a few years the increased productiveness of his farm has recouped him the capital expended, and that during the remainder of his lease, his rent being of course as at first, he reaps a high rate of profit on his improvements. When his lease expires the farm thus improved falls back into the hands of the proprietor, who revalues it, and finds the rent may be considerably increased. The proprietor himself perhaps has done nothing whatever to improve his land, but the tenant has done everything. It is perfectly evident, therefore, that the inducements to improvements under such a system cannot be nearly so strong as under one where the proprietor himself is the cultivator ; for whereas the tenant calculates on and obtains only the ordinary reward due to the investment of capital (it may of course be more or less) the proprietor finds the value of his land without any sacrifice to be greater than it was at the commencement of the lease.

When land is held from year to year, on the other hand, the farm is liable to be revalued at any time, and the rent may be so increased as to strip the farmer, should he remain tenant, of the ordinary profits of trade. Rather than remove, however—a thing undoubtedly extremely inconvenient to him—he may remain at a comparative sacrifice. But wherever an uncertainty of tenure exists there must necessarily be also a great hindrance to the carrying out of the most important kind of improvements. It has frequently been proposed to overcome this dis- advantage by enacting that a valuation of the improve- ments effected shall be made at the termination of leases, so that a fair remuneration shall be given to the tenant for that capital he is obliged to leave in the soil. High authorities, such as Mr. James Caird, however, think such a system to be impracticable ; and others, such as the Duke of Argyll, believe it to be unjust. Its operation in Ireland under the Land Act of 1870 has probably failed.

It appears, therefore, that the most certain means by which improvements will be made upon the land so as to render it productive in the maximum degree, is to confer upon the actual cultivators as large a share of the benefits of proprietorship as is consistent with justice. In a country where land is not perfectly freely bought and sold, where artificial restrictions exist to prevent its falling from the hands of a particular family, or to hinder its being acquired by men of capital, and by those who are in the best position to improve it, the proper and

natural inducements to improve it are taken as much
as possible away, for the cultivator cannot in general
readily purchase his farm at all.   It is said that the
farmer, if a tenant, is in a better position to cultivate
successfully than if he were proprietor, for his capital is
not shut up in the purchase of the soil, but is free in
his hand for its improvement.   When, however, a man
owns real property he ought to be in the best position
to command the most extended credit, and the capital
he may require for the improvement of a particular
farm he cultivates will not generally stand in any considerable relation to the value of the ground itself, so
that the proprietor is in a specially happy position to
cultivate his own property so far as the ability to command capital is concerned.   On the other hand, a farming
tenant in Great Britain is under disadvantage of a special
and artificial character.   In Scotland he is subject to the
law of Hypothec, in England to that of Distress, and
these have similarly an unfortunate and prejudicial effect
on his credit.   The tenant's credit is prejudicially affected
by the primary claim which the landlord possesses, so that
he cannot get the use of capital he otherwise would be
in a position to borrow on such security as he might offer.
Thus those improvements which would be carried on
regularly and constantly were the land in the hands of
cultivating proprietors, are only proceeded with irregu-
larly and slowly; for under the present system the
farmer chosen may be a man without either capital or
credit, and therefore not in a position to improve the
land in any appropriate degree.   The landlord, regarding
the advantages which are offered by the highest bidder
and the security he has for the payment of his rent,
possesses the least inducement, however he may act, to
select a substantial and experienced farmer.

P

But it has been recently asserted[1] by the Duke of Argyll that ' " Feudal feeling"—the dislike of doing what is disagreeable to friends and neighbours—mere laziness, and procrastination—all tend to make many English owners postpone the day of revaluing farms,' and that therefore tenants dislike leases, for a certainty of revaluation at a specific date would take the place of present uncertainty. And it is also contended that when farms are revalued under the present system of yearly leases the rents are commonly abated below the sum they would fetch in the market, and that such abatements, ' which are direct allowances of money from the owner to the occupier over and above the average profits of cultivation, ... represent very large sums indeed.' Such are given not specifically, but really as compensation for improvements. Now, when following out these statements, the Duke says :—' It is quite obvious that a tenant can better afford to lay out money on improvements who holds his farm at a cheap rent, than the tenant that holds it at a dear rent.' But, then, again, he says, in the course of the same essay :— ' It will be found that improvement is most active where the rent is not specially abated from the full value of the land in its unimproved state, but, on the contrary, where the rent is kept fully up to that value.' That is to say, that landlords generally pursue a generous policy of under-renting their farms with the view of encouraging tenants to improve them, or, at any rate, in view of probable prospective improvement ; but nevertheless it is found that improvement is most active where such generosity has not been manifested and abatements have not been made. It does not appear that landlords, as a rule, would act without sufficient motives ; and if it is found that the

[1] *Essay on the Commercial Principles applicable to Contracts for the Hire of Land,* by the Duke of Argyll, K.T. Published by the Cobden Club, 1877, p. 45.

improving tenants are generally those who have had no abatement from the market value of their farms allowed them, then there would be no motive for landlords making such abatement as the noble author says is generally granted. It may rather be supposed that landlords, like other human beings, will, on the occasion of revaluing their farms, require a fair and reasonable rent from the tenant, such as would be got in a free market, and that they would not be disinclined towards maintaining this position by the knowledge that the tenant could not remove to another farm without additional expenditure and inconvenience.

Again, the Duke says, in the same essay :—' It is evident that the profit to the tenant must be both higher in amount and more immediate in enjoyment than any profit which the owner can secure. The capital which he lends to the tenant in the value of the soil is lent at a rent which rarely exceeds the rate of 3 per cent. Whatever additional capital he may contribute over and above this is lent also at about 3½ per cent. in all those cases in which the tenant agrees to pay for improvement loans at the rate of 6½ or 6¾ per cent., because this is a rate which represents both capital and interest. It is evident also that from the capital so lent to the tenant he must derive a very much higher rate of interest, since generally he finds an ample profit from the increased returns, after paying the interest of 6½. What the average rate of interest may be upon capital employed in farming it would be difficult to say ; but we shall see presently that a farmer of great experience and skill estimates the rate which he calculates upon in his own case at 10 per cent.

' Accordingly we shall find from numerous recorded cases that the permanent improvement and reclamation of land, which is the most conspicuous and costly kind of improvement, is very often amply remunerative to tenants

under a nineteen years' lease, even when the whole supplementary capital over and above the value of the land is
advanced in the first instance entirely by themselves.'

Now we have already seen that there is, according to
the Duke's view, no basis in the fact of a superior rate of
improvement to farms by tenants, to the statement that
landlords generally let their land at an abatement on its
market value, and even if there were such a basis it would
be difficult probably to recognise it ; for, as the Duke says,
' What the average rate of interest may be upon capital
employed in farming it would be difficult to say ; ' and, that
being so, it is equally difficult to say what ought to be
the rate required for the use of the land, which is
considered by the Duke to be the most ' fundamental '
part of the capital employed by the farmer. Surely,
therefore, it is not easy to come to such conclusions
as the Duke has done with reference to the system of
abatements that are asserted by him to be so generally
practised by landlords. We have no reason to suppose
that owners who act rationally—as no doubt owners, like
occupiers, generally do—do not often prefer to have one
individual before another as tenant farmer, and even at a
pecuniary sacrifice ; but the reason must be apparent—the
preferred one promises by his character, his experience,
his capital, or some other well-known advantageous qualification, to be by so much the better tenant of the two,
and the common sense of the landowner asserts itself
even in the presence of vicious laws, framed, or at least
now maintained, though their tendency must be to
place the man of straw on the same level as the man of
substance.

But to return to our consideration of the mode and
means of improvement. In what circumstances does the
cultivator improve the land in the greatest degree? The
Duke of Argyll, in the sentences just quoted from his

essay, asserts that the profit of the farmer is both higher
and more immediately realised than the profit of the
owner of the land.   Let us, then, follow the steps of the
illustration given.   First, the land is let to the tenant at
or under 3 per cent. ; and, secondly, the capital lent for
improvement is lent at about 3½ per cent. ' in all those
cases in which the tenant agrees to pay for improvement
loans at the rate of 6½ or 6¾ per cent.'   Now, as regards
the first proposition, it may be remarked that land is
not solely valuable on account of its agricultural fertility, for, as everyone knows, it is let a second time occasionally for sporting purposes, and it is undoubtedly
estimated at a certain value on account of the social
position which it confers on its proprietor, or on the
amenity it bestows on a country residence, or, indeed, as
is obvious in other ways ; and if it were not so, land
would probably be let for agricultural purposes at a
higher percentage on the purchase money than it is.   But
does every proprietor reap only 3 per cent. on the purchase money, or does he reap 3 per cent. on the modern
valuation ?   Doubtless on the latter, and the difference
in this country between these two ways of regarding
the principle upon which the percentage is reckoned is
over a few years considerable.   Land, indeed, is, as the
number and wealth of the population of these islands
increase, constantly rising in value ; so that if we regard
it prospectively, and can account the future gain, it is
probable that the rate at which farms are let, considering
the great security, is not a low one from a proprietor's
point of view.   It cannot be said, then, that any argu-
ment can be founded on this basis as regards the relative
rate of farmers' profits.

    Again, when proprietors lend capital it is said to be
at a low rate ; and doubtless if the rate being 3½ per
cent. per annum were a perpetual one, payable by every

succeeding cultivator, it would be a very good and favourable one for the farmers. But such is not the case : the present tenant pays off both principal and interest, and the future payment of $3\frac{1}{2}$ per cent. or more is made by the cultivators to the proprietor in name of improved land, all of which improvement has really been effected by one tenant in course of a single, say nineteen years', lease, and the proprietor therefore has expended nothing, for the money may be obtained from the State on the security of the land.

It is, therefore, not the fact that the proprietor earns a less, or a less immediate, return for his capital than the tenant ; for in all these improvements where he does not advance the funds himself—and he has no great induce-ment when improvement loans are to be had on easy terms to do so—he actually gets them executed for nothing, and therefore their value is to him a pure gain, and does not possess the character of a percentage at all. It is said, however, that had it not been for the inherent qualities of the soil those improvements could not have been effected ; and those qualities being recognised by the tenant, he utilises the capital expended during the currency of the lease to his own satisfaction, deriving from its employment a proper marketable return. That, no doubt, is often or generally quite true ; but it is none the less so that he does not derive that benefit from the continual improvement of the soil which he would do if it were his own, and if he were the cultivating proprietor, and that in consequence he has not that inducement to its improvement brought so strongly before him as if he shared continually in its results, instead of expecting only to receive the marketable return for the employment of his capital.

The interest, therefore, which the cultivators of a country possess in its rapid and constant improvement,

when they are the proprietors of the soil, is lost when
they are simply tenants, and expect to reap, and do reap,
only a reward for their own toil and the employment of
their capital. The gradual increase of population and
wealth which takes place normally in a country enjoying
a stable government and a settled condition, thereby
raises the value of the soil for agricultural purposes ; and
that value ought, with respect to the highest considerations of economy, to be reaped at least chiefly by the
agriculturalists, and that can be attained only in the
maximum degree when they are the proprietors of the
soil.

When, however, upon the other hand the agriculturalists are not only tenants, but tenants-at-will, and
subject to their rents being changed at any time, then
indeed there is no prospect for them of permanent
improvement, and no prospect either of the land being
made to produce an increasing crop by which an increasing population, whether agricultural or industrial, may be
adequately clothed and fed. And, as we have already
seen in Ireland, and to some extent in Britain, these
unfortunate conditions are at work.

We have, therefore, before us the vices and virtues of
the two systems of extensive estates farmed by tenants,
and of small subdivided lands farmed by proprietors, and
we see that the circumstances of their profitable existence
are essentially dissimilar.

However, if we regard tenancy and proprietorship as
cultivating where the country is for the most part agricultural, we shall see that where the former, as it largely is,
is subject to alteration in its conditions within short
periods affecting the amount of produce that falls to the
cultivator, it is completely unsuccessful ; and where the
latter exists, even though to a limited extent, the country
generally is fully cultivated, and the maximum of exer-

tion in cultivation, and of prudence and thrift in saving, is exhibited by the cultivators.

The condition of contentment which thus appears to have its being in a certain secure possession of an amount of land sufficient to enable its cultivator to procure, jointly perhaps with an additional occupation, a competence for himself and his family, is one which lies at the root of social stability. As in France, where the contented cultivator tills his own land, depending on its produce alone, so elsewhere, when the inhabitants are peasant proprietors, and not industrial workers, the condition, though contented, is not rapidly a prosperous one, and the population is one verging naturally on the stationary condition. In a country such as Great Britain, however, where country life is not so attractive as in the South, the rewards of industrial life will be relatively all the more prized ; and particularly will this be so when the ability to apply capital to industrial undertakings is, where mineral wealth is so abundant, so perfectly easy. We should therefore expect to find that the workmen of the North would be, on the whole, more prosperous with a comparatively small-sized holding—a large garden or small field of perhaps from one quarter to half an acre, that would fitly form rather the occupation of a meagre but joyous leisure than the sphere of severe and prolonged exertion. The change that is actually taking place where there is sufficient freedom, appears generally to be towards a union of the two kinds of occupation. Where rural employments have been hitherto the sole resource, as in Norway, the inhabitants are becoming alive to the great advantage which industrial employments would present, and they are therefore successfully endeavouring to introduce manufactures by co-operative associations. In this country, upon the other hand, the desideratum is an addition to the present too exclusive town life, and confinement of a certain measure of rural employment; and this would be, as we have already seen, immensely beneficial to those workmen who could contrive to purchase their own little properties. Contentment would then reign in the minds of the people. That chronic quarrelling with his position, which unfortunately is to a large extent the characteristic feature of the British workman, and the perpetual inclination to strike work which is often disastrously followed by action, would disappear at least largely; for when the possibility of an individual being dispossessed of his freehold as the result of an unsuccessful strike, would present itself to his mind, there would undoubtedly be less inclination manifested to do battle with present fortune. There would be less improvidence and recklessness in the conduct of trades unionists than there is at present, and a more conservative spirit would grow up that would foster action tending to enrich the workman as well as to preserve him contented.

There is an elasticity about that system of binal occu-pation which exists in many continental countries; for the possession of patches of land by workmen, besides engaging their spare labour, which is indeed a refreshment to them, forms a resource in periods of industrial adversity that cannot be estimated too highly. Such plots or patches would afford the workman an opportunity of remuneration in proportion to the exact amount of the labour expended, so that they would form a school wherein the greatest stimulus to exertion would be supplied. It is unfortunately too clearly seen that, the more extensive the ramifications and dimensions of trading operations become, the larger are the fluctuations which characterise them; and while the capitalist may wait easily, it may be with some loss of capital, for the return of the tide, the workman, if he possesses savings,

receives, from any investments he may have made, no
sufficient or suitable return. The result, therefore, to
him is entirely disastrous ; there is nothing left upon
which he may break his fall, or assist himself again to
rise. It may be objected here that trade union funds do
so ; but unfortunately in their character they rather tend
to render the workman more reckless, for they are essentially communistic ; they belong to no one in particular,
but to all ; therefore no one individual cares to exert
himself rather than expend them.

In the one situation, therefore, which is happily that
of many countries, where the workmen possess and cultivate pieces of land, there is a material relief in periods
of industrial adversity afforded in a healthy way by their
produce ; in the other situation, which is that of Great
Britain and Ireland, there can be no such satisfactory
relief ; and if the manufacturer chooses to stop his
works rather than to proceed at a loss, his workmen are
thrown idle, there are no resources for their energies, and
material followed by moral wretchedness and despair
seize them. The tendency then will be towards a pauperisation of those who are thrown out of employment,
and a consequent reduction in the efficient working
strength, or the effective population, of the country.

It may, however, be noticed that though the present
state of the law practically prohibits the workman or
even the middle-class individual from purchasing a suitable plot of ground—for there are no such plots to be
had, and if there were he knows that the expenses of
transfer would be too considerable and uncertain—a
system of allotments has been already extensively adopted
in the agricultural districts. This system has been introduced in face of great opposition and in spite of powerful prejudices, for it was supposed that the agricultural

labourer would be apt to neglect his proper work were he furnished with a piece of ground he might cultivate for himself. But the result of the system so far, as already introduced, has undoubtedly benefited the labourer without interfering with the execution of his other more important duties, unless indeed when the allotment has reached an undue size. By the census of England and Wales for 1871, it appears that in the seventeen representative agricultural counties, there were 91,492 allotments detached from a cottage or house, in addition to the gardens or lands attached; and, as there were 201,903 farm labourers in these counties, it follows that a large proportion of these must already be in the occupancy of a plot of ground, and that the allotment system is now capable of producing an ameliorating influence upon the condition of the agricultural labourer, though it must be in no degree similar to that which would take place were the allotment the labourer's own land.

Mr. T. E. Kebbel writes as follows upon this important subject :—' On the whole, we may say that if all the good which the system is thought capable of effecting has not yet (1870) been realised, little of the evil which was predicted has yet ensued ; while, if setting aside for a moment its purely economical aspect, we look only to its moral effect, the picture seems without a drawback. While cultivating his potatoes, his turnips, and his wheat, to say nothing of fruit and flowers, the labourer is merged in the husbandman, and begins to understand for the first time what is meant by the dignity of industry. The plot of ground, too, is a source of common interest to the whole family, and the pride they take in it sheds a humanising influence on the otherwise cheerless tenour of their lives. That the garden is a formidable rival to the

public-house is a point in its favour which none can be
so ignorant as to question.'[1]   And the Commissioners on
the Employment of Children, Young Persons, and
Women in Agriculture, in their third Report, dated 1870,
say (p. 16) :—'With the gradual disappearance of the
small farms, which economical causes cannot fail to
cause to continue, it is of the utmost importance to the
welfare of the class that have thus changed their position, that, for the sake of their children in particular, one
advantage which they derived from their small occupations should in some form be preserved to them.   The
abundance of milk as an article of diet, and the occupation afforded by the dairy to the females of his family,
are very valuable elements in the condition of the small
farmer.   If arrangements are adopted by which, when
he becomes dependent on daily wages as an agricultural
labourer, he can keep a cow, he would, according to
the best opinions, if in constant employ, have no reason
to regret the change.'   And again :—' Great progress is
being made in all parts of the kingdom in the improvement of the labourer's cottage home ; and where his
dwelling in size and accommodation admits of due
attention to the decencies and comforts of life ; where
he has a good garden attached or near to his cottage ;
where, either by the privilege of a "cowgate," or any
other arrangement, he has a sufficient supply of milk for
himself and his family ; where, in default of a garden, he
has a suitable allotment or potato ground ; and where he
is in regular employ at good wages—his material condition
is better than that of a small farmer.'

It may, however, be supposed that although circumstances are favourable to one class of labourers—namely,
those who dwell and labour in the country, being in a

---

[1] *The Agricultural Labourer*, by T. E. Kebbel, 1870, p. 71.

position to profit by the occupation of a garden or allotment of ground—circumstances are not equally favourable, and are indeed adverse, to the workmen of the towns
possessing similar advantages. It may be said that in the
large cities the distance to the country is so great that the
mere cost of travelling backward and forward daily would
render the plan impracticable. The larger the city, however, the more costly are the dwellings, and we find that
the mere ground rents of workmen's houses in London vary
from $1\frac{1}{4}d$. to $1s$. $6d$. per family per week. The means of
communication are now so complete between large towns
and the adjoining country, that the additional cost of
transferring workmen from their homes in the country to
their work in the towns and back, should not be a fatal
obstacle, for some railway companies at the present time
carry workmen at the rate of one penny for at least ten
miles. There are at present numerous classes of tradesmen in London who reside at a distance of from eight to ten
miles from town. Mr. Sutliff states that 'the experience
of the Metropolitan (Building) Association is that the
ground rents of cottages in the country are $3\frac{1}{2}d$. per
family per week, while those in London average $8d$. per
family per week; and also that cottages in the country
can be constructed at $34l$. per room, while the construction of dwellings in London costs on the average $46l$. per
room. And these cottages (of the Metropolitan Association, which are situated at Beckenham), accommodating
164 families, are semi-detached and possess gardens
20ft. by 80ft. The financial success of the experiment in
the construction of these suburban workmen's cottages in
the neighbourhood of such a city as London amply
proves the practicability of the system.

It may be asked, however, how such a system, if
extensively adopted, would affect the occupation of the
country as a whole; would not its adoption largely

reduce the extent of land available for the common purposes of agriculture? In order to reply to this question,
we must first ascertain the number of families which
would probably be in some degree likely to take advantage of a country life, and possess a garden or field with
a dwelling.

In England and Scotland in 1871, there were 4,750,000
inhabited houses; and we may reckon as the highest
maximum that one-half of the families inhabiting them
suffer from their having no interest in or enjoyment
from the possession of land, and that they would be prepared to embrace the opportunity that might be afforded
to acquire a small plot of their own. Now, in most
cases, so far as the evidence laid before the Commissioners on the Employment of Women and Children in
Agriculture has led them to form a conclusion, one rood
of ground, being five times the size of the gardens of the
Metropolitan Association at Beckenham, is a fair measure
for each family to possess; for beyond this limit the
workman is apt to neglect his common work in order to
attend to the cultivation of his ground. But if we allow
one-half acre to each family, and we suppose a universal
system of allotments or holdings to be instituted throughout Great Britain, it would result that not over 1,187,500
acres would be thus occupied—an extent equalling
less than 1-25th part of the cultivated land of the
country. There can be nothing, therefore, in the objection that the introduction of such a system would trench
on the food supplies, for the ground thus occupied would
doubtless be most profitably utilised. In other countries
the land generally is relatively to the population more
extensive than in this; and the gradual occupation of the
suburban country districts might, therefore, become
general without affecting the food supplies to any prejudicial degree.

But, on the other hand, it may be objected that the workmen themselves would not desire to live in the country, or care to possess ground of their own in preference to dwelling in the town adjoining their factory or workshop. Every new taste it may be said, however, has to be created, and every new experience must become customary before it can be a profitable one. But there is inborn in everyone a love of nature and of the open fields, the richly blossoming gardens, and the fresh, healthful, and fragrant air of the country. There is in truth, then, no new taste to be created, and the experience would, even if at first comparatively unsuccessful, be soon productive of benefit. The example and emulation of neighbours already settled in their little freeholds would soon encourage and teach the uninitiated. New pleasures would arise from the cultivation of the ground which would withdraw the workman from the public-house; the domestic animals would supply a source of interest, recreation, and light labour to the wife, and the children would grow up amid surroundings infinitely more healthful and joyous than those of the town, while they would add to their former good feeding the healthy exercise which is the prime requisite towards a lusty growth. What can be more pitiful than the sight, which is so common in our great towns, of children in hundreds, dirty and in rags, painfully amusing each other in the gutter, so that 'gutter children' is a phrase that expresses a view of human misery only to be seen in perfection in Great Britain? If we pass to the neighbouring shores, where the wealth is comparatively small, we find an amount of self-regard, cleanliness, and healthfulness very different from the misery, squalor, and drunkenness so prevalent in our streets. But beyond the physical pleasure and the moral benefit derivable from the general adoption of such a system, so far as it might be found practicable, there can be no doubt that the capacity of the workman would be improved both in body and mind. His energies would be enlarged, and he would, in the course of a few years, be capable of turning out more work than formerly, with more ease to himself and more profit to his employer.

What can be expected from the masses at present when they are, as in Liverpool, packed together in dark courts and alleys—containing from about six to twenty houses in each, with their 'public conveniences' for all the inmates of such houses—at the rate of about 600 persons to the acre?[1] It is, indeed, impossible to expect material and moral results other than disastrous.

The first steps necessary are those of wholesale removal of considerable proportions of the population to districts where more light and air are to be had ; and, in order to effect this, the locomotive and steam-car must be called into requisition. However difficult such steps must be, there appears to be no other method of undertaking the much-required improvement. Large organisation is called for ; and it is a question whether the municipal authorities are competent, even were they always disinterested, to undertake such. It may well be a problem demanding the immediate attention of the Government, and assuredly there is none that more eminently affects the national well-being.

[1] See Letter by Mr. R. W. Pitcher in *Times*, December 4, 1877.

CHAPTER VII.

THE SUSTENANCE AND ABILITY OF THE INDIVIDUAL WORKMAN.

THE inhabitants of different countries are extremely dissimilar, and one of the most striking dissimilarities consists in their relative working power. As a whole, the people who dwell in temperate climates are able as labourers to work most energetically and successfully. In the same country, however, particularly before the construction of railways, striking dissimilarity in the working powers of individuals must always exist.

The degree of prosperity which the labourer enjoys must be measured not so much by the position he occupies relatively to other labourers in his own or in another country, with whom he has probably no immediate connection, as by the fact of progress or retrogression having taken place in his own condition. If the fact of gradual progress be not ensured, then he is in a miserable position indeed; where the individual energy he possesses has not a fair field for its exercise, then individual prosperity cannot result, and stagnation or retrogression ensues. When, however, the exercise of labour is constantly stimulated. by an enlightened self-interest, there will be an accumulative progress in everything which can benefit the labourer. And if the labourer be benefited, everyone around him with whom he has to deal must also be benefited, and moreover contentment and security reigns.

Where war and violence frequently disturb what

Q

peace a people enjoys, there will be continually a certain degree of insecurity felt, and there will, therefore, be the less inducement presented to the labourer, for he can never be sure that the fruits of his toil can be perfectly safe ; he may fear that, when violence breaks out, the fruits of his life of toil will be relentlessly swept away. In consequence of this, there will be a tendency to work only to supply the immediate necessities of life, but not to lay up for the future. There may thus be little capital accumulated, and all those helps to labour which capital supplies will be afforded in the smallest degree. The labourer will apply himself to his labour with only the rudest instruments, and the consequence will be that with hard toil he will be able to produce only a small result. The disinclination, therefore, to work so as to lay up savings for a future period that arises from insecurity, causes ultimately a necessity for a disproportionate degree of toil in order to provide mere daily subsistence. It is, therefore, apparent that where a country is secure from spoliation, there ought to be, *cæteris paribus*, the greatest accumulation of savings, and, therefore, the greatest facility in producing a livelihood and something more ; and conversely, where lands are apt to be ravaged by wars, the people will have a harder lot, their toil being comparatively unproductive.

And since this must be the case, it is equally plain that where wars and violence burst out periodically, the people will be relatively poorly fed, and also relatively incapable of active and prolonged muscular exertion.

There appear to be important and striking differences between the physical capabilities of men in different parts of the globe. In India, the labourer works feebly, but he spreads such energies as he possesses over a very long day of work. In Eastern Europe the product of a day's labour is not so great as it is in Western Europe, though upon an average the hours of labour are more prolonged. In Britain and America, the labourer applies himself with energy, and produces more work in a nine or ten hours day than his competitor in Western Europe does in one of eleven or perhaps even twelve hours. But in each of the quarters referred to there exist minor differences, for men have not even within the same country the same ability to work effectively; and this difference is seen even in England at the present time, the agricultural labourers of the south being not so robust and energetic as those of the north.

With man, indeed, it is as with the horse and the ox : his powers of enduring exertion depend upon the amount and kind of food he assimilates. There is a great gap between the position of the civilized man and of the savage; and while the latter necessarily possesses a disproportionately large alimentary system in consequence of the crude character of the food he eats, and the irregular intervals at which he secures it, the former enjoys a system developed to give a maximum amount of external strength. The latter inevitably consumes a large portion of his physical energy in digesting food taken when secured in enormous quantities, and wastes the most part of the remainder by enforced fasts; the former possesses at short and regular intervals a food already cooked, and, therefore, easily digested, so that there is no unnecessary loss of strength in assimilating it. But while there exists this great distance between the physical construction of the savage and of the civilized man, the latter is not by any means uniformly the same as regards his capacity to assimilate food and to produce work.

In Europe generally the common labourer subsists upon a vegetable diet, or where animal food is added, it is of a crude and cheap kind. Thus, in Belgium,

we find that 'very many have for their entire subsistence
but potatoes with a little grease, brown or black bread,
often bad, and for their drink the tincture of chicory.'
. . . . 'Sugar is seldom seen, and milk is a luxury
afforded by only the better class of workmen.'   'The
hucksters constantly adulterate everything they sell,
thereby undermining the health as well as the pocket of
the unfortunate workman.' . . . . 'When the wife has
to work she has not time to attend to the cooking of the
food, such as it is, nor can she mind the children, who,
therefore, grow up in a state of misery both physical
and moral.[1]

'In the four large sewing-thread factories of Alost,
wages are 40 cents and 50 cents to 2 francs for men, and
40 cents and 50 cents to $1\frac{1}{4}$ francs for women; children
are employed from six to seven years.   The factory
operatives here live wretchedly; their chief food consists
of potatoes and dry bread.   They inhabit small huts,
many of them unfloored, and sleep on sacks filled with
straw, with a sort of blanket made of coarse tow for
bed covering. . . . . All mill hands wear blouses and
wooden shoes, and clothing costs a spinner an average of
50 francs per year.' 'At Ninove ignorance and misery
prevail; the food is the same as at Alost.' 'The position
of the operative is perhaps worse here (in Alost, Ninove,
and Termonde) than elsewhere in Belgium.   A first-
class hand earns on an average about 28l. a year, whilst
the smallest expenditure on which a man can exist
involves an expenditure of about 20l. a year. . . . .
Indeed, the possibility of existence on such wages is only
to be explained by the large proportion of children employed, who add to the resources of their families, and

[1] *Reports from H.M. Diplomatic and Consular Agents Abroad respecting
the Condition of the Industrial Classes, &c.*   Report by Mr. Pakenham.
Brussels, 1871.

also in the country and smaller manufacturing towns, by the possession of a small garden, where vegetables, chiefly turnips and carrots, and sometimes potatoes, are raised.'[1] ·

The cheapest thing in Belgium appears to be gin, which is entirely free from taxation, and costs about $\frac{3}{4}d$. per glass.

'In the Netherlands, the artisan can live comfortably and contentedly on what would ill suffice to satisfy the wants of an English labourer. A carpenter, joiner, or plumber gets 16s. a week in the larger towns, his wife adds 3s. or 4s. by washing, and the man by working out of hours on odd jobs often adds another one or two shillings. In the smaller towns, artisans may have only 10s. a week, yet the country holds by protection and things are dear.' 'Breakfast consists of a sandwich made of a thin slice of a peculiar highly-flavoured but not unpalatable black bread between two thicker pieces of brown or white bread and butter, and coffee with milk and sugar. Dinner always begins with potatoes, after which comes a mess of carrots, turnips, or other vegetables, boiled together in a liberal allowance of fat; fish when in season : and it is followed by a cup of tea. Beer is not drunk at meals as with us; there is plenty of water, and the gin-shop, if at a convenient distance, is doubtless occasionally visited before returning to work. The evening meal resembles the morning one. . . . . Meat is rarely tasted by the working classes in Holland. . . . If ever indulged in, it is at the Sunday meal, when the whole household share the delicacy.' 'Each has his own house, which is sometimes very small, not wider than the length of a good-sized bed.'[2]

[1] *Reports on the Condition of the Industrial Classes, &c.* Report by Mr. J. G. Kennedy, November, 1872.

[2] *Ibid.* 1870. Report by Mr. Sidney Locock. The Hague, December 10, 1869.

Again, in the Netherlands a special committee, appointed by the Arnheim Branch of the 'Netherlands Society for the Promotion of Industry,' came to the conclusion that the average bare necessaries of an ordinary workman with an average family, amounted to 15s. a week, while his average wages did not exceed 11s. if he was a skilled, and 8s. if he was a perfectly unskilled workman ; that there thus remained a deficit of 4s. in the one case, and 7s. in the other, which had to be provided for by the man working out of hours, or by the help of the wife or children. . . . . It is not to be wondered at that the conclusion which the Committee arrived at was 'that the average rate of wages within the district was not in proportion to the cost of the necessaries of life; in other words, their wages were too low.' These labourers work from ten to twelve hours per day, and it is not difficult to form an idea as to the amount of efficiency of labour which is so poorly sustained.

'To the industrial classes in Holland, animal food, cheese, eggs, beer, currants, raisins, sugar, &c., are luxuries of which they partake only on Sundays, and then but sparingly, and in some instances not at all. They live chiefly on potatoes, cheap vegetables, such as carrots, turnips, onions, cabbage, &c., stewed with lard, and bread both wheat and rye. When cheap vegetables are not procurable they vary their meal by dried peas and beans of various kinds, or rice, barley, and flour prepared with buttermilk and treacle. . . . . Nor do the labouring classes in this country in general work with the energy and activity of Englishmen, so that, notwithstanding the cheapness of labour, the work when finished costs nearly as much per yard or foot as it would in England. . . . . The employers of labour take the very decided view that the quality of work turned out by the Dutch artisan is inferior to that of German, Engglish, or French.'

The result of this condition of feeding in Belgium and the Netherlands is that the amount of work performed. is much below what it is in the neighbouring countries, though probably the amount of application is no less severe.

In Saxony, again, 'the feeding of the agricultural labourer is good and plentiful, consisting of rye bread, soups, cheese, lard, butter, and, once or twice a week, pork or other meat. The wages of the labourer who keeps himself vary from 1s. 1d. to 1s. 3½d. per diem, that of the fed labourer from 6d. to 7½d. The expenses of a working man with a wife and three children amount to 1l. 0s. 1¾d. per week. 'I shall be asked at once,' says the reporter, 'how it is possible for a married man earning very much less than 1l. per week to live. The reply is quite simple. What the man does not earn must be made up by his wife, and if she is disabled the household gets into debt. There are not two opinions on the subject in this country. Something may be won, and no doubt is often won, by the married man letting one or two beds to journeymen, at the rate of 1s. a week for a bed, but this is an uncertain profit.' 'The women here chiefly nourish themselves with weak coffee, often made from roasted barley, or grounds bought in hotels or taverns.' . . . . Saxons as a rule do not turn out as much or as finished work in a given time as the Englishman. I allude here more particularly to work requiring muscular exertion.' [1]

In Norway, 'the small farmer and his housemen differ but little in their means and habits from the English day labourer. . . . . The food both of the master and

[1] *Report on the Condition of the Industrial Classes, &c.* Report by Consul-General J. A. Crowe. Leipzig, November, 1870.

labourer is of an inferior description, consisting of coarse rye or barley bread, porridge of barley or oats, potatoes or salt fish. Fresh meat is but seldom seen on the table of the small farmer, and to the labourer it is a rare luxury. Coffee alone is much consumed, both morning and afternoon, in the poorest cottage. . . . . All is stint and parsimony, but the eye of the observer is not often shocked by scenes of distressing poverty.'[1]

In Sweden, ' the average wages of a common labourer, estimated at 2*l.* 10*s.* per month, will enable him to keep himself, wife, and two or three children in a decent way. Of these 2*l.* 10*s.*, 10*s.* per month goes for house rent, 1*l.* 10*s.* per month for provisions, leaving 10*s.* for clothes and incidental expenses.'[2] And Mr. Jocelyn remarks of the labourer's ability as follows :—' Although the Swedish workman, if he exerts himself, can doubtless vie with his rivals of any nation, still I cannot say that from my experience there appears to exist here that spirit of emulation in producing the best possible workmanship which obtains in England.'[3]

In Sweden the climate, and therefore the mode of living, differ greatly. ' Thus in Skania and the districts of Calmar, Gothenburg, and Bohas, the agricultural population subsist chiefly upon potatoes, rye, oats, and barley ; beans and peas being also cultivated upon the north seaboard. Salt herrings are much used, but meat is seldom seen, and then consists of smoked pork, as the farmers are generally breeders of pigs. Oatmeal cakes are baked ; and, the other food being wrapped up in them, the whole forms a tolerably palatable meal. In the far north, however, this is modified. For there barley is the only cereal available, everything else having to be transported

[1] *Report on the Condition of the Industrial Classes, &c.,* 1870. Christiana, Report by Consul-General Crowe.
[2] *Ibid.* 1870, Gothenburg. Report by Consul C. F. Engström.
[3] *Ibid.*

thither.   Potatoes are grown, and salt fish is stored up
for winter consumption.   One article of food, moreover,
is to be found everywhere, and in many districts in great
abundance ; this is milk, which forms a wholesome sub-
stitute for meat, and becomes a universal source of nutriment when converted into cheese.' [1]

' The wants of the Wurtemberg working man are very
modest.   While in England almost every workman can
manage to procure a warm meal daily, many workmen
in this country can only do so on Sundays, and during the
week readily content themselves with bread, cheese, and
cold sausage, washed down with copious libations of beer.'
The wages of ordinary labour in Wurtemberg ranged,
in 1870, from 1s. 8d. to 2s. a day, but ' the ordinary
day labourer can lodge and feed himself at from 30 to 36
kreutzers (10d. to 1s.) a day, his daily expenses being
distributed as follows :—breakfast 6 kreutzers, dinner 12,
supper 8, bed and lodging 4 to 6.'   The expenditure of
apprentices is reckoned at 18 kreutzers (6d.) a day ; these
include ' 1 cup of coffee and bread in the morning 3
kreutzers, dinner 8, supper 4, and bed 3,' but according
to the report of the Apprentices Home at Stuttgardt,
published in 1870, ' experience has unfortunately shown
that many masters remunerate the apprentices and errand
boys so insufficiently that even this trifling expenditure is
scarcely within their means.'   ' Dr. Pfeiffer assures me (Mr.
Charles O. Scott, the reporter) that many employers have
admitted that, when they have reduced the hours of labour
from 12 to 10, they have generally obtained an equal
amount of labour in a day as they did before the reduction.   They have consequently effected a clear saving in
the items of fuel, light, and the use of the machinery.'
Here the ' local diet is much lower than in England. '   ' It

---

[1] *Reports on the Condition of the Industrial Classes,* 1870.   Report by Mr.
Nassau Jocelyn.   Stockholm, December, 1869.

may be stated that the entire economical position of Wurtemberg differs widely from that of other industrial countries. The fact that a large proportion of the small artisans, the workmen in factories, and the agricultural labourers, are at the same time in possession of a small amount of landed property, acts as a great relief to the working classes in times of distress, as when trade is slack. Many thousands of weavers, for instance, are only in work five or six months during the winter, while in the summer they work on their plots of land or on farms.'[1]

And, comparing the condition of the operative in Wurtemberg with his fellow in England, we find the reporter remarking as follows :—' The discontented gloom with which he (the labouring man in England) has of late been sometimes disposed to regard his victuals, might, perhaps, be somewhat dissipated by a wholesome contemplation of the denizens in other lands. While the Wurtemberg operative is happy with brown, black, or rye bread, in England even the inmates of workhouses are regaled with white. While the Suabian is contented with meat once or twice a week, the Englishman looks for his quantum of flesh with each returning noon. . . . . Twelve years ago, while the individual wages were 100 per cent. higher in England than in Wurtemberg, yet the cost per spindle was at the same time only 13 to 20 per cent. lower in the latter than in the former country. . . . . England, in fact, paid each individual man, woman, and child greater wages than these same classes received in Wurtemberg, in the proportion which $111\frac{1}{4}$, 49·6 and 23·8 respectively bear to 45, 30 and 20, and yet the wages cost per spindle in England was all the while only some 15 per cent. higher than in Wurtemberg.[2]

[1] *Reports on the Condition of the Industrial Classes, &c.* Report by Mr. E. O. H. Phipps. Stuttgardt, December 31, 1869.
[2] *Reports on Factories Abroad*, 1873, part i.

In Saxe-Coburg, ' comparatively speaking, little meat is eaten even in the houses of the middle class. Many tradespeople, even clerks in public offices, cannot afford to eat it, except, perhaps, on Sundays. They live principally on porridge and dumplings, potatoes, bread and beer, of which much is consumed by all classes. The people here are very frugal.' [1]

Again, in Prussia, ' the ordinary or unskilled labourer in Dantzic or Elbing gets from 1s. 6d. to 2s. a day in summer, but the average price of their day's work during the year cannot be estimated higher than 1s. 7½d.' for a day of 11 working hours with the exception of Saturdays, when it is an hour shorter, namely from 6 to 6.' In Prussia generally, ' petty tradesmen, or artisans, in the small towns and rural districts, in addition to their ordinary business, frequently turn their hands to agriculture . . . . and sometimes become day labourers. . . . . Under such changing and precarious conditions of labour, it is not surprising that perhaps half of the families of the artisan class which I have described live in comparative indigence. Fresh meat is an exceptional luxury with many of them, their household economy is of the humblest kind, and indulgence in spirituous drinks, even in moderation, beyond their means.' [2]

With regard to the condition of the common labourer in Denmark, Mr. Rowan, one of Mr. Brassey's, the railway contractor, agents, wrote :—' It must be observed that they take their time to do their work in, beginning in summer at 4 in the morning, and not leaving off till 8 in the evening. . . . . The Danish labourers have five intervals of rest in the day, these intervals lasting each for half an hour. . . . . In Denmark, rent is cheap ; and the food of the common labourer, chiefly consisting of

[1] *Reports on the Condition of the Industrial Classes, &c.* Report by Mr. Charles T. Barnard. Coburg, November 20, 1870.
[2] *Ibid.* Report by Mr. George Petre. Berlin, December 8, 1869.

black bread, is also cheap; but fuel and clothing are
dear.'[1] Mr. G. Strachey reports on the same subject
as follows: — 'It is not . . . . surprising that the
Danish operative's position should be painted in gloomy
colours. An authoritative writer has lately asserted that
of ten old and decayed workmen, nine have to go to the
parish for relief. . . . . In 1867, 1 inhabitant in 4
of the people of Copenhagen received public relief of
one kind or other. In the poor quarter of Christianshavn,
out of 15,000 inhabitants, 5,000 were receiving parish,
and probably 2,000 more were receiving private, charity.
. . . . The material position of the Danish operative
is decidedly inferior to that of his fellow in England.
. . . . If the Danish operative be more sober and more
moral than the German, he is also less industrious and
less frugal. No fact in my report is more certain than
that the Dane has yet to learn the meaning of the word
" *work.*" . . . . This is why the Swedish artisan can so
often take the bread from his mouth.'[2]

In Italy, the labour market is generally over-crowded.
'Agricultural labourers receive from $8\frac{1}{2}d.$ to 1s. $10\frac{1}{2}d.$
per day, bricklayers and masons from 10d. to 1s. 3d., and
carpenters from 1s. 3d. to 2s. 1d.' 'The hours of labour
are usually from sunrise to sunset, with intervals for meals
of two hours in winter and three in summer ;' and according to the report of a Commission appointed to examine
into the working of the co-operative clubs, dated January
20, 1872, the Italians 'are less assiduous, less laborious,
less instructed, and possess less dignity and self-respect,
than the English and French workmen.' 'The ordinary
diet of a workman here (at Genoa) which consists of a
" pasta " soup twice a day, and a piece of bread with a
piece of cheese, or lard, or fruit, or a pint of their wine,

---

[1] *Life and Labours of Mr. Brassey*, by Arthur Helps, 2nd edition,
1872.
[2] *Reports on the Condition of the Industrial Classes.*

would certainly not suit an Englishman. As far as my (Consul Brown's) experience goes, Englishmen, to be able to stand work in this country, require to feed very much as at home. . . . . Their (the agricultural labourers') mode of living is very simple ; they subsist chiefly on bread made of the Indian corn, pilchards, and water ; a poor sort of wine manufactured from the washings of the grape husks, and called *vinello*, is only occasionally indulged in.' [1]

From the evidence of Mr. Thomas Brassey's agents abroad, we find that the Neapolitans ' would not take any *heavy* work. They usually earned a franc a day. . . . . They ate bread and vegetables, and drank only water. They had also tobacco, a little coffee, and a small quantity of goats' meat now and then.' [2]

In Sicily, ' when no village lies within his reach, the agricultural labourer often inhabits a conical hut of reeds, with no furniture beyond a few utensils for cooking and drinking. The workmen in the mines also, when these are not accessible from any village, after toiling all day in the bowels of the earth, come to the surface only to pass their nights in holes or caves hollowed in the hill side, and more like the dens of wild beasts than the habitations of human beings.'

' The Sicilian artisan, though receiving moderate wages, considers himself, and in truth is, a respectable member of society, frugal, sober, hard-working, and self-respectful. He lives on bread and maccaroni, cheese, pulse, vegetables, and fruit. Fish he purchases only when abundant and cheap ; in meat he indulges but once a week.' [3]

In Spain the diet of the workmen is ' principally the

[1] *Reports on the Condition of the Industrial Classes.* Report by Consul Brown. Genoa, 1872.
[2] *Life and Labours of Mr. Brassey,* by Arthur Helps, 2nd edition, 1872.
[3] *Reports on the Industrial Classes, &c.* Report by Consul Dennis. Palermo, 1872.

" puchero," a kind of soup composed of vegetables, a little coarse meat, or stock fish, oil, and peas, and good bread.'[1]

Mr. T. Percy Ffrench reports with regard to the province of Andalusia as follows:—' The position of the labouring classes in this province is morally and physically bad. Their pay is generally insufficient, their food scanty, and their wearing apparel of the coarsest and commonest description. They live on bread and vegetables in the winter, and principally on " gaspacho " (a species of cold soup composed of slices of cucumber and bread steeped in vinegar and water). They are in general very ignorant, albeit intelligent, 80 per cent. of them being unable to read or write. They are prone to idleness, proud and independent, and very excitable, but generally speaking not disaffected towards their employers.'[2]

In Portugal, ' the food of the workman is varied and wholesome, but, when compared with the British workman's dietary scale, it is not liberal. Bread, composed of a mixture of maize and rye meal coarsely ground, is the invariable bread food. Meat and bacon, or lard, are used only in the form of broth, made with the addition of one or more of the following ingredients : cabbages, rice, haricot beans, gourds, turnips, or onions. This broth (in the case of working men oftener made without meat than with it) is the staple of the dinner of nearly every Portuguese of all classes. Dried and salted codfish, pickled sardines, and dried cuttle-fish are likewise parts of the Portuguese workman's diet. The common red wine of the country, acid, rough, and astringent in its character, is the only drink. It is possibly more wholesome than beer in a hot climate. It hardly exceeds the beer drunk by the English workman in alcoholic strength, and in nourish-

---

[1] *Report on the Condition of the Industrial Classes.* Report by Consul Young. Bilbao, 1872.
[2] *Ibid.* Report by Mr. Percy Ffrench. Madrid, 1870.

ing qualities it is certainly inferior to it. Few working
men, except of the better paid classes, use tea or coffee.
Gin, made of raw grain of several kinds, or of figs, is used
occasionally as a dram, but its abuse is very rare indeed.'[1]

In Turkey, 'the frugality of the Armenian hamel
(porters) is proverbial ; bread, olives, cheese, onions, and
salad are the staple of their food, and it is only on the
celebration of some holy festival that they indulge in
excess in strong drink.'

In Wallachia, ' the statement (official) that there are
only about 120 butchers and bakers among a rural population of some two million souls, is accounted for by the
fact that the peasants seldom eat either bread or meat,
their food being *mamilagu*, a porridge made of maize.'[2]

In Roumelia, ' the meal of the day labourer and peasant
is composed of a dish of stewed beans or lentils, which,
with the addition of onions or leeks, salt pickled cabbage
and green pepper, and garlic and red pepper as a condi-
ment, are eaten with the half-baked bread of mixed grain
—maize, wheat, barley, or oats, in varying proportions—
which constitutes the staple of their food. Very many of
the labouring classes subsist entirely upon bread, of which
they are capable of consuming four or five pounds a day.
Olive, hempseed, linseed, and sesame oils, salted cheese,
and other preparations of milk are likewise occasionally
eaten. Meat, wine, spirits are taken habitually only on
festival days.'[3]

With regard to the general condition of the labouring
classes in Russia, Mr. Egerton reports as follows :—' There
is, perhaps, no country where the hours of labour in
every branch of industry are so long as in Russia ;

[1] *Reports on the Industrial Classes.* Report by Consul Oswald Crawfurd. Oporto, 1870.
[2] *Ibid.* Report by Mr. I. Green. Bucharest, March 20, 1872.
[3] *Ibid.* Report by Mr. Charles J. Calvert. Monastir, November, 1869.

thirteen hours per day being the general average, children generally working the same time as men. . . . . In England a spinner at the mules, with his helps, will attend to about 2,000 spindles; in Russia he is never given more than 1,000 spindles, generally 500. Again, in the weaving mills a Russian rarely has the care of more than two looms, whilst in England a weaver will frequently look after six; had the Russian six looms under his care he would earn about 6s. or 7s. a day. These large earnings would find their way to the "vodki" (brandy) shop, and irregularity of attendance would be the result.'[1]

And from a memorandum by Sir A. Buchanan, we learn that, 'as a rule, in the neighbourhood of large towns (in Russia) the people live generally at an average rate of about 1l. a month per man; at other places, however, the living is very wretched, the food consisting of little else besides black bread and water, and occasionally only a little tea, the living in this case costing only about 5s. or 6s. a month.'[2]

The condition of the working classes in Switzerland is thus described:—'The average rate of wages for men, women, and children, taken altogether, may safely be assumed to be from 33 to 40 per cent. lower than in England, and 10 to 15 per cent. lower than in France. . . . . The average rates throughout the country would seem to lie betwen 1s. and 1s. 3d. per working day, and taking the men only between 1s. 5d. and 1s. 7d.' 'The food of the working classes in Switzerland consists principally of bread of very fair quality, of cheese, potatoes, vegetables, and fruit. They seldom eat meat above once a week, and even then in very small quantities. . . . . The

[1] *Report on the Industrial Classes, &c.* Report by Mr. Egerton. St. Petersburg, January, 1873.
[2] *Ibid.* 1870.

meals are :—Breakfast, taken before beginning work, or at a very early hour, generally consists of coffee with milk, but without sugar, and a large piece of bread. Those who are highly paid add cheese, butter, or fried potatoes. The whole population, from the highest to the lowest, dine between eleven and one o'clock. At this meal the working classes take soup, potatoes, vegetables, and bread, with a bowl of coffee without either sugar or milk. The last meal is in all respects the same as the first. The above statement is liable to not a few modifications.'[1]

Again, in regard to France we find that ' the rural population of the central division comprises four-fifths of the whole. . . . . The average agricultural wages are about 1s. a day. The food of the labourer is very bad and insufficient.' ' If the workman's pay in England is higher (than at Vannes in the Western Division of France) it is because he possesses greater muscular strength, which he could not maintain on the poor Breton fare.'[2] ' A British workman will get through more work in a given time than the people here (at Bayonne) ; in case of field labour a man would not do more than two-thirds of what a labourer in England would do.'[3] ' As to labour here (at Bordeaux) native mechanics in the branches of building, furnishing, and clothing are paid between 2s. and 5s. a day, while in the same trade British workmen get between 5s. and 8s. a day, and are found to do more work and earn their wages better than the French. Thus the effective value of an Englishman's labour is in the ratio of 26 to 14 as compared with a Frenchman's. This is a practical result, derived from the experience of employers and worthy of acceptation as a rule.' ' Frenchmen live for less (than

[1] *Report on the Industrial Classes, &c.* Report by Mr. G. F. Gould. Berne, February, 1871.
[2] *Ibid.* Report by Lord Brabazon. Paris, 1871.
[3] *Ibid.* Report by Mr. F. J. Graham. Bayonne, 1872.

Englishmen), in giving to vegetables at one penny per pound the place of the Englishman's meat at ninepence ; but the latter finds that he cannot make this change in his life-long habits, and keep up to the quantity of work he is now paid for.'[1] ' It may be remarked that for certain trades (in Paris), especially those in which taste is the predominant quality required, English salaries are far superior to the French—in the ratio of 10 to 7.'[2] ' I (Consul J. T. Elmore) must say . . . . that the amount of work effected here (at Nice) is certainly not two-thirds of that done by an average English workman in one day.   The work itself, with rare exceptions, per-formed by all classes, is ill-conditioned and slovenly, and would not pass inspection in England.. . . . . The amount of work he effects in one day is but little ; this may arise from the fact that in general he is ill-fed, for he will attempt to save from very low wages.'[3]

Mr. Brassey, in his ' Work and Wages,' supplies many illustrations of the superior energy of the British work-man over his fellow on the Continent.   He says :—' On the whole, wherever the English have been employed on the Continent they have received much higher pay than their fellow-workmen, the natives of the country ; and the difference in the pay has been fully represented by their superior skill and marvellous energy.   Great pains were taken to ascertain the relative industrial capacity of the Englishman and the Frenchman on the Paris and Rouen line, and on a comparison of half-a-dozen pays it was found that the capacity of the Englishman to that of the Frenchman was as 5 to 3.'

Sir John Hawkshaw, the eminent civil engineer, says, when ' speaking on the relative value of unskilled labour

[1] *Report on the Industrial Classes, &c.*   Report by Consul Hunt.   Bor-deaux, 1871.

[2] *Ibid.*   Report of Consul Clipperton.   Nantes, 1872.

[3] *Ibid.*   Report by Consul Elmore.   Nice, 1872.

in different countries, I have arrived at the conclusion that its cost is much the same in all. I have had personal experience in South America, in Russia, and in Holland, as well as in my own country, and as consulting engineer to some of the Indian and other foreign railways I am pretty well acquainted with the value of the Hindoo and other labour, and though an English labourer will do a larger amount of work than a Creole or a Hindoo, yet you have to pay them proportionately higher wages.'[1]

In the United States ' the unit of labour of all hands in cotton factories may be affirmed to be at the present time (June, 1873) a dollar (3s. 9d.) a day of eleven hours for a year of 300 working days. . . . . The census returns indicate the same rate by showing an actual average annual wage per hand of all kinds of only 288 dollars, or about 54l. sterling.' ' In the United States it is usually asserted as regards many industries, apparently with reason, that two Americans will do as much work in a given working day or week as three Englishmen.' ' Taking the cotton manufacture through, it can be fairly stated that in the United States the hands, as a rule, tend more machinery, especially looms, than in Europe, and, in some cases, than in England.'

' In some returns showing lost days per hand in a month, the average showed 23 lost working days in a year; they may be generally reckoned at 30. . . . . The reasons of this shortening of the working period were sickness, looking for work, paying visits in particular, and taking holidays in general. This last reason accounts for many days in the year. The girl weavers often go home for five or six weeks' holiday in the year.'

' I (Mr. J. P. Harriss-Gastrell) am inclined to think that although the American cotton operative works eleven hours per day, he does not in the aggregate work a longer

[1] *Life and Labours of Mr. Brassey,* p. 96.

R 2

period in the year than does the English cotton operative, whose working day is only ten hours.'[1]

With reference to the introduction of Chinese labour in America, Mr. Harriss-Gastrell quotes from the 'San Francisco Bulletin' of 1869 as follows :—'Chinese labour gives the mills here a great advantage. " John " is peculiarly adapted to running machinery, and he never strikes, never wants a holiday, never has a sick wife or family, or goes " on a bender." Pay him his 25 or 30 dollars a month promptly, and he will work his ten, twelve, or fourteen hours, and average 26 days a month out of every twelve the year round. He has no little story to tell, pipe to blow, or horse to swap, or gossip to reel, but knows nothing or nobody, except the " machine-ee." We have about 80,000 of them now on the coast, and I know of nothing they can't or don't do.'[2]

Mr. Rowan, one of Mr. Brassey's agents on the Grand Trunk Railway of Canada, says of the French Canadian from Lower Canada :—' They could ballast, but they could not excavate. They could not even ballast as the English navvy does, continuously working at filling for the whole day. The only way in which they could be worked was by allowing them to fill the waggons, and then ride out with the ballast train to the place where the ballast was tipped, giving them an opportunity of resting. . . . . They could work fast for ten minutes, and they were " done." This was not through idleness, but physical weakness. They are small men, and they are a class who are not well fed. They live on vegetable food, and they scarcely ever taste meat.'[3]

From these extracts, the value of which, I think, justify their being made use of so copiously, it will be

---

[1] *Report on Factories in the United States,* by Mr. J. P. Harriss-Gastrell, 1873.

[2] *Ibid.*

[3] *Life and Labours of Mr. Brassey.*

clearly evident that a vast difference exists between the condition of the labourers of the various countries enumerated. The British workman, by such 'a whole-some contemplation of the denizens in other lands,' as the perusal of these descriptions of their fellows in other parts of the world might induce, might possibly conceive after all some love, or, at least, less dissatis-faction than he often does with his own lot. There can be no question that his style of food, clothing, and lodging is much superior to the greater part of the inhabitants of the European continent, and that alone is the reason why he is universally credited with a very superior amount of strength, skill, and taste.

M. Maurice Block, in his 'L'Europe Politique et Sociale,' supplies a probable estimate of the average revenue per head of the population of the countries named, which in figures may afford a clearer idea of the relative wealth of the various populations, although, owing to the superior incomes derived by the upper classes in this country, the rate may express (if otherwise near the truth) too high a ratio for the prosperity of the working classes. The estimate is as follows :—

The United Kingdom, average income, 685 francs.

France .	.	.	.	„	598 „
Prussia	.	.	.	„	455 „
Austria	.	.	.	„	375 „
Russia .	.	.	.	„	161 „
Italy .	.	.	.	„	125 „

The consumption of considerable quantities of nutri-tious food is not so necessary in the southern part of Europe as it is in the middle and northern parts, for the constitution is not called upon to resist the same amount of cold. The external temperature being nearer to that of the body, there is in the south on this account generally less functional expenditure than in the north. In tropical countries there is a correspondingly less

inducement to work, for the natural produce of the soil
supplies nearly every want. In Sicily and in some parts
of Italy about one-fourth of the lower class of labourers
can continue to exist while spending the greater portion if not the whole of their time in idleness. In the
north, however, where the climate is severe, and its
vicissitudes are considerable, the constitution of man
must be fortified by a food more condensed and nutri-
tious, and, therefore, more expensive than that which
proves sufficient in the south. In proportion as this
kind of sustenance is not obtained, the alimentary system
must be called upon to assimilate a greater quantity of
comparatively inferior food, which it must needs do at a
relative mechanical loss. That is to say, that the strength
or force which is required to sustain the heat of the
body is obtainable by those who do not make a profitable livelihood by systematic labour, from a larger mass
of cheap and comparatively innutritious vegetable food,
and that the expenditure of force required to digest and
assimilate such is necessarily greater than in the case of
more nutritious vegetable and animal food being employed. The superior kind of food, however, is just that
which the very poor man in northern latitudes cannot
obtain. He has, therefore, to perform a certain amount
of internal organic work in disposing of his food over and
above his fellow, who is well remunerated for his work,
and can, therefore, feed himself better. To sustain the
animal functions merely, a certain amount of force is
required, and every development of force beyond what is
so required may be utilised in productive labour. It
follows, therefore, that he who is well remunerated for
his labour is provided with means whereby he can sustain the force necessary to continue his labour at a relatively less physical cost than he who is ill remunerated.
There being a certain fixed amount of expenditure

required to maintain the organic functions against the external influences of climate, the balance of strength which is utilisable for external physical or mental work must increase in a greater progressive ratio than the increase in the amount of food assimilated; and that amount is more likely to increase not only when it is abundant, but when it is of an improved, concentrated, or properly prepared kind. It is just as if we had to deal with two locomotive engines, one of which belongs to a poor man, the other to a rich one, and they are treated according to their respective means. In the one case the machine is kept not only in thorough repair, but it is supplied with the best coal, oil, and tallow, and these in abundant quantities, so that there is a maximum of work obtainable from it; in the other, the machine has suffered not only from a poor supply of these indispensable articles, but from a bad quality of them. Besides, it has been accommodated in all weathers under a rickety shed instead of within a proper engine house, and add to this that, when something has gone wrong, the mechanic has not appeared soon enough to make the repair, and the result is the machine is chronically out of order, and drags along with an undue amount of friction. It requires a less force to start and work the one machine than the other, and that force is obtained from materials which produce it more economically. Hence, whatever force is developed so as to propel a train is, relatively to the fuel and lubricants employed in either case, very much greater with the engine that is well attended to, than with the other that is partially neglected. It is, then, as we might expect, found in practice where tools and engines of all sizes and descriptions are employed, that it is cheaper to uphold a first-class machine in first-class style, than to employ a second-hand tool, though its first cost may be cheaper, to do the same kind of work; and the result is that men of capital who can possess the best of everything, obtain a most material advantage in this respect over men of moderate means. It is with animals as with machines ; and he who possesses good cattle, which he takes care to nourish well, finds out by experience that he can perform his work through their assistance more cheaply, certainly, and easily than the poor man whose cattle, perhaps, suffer heavily in their more arduous and less successful exertions. This, then, is an important principle which we cannot recognise too clearly or assert too emphatically ; for, when it is generally understood and practised, one of the principal causes of hardship and suffering endured by the labourer will be seen to proceed from false assumptions, from the belief that the less wages that are given to the labourer the cheaper is his work, forgetting all the while that the labourer's first interest must consist in nourishing himself till he feels comfortably full of health and strength.

From what has been said, we would naturally conclude that the labourer who rises from a position of great poverty will have his capacity for remunerative labour increased in a greater ratio than his additional cost of maintenance, and that appears to be—so far as it has been observed or discovered—the actual state of the case. Everyone who has the management of workmen will acknowledge that the old, decrepit, or infirm are disproportionately the dearest workmen. Even men who, according to the present system of conventional equalisation which is often too hardly stereotyped by the regulations of trade unions, are paid from week to week the same rate of wages, are often very unequal in ability. This inequality is consequent upon the dissimilar antecedents of these men, or it may be because the same amount of wages has to be spread over a different number of dependents. Workmen in this country are generally well remunerated, and, if economy is practised, there is little difficulty in their supporting themselves so as to work efficiently. But if the ill-supported individuals of another country come to this, or emigrate to a position where superior work and wages is afforded, they will improve within a comparatively short period considerably, though it cannot be expected that the effects of semi-starvation for generations can be repaired in a few months. The progress of this country has been lately so rapid that many men of this description have been of late years flocking from the poverty-stricken outlying rural districts to the industrial centres, and it is impossible that these should equal in ability at once the strength and skill of workmen who have been well nurtured for years or generations. These essential differences are noticeable everywhere, and must continue to be very considerable. The principle of physical improvement, however, of which we speak, is not thereby impugned. The manifestation of its action is, perhaps, the most considerable, when the individuals who are affected by it are the lowest in the scale, for then the difference is the greatest. Human beings will indeed continue to exist, particularly in such countries as India, and during famines, on very little food. If we call upon them to exert themselves in what are called relief works, they require more food, and their labour cannot be profitable. Should such individuals, however, be sustained by a full and wholesome diet of appropriate food for months, they will then begin to labour with profit to their employers; and ultimately, as their condition improves further, the profit will be still more, though in a less relative proportion than at first, when the labourer had just changed from a starving man to a satisfied one.

It may perhaps be observed, however, that although

wages are increased, they may be increased, as the reporter on the Russian factory worker asserts, only to be
spent on ' vodki,' or drink. If that be so—at any rate to
an immoderate degree—the result must be pernicious.
It is indispensable that the labourer should feel the
necessity, and the inclination as well, to appropriate the
produce of his labour in the right direction—namely, to
the suitable sustenance of the bodily frame. Another
observation again may be made—namely, that the funds
obtained by an increased rate of remuneration may be
spent on providing an additional and excessive amount
of leisure ; in fact, may engender idleness. In such case,
the question will arise whether these hours be spent profitably ; and this may be tested by ascertaining whether
the occupation of these hours tends to improve the
physical and mental powers of the labourer, so as to
make him more qualified for the performance of his
duties than before ; for if they are squandered in mere
idleness, or dissoluteness, then they can only be hurtful,
and in the interest of the individual, of his employer,
and of society, they ought to be curtailed. If, however,
they are spent profitably, he will to this extent not
only qualify himself more fully for his present work, but
may qualify himself for a better one. And when the
practice of self-control and the desire of self-improve-
ment is developed to its fullest extent, the individual
will possess the power of raising himself by the constant
exercise of virtue to a position more and more elevated,—
where, indeed, the unlimited powers of mental action will
begin to take the place of the restricted and mechanical
labours of the body. The misfortune is that the masses
of humanity generally do not possess those opportunities
at all, or possess them only in a very limited degree, and
the principle of progressive improvement which is consequent upon the intelligent appreciation of opportunities

that exist, is scarcely possible. Great multitudes are held
in bonds by systems of government that are more or
less repressive; and even when these are light and produce no heavy burdens, the presence of erroneous popular theories—the result of abounding ignorance—insists
upon the application of restrictive rules and laws that
depress rather than protect. The abundant evidence
which we have adduced of the very deficient food, clothing, and housing of the labouring classes of Europe
generally, and their consequent comparative inability to
labour actively, strenuously, and continuously, is sufficient
proof that their position is not the best. Unquestionably,
however, the situation of the poorer classes in Western
Europe has of late years greatly improved. We have
seen that generally their emancipation from serfdom has
occurred within the last one hundred years, and the
abolition in industrial life of the trade guilds has no
doubt had a largely beneficial effect. The petty vex-
ations and costs that met the merchant at every turn, and
prevented the tradesman from carrying his abilities freely
to the best districts, which resulted from the divisions of
Germany and Italy, have been got rid of. There has,
therefore, been a very large movement in favour of individual freedom, and the development of individual interests, which undoubtedly is the solid basis upon which
alone society may be securely built up.

In Ireland, and the outlying rural districts of Scotland, we have seen that this basis has not been generally
attained. There, as well as indeed over Great Britain, the
monopoly of the land, and whatever mineral riches it may
contain, is practically maintained in the possession of a comparatively few wealthy individuals, who are therefore so
rich that they do not feel exertion to be a necessity; while
the poorer classes, from their inability to reap directly any
share of the fruits of the soil, agricultural or mineral,

have any inducement to superior exertion, as well as to the practice of thrift, to a large extent taken away. Workmen engaged in mining are undoubtedly well paid ; but that is because the prize to the landowners and the capitalists who may possess the mines is large, and they can afford to pay, and must pay, high wages in their competition with each other. The treasures which much more than pay the labour of unearthing, because of their great value, cannot be allowed to lie dormant ; and labourers are employed at high rates so long as the work has to be done. When, however, the period approaches when these treasures become considerably less and more difficult of realisation, the demand for the labourer will droop, and his wages will fall in amount and begin to approach the level of those who labour in a country not possessing mineral resources. The position of the labour market, therefore, though high now, is so on account of the exceptional conditions chiefly of the mining enterprise of the country, and affords no criterion of what it would be if the mineral resources were no greater than those of France. What is to be observed is, that the manner in which the masses of the population derive their income is the one least likely to produce the maximum of labour, thrift, and prudence, because it appeals in the least degree to self-interest ; and where this is the case so extensively, the material and moral position of the people cannot be of the most satisfactory kind.

In this country, we have experience of workmen of all grades, from the lowest paid and most uncouth rustic, to the highly skilled and energetic mechanic, and we find that as the population recedes from the industrial and mining centres, the rate of wages constantly decreases, and the quality of the men deteriorates. In Ireland, it is often difficult for the people to realise a comfortable livelihood, and periodically they are threatened with starvation. In consequence, therefore, of this state of things, we have seen in a former chapter there is a constant emigration. When the Irish go to America, or cross over to this country, they have the opportunity of improvement, but in the process of improvement they are often unfortunate. The curb of necessity being relaxed, they incline to indulge too freely and recklessly, and the character of simplicity which they possess in their native country is too soon spoiled when they emigrate. A change in their mode of life, consequent upon the advent of systematic labour, is necessary. Whereas they existed formerly chiefly upon potatoes, they are now compelled to betake themselves to a more nutritious diet, and, by gradually feeding more and more upon animal food, they largely increase their activity and powers of endurance. This change may be accomplished, as already indicated, so as to allow the labourer to produce an amount of work whose scale of remuneration will admit of a margin beyond the necessities of improved living. The labourer will now have become a more economical machine, and a more comfortable and satisfied individual. If he should proceed to America he may now be the cultivator of his own land, and have every inducement to continued improvement; in this country, however, he will probably find that day's wages and labour in the employment of another afford sufficient for self-indulgence without affording a compensating inducement to a superior amount of labour and prudence. There can be no doubt that the introduction of piece-work stimulates a man to greater exertion, and gives him more remuneration, but it does not induce him to be more prudent and thrifty. In consequence, therefore, as in Russia so in Britain, the surplus wages are spent on drink or other coarse indulgence, and the man is brutalised instead of being elevated.

Mr. Thomas Brassey says in his ' Work and Wages' :—

'This I say, that all experience shows that with proper supervision, and with an equitable scheme of prices for piece-work, the best paid workman does more work for a given sum of money than the underpaid and, therefore, underfed labourer can by possibility accomplish.'

In the third report of the Commission on the Employment of Children, Young Persons, and Women in Agriculture, dated March, 1870, we find Mr. Culley, one of the reporters, saying :—' The man who, upon a diet of potatoes, oatmeal flummery, and barley cake was worth 6s. or 7s. a week to the farmer, became, when fed on wheaten bread and meat, worth 12s. a week to the railway contractor ; and, having tasted the more generous diet which farm wages would not buy, he set the example of an exodus which has been going on to a remarkable extent of late years from the rural districts of South Wales. . . . . Mr. Sewell Read, speaking of twenty years ago, when farm labourers' wages in South Wales were from 6s. to 7s. a week, says :—' Piece-work cannot be done cheaper in Wales than in the east of England.' ' Now when wages in Pembrokeshire and Carmarthen have gone up to something like an average (all told) of 12s. a week, such piece-work as the Welsh understand— as for instance, mowing corn and hay, as well as carpenters' and masons' work—is cheaper (according to the evidence which I received on the subject) than in any of the English counties which I have inspected.'

There is still another advantage resulting from the employment of superior food in abundance, and that consists in the strengthening of the constitution against the attacks of disease.   Mr. T. G. Bush, the medical officer of the Narberth Union (Wales), in answer to the question, ' Is the change of food gradually taking place for good or for evil ? ' said :—' Most decidedly for good. I find that since the potatoes and porridge diet (which was up to the time of the outbreak of the potato disease the prevalent food of the agricultural labourer and cottager) has been to a great extent abandoned, and replaced by bread, butter, and cheese, that the labourer is more able to resist the influences of weather ; and when he is struck down by disease, there is a far greater rallying power in the constitution than formerly, so that he is able soon to resume work.'[1]

We may therefore conclude from the evidence that has been adduced, as well as from *a priori* considerations, that the individual becomes a more efficient labourer and a more comfortable one in the degree that he is properly clothed, fed, and housed. He is also a more economical one, except when he is too prone to self-indulgence. This proneness will be the more developed under two conditions. First, on account of his not having sufficient inducement to save his earnings; and, second, when, this being the case, those earnings are considerably greater than he has been accustomed to.

There is no country in the world where these conditions exist so fully as in Great Britain, and particularly in the mineral districts of it. There, wealth is increasing by leaps and bounds, high wages are going, but there is no great inducement for the workman to save. The bank in which he would readily deposit his money, namely land, is not to be had, and the money is, therefore, generally squandered, and he and his family are thereby debased instead of being improved. The ability to work, which should have gradually increased, becomes impaired.

The difference between the working powers of the Englishman and the American is not attributable to a lower rate of remuneration to the former. The following

---

[1] *Third Report of the Commissioners on the Employment of Children, &c., in Agriculture,* 1867.

is the opinion of Dr. Edward Young, Chief of the United States Bureau of Statistics, contained in 'Labour in Europe and America,' published in 1875 :—' Does a workman in the United Kingdom accomplish as much work in the same space of time as one in a similar employment in the United States? This branch of the investigation engaged the attention of the author before and during his visit to the manufacturing towns of Great Britain, and he endeavoured to gather such facts as would enable him to determine this question. Through observation and inquiry the conclusion was reached that, in most industrial pursuits, a workman in England does not perform so much work in, say nine hours, as another of equal knowledge and skill in the same branch in the United States. The reasons assigned for this were various, some of which are here presented.

' Mr. Sellick, the United States Consul at Bradford, is of opinion that workpeople will not perform as much work in a week as similar workmen in the United States. The English workpeople, he stated, lack intelligence, waste time, and by their intemperate habits injure their health, and consequently lessen their ability to labour.

' The same reply, substantially, was made by the Consul at Sheffield, and by others elsewhere, each possessing such an acquaintance with the subject as enabled him to express an intelligent opinion. . . . .

' It is evident that the intemperate habits of the men, and the loss of time consequent thereon, prevent them from performing a full week's work. True, while at work, especially during the latter part of the week, the men work as rapidly as those in the United States ; but in the earlier part of the week this is not the case with men who drink to excess. Even if men of such habits do not observe the festal day of their patron, Saint Monday, they are unable to perform a fair day's

work so soon after the dissipation of Saturday night
and Sunday. This is especially true of the men in
Sheffield. . . .

'The fact will not, perhaps, be disputed, that in most
branches of manufacture, especially at machine and
engineering work, and in the fabrication of hardware,
cutlery, and other manufactures of iron and steel, the
workmen perform less work per week, on an average,
than an equal number in the United States.

'The next inquiry is, what percentage of reduction
should be made in the computation? From observation
and inquiry the author is led to the conclusion that it
amounts to 10 per cent.; in other words, that on an
average 900 men in the United States, employed at the
branches indicated, as well as at many others, will
accomplish as much efficient work per week as 1,000 in
England.

'In this connection it may be stated that, after the rise
of wages in England in the year 1872, it was ascertained
that the men in many branches of industry performed
less work than when the rates were lower. An illustration of this fact is given by a correspondent of the *Leeds
Mercury*, who presents an interesting comparison of the
work done by colliers in 1864 and 1873 :—

' " In 1864 the average product of our coal-mines gave
for each person employed 327½ tons, which, for 313
working days, is equal to 21½ cwts. for each person
per day.

' " In 1868, the average product gives for each person
317 tons, which, for 313 working days, is equal to 20
cwt. for each person per day; and in 1873 the average
product gives for each person only 271 tons, which, for
313 days, is equal to 17½ cwts. for each person per day.
It will thus be seen that in the first period of five years

(1864–1868) there was a diminished output per person of about 7 per cent.—21½ to 20 cwts.

'"In the second period of five years (1869–1873) the output had declined by 12½ per cent.—20 to 17½ cwt per day for each person. So in the 10 years each person employed about a coal-mine has reduced his labour by nearly 19 per cent.—21½ to 17½ cwt. per day. It is a remarkable fact that, while there has been so great a reduction in the amount of work performed per man in 1873, the rates of wages have advanced from 30 per cent upward!"'

Then, again, further on in the same report, Dr. Young says, describing the style of habitations:—' In Birmingham and Wolverhampton, and in most parts of the " black country," in parts of nearly all the chief manufacturing cities of England and Scotland, the tenements to which the tired labourers return at night, and where they should have comfort and repose, are in many cases unfit for human habitation. In some instances these belong to the corporations owning the mills, mines, or works, and were erected in low grounds destitute of drainage and of proper sanitary regulations. In other places they occupied rooms in poor buildings in the outskirts of the town, or in the most crowded thoroughfares, redolent of filth and dirt. Confined to two or three rooms, or, as in Glasgow, to one, or, at most, to two rooms for a family, comfort, cleanliness, and even decency, are impossible.

' What wonder, then, when the husband and father, fatigued with his day's toil, returns home to partake of his frugal evening meal, finding his wife irritable in consequence of hard work, the care of wayward children, and the deprivation of ordinary comforts, that he visits the ale-house, where he and his fellow toilers, similarly circumstanced, drown their cares in the beer-mug and squander their hard earnings, which should have been devoted to the comfort of their families!'

The style in which the American workmen live is in general strikingly different; though in New York, and perhaps some of the other larger cities, the condition of numbers is not dissimilar from that of their fellows in the large manufacturing towns of Britain. In these exceptional cases, however, the crowding is caused greatly, if not altogether, by the immense immigration of poor Irish which is generally taking place.

The result, therefore, of such compression of the working classes within the towns of Great Britain, which is unquestionably caused by the difficulty and cost of extending freely into the neighbouring country, is that there exists a prevailing imprudence, recklessness, and drunkenness.

The atmosphere of Glasgow has lately been tested experimentally, and found to contain components eminently prejudicial to health. In cold, foggy weather these gases accumulate in the highest degree, and, together with the lowering of the temperature, affect the vital powers of the poor so seriously as to raise the death rate for the whole population to nearly three times the average. What wonder, then, that living in such an atmosphere, and within such dwellings, where for the most part, too, they are religiously immured on Sundays, the working classes are given to intoxicating habits! Men are cut off from the country, and from those innocent and refining pleasures which natural beauties create. They are confined for six days, and on the seventh they are prevented by every power, but the arm of the law, in this country from breathing at least once a week the fresh air of heaven. The streets are crowded with children, many of whom are to be seen disporting themselves in the gutter, and marked by squalor and disease.

The workmen themselves are dull and dispirited, if not drunken and wretched. The *Times*, referring to the drinking habits of the working classes in 1872, writes thus :—' We drank, it appears, last year in spirits, malt liquors, wine, cider, &c., more than seventy-two million gallons of pure alcohol, at a cost, in round numbers, of 120,000,000*l*. It is calculated that at least half of this money is spent by the working classes ; and as they desire principally strength or quantity in their drink, we shall probably not be wrong in assigning to them very much more than half our entire yearly consumption. There is no more alcohol in a bottle of wine than in half a pint of ardent spirits, and the cost of the one may be a guinea, and of the other ninepence or a shilling. It is clear that if the working classes have spent their 60,000,000*l*. in a cheaper form of intoxicating drink, they have got much more for their money, and may probably be debited with 50,000,000 gallons out of the entire seventy-two millions of the year. It will be seen, if the figures are compared with those of 1871, that the total amount of the past year is not only very large in itself, but shows a considerable increase on the year before it. We spent in 1871 only 108,000,000*l*. on the same subjects, and received for our money, in various forms, somewhat less than sixty-five million gallons of alcohol. The rise is certainly considerable. It has been due, probably, to the increased wages of labour, which have allowed the working man to indulge himself in more luxuries.'

Thus, then, the improvement which is taking place with the individual workman, in consequence of the ancient hindrances, oppressions, and monopolies being removed, is one that is consequent upon a more full reward being bestowed upon his labour ; but this improvement may be interrupted or impeded, as is unfortunately the case with the British workman, from the absence of a requisite amount of thrift. Not only in this case is the labourer a more unsatisfactory one, but he is himself less satisfied; he saves little and he enjoys little. His labour, instead of being filled with hope, is one monotonous round of slavish toil; he feels he works from necessity to preserve a lot that is generally dull, sometimes wretched, instead of from choice directing his energies with the utmost economy and force with the view of gaining a plot and dwelling of his own, or some such other equally worthy object of ambition, wherewith his legitimate expectations should be fulfilled and his hopes gratified.

CHAPTER VIII.

WHAT ARE THE BEST ECONOMICAL CONDITIONS OF SOCIAL WELL-BEING?

Of all the subjects which come under the consideration of a political economist there appears to be none of more importance at the present day than that of the mutual relations of capital and labour, the capitalist and the labourer. Many able writers have already treated this subject with fulness, but it would seem that all such literature has had extremely little influence upon those for whom it was chiefly intended. The prevalent idea abroad is that capital is a hydra-headed monster, capable, if it could only have its own way, of eating up the earnings of the labourer, and of leaving nothing behind but the endless and hopeless labour of the slave.

The subject is in itself not a difficult one; but, in the application of its lessons to human life, the eloquence and persuasiveness of a superhuman being would almost appear to be required. We can only add a view of the subject from the point at which we have arrived in the description of the influences that affect the position of the civilized labourer.

In the earlier chapters of this volume, we have endeavoured to show how at first the existence of commerce consolidated towns lying in a favourable situation, through the influence which the capital derived from that commerce promoted; how these towns grew from the increasing wealth obtained from manufactures and trading;

how these occupations called for additional labourers, who escaped from their condition of serfdom in the country to experience the condition of freemen in the towns; how gradually the influence of commerce spread itself over the country, eating out the spirit of feudalism and war, and replacing it by one of civil employment and peace; all of which changes having taken place gradually, through the power which the accumulating wealth of the town has continually exerted upon the comparative poverty of the country.

It must thus be acknowledged that capital has been the great instrument whereby first the towns have become the asylum of free labour; second, they have extended ramifications of the same influence, and subdued the genius of feudalism throughout the country; and, third, with a people thus freed, the standard of living has been gradually raised throughout Central and Western Europe. We have further endeavoured to show how, owing to the rare security which this country enjoys from the existence of a sufficient margin of ocean to make attack difficult, that capital has uninterruptedly accumulated, and that Britain is now, not only the wealthiest country in the world, but that she is or has been hitherto very much the workshop of the world, employing an industrial population probably seven times greater than her agricultural; and we have endeavoured to show how the gradually accumulating capital of the peasant proprietors upon the European continent is enabling them to increase the productiveness of their lands—a result that, besides producing the most beneficial effects upon the proprietors themselves, allows a larger proportion of the products of agriculture to every individual of the community.

Freedom and well-being, with their attendant moral and material benefits, have, therefore, been the results of the presence of capital in the past, and the results in the future must correspond thereto. The origin of capital agrees with its results; for the production of it depends upon the exercise of labour and prudence, and its accumulation depends upon the continuation of these virtues.

This is already testified at the present day by the combined labour and prudence of peasant proprietors; but it is none the less testified in this and other countries where the great endeavour of each individual is, when there is a tolerable opportunity presented to him, to lay up funds upon which he may depend at a future time for help and sustenance. It is only when the benefit to be derived does not appear to be worth the effort that men do not endeavour to lay up savings; and this may arise from various circumstances—either that little or nothing can be saved, or because, when so much is saved, it cannot be profitably invested, so as to produce the legitimate results of husbanded labour. Either the one or the other of these may be effectual as a bar to prevent large portions of the community saving; and therefore they who can and do, namely the comparatively rich, are regarded by the masses with envy, jealousy, or hatred. And if we may judge at all from the sums of money deposited in savings banks, we may assert that the labouring classes of the United Kingdom do not save one-half as much as the corresponding classes in America, and only two-thirds as much, and not so generally, as those of Switzerland, while in each of these two countries, particularly the latter, the same classes are also in possession of realised wealth.

Those causes which tend to prevent the accumulation of savings by the masses of the people, ought, therefore, as far as possible, to be immediately removed. If wages are so low that no one can save from them, every penny being required for the immediate sustenance of life, the condition of the labourer, and of the com-

munity of which he is a member, must be in some degree
diseased, for a time must in the life of the labourer be
expected to arrive when his powers will diminish and
the rate of his wages be reduced. Then the sum he
receives cannot longer support him, and he falls upon
the aid of public charity, his relatives being presumed to
occupy the same position. Such a condition is in essence
that of the slave. The employer supports the labourer,
and must be supposed to reap the whole benefit of his
exertions; for the labourer is permitted to exist only to
work, and when he can labour only inefficiently, or his
days of labour are interrupted or ended, some extraneous
source of support must be provided for him. Such a
condition the labourer can exist in, but cannot profit by,
or raise himself from, and it is indeed one of hopeless,
endless slavery, though it be regarded, from the effects
of custom, as the normal and proper state.

In this country the greater number of the agricultural
labourers of England, and particularly those of the south,
where wages are at the lowest, occupy a position similar
to that described. In the southern counties there has
been no improving influence at work similar to that in
the north, where manufacturing enterprise has indirectly
benefited the agricultural labourer considerably. In
1852, Mr. James Caird estimated the difference between
the rates of wages as paid to the agricultural labourers in
the north and south as 37 per cent., being in favour of
the former. That difference is still maintained, if not
augmented. Mr. Stanley James says, in 1874, that the
hours of labour have been reduced, and that the rates
vary from 12s. to 14s. per week, sometimes lower, in the
south, to 18s. per week in the north. In some counties
in the south, however, they had not risen beyond 11s. per
week; a sum that, in estimating the enhanced price of
provisions, must be acknowledged to be quite inade-

quate to supply current wants in any kind of satisfactory way.

The improvement which has taken place has been solely on account of the manufacturing and mining enterprise of the north, the improvement ceasing 'where coal ceases to be found.' This is the more clearly recognised when we find that in 1770 the average wages, according to Arthur Young, were 6s. 9d. in the northern counties and 7s. 6d. in the southern. The average rate of remuneration has risen in the former about 250 per cent., while in the latter they have risen only about 60 per cent.

In the south, the labourers have not sufficiently declined in number relatively to the work to be done, and the farmers, to escape the poor's rates, sometimes, as Mr. Caird describes in his 'English Agriculture,' divide the surplus hands among them, so that there may have been sometimes from 30 to 50 per cent. more labourers upon a farm than were required. The recent agitations and the endeavours of Mr. Joseph Arch undoubtedly have, at least by causing an unwonted emigration, benefited the labourer, and probably there is some improvement at the present time. How long that may last is very problematical, for the prospects of the farmers are not regarded as now very bright, and it would appear that the same conditions will only too surely produce the same results. Man is of all animals or goods the most difficult to move about, and when he is ill-paid, ignorant, and hopeless, he is the more so. Unless some permanent extraneous organisation therefore takes the condition of the agricultural labourer in hand, it does not seem probable, till radical reforms are made in the transfer and tenancy of land, that his lot will be permanently ameliorated. At present, the old labourers, when no longer able from gathering frailty to work in the fields, regard the workhouse as their last

home, the refuge the parish is bound to provide for them,
and which they have a right to claim from it. This deplorable condition of things has arisen, as has already
been pointed out, from the unfortunate dissociation of
the people from the soil, the result being to leave upon it
a redundancy of labourers. This statement may appear
paradoxical; it is nevertheless true. The people who
cultivated the soil had, up to a certain period, derived
immediate benefit from its produce. But when the change
formerly described took place, the ground tilled was
largely thrown into grass, and the labourers who remained
stood in too high a proportion to the work to be done.
Some change was required in the opposite direction. The
poor laws of England have, however, only helped this
mischief by supporting useless labourers until in some
parishes the actual revenue from the land was at one
time found to be insufficient for the labourers and the
poor.

The inducements to prudence having been removed,
the agricultural population became imprudent with the
ultimate result, as in Ireland and the outlying districts of
Scotland, of multiplying beyond the means of support.
The condition of life in which these labourers exist is a
low one,—one that is not comfortable to themselves, nor
economical to their employers; and, should emigration
diminish, it might become largely worse, and prove disastrous to the interests of the landowners. The people
in such circumstances are supposed to possess the full
necessaries of life; but, when the wages of so many hands
must be divided amongst a disproportionate number of
mouths, it is obvious that the standard is relatively reduced, and more expenditure is directed merely towards
supporting the functions of life, than in rendering the life
so sustained profitable to themselves or others. The
labourers are thus sunk lower than they should be to

labour with an adequate degree of efficiency, and, therefore, they are so far removed from that position wherein
they could begin to save anything for a future day; and
not only is this so, but capital is expended unnecessarily
in supporting labourers that individually live uncom-
fortably and labour unprofitably, and are in the aggregate
redundant.

But this evil is so far corrected as we approach the
manufacturing and mining centres of industry; for then
there is a superior demand for labour, and therefore the
superabundant hands employed in agriculture gradually
are reduced, and those remaining receive a higher remuneration and attain a greater efficiency than before. This
we shall see is strikingly true.

It has been remarked that the amount of skill and
knowledge required in various trades such as the
mechanical, does not very greatly vary from that required
by the agricultural labourer. The latter must deal with
a much greater variety of circumstances and appliances
than, for instance, the riveter, the smith, or the mason,
and I conceive the remark on due consideration will
be found to contain indisputable truth. There may be
a greater amount of muscular force required by the
riveter, the smith, or the mason; but then, as a compensation for this difference, their hours of toil are considerably less than those of the field labourer. Their work,
therefore, should not differ much in intrinsic value. The
low rate of remuneration of the agricultural labourer, as
compared with that of these tradesmen, may, therefore,
be largely explained in the way stated, the other remaining reason arising from the cheap manner in which the
agricultural labourer residing in the country can subsist.

But what are the facts? While the agricultural
labourer receives somewhere between 10s. and 18s. per
week, the riveter receives on an average in the chief

towns of the United Kingdom (1873), 30s.; the smith,
33s.; and the mason (in Scotland, 1874), 32s. But to
set the contrast in the most striking light, we shall take
the wages of farm labourers and tradesmen in the counties
of Durham, Nottingham, and Middlesex, which, in 1874,
were as follows:

			s.	d.
(1) Durham: Farm labourers (average rates per week, winter and summer)			15	6
Blacksmiths (reckoned at 6 days per week)			31	0
Miners	„	„	35	0
Machinists	„	„	32	6
Carpenters	„	„	32	0
Bricklayers and Masons, reckoned at 5½ „ .			32	0
(2) Nottingham: Farm labourers (average rate per week, winter and summer)			19	3
Blacksmiths (reckoned at 6 days per week)			33	6
Miners	„	„	29	0
Machinists	„	„	34	9
Carpenters	„	„	33	6
Bricklayers and Masons, reckoned at 5½ „ .			33	0
(3) Middlesex: Farm labourers (average rate per week, winter and summer)			11	6
Blacksmiths (reckoned at 6 days per week)			34	6
Miners	„	„	—	
Machinists	„	„	43	0
Carpenters	„	„	37	5
Bricklayers and Masons, reckoned at 5½ „ .			37	0

The above information, which has been derived from
Dr. Edward Young's Report to the Government of the
United States on 'the rate of wages, the cost of subsistence, and the condition of the working classes in Great
Britain, Germany, France, Belgium, and other countries
of Europe, also in the United States and British America,'
dated 1875, will show the reader at a glance the immense
gap that exists between the condition of the agricultural
labourer on the one hand, and all those classes of
labourers upon the other which are connected with
thriving industries that find the numbers of their workmen to be no greater than is required, though still so
abundant that it is quite a regular occurrence for
members of such classes to emigrate.

The perfectly unsound condition in which the English
agricultural labourer exists may be further indicated by
contrasting it with his fellow in four of the eastern
manufacturing States of America, and in showing the
relation which the latter occupies towards the skilled
workmen in the same States. Thus, if we take New
York, New Jersey, Delaware, and Connecticut, we find
that the average wages of the agricultural labourer in
these States (taking experienced and ordinary hands
together over the whole year) amounts to 6s. 7d. per
day without board, and if we take the experienced hand
in summer the rate is 8s. 6d. per day. On the other
hand, the average daily wages of blacksmiths, bricklayers
or masons, carpenters, and wheelwrights respectively,
are (when employed in full work) 10s. 9½d., 13s. 10d.,
11s. 8d., and 10s. 9½d., the average of the four being
11s. 9½d.[1]

We are now in a position to contrast the rates of
remuneration of the two classes of labourers in either
country. First, then, the average of the agricultural
labourers' wages in the three English counties enumerated
stands to the tradesmen's wages as 15s. 5d. to 34s. 4d.,
the latter being 123 per cent. above the former. Second,
the average of the agricultural labourers' wages in the
four American States enumerated may be stated at 8s.
per day, while the average of the tradesmen's wages is
11s. 9½d., thus showing a superiority in the latter of only
48 per cent., and this result, notwithstanding the artificial
stimulus given to the industries of the tradesmen by the
establishment of a prohibitive tariff levied on foreign
manufactures. If, however, we take into account the
fluctuation of occupation that exists in the industrial
centres of these four States, it is very questionable

[1] *Reports on the Industrial Classes.* Report by Mr. E. M. Archibald.
New York, March 18, 1872.

whether the remuneration of the tradesmen ought to be reckoned so high as the figure stated.

These facts can bear, then, only one interpretation, namely, the one we have already assigned—that the ill-paid labourers in England are superabundant. If, therefore, those who are well paid—namely, the tradesmen— receive just the natural and proper amount of remuneration, which is in general testified by the fact that the industries in which they are engaged continue to prosper, it is obvious that the ill-paid are only half-paid, and that their condition in every respect must correspond with such a miserable rate of living.

What proportion of the inhabitants of the United Kingdom occupy such a position? It would be difficult to reply to this question with accuracy. Still, it may be said generally, that the greater proportion of the inhabitants of Ireland residing in the purely rural districts, almost all those of the insular and northern districts of Scotland, and the greater proportion of the farm labourers of England, must occupy this comparatively backward condition. Indeed, the medical officer of the Board of Health declared some years since, after a most careful investigation, that one-fifth of our popula tion have not a sufficiency of food and clothing.

There must therefore be a resulting loss to the country as a whole, imperceptible though it be, of considerable moment; for all these inhabitants exist below the natural standard of comfort and efficiency. Whatever improvement their condition undergoes must be in the direction of raising them higher as individuals; additional and improved supplies of food, clothing, and housing, which means increased remuneration, must first go to produce additional health and strength. The wealth that is presently expended on the payment of their labour would become then more remunerative, until gradually the labourers would find themselves little by little in a position to lay by something of their own, sparing from their immediate necessities some realised strength for sustenance in the future period of increasing weakness.

When this condition had been attained, the savings of the multitude might begin to be added to swell the resources of the country.

But there is another condition equally necessary to the healthy existence of such a state as that wherein saving would become the rule, and the contribution of capital by the masses would be efficiently stimulated. That other condition consists in the formation of sufficiently powerful habits of thrift. The labourer may be efficient, and he may derive the full remuneration due to his efficiency; he may work with ease and comfort to himself, and with profit to his employer and to the community; but unless he go further and exercise prudence to save some of his earnings against a future period, and even with the view of benefiting his children, he cannot be said to derive that advantage from his improved situation that he ought. But there must be strong and palpable inducements to create thrift. No lectures on the moral beauty of economy can be expected to change the practice of men who have been accustomed to feel only the comfort and gratification of self-indulgence. They must first feel that their savings will be secure, and the institution of postal savings banks has done immense good by creating the necessary confidence. The old private banks could not thus be relied on, for there were frequent and disastrous failures. The difference of security was felt and appreciated strongly, as is testified by the fact that after the establishment of the government banks, in 1862, the number of depositors in the private banks diminished, and in ten years there were as many depositors in the former as in all the latter together, and thereafter the number of depositors in the government banks became rapidly preponderant.

But there is one especial engine by which the necessary virtues of thrift may be cultivated, and we have already described the powerful influence which it exercises upon the continent of Europe. That consists in the ' passion for land,' which has been found capable of counteracting other passions that are gross and reckless. The cultivation of this passion for land demands only field for its exercise; but where it is not, there must be expected to grow up, as there has grown up among the working classes in this country, a spirit of recklessness that is not manifested on the Continent. Let, however, the passion for land take hold of the people, and they will become, as possessors of patches, perhaps originally of little value, thrifty, contented, respectable, orderly, and conservative members of society.

So much for the moral influence of this passion : its economical influence is calculated to be quite as marked. Instead of the immense sums that are, as already described, presently squandered upon drink, there would arise a strong competition for the acquisition of land. The face of the country, where land would be accessible to the workman, would be interspersed with gardens, which would produce those fruits and vegetables of which there is now such a poor supply, and of which so large a proportion is presently imported from the adjoining countries, where workmen generally are owners of land. But the present landowners would benefit largely from the opening up of a competition for the article they hold that had never before been felt, and, as I think Mr. John Bright remarked in one of his late speeches, it is surely not too much to ask a reform affecting the landowning classes that can act no otherwise than

T

beneficially to them. All who are not at present in easy circumstances cannot afford to buy land, for, as in England more particularly, the costs of the transference are too heavy and uncertain.

At the present time immense sums are sent abroad to foreign countries, and these for the most part represent the savings of the middle classes. Such are not uncommonly lost altogether, and the community is thereby rendered so much the less prosperous. Were the opportunities of development that would arise from a more general possession of the soil of the country by the people fully realised, the capital that is presently sent abroad might, to a large extent, be advantageously retained at home, and the resources of the country and of its coasts, which are being opened out now comparatively slowly and fitfully, at least where there are no minerals, would be more rapidly and fully ascertained and utilised. There can be no question that one great evil which afflicts the outlying agricultural districts is the want of capital, and the want of capital is caused to a large extent by the vastness of the estates of individuals who are accustomed to a large personal and family expenditure, and who cannot take any appreciable commercial interest in the development of every part of their large estates. As one instance of how such a change would influence the prosperity of the country, we may refer to the facts that were elicited in the evidence lately given in the inquiry of the Herring Fishery Commission. The want of proper harbour accommodation appears, according to that evidence, to be the reason why the fishery is unduly restricted. The fishermen caught in a storm cannot find over long tracts of coast any secure refuge, and even at ordinary times, the accommodation for the conduct of their trade is inadequate. The fishermen themselves have never contributed much towards the construction of such necessary

adjuncts to their occupation, partly it may be on account
of the great cost and the dreaded possibility of failure
in the object desired, but generally on account of their
having saved nothing at all approaching to the necessary
expenditure.

It is sometimes the case that the great landowners
undertake such works; but not, I think, generally, if at
all, with a view to commercial profit, but rather as an act
of generous humanity, and there are at present some rare
instances of such landowners. There are, however, on
the other hand, landowners who allow the harbours that
are already constructed to fall to pieces, when a trifling
expenditure would be sufficient to maintain them in an
adequate state of repair and efficiency. The community
in either of these cases is helpless as regards their own
condition of progress and improvement. In the one case,
by the construction of large and costly works, it may
receive a valuable and lasting impulse in the direction
of new industries and the development of such as may
exist, while in the other it suffers irretrievable ruin.
These conditions, however, cannot be of the people's own
making or unmaking, for their present opportunities preclude that possibility. The actions of great landowners
can never be counted on as regular, for their interests
are scarcely affected by the condition of any one part of
their estates; their personal expenditure is generally too
great, and their commercial spirit too little, to admit of
adequate improvements being regularly proceeded with.

But if, on the other hand, there are a multitude of
interests, each of which has its whole centre in or near
the district which calls for development, then the whole
of those interests will naturally more or less gravitate
towards the development of resources that may have
been hitherto neglected or only opened out partially.
For whatever would tend to improve the particular district

T 2

must necessarily improve the whole of the comparatively small properties within it, and, therefore, from a commercial point of view, the necessary outlay of capital by the proprietor would be more than repaid, for it would benefit his whole property indirectly, as well as that portion of it thus expended, directly; he would, in fact, not only receive the ordinary profits on the undertaking in question, but he would feel an indirect benefit on all his estate.

In this way, then, the capital of the country would be to the greatest extent regularly employed upon the development of the country; the masses of labourers that are presently ill-fed, ill-clothed, and ill-housed, would then have opened up to them fuller and more remunerative employment than they can have at present.

But we have to consider the manner in which the capital of the country affects the position of the labourer, and it may be said at once that the more capital there is disposable in any particular occupation or district, the better position does the labourer occupy. The reason of this consists in the fact that the capital cannot be rendered productive to the capitalist unless it is first paid as wages to the labourer; and the oftener it can, as circulating capital, be paid to the labourer the better it is for the capitalist. They are embarked in exactly the same interest then as regards the presence of capital, and it follows that the more of it that is realised, the more is it competent to benefit the labourer, so long as it is expended in the occupation and district in which he is engaged. If, then, this be true, it follows also that the more that capital is sent out of the country, district, or trade—and this will depend on its prospects of profit in either—the less advantage will there be from its realisation to the labourer.

It is necessary to illustrate these propositions: first,

then, the more that incomes are saved from, the better for all, for, if they are spent, the capital is consumed once for all. Thus, if an iron-master realise 50,000*l.* a year for a few years of good trade, and saves three-fourths of it, he has wherewith to improve his works materially, and he may introduce the newest machinery, and produce the iron bars, plates, or rails as cheaply as possible. He will then occupy the best position in the trade ; he will sell his productions most readily, and receive the best price for them; in other words, his business will flourish and extend. As a necessary consequence the men engaged in his works will receive a higher rate of wages, for unless he raised the rate, it would not be in his power to increase the numbers of his workmen or to select the best that are to be had.

If, however, upon the other hand, the iron-master be supposed to spend all or the greater part of his income upon himself, he will not be able to prosecute improvements in the way just described, for the money spent, it may be in increased personal luxuries, will disappear. Thus, if he spend his income on lands or houses, or in laying out or furnishing these, his resources will be no longer available for trade purposes; his capital, as political economists express it, will become fixed, and that without profiting the community. Should he devote three-fourths of his income to the construction of public works, such as railways, roads, harbours, or canals, his capital will become equally fixed as before, but then it may profit the community, perhaps, very highly.

Again, should he spend his funds several times a year in the payment of wages to the men at his works—a thing he may do from his ability to dispose of his manufactures that number of times, and thus turn over his capital, which is now circulating capital, frequently—it is clear that the labourers will profit most largely.

What, then, is the limit to such a method of applying the capital realised from manufactures, mining, or commerce ? The limit depends primarily upon the amount of profit the capitalist receives from the application of such further supplies of capital. Should the rate of profit fall, he has the less inducement to go on saving from his personal expenditure in favour of his business. The least difference in the rate of profit must inevitably make a sensible difference in the amount which he spares from his own enjoyments. He reflects that the money may be expended immediately upon personal objects, and he exercises self-denial now only in prospect of obtaining an enhanced reward afterwards. That is the way with human beings universally, and is not peculiar to large employers ; it is only regrettable that the spirit of denying one's self present enjoyment in prospect of future good does not act more universally. This is the special mark of civilized as distinguished from savage man. When, however, there is little expectation of receiving an augmentation of present good by waiting for it, the present good will be rightly realised. In the case which we are considering, and which is indeed a case typical of conditions that exist universally in business, the employer will act according to the circumstances that present themselves to him. Should he find that the self-denial which saving demands is not amply repaid, he will deny himself no longer. Thus, the business and the workmen in it will suffer enormously in the future by even a comparatively slight reduction of profits in the present. For this reason industrial battles between employers and workmen must produce, independently of the ruinous consequences they often bring at once, ultimately an infallible fall in the demand for labour. Capital is one of the most reasonably timid creatures in existence: whenever it scents the smell of danger or of ill-treatment, it will, like a frightened deer, disappear.

But the case is not yet fully represented. Capital will not come into existence at all, if there are not already existing favourable conditions to create and foster it. It is the story of the goose and the golden eggs, with an addition to it : the goose will not only be killed in a premature endeavour to get the eggs, but no other geese will ever again present a like opportunity.

I think—and I venture to differ from some economists in this respect—that strikes must invariably affect the interests of the workmen perniciously. Capitalists cannot be compelled first to strive hard to realise capital, and then to spend the most of it in extending their business ; and unless these two conditions conjoin, it is impossible that the policy of strikes under any circumstances can ever be a successful one.

The abundance of capital is the workman's opportunity, the scarcity of capital is the employer's opportunity. In the first instance the working community will progress from one degree of prosperity to another ; in the second, their position will be non-progressive, and may be that of serfs, bound hard to perpetual labour, and never able to rise above a certain daily round of hopeless drudgery. The policy of working men, therefore, should constantly be to encourage the accumulation of capital in every possible way, and to encourage its presence and expenditure to the utmost in their own particular trade. Even, however, though it should not be expended in their own particular trade, it is still, if spent in their district or country, of benefit to them, because it improves the machinery and renders more efficient the production of other trades, whereby articles are cheapened, and they are thereby enabled to obtain a greater supply of them than before. In the first case their wages are raised; in the second, the articles on which their wages are spent are cheapened, whereby with the same wages they are able to purchase more of them.

May there, then, be no case in which the workman shall resent by a strike an attempt reckoned to be unjust, to damage his position as a workman? Employers are unquestionably not all alike, and some may act with comparative illiberality or occasional caprice toward their workmen, the result being perhaps an inadequate remuneration. But such employers will not be able to retain the services of the best men, for these will gravitate to the best positions. That is a natural mode of rectification that must always be in operation. But generally the question comes to be, how the workman arrives at the conclusion that the attempt of the employer is unjust. Lord Moncrieff, in his late adjudication, or, as he called it, friendly advice, given to the carpenters locked out on the Clyde, said that from his knowledge of the state of the ship-building trade, as the result of his study of the circumstances in which it had been placed for some years, he was certain an advance in wages could not be given, and, moreover, that if the carpenters had been able to know what the circumstances of the trade were, he was equally certain they would never have made the demand, and never have incurred the loss and the suffering entailed upon them by the strike and lock-out. Now it may be asked, how can the workmen ever know that the reduction of wages proposed, or the rise denied, is unjust and unnecessary? The employers feel the pinch of bad trade, but the workmen cannot feel it except by a reduction in wages. But when a reduction is proposed they are apt to think it proceeds from some other cause, for they cannot, as the employer does, feel the necessity for it.

Now, employers are, of all others engaged in business

transactions, apt to be jealous of each other, and to seize from each other an advantage when the opportunity presents itself, and in no other way can they do this better than in tempting, legitimately it may be, the best hands from their neighbours' works. In face of this constant jealousy, it is impossible that employers will concert together successfully to reduce wages unless they feel it to be an absolute necessity, and even then sometimes the reduction is delayed as long as possible. Besides, there must always exist a strong dislike upon the part of an employer to take the initiative in a measure so extremely unpopular as that of the reduction of wages. If, however, the workpeople themselves unite together to resist a reduction of wages, they may long maintain a rate only applicable to a prosperous and sometimes to an inflated condition of trade. The capitalist must then suffer loss, relative or absolute, which he will, of course, endeavour, by increasing the price of his productions, to share with the public. But the public will limit their applications for such productions as become higher in price. It therefore follows there will be a restriction in the amount of business done. There being then less work, fewer workmen will be required. Some of the workmen will now be paid off, and those will be the most inefficient, and therefore the least able to obtain suitable work elsewhere. The burden of their support will now fall either upon their friends or upon the community. But the community have more to pay for the goods of that business, and, therefore, they will be in a less favourable position to support those who are thrown out of its employment, and from an equitable point of view there could be no claim either upon public support or sympathy.

The artificial maintenance of wages, therefore, at rates which are not justified by the condition of trade is an

evil which must be felt pre-eminently by the workpeople
themselves, for if the system were to be generally adopted,
the workpeople, who form the greatest portion of the
public in every country, would be called upon to support
all their fellows thrown out of employment at a time
when they would have to pay an increased price for most
of the articles of daily consumption.

The result would therefore be, first, that the poorest
part of the workmen would become impoverished, and
possibly become paupers; second, the remainder would
be placed in disadvantageous pecuniary circumstances, for
while their wages were relatively high at the one end,
they would not go so far from the increased prices of
articles at the other; and, third, an increased contribution
would be demanded for the support of the poor.

These evils would be avoided by leaving the rise and
fall of wages to the operation of natural law, and natural
law is as powerful in human society as it is in physical
nature.   There frequently exists, however, an idea in the
minds of workmen, that the large employer is continually
striving to gain ends that are inimical to their prosperity.
I conceive there is no greater fallacy, and none more
competent to produce evil and disastrous results.   Men,
indeed, everywhere work upon the lines of self-interest,
and the more they do so without trenching on their
neighbours' rights, the better for all.   That self-interest
may indeed change into selfishness, but that will be
chiefly when restrictions and monopolies exist; for where
there is perfect freedom, the aggregate action of self-
interest produces the maximum of public good, and reduces
individual selfishness.   The greater number of free and
equal transactions there are between men, the more will
individual self-assertion and offensiveness of all kinds disappear, because their owners will find out soonest their real
nature and their unprofitableness.

We are therefore perfectly able to judge from *a priori* considerations what will happen in particular cases; whether or not, for instance, employers will carry their works on as fully in times of adversity as in times of prosperity, thereby losing wealth as rapidly as making it.

While, therefore, the great law of self-interest acts in the world of human society as that of gravitation in the natural world, there are modes of action that can be prognosticated as certainly in human affairs as in the phenomena of terrestrial motion. The great operating forces in human affairs are nowise more irregular or capricious in their action than are the material forces. The possibility of interruption in the result of the action of these two forces is, however, always to be kept . in mind. There may be minor forces that would be more apt to escape our notice than the major ones, but for the fact that they act so as to produce aberrations in the movements we look for from the operation of the first purely. It is just as if a disturbing force was detected in the solar system producing aberrations in the movements caused by the bodies which are already known, and such indications of disturbance lead to the discovery of smaller planets.

In describing some of the great influences which affect the prosperity of the people, we must endeavour as far as possible to ascertain how these influences are set in motion. There can, we conceive, be no considerable force at work to disturb in any material degree the operation of that all-prevailing force, self-interest. We therefore compare it to that of the gravitation of the planets towards the sun; and as astronomy can predicate the movements of the planets, so can political economy predicate the movements of men in their dealings with each other. It is the duty of wise men to acquaint themselves with the action of natural law, whether it be in material or moral nature, for then only may the great masses of men be guided so as to frame their course in harmony with it. If natural forces are defied or neglected, there can be no doubt of the result being equally disastrous ; otherwise, if understood and consulted, they may be utilised.

As to the standard of wages, it must be ultimately regulated at all times by the operation of the natural laws working within human society. Whether the market falls or rises, the operation of the law of self-interest operating in the minds of the employer, the employed and the public will inevitably bring about, when there is no artificial action, a constant close approximation to the natural rate.

It is said, however, for instance, that when there is a sudden stream of prosperity, the employer for a time enjoys higher profits in relation to his expenditure upon wages than before, and that therefore, by a sharp and combined action on the part of the employed, the divergence that would for a time take place from the natural rate to the prejudice of the workpeople, might be corrected. This is an exceptional occurrence. Shall we correct this temporary rise in profits by demanding immediately a higher rate of pay than would take place otherwise? If we could always be perfectly certain of the character of the occasion we might do so ; but it must be acknowledged that it is impossible for the employed to know exactly when the market prices rise sufficiently to afford a disproportionately high rate of profit.

The workpeople, however, it may be said, might advantageously act upon the advice of others who profess to know. The chance of error, however, in following such guidance must always be serious. Good news is always too eagerly welcomed, and therefore there is a likelihood of a multitude of advisers who will prophesy fair things. Those who rely upon such are too likely to be deceived and to follow advice which is pleasant merely. It is unquestionably a much safer course to wait for the gradual increase in the rate of remuneration which must take place. For the increased expenditure of capital on new machinery and premises, which must always in time of improving trade take place, will be the inseparable antecedent to the demand for more labourers and the necessary addition to the present rates of remuneration, for without the latter the former cannot be had. It is a safer course, because the accession of new capital cannot be utilised till new hands are employed, and the capitalist knows that the cost of the new works is justified by the prospect of a continued increase in the manufacture, otherwise they would not be proceeded with.

If, however, every attempt at an extension of the works and business of an employer should be nipped in the bud by premature demands by the workpeople for a rise of wages, it must be obvious that the self-interest of the employer will incline him against staking the outlay of further capital; he will feel his position to be insecure, and he will therefore divert more capital from his own business to some other, to his private uses, or to some foreign investment than he would otherwise do. In each of these cases the workmen of the particular employment will suffer permanently from the non-progressiveness that follows. In what has been already said, capital has been regarded as already existing in definite quantities available for some one purpose or other. But employers frequently become bankrupt, and when they suffer total or partial loss of property, the workmen suffer also, though it may be in various degrees. It is true that the workman may, when his employer stops payment, find employment elsewhere. When trade is in a declining

condition, the workmen may fail in procuring sufficiently
remunerative employment, and in the degree in which
capital is lost will this tend to become the rule.

Without failing, however, the capitalist may close his
works; for, unless he be receiving a certain compensation
for the use of his capital, he may find it less perilous to
stop temporarily than to proceed. At such a time wages
must be pitched too high, and the claims which workmen
are often too apt to put forward in prosperous times may
of themselves tend to produce, if too long pursued, a
disastrous collapse. It would not be too much to say
that the continuance of periods of bad trade and general
adversity must proceed from the too heavy demands of
the workmen upon the employer. It not unfrequently
happens, as it has happened lately in South Wales, that
the workmen of a district that has risen from poverty to
comfort if not affluence in the course of a single generation,
forfeit that success by a too greedy pursuit of their own
claims. They are often tempted to think, in the pride of
conquest, that everything will fall to them if they are but
sufficiently united. They therefore demand higher and
yet higher remuneration. The employer is now between
two difficulties; he may resist the demands made, and his
capital as the result of a strike may lie idle perhaps for
months; or he may accede to the demands of his workpeople, feeling that his enterprise is thereby disheartened
and crippled. Should he ultimately stop his works, the
workmen lose all, and must seek out new fields of labour.
In the case supposed, the employed have overstepped the
bounds of action defined by an enlightened self-interest, and
the result has recoiled upon them disastrously. Such a result doubtless may not often occur, but nevertheless the tendency of such action upon the part of workmen is always
in the same direction. Self-interest with the employer will
dictate the continuance of business operations as long as

possible; if he stops, it must be either on account of an overwhelming competition which has in combination with bad trade attenuated his profits too greatly; new works may have arisen in periods of prosperity that are now strangling each other, being assisted in that process by the unreasonable demands of the workmen. There is therefore quite as much necessity on the part of workmen to realise the presence of adversity as to seek diligently after the fruits of prosperity.

The employed suffer, however, from fluctuations of trade that are greatly caused by actions outside of those they have cognisance of, or can control. What is the reason why business operations periodically undergo violent fluctuations, sometimes being active, at other times being languid? Men may conduct their operations by the use of capital or credit. Upon the basis of the former the latter may be largely used, but sometimes the latter is used without sufficient basis. Accommodation bills and bills at long dates are often too freely obtained, so that when any ill success arises, the arch of credit falls suddenly for want of the keystone—capital. When this system of trading grows unduly, as it periodically tends to do, one break-down is often sufficient to precipitate the whole edifice of credit to the ground. There is a sudden interruption of confidence which arises from the knowledge that many are trading beyond their means; so that when one falls, it is never known who or how many he will drag down along with him.

There are other causes which produce a similar result. Capital may be expended too rapidly upon the construction of permanent works where it is permanently sunk. It then can never be paid out as wages. It is practically irrecoverable. But by the facility which the works upon which it is expended create in means of transport, manufacture, or otherwise, there is a considerable saving, and capital benefits by realising a portion of this saving. But if capital is spent too rapidly, or upon ill-judged works, it does not create the expected facilities; there is little saving, no dividend, and it may be temporarily as good as lost. Thus railways have been constructed throughout the Western States of America too rapidly and often prematurely.

Natural resources cannot be developed immediately—time is a necessary element in the calculation. But time is what capitalists cannot allow; everyone calculates on a revenue from the first. There follows after periods of railway or other mania, therefore, necessarily a corresponding impoverishment. Capital that ought to have returned so much in the circulating form, returns nothing, and is itself irrecoverable. Everyone is thereby temporarily impoverished, there is a diminished demand everywhere for articles of consumption, and trade languishes. When a revolution of this kind has come about, it is too apt to be intensified and prolonged from other causes. In periods of antecedent prosperity, workmen have become accustomed to regard former luxuries as present necessaries, and their new rate of wages as one indispensable to their comfortable and decent subsistence. There is, therefore, an extreme reluctance to face the actual facts, and to consent to a fall in the rate of remuneration that may be the necessary prelude to the desired improvement. Wages are often maintained, therefore, at or about the high rate attained in the previous times of prosperity. The shorter hours that may have been struggled for are also naturally enough clung to with tenacity. Human expectations, when once firmly elevated, are difficult to disenchant. Hence the result is necessarily to restrict trade still further. Men continue to receive the nominally high wages of former days; but they gradually find that these wages become week by week of less value to them, for their purchasing power is diminished. Workmen do not readily recognise that at the time their wages are high those of other trades are also high, and that there is more to be paid for what they consume on account of such prevailing high wages. Then those with fixed incomes cannot purchase so much as before ; so trade becomes or continues dull, and the workman suffers severely, at times of high prices. But when, additionally, the hours of work are reduced, the fixed capital invested in works and machinery cannot be utilised so fully as before. Thus, when the working day is reduced from ten to nine hours, machinery is utilised only to 9-10ths the extent it was before the change. But the manufacturer, to reimburse himself, raises the price of the articles produced, which creates in its turn a weakness of demand, and, therefore, fewer articles being wanted, the trade becomes dull and workmen are paid off. Thus the workpeople are not only no gainers, but are actual losers, and the policy that would promote their welfare in the fullest degree is that of a resumption of the former hours of work and the former rates of wages. Trade would then immediately revive, and the workmen would derive the greatest advantage possible in the circumstances of their particular employment.

The real basis upon which the prosperity of workmen can be built up solidly is that of intimate association with the largest possible expenditure of capital upon the implements and appliances of their business ; and when this capital is attacked, the maximum of damage must inevitably follow. A little reflection will prove this. A workman without tools, however expert, is practically useless, and this is why barbarism is so much weaker than civilization. But when invention has proceeded as the result of leisure, education, and thought, and capital has been expended in the realisation of the idea of the

U

inventor, work is facilitated, toil is abridged, and remuneration is increased.   Capital can be expended profitably
only in this way, and the benefit of such expenditure cannot be withheld from the very poorest.   Although the
actual wages were now paid by the same amount of gold
of the same quality as before, the receiver would be
enabled to purchase a greater number of better articles
than before.   This is because machinery is now employed
to perform quickly and well operations that were executed formerly by hand labour.   Consequently, at
the present day twenty articles may now be turned out
at the same cost as ten, five, or even one some years
since.   This result, so highly beneficial to everyone, could
not have been attained without the continual expenditure
of capital; and had this expenditure been interrupted or
checked, the means or comforts of civilization would have
been in some degree lessened.   But when articles of
general consumption are thus cheapened all over, everyone is able to purchase greatly more of them than formerly, and thus there is a greater demand for labour, and
wages rise.

The influence, then, of capital is of two kinds : first,
it cheapens everything which is the product of labour;
and, second, it increases the reward of labour.   He,
therefore, who attacks capital is an enemy of society
and of the workman in particular, for he derives the most
perceptible benefit from its application.   With him it
changes poverty into comfort; with the wealthy it produces only a superior degree of ease or enjoyment.   This
idea is well stated by M. Frederic Bastiat, in his 'Essays
on Political Economy':—'If there is a class of men to
whom it is more important than to any other that capital
be formed, accumulate, abound and superabound, it is
certainly the class which borrows it directly or indirectly ;
it is those men who operate upon *materials*, who gain

assistance by *instruments*, who live upon *provisions* produced and economised by other men.' And again :—' It is never more possible for capital to tyrannise over labour than when it is scarce, for then it is it which makes the law,—it is it which regulates the rate of sale. Never is this tyranny more impossible to it than when it is abundant, for in that case it is labour which has the command.'

While all this, however, may be acknowledged by the workman to be true, there may still lurk a feeling of dissatisfaction with the idea of complete resignation to what is accounted to be an unsatisfactory condition of things. Capitalists who have made capital rapidly are too apt to lose sight of their real position; too apt to forget from what they have sprung, and how they have risen. They are too apt to credit their own personal abilities with the change, forgetting that circumstances often unseen and accidental have had everything, or a great deal, to do in the matter. The air of haughtiness which is often adopted by the *nouveaux riches* as employers towards their workmen becomes all the more insufferable when the change in the position of the former has been witnessed in all its stages; and the old men particularly cannot easily regard an air of pride and superiority on the part of him who was perhaps their former associate, with equanimity. In these circumstances, an abrupt message to the workmen that they are required to work so much additional time, or receive so much less remuneration, cannot fail to act like a match to gunpowder. The demand is resented as an insult, and there arises perhaps an industrial war, pernicious if not disastrous to both sides.

Now, upon the continent of Europe there are not so many new capitalists, for industrial undertakings do not often lead so rapidly to the accumulation of large fortunes, and there is in general much less jealousy existing between employer and employed than is the case in Great Britain. And the friction is not so great, partly because there is often a systematic effort made to avoid it. Masters meet their men face to face in the Conseils de Prud'hommes, which are boards established to conduct business between both sides in a conciliatory manner. In some countries, trade combinations are prohibited by law.

In Holland, the law prohibits combinations amongst workmen, which have the raising of the rates of wages, or the reduction of the hours of labour, for their object. Yet the general impression in that country appears to be that 'the working of this law, as compared with the results of an opposite state of the law in England and in some other countries, is such that there is little probability of any change being made for some time to come. . . . . The law as it now stands is not found to work badly or oppressively ; . . . and where masters and men are forbidden to fight, they learn to arrange their differences by more gentle and civilized means.'[1] And in a later report, dated 1870, the same reporter says :— 'Workmen's clubs and trades unions abound in every town in the country. Every trade has its society, and every tradesman, citizen, and labourer is a member of one or another. The law allows such societies to discuss with full liberty all questions connected with the relations of master to man, and to use all amicable and legitimate means for effecting a change in those relations. What it prohibits is a hostile demonstration of a whole class against another, or of a whole body of workmen against a common employer. This law is respected by all parties, and meets, I have reason to believe, with general approval.'

In 1806, the Conseils de Prud'hommes were first

---

[1] *Reports on the Condition of the Industrial Classes, &c.* Report by Mr. Sidney Locock, dated The Hague, December 10, 1869.

legally established in France, and they were established
with the view of putting an end, by means of conciliation,
to the small disputes which arise, either between employers and workmen, or between foremen, workmen, and
apprentices.

These boards have proved eminently successful in
attaining the object stated, for it is ascertained that upon
an average 19-20ths of all disputes that come before them
are thereby amicably settled.　Parties bringing cases
before these courts must appear in person, not through
the intervention of a lawyer.　Should the court of conciliation fail to arrange matters, then the case is referred
to a court of judgment or arbitration.　In either of these
courts, or in any committee that may be delegated by
any of them to arrange matters—for small committees
are often appointed to effect the same objects—the number
of judges on either side is the same; that is, there are
an equal number of employers and workmen who act
together.

Mr. Frederic Bernal reports from Havre, on March
1st, 1872,[1] in regard to the nature and operation of these
boards, as follows:—'The Conseil de Prud'hommes,
or board of experts, is an admirable institution, and
might, with certain modifications, be advantageously introduced into our own industrial legislation.　Instituted in
1806, the board is divided into two divisions, and consists
(in this town) of a president, vice-president, secretary,
and 24 judges.　The president and vice-president are
appointed by the central government; the secretary by
the préfet of the department, and the judges are elected
by the qualified voters.　The election for these latter
takes place every three years, when one-half of them
retire, being, however, eligible for re-election.　Half of
the judges are masters, half workmen, · each side electing

[1] *Reports on the Condition of the Industrial Classes, &c.*

their own judges. The election is held in the ordinary manner, and is presided over by the sous-préfet, or mayor. The qualifications for a voter are—for a master, that he be 25 years of age, able to read and write, holder of a license during five years, and a resident in the district for three years;—for a workman, that he be 25 years old, able to read and write, and engaged in his trade for five years. The qualifications for judges are the same, with the exception that they must be 30 years of age.

'The Conseil de Prud'hommes is essentially a tribunal of conciliation. The first bureau endeavours to arrange disputes amicably; but, should it fail to do so, they are sent before the second bureau, whose decision is final, unless the sum in dispute exceeds 200 francs (8*l*.), when an appeal can be made to the tribunal of commerce. They have, otherwise, full power to enforce their decisions. The cases brought before them comprise every kind of dispute between masters and workmen, but not domestic servants, and the average number per annum in this town (Havre) of these cases is about 1,000.'

In this country, Mr. Mundella, M.P., possesses the honour of being the first to introduce the system of conciliation. In 1860, the first board was started in connection with the trade of hosiery, in which he was engaged, with the object of endeavouring to arrest the evils that arise from industrial conflict. The consciousness of a good cause has fortified the resolutions of those who have inaugurated the system of conciliation in this country, and has led them to combat successfully many difficulties and discouragements.

The masters and men meet and mix together, and talk over the differences that may have arisen, and settle them by mutual concession in the spirit of forbearance, avoiding, if possible, even the voting against each other.

When committees of masters and men thus meet together
in a friendly and informal manner, and at regular stated
periods, the changes that take place from time to time
are discussed, and the rates of wages and hours of work
are fixed accordingly. Thus, there is no room left for
the brewing of discontent, nor for the origination of
strikes   Trades unions still have functions to perform,
but in their action they become entirely beneficial.
Without them, indeed, boards of conciliation could not
act effectively, for they would have no responsible body
upon which, unless government interposed, they could
rely to see their decisions carried out by the men. The
organisation of the trades unions is therefore essential
to a reliable settlement of difficulties.   Mr. Henry
Crompton, in his valuable little work on ' Industrial Conciliation,' writes on this subject as follows :—' We have
come to the conclusion that permanent boards, either of
conciliation or arbitration, are not possible unless the
operatives are united together in some form of permanently established organisation, without which there is
no guarantee that the men will abide by the decisions of
the board, and that the system has the best chance of
success when the employers are also associated together.'
Sometimes it has been the case, indeed, that the men
have proved refractory ; but with a sufficiently organised
union instances of this kind will, in the future, become
less frequent.   It is not a hazardous allegation that the
chief disputes arising between masters and workmen arise
on account of ignorance and prejudice, rather than dis-
honesty.   And this ignorance and prejudice begins to
disappear when the parties concerned come together with
honest intentions to discuss their views.   Thus Mr.
Mundella testified :—' The very men that the manufacturers dreaded were the men that were sent to represent
the workmen at the board.   We found them the most

straightforward men we could desire to have to deal
with ; we have often found that the power behind them
has been too strong for them ; they are generally the
most intelligent men ; and often they are put under great
pressure by workmen outside, to do things which they
know to be contrary to common sense, and they will not
do them.   They have been the greatest barriers we have
had between the ignorant workmen and ourselves.'

In the adoption of this system we see the predominance of reason over brute force, and, as the result of the
establishment of reason, the existence of harmony instead
of customary suspicion and distrust, varied by occasional
war and disaster.   Should the means of conciliation fail
on particular occasions, there is a reference to an established arbiter, whose decision is final and binding upon
both parties.   The possibility of war, therefore, is avoided,
and men live in peace, enjoying a resulting prosperity.
Mr. Henry Crompton thus describes the change that has
occurred in the condition of the Nottingham and Leicester
trades that had adopted this system :—' The change has
been from war to peace.   Confidence and goodwill have
replaced suspicion and open hostility.   The constant
reference of differences and disputes to an acknowledged
authority for decision upon the basis of reason and proof,
and the abiding loyally by an adverse and disappointing
award, is truly a great moral lesson.   Besides this, the
lesson has a valuable intellectual influence, in teaching
the working classes to look further into the future than
they are wont to do.   The moral and social advantages
of a board of conciliation cannot be disputed.'   At the
present·time there is a board of conciliation established
at Darlington for the iron trade, which represents 35
works.   'The works represented by the board,' Mr.
Crompton says, ' contain no less than 1,913 puddling
furnaces out of 2,136, the number in the whole district.

The board has a representative constitution, each " works" sending two representatives—an employer and an operative, the latter being chosen by ballot for one year, but eligible for re-election.   A president, vice-president, and two secretaries are chosen by the board for a year.   They are not entitled to vote, but the " works " for which either was elected is entitled to nominate another representative in his stead.   If the employer-representative of any " works " happens to be absent, the corresponding operative-representative is not allowed to vote.   A standing committee, consisting of five employers and five operatives, the president, and vice-president, is appointed by the board, and is exactly analogous to the "committee of inquiry," in the lace and hosiery trades.   Its functions are well defined by Rule 11 :— " All questions shall in the first instance be referred to the standing committee, who shall investigate and endeavour to settle the matter so referred to it, but shall have no power to make an award except by consent of the parties."'[1]   Failing settlement by the committee, the dispute is at once referred to the board.   In 1875, this committee settled more than 40 disputes.   Its decisions—or, to speak correctly, its recommendations—are generally accepted ; appeal to the board is exceptional.   If the board fails to agree, it appoints an independent referee to settle the dispute.   The action of the board has produced the most salutary results, and there has been no strike notwithstanding the numerous reductions in the rates of wages that have necessarily taken place during the recent unprecedented relapse in the condition of the iron trade.

Until general councils are established to embrace many trades, it appears that each trade would require to appoint its own board, and to act without reference to decisions in other trades.   This condition of things would be a

---

[1] *Industrial Conciliation*, by Mr. Henry Crompton, pp. 57, 58.

step in advance of the present condition ; and a most important and beneficial step, for the greater number of trades at the present day have not yet found their way to establish permanent boards, on the principle of settling disputes conciliatorily as they arise.   The machinery that is presently employed, when any is employed at all, is that of arbitration, specially erected for the purpose at the particular juncture ; and that machinery may work well or ill, may inspire confidence or not, and, indeed, does often disappoint the expectations of both sides ; for, as it is sometimes said, the arbiters have not clearly apprehended the question in dispute, nor fairly decerned upon it.   Those complaints flow from the fact that the individual appointed as a referee is one generally, if not always, unacquainted beforehand with the trade and the circumstances in which the dispute upon which he is called to arbitrate has arisen.   He has to learn his position as well as he can ; and it is not to be expected that he should always, however able and honest he be, apprehend exactly the particular points for adjudication ; at least, he possesses no advantage comparable to that which the employers and employed themselves possess.

For these reasons, boards of conciliation, composed of an equal number of employers and employed, ought to become more general in the future.   It is not essential that every master or workman should be therein directly represented ; for, if the great body of the trade is represented, the outlying pickets of it may also be guided by the common action.   Thus, when there are a number of tradesmen within an establishment whose divisions comprise various trades, the master, who is for instance an engineer or shipbuilder, may be guided by the decisions of the various trade boards.

When, however, the period has arrived when the various trades possess each their respective boards, the

establishment of a general board for all would amalgamate
the interests of all concerned more closely than by any
other process. For, at the present time, and even perhaps when boards for the various trades have been established, it is not to be expected that there will never arise
occasions on which harmony may be interrupted, and a
strike take place. But when this occurs in one trade, the
workmen in the others will in many cases, when working
conjointly with the workmen of the trade in which the
strike takes place, be thrown out of work, suffering loss of
wages. There exists an actual interdependence between
the workmen of different trades, and this interdependence
demands its counterpart in a junction of councils; and that
this junction should act in the most efficient way, it should
be permanent, not occasional; for, when permanent, its
function will enable it to take cognisance of all the current
facts of all trades, so as to be ready with the maximum
of experience and intelligence, to discuss and settle disputes of all kinds in every trade. But, additionally, the
acerbity of feeling which may arise occasionally in the
breasts of the members of either side in one trade, will be
reduced and controlled, more or less, by the juxtaposition
of the members of other trades in the same council, whose
feelings are calm, and whose interests are opposed to the
adoption of violent measures that might, if these dangerous
feelings were to remain unchecked, follow from them.
And, still further, the interests of the community as a
whole, of which working men always form the major
portion, would be consulted by the establishment of such
a permanent general board for each district or country;
for there would arise advantageous opportunities for the
discussion of general questions, separable from strictly
trade questions, so that the functions of such boards
would, doubtless, develop towards the advantageous consideration of all those matters that affect the general

commercial and social prosperity of the community of which the board formed the centre.

To say that there will be a rapid adoption of such m eans for rendering the clashing interests of employers and employed amenable to rational counsel—intelligent in its character, and regular in its action—would be, perhaps, too sanguine a prediction. Surely, however, we are warranted in looking for a more rapid realisation of them in the future than in the past. Employers have often hitherto regarded the claims of the employed to union, and their action in that direction, as an attack upon their interests. Whenever this idea is laid aside, another idea—that of dealing with such unions most effectively — will take its place. Employers naturally must possess more education and development of the intelligence than the employed; and it is, therefore, from their side that the advances in the direction of supplanting brute force by reason are naturally to be looked for. Yet necessity has sometimes led the workmen to make the first advances. When intelligence on the one side and necessity on the other incline bodies of men towards each other, there but remains that application of special knowledge and energy, on the part of a few leading individuals, to cement a union. It is for some of the more prominent employers to do this, and the recognition of the responsibility will be the first step towards it. There can probably be no more successful way in which to cause that responsibility to be felt, than by the promulgation of the doctrine that every one who has attained a position of comparative comfort is bound to extend his hand toward others and towards the masses of the community who labour with their hands, and who have only a feeble opportunity of ever looking beyond the limited circle of their own daily wants. Men who toil with their hands from week to week, and month to month, have little opportunity of seeing far around them, so as to discern the general influences that affect their position for good or for evil. But men who have attained the position of large employers, who in the very course of business need to consult many men and consider many interests, and who, besides, have always more or less of leisure in which they may take a more extensive view of the situation, are they who must naturally guide those who are unable to guide themselves. From large employers, therefore, the first movements towards the adoption of specific measures for the general benefit should come.

Masons are probably more refractory than other classes of workmen, which arises doubtless from the fact that they have a·virtual monopoly of work within their district, for the articles of their manufacture—viz. stone buildings—cannot be imported, like the articles of most other trades, from a distance. Yet they are amenable to reason, and they must, like other workmen, feel the severity of strikes when they occur. Mr. Crompton says :—' The opposition of the masons is to be overcome. The leaders are most desirous for a permanent system of conciliation, to replace the present antagonism. They would do all that in them lies to influence their men in the right direction. It cannot be doubted that if the master builders in London were really to advance towards the men, to establish a board, inviting the masons to join with the other trades, the force of public opinion and that of their fellow workmen, and their own common sense, would sooner or later produce a great impression upon them. All men on these subjects have undergone great change, and there are plenty of reasons why certain changes should be made less rapidly in some trades than in others.' [1]

And, again, Mr. Crompton says :—' To me it seems

[1] *Industrial Conciliation*, pp. 115, 116.

difficult to point to any set of men in history, certainly to
none in modern history, on whom a greater and more
important duty rested, than at the present moment de-
volves upon the English capitalists.   They have to solve
the industrial problem of the world ; to discover the truths
on which it must depend ; and, putting aside the precon-
ceived notions and prejudices of the past, to urge forward
the final, and industrial, and social reorganisation towards
which we are now moving.   There cannot be a nobler
or more sacred work for men to do.' [1]

At the present time there generally exist two separate objects in the organisation of trades unions.   One of
these is to establish concerted action, and to accumulate
the funds to maintain such action in the event of a strike,
a lock-out, or sometimes inability to procure work ; the
other object consists in the creation of funds by which
those who are sick, or are superannuated, are relieved,
and also for insurance against death, commonly with the
view of meeting the funeral expenses.   But these means
and funds are not kept as applicable to the separate objects contemplated, but generally form one common fund,
the result being that the members may at any time lose
all their contributions towards benefit objects from the
necessary expenses of a strike.   All the funds that have
been contributed for both purposes are expended on the
one, and the law provides no remedy to the sick or dying
workman.   As Mr. William Thomas Thornton remarks :—
' All unions which seek, as most do, to combine the purposes of " benefit " with those of " trade " societies, rest
upon bases financially unsound.   The incomings of the
richest among them are insufficient even for their ordinary
and calculable liabilities ; and they are liable, in addition,
to extraordinary calls, the amount of which cannot possibly
be calculated beforehand.   Few, if any, other unionists

[1] *Industrial Conciliation*, p. 166.

tax themselves nearly as heavily as the amalgamated engineers and the amalgamated carpenters, who pay 1 s. a head weekly, or three or four times the more usual rate of 3d. or 4d.; but, according to the principles by which the proceedings of ordinary insurance companies are regulated, the taxation of these engineers and carpenters ought to be three or four times heavier still, in order to provide duly for the allowances which their associations are pledged to make for the support of sick and superannuated, and for the burial of deceased members, independently of their miscellaneous obligations towards members who are desirous of emigrating, or who have lost or broken their tools. It is true that the proportion of its promises to pay, which a " trades " union is likely to be called upon to keep, is smaller than that of an ordinary life insurance company. Almost every one who has begun to insure his life, goes on regularly paying the premium, until, on his death, the company has to pay in turn to his heirs ; whereas, it is a very common thing for unionists, after paying their weekly groats or shillings for a year or two, to stop their subscriptions on changing their place of residence, and thereby to forfeit all future claim upon their society, leaving to it all their past contributions as so much pure gain. The amalgamated engineers during the first sixteen years of their existence profited in this manner at the expense of 13,317 of their members.'[1]

And, again, Mr. Thornton says:—' No definite provision can be depended upon for an indefinite drain. No subscriptions, no accumulations can afford complete security for ordinary claims, if these are liable at any moment to be indefinitely swollen by irregular and extraordinary claims of unforeseeable amount. As long as the cost of a strike or a lock-out is held to constitute a first lien on

[1] *On Labour*, p. 328.

union funds, no unionist can be certain that his application for the superannuation or other allowances, to which
he may have become entitled, will not be addressed to
an empty exchequer.'[1]

In the evidence given by the Right Hon. Robert
Lowe, M.P., before the Friendly Societies Commission, he
says:—'A great many trade societies are formed as a
benefit society and a trade society, and the benefits
which they promise are out of all proportion to the payments, and can only be made up by arbitrary calls in a
case of emergency. Hardly one of them will stand an
investigation. I think that that is a great cruelty and a
great fraud upon the working classes, and one which it
is quite in the power of the government to stop.'

A correspondent in the *Pall Mall Budget*, of October
19, 1877, remarks upon the abuses that are possible at
present as follows:—'The Trades Union Act of 1871, as
first drawn, provided that, as in the case of insurance
companies and friendly societies, the funds contributed to
the unions for distinct and specific benefit society purposes should be kept apart, and not all confused in one
fund applicable as a primary object to fighting or strike
purposes. Surely, nothing could be more reasonable or
honest. . . . . But the trades union leaders did not see
the case in this ordinary light; . . . . the Act was allowed
to pass with special clauses which permit trades unions
to be exempt from the obligations placed on insurance
companies and friendly societies as regards the separation
of funds received as the purchase money of specified
benefits. Nay, more, trades unions need not be registered,
nor require security from their treasurers, nor separately
provide for expenses of management; and, still further,
the Act provides that no court of law shall have power
to give redress to any member who considers himself

[1] *On Labour*, p. 331.

aggrieved under the rules of the union. The meaning of all this is, that the leaders of the unions have full and uncontrolled power over all the funds, whether collected under the promise of benefit objects or otherwise, and they have also full control of expulsion over any members who become impatient or inquisitive.'

The writer proceeds to describe a case in which a poor widow sued the officials of a trades union for a sum of money consequent on the loss of her husband by an accident. The judge gave a decree against the widow, because he had no power under the law to compel the fulfilment of an agreement made between a trades union and one of its members. The case was a typical one representing some 300 widows and 600 orphans, who had similar claims on the union. Such a state of things ought not to be permitted to exist, for it virtually allows the establishment of numerous little despotic governments within a free country.

But even with benefit societies pure and simple, whose funds are not liable to be thus abstracted for trade purposes, there is too much danger that funds which are intended for benefits to be conferred many years after they are paid in, may be lost or greatly reduced before the period of the benefits arrives It has been found that many of such institutions have been compelled to dissolve, and such is not wonderful when we consider that both the technical knowledge, and the stern commercial principle required in their administration, cannot well be fully present in small societies, particularly in the rural districts.

Mr. T. E. Kebbel writes as follows with regard to the influence of these societies in the rural districts [1] :—'That benefit societies are frequently the reverse of beneficial to the unfortunate labourers who belong to them, is what

[1] *The Agricultural Labourer*, p. 64.

every one is now aware of. But still the principle itself
seems sound enough, and if the machinery were amended,
they would be properly included among the ameliorating
circumstances of agricultural life. At the present time
(1870) they seem to have gone altogether wrong. They
do that which they ought not to do, and leave undone
that which they ought to do; they squander their money
upon beer, and repudiate their just debts; they lead a
jolly life for a few years, and as soon as the necessity for
meeting their original engagements begins to threaten
them, they are dissolved, and the funds evenly divided.
The young members join another club; but what becomes
of the old men, who had pinched themselves for many
years to secure a provision for their old age? This
selfish and dishonest practice is so general throughout the
country as to have caused the Commissioners to report
most unfavourably of the operation of benefit societies.'

Again, the Hon. E. T. Stanley, one of the Assistant
Commissioners on Friendly Societies, reports (1874) respecting the general character of the management of
these societies thus:—'They have been hindered by
causes besides their own neglect from doing what they
might have done for sick insurance. They have suffered
much from fraud, through the want of protection afforded
them by the law. Even now, unregistered friendly
societies are very much at the mercy of fraudulent secretaries or trustees, for the remedy by indictment is a poor
consolation, and is only throwing good money after bad.'

When the various affiliated Orders manage benefit
funds in the interests of their members, there is not the
same liability to abuse as when the funds are in the hands of
trades unions or the smaller benefit societies. The Orders
have gradually developed from secret societies professing
loyalty, but chiefly held together by their convivial tendencies, into such benefit societies as they now happen to

be, having more or less profited by the experience of past failures in this direction. Yet even the various Orders —except when containing a large number of members, such as in the case of the Manchester Unity of Odd Fellows and the Ancient Order of Foresters, which together contain two-thirds of the whole membership of these Orders—are not in a position to furnish that perfect security that ought to be insisted upon. 'Unfortunately,' the Hon. E. T. Stanley says, ' in these small societies there are local ambitions to satisfy which tend to the multiplication of branches, and consequently offices which are sought, not for the salary, but for the sake of the petty importance and the high-sounding title. Few things are more needed than the amalgamation of small lodges, and few things are more difficult to accomplish.' If then, even in the most favourable circumstances, these societies do not generally succeed, but rather bring disappointment and loss to the members, nothing else than constant failure can be expected when the management is entrusted to the officials of trades unions, who are not only unqualified, but irresponsible.

One of the chief objects of Government is to protect the citizens from loss and damage, and when these citizens are poor and ignorant, the more prominently ought that function to be called into exercise. The community employs, through the State, machinery and officials to perform the services of watch and guard. Were these agencies withdrawn, society would suffer disproportionately, for then property generally would be exposed to all kinds of depredations. There are enemies within the State as well as without, and it is impossible that poor persons can defend themselves always successfully against the former class. It is impossible for poor persons to investigate for themselves either the particular facts or the general principles on which a benefit society

x 2

is founded, and unless they can feel from day to day that its benefits are being fairly distributed, there would appear to be a duty devolving on the State. The State may then protect them in either of two ways. It may investigate for them, or it may itself manage this kind of business. In the case of the administration of sick funds alone, small societies ought to be sufficiently regulated by the watchfulness of their members, although, as men become oftener sick the older they grow, there is a liability of the funds that were found ample when the members were young, being found the reverse as a proportion of them become old. Mr. Scudamore has pointed out, in his evidence given before the Friendly Society Commission, that the difficulty of detecting malingering in the members of such a society virtually precludes the possibility of Government conducting sick benefits. With objects, however, which cannot be fulfilled till many years have passed, there is an imminent risk of all private societies, particularly small societies, failing to meet them. Then the State may demand either the fulfilment of certain qualifications in the nature of guarantee before the authorisation of such societies is granted, or it may undertake the functions of these societies itself. The former method is, to a certain extent, adopted already, but however perfect such a machinery of registration may be, the degree of security will still be very imperfect, and in cases of failure the members might fairly conclude that the State had contributed by its authorisation or registration of such societies as afterwards failed, to bring about their loss, for it had, in fact, set its mark of approval upon a society that should have been discountenanced. The second method, namely the undertaking of the functions of these societies, is the one most open to the State, and not subject to such objections.

In the words of Mr. Frank Ives Scudamore's evidence

before the Friendly Societies Commission :—' I think that the Government has a peculiar right to get the insurance business for this reason, that insurance business deals with the remote future, and although the future of no Government is absolutely secure, the future of this Government is a great deal more secure than that of any private institution can ever hope to be.   Government can give far greater security than any private institution can for something which is to occur at a remote period of time.'   We have already noticed how the superior security afforded by the Government savings banks has been appreciated by the people, and there can be no doubt that were the limit of amount at which any one may insure his life reduced from 20*l.*, which it is at present, to 5*l.*, an immense boon would be conferred on the working classes.   Working men cannot, and scarcely ever do, insure for so high a sum as 20*l.* ; for, as a rule, they calculate only on leaving their families free of debt, and, therefore, such a sum only is required as will re-imburse the outlay on the funeral expenses.   As yet, however, the working classes receive no benefit from anything that has been attempted by Government in this direction.

Trades unions are then on no grounds the appropriate organisations for the management of such funds, even though by law they should be decreed to be preserved separate and distinct from those intended for trade purposes.   Mr. William Thomas Thornton states the case clearly when he says :—' A modification . . . . is that unions, without formally dissolving in order to reconstitute themselves as independent societies, should keep the funds destined for different operations completely separate, so that the provision for provident purposes should no longer be liable to be swept away in trade disputes.   This plan is pronounced by experienced unionist functionaries to be impracticable : whether really so or not it would certainly prove ineffectual. The proposed separation, if made, could certainly not be maintained. It is not to be supposed that when reduced to extremity, unionists could hold any money of their own sacred, or that they would scruple to use to-morrow's provision for to-day's sustenance, when the only apparent alternative was their doing away with to-morrow's need by perishing immediately from starvation.'

The interest of the masses of the people, therefore, demands that benefit societies having their benefits realisable only after a lengthened period of years shall be supplanted by the State. The State could with the largest amount of benefit to everyone concerned conduct the business of life-insurance, deferred annuities, and deferred endowments, as well as banking, which it has already undertaken. The security would then be as perfect as possible, and in consequence the prudential habits of the working classes would be stimulated, and their material position appreciably improved.

Trades unions would then be relieved from such functions which, we have seen, they can never perform to the assured benefit of their members. What, then, in that case, it may be asked, would be left for trades unions to do? Important duties would remain, which they would be able to perform all the more successfully that their hands were relieved from the performance of others which do not properly belong to them.

Thus, there would still remain a necessity for organisation and for meetings, and contributions among the members, in order that the position of the particular trade with reference to the relations between employers and employed should be discussed : representatives, again, must be appointed to sit at the boards of conciliation, so as to put forward the views of the workmen, which they would be fully acquainted with from the course and

points of the previous discussions. Then in cases of accident, the unions would meet to determine how the subject
of the accident is to be relieved ; and in cases where
neglect on the part of the employer is alleged, an investigation might be demanded, and parties appointed in the
interest of the members and of those injured or killed, to
watch the course of such investigation. There are also
the interests of the workman as regards political influence
to be considered, and then the employment of such in the
procuring of laws to reduce existing abuses, or to establish the most healthy practicable conditions under which
work can be carried on. By the combination of various
trades unions, building societies might be successfully
established, also benefit funds for sickness ; for in the
first, a large corporate power is required to deal successfully with the business of acquiring land, entering into
contracts, borrowing money, &c. ; and in the second, it
is a necessity in order that cases of malingering should be
readily detected and reported, that the members of a
benefit society with such an object should live as closely
together as possible, for even in the best of circumstances
it is found difficult always to detect such cases.

These and many other duties will lie always fairly
within the province of a trades union, or a combination
of such unions. Such organisations, indeed, appear to be
indispensable to insuring the best practicable conditions
in which the workman shall expend his labour, and thus
in securing to himself the maximum of benefit from such
expenditure, he will also secure to the community as a
whole a more ample share of the product of his
labour.

It may be objected that the system of conciliation as
above described is regarded with too great an amount of
favour, as too complete a panacea, as it has been termed,
for the industrial ills which afflict the workman.

There are other systems which are often regarded as affording the workman the best prospects in the future, and we shall now endeavour to describe these, and estimate them at their true value There are, first, those of co-operation, and, second, those affecting the distribution of a proportion of profits among the workmen.   The former have already been tried, and with very varying success.   They have thriven well when the circumstances have been very favourable, but they have often succumbed to adverse influences, and it may be said generally that the ground must be prepared beforehand in a special way for their reception. When they do succeed, it is because a special effort has been made by special men, because they adopt principles of action greatly healthier than those otherwise at work, or because the circumstances in which they exist are abnormal.

It will be necessary to illustrate these statements. There are, then, three several systems of co-operation, namely, co-operative distribution, which flourishes chiefly in Great Britain; co-operative production, which has thriven pre-eminently in France; and co-operative credit, which has extended itself remarkably in Prussia and Germany.   The first of these systems, namely co-operative distribution, is that which is best known in this country, for it has been adopted both by rich and poor, and it has found a footing in almost every average-sized village throughout the country.   By its means, the distribution of the various articles of household consumption of a good quality and at a cheap rate has been carried on with great advantage to the community that has adopted it.   But the reasons for such success are not difficult to discern.   In retail shops generally there exist three disadvantages, with which the business they conduct has to contend.   First, the system of credit is almost always that on which purchases are made, the result being that

there are bad debts incurred, the losses on which must
be recovered by the retailer from the bulk of his customers, thereby enhancing the price of goods; and,
further, as the circulating capital of the dealer cannot be
turned over so fast as if he adopted the system of cash
payments, he must have more of it to conduct the same
amount of business, and the interest upon the use of the
addition must be charged in the further enhanced price
of his goods.   Second, there are frequently, and particularly is this the case with country shops, an unnecessary number of hands through which articles pass from
the wholesale, it may be importing merchant, before they
can reach the retail dealer, all of whom must draw off
some profit, so that the prices of the articles are considerably increased before they can reach the hands of
the customers; and third, there are an unnecessary
number of retail dealers, the maintenance of whose shops
must entail an increased expenditure that can only be
recovered by a further addition to the prices of the
articles sold.   It is astonishing how prices are raised by
these causes, and the further we recede into the outlying districts, where the people are relatively unable to
pay high prices, the greater is the amount added to the
original price of the article.   A heavy tax is thus imposed
upon the poor customer.

When co-operative shops are established these three
disadvantages are avoided, and the membership, which
is generally large, has its work of purchasing and retail
distribution performed at a very small cost, and consequently the prices of the articles are low, their quality is
good, and there is found to be a saving at the end of the
year, upon which a small bonus is frequently given to the
customers in proportion to the extent of their accounts,
thus inducing regular and abundant custom.   It is not
wonderful, therefore, that these establishments have

become popular with the working people, and not with them alone.

But the question arises, how is it that retail dealers exist in such numbers as to be able to conduct their business only at such disadvantage? Probably the principal reason why retail shops so predominate in the towns and particularly in the villages and country districts over the requirements of the inhabitants is because the people are unable on account of the artificial obstructions that exist to settle in the country districts or suburbs on suitable patches of land of their own. There are therefore a disproportionate number who reside in the towns, and resort to the retail trade to obtain or to eke out a livelihood. Retired ship captains and sailors form a class who would greedily invest their savings in land, instead of in a town's business, if it were in their power to do so. That is the case in the Channel Islands; and where the agriculturalists have been able to possess land in Ireland the capital is probably chiefly acquired at sea. The large numbers of small shops therefore must be regarded in this light as an indication of an abnormal condition of things, without which the co-operative stores would not possess such preponderating advantages as they are known to do.

Societies or combinations of workmen for the purposes of production flourish chiefly in France, and they have also been successfully established in Sweden. Where property on the whole is not very unequally distributed, the circumstances for the existence of societies of co-operative production will be most favourable, for then there will be the less difficulty experienced in obtaining the capital necessary to start and maintain them, and when that capital is obtained, they will not be so likely to be outdone by the competition of very large and therefore more economically conducted works. Additionally, however, as regards France it may be said that many and strong efforts have frequently been made to set on foot such establishments, and State aid has been asked and extensively granted. The total result has, however, been that few of the whole number that have been started have survived more than one or two years, and the members of those who have have distinguished themselves by their extraordinary perseverance and heroic resolution in combating the most dreadful privations. The exceptional exertion and self-denial have produced in this direction, as they are capable of doing in all other directions, exceptional results. In England, these societies have generally, though not always, failed, and they have failed in spite of the extraordinary exertions of their members, on account of their having to run in competition with the works of capitalists, whose advantages must, because of their ability to do everything in first-class style and on the largest scale, be always overwhelming. Some co-operative societies for production in this country have not been able to withstand the temptation of denying themselves the benefits of an extended employment of capital. It has been felt at these times that the capital and credit of the working members were insufficient to enable them to reap the fullest benefit from the labour expended. The result is that subscribers to the capital who do not partake in the labour of the work are admitted. The interests of these members are necessarily in some degree different from those of the workers, for if a comparatively high bonus be paid to labour they begin to feel that so much that might have been added to swell the profits of capital is lost. These diverse interests then gradually pull different ways, till at the time that the work is gaining the fullest advantage from the employment of ample capital, a struggle commences, which ends either in the expulsion of the new capital held by non-workers, which will generally, if not always, be impossible, or in the conversion of the concern into a joint-stock company, wherein the principle of co-operation is necessarily abandoned.

Whatever associations for co-operative production have succeeded, have succeeded through the energy and self-denial of their original members; and when they have passed the initial stage, and the particular trade in which they are engaged remains in a healthy condition, a continuance of the same exceptional exertion will eventually produce a great success, for every step in advance, owing to the gradual accumulation of capital, is an easier one than that which has preceded it. We thus see a few wonderful examples of the success of this system, at which its advocates point, full of hope; but there remain still only a few,—out of the large numbers that have been started. It may be said, then, that 'there is no record of experience, nor any process of economical reasoning, to convince us that any large number of manufacturing enterprises can be conducted upon what are known as "co-operative principles." . . . They are essentially exceptional undertakings.'[1]

In Prussia, through the extraordinary and persistent exertions of M. Schulze-Delitsch, a system of credit co-operation was established among the working classes. This system has spread considerably, and is reckoned to have produced very advantageous results to the members of the various societies. The principle adopted is that of mutual credit, whereby every one enrolled becomes responsible for the debts of the whole society, so that when it consists of many individuals, every one of them possesses an amount of credit he could not otherwise enjoy. The society receives contributions from the members, that form a fund, upon the basis of which it borrows capital on credit. With such capital, the members are in a comparatively favourable position

[1] *Times*, December 29, 1875.

to supply themselves with the tools, machinery, and appliances of their respective trades. At the present time, the credit of these societies is able to procure ample funds in the open market on favourable terms. It is the same principle that has been adopted by the Government of Russia in carrying out the emancipation of the serfs. Each individual was made amenable to his commune for the payment of the redemption dues on the land, and the commune was made responsible to the State, so that the credit of the aggregation of individuals in the commune was conferred upon the unit. The same principle is also adhered to in the transaction of business generally wherever possible, although individuals trading with each other continually become accustomed to put faith in each other to such an extent, that so far as it is found to be inconvenient or not easily practicable, the principle begins to be lost sight of. The spreading of responsibility over numbers acts as a safeguard, and the amount of security thereby obtained is valuable to the co-operators, and it becomes all the more valuable and all the more necessary in proportion as the co-operators are men of indifferent means.

But the necessity for the establishment of such co-operative credit societies is only apparent when capital is not introduced amongst a population in the usual way. Capitalists, if alive to their own interests, will prefer to invest their capital where the most profit will be expected from it; and if there are good means of communication, and equal advantages in other respects, capital will be distributed over a country pretty uniformly. There are always, however, centres of industry where trades locate themselves, because for one reason or other they derive special advantages at these. In the country districts, however, unless minerals are to be readily found, there is a relative dearth of capital experienced. In purely

agricultural districts, especially where the winter is long
and dark, the people may generally be without full means
of employment, and indeed in many European countries,
while they may possess full work during summer upon
their farms, there is little remunerative work to be had
in the winter. In these circumstances credit co-operative societies do good, for they enable the people to
procure tools, machinery, and appliances that assist
them to work most profitably in the winter time; and
even in the summer their field occupations are conducted
much more successfully on account of the fuller employment of capital that is so obtained. In England
there appears to be no appreciable space or occasion for
such societies, for large works, the productions of large
capital, exist at frequent points over the most part of the
country except in the outlying rural districts, and otherwise the poorer classes do not possess any lands of their
own upon which they may apply capital.

Thus, then, there does not appear to be any prospect
of a permanent and regular advantage derivable from the
adoption of the principle of co-operation by the working
classes, unless when the circumstances are exceptional;
and when they are so, it is often, if not always, on account
of an unhealthy, or at any rate a not very robust, condition
of the industrial community. Where capital is made, it
will tend to reproduce itself more easily in the future, for
it facilitates labour, and the labourer must therefore, in
preferring his own interest, prefer to work by its unstinted
aid. The system of co-operation in a degree prefers a
combination amongst labourers to the most profitable
kind of combination between capital and labour; in the
first case a distinct sacrifice is made, but with the view
that what remains shall be securely divided amongst the
labourer recipients, who have therefore a greater inducement to work hard and spare penuriously. From another

point of view, it may be seen that the principle of co-
operation can never be generally adopted, for should it
tend to do so, capital would become so very cheap, that
the disadvantages of working without the largest practicable application of it, would become too severe to allow
the working co-operators to survive in the competition.

Without, however, it being necessary for the labourer
to dissociate himself thus far from the advantages which
capital when fully employed must always present, he may
benefit by its employment most amply, receiving, at the
same time, full remuneration for his daily labour. That
is to say, he may receive in addition to his nominal wages
—which may be the current rate—a sum in the form of
part-profits of the business in which he is engaged, for the
effect of his knowing that he shall receive such will cause
him naturally to apply himself more regularly and earnestly to his work than he would otherwise do, and it
will also cause his interest to lie in detecting and reporting any idling in others engaged in the same business.
By these means the position of the employer would be
improved, for his capital would undoubtedly be rendered
more productive, and therefore he would be enabled to
grant such a bonus to his labourers, not only without loss
but with additional profit to himself. It is, however, not
easy generally to carry out such a system in practice, and
in many businesses it is impracticable. With some, however, an adequate measure of success depends very largely
upon such a mode of payment being adopted. Thus in
the case of whale-fishing, there are rates paid to each
class of men engaged according to the produce of the
fishing additional to a fixed though low rate of wages, and·
these in a successful year represent a hundred per cent. of
additional remuneration. But though the whaling vessels
may return home ' clean '—that is to say, when the fishing
has proved a failure—the men do not lose any portion of

their wages, they simply do not gain their percentages. In this way, there is created a very great inducement to the exercise of watchfulness, diligence, and enterprise.

In many businesses, however, this mode of remuneration cannot be practised, for the profits may, in periods of bad trade, or in cases of contracts where contractors miscalculate, be converted into losses, when it would be found impossible to deduct anything from the wages of the labourer, so as to make up the deficit caused by these losses. Where, however, this system of dividing part-profits can be practically carried out, its influence upon the interests of both employer and employed must be beneficial. A modification of the same principle as that embraced in the distribution of a proportion of the profits amongst the employed, is that of piece-work, which is more extensively adopted and better known than the other. It differs in its action from that of payment of part-profits in two particulars—namely, that the capitalist cannot have the same reliance on the quality of work performed by his workmen, wherefore its operation cannot be so beneficial to him, and that the workman may altogether disregard the performances of his neighbour, when he is remunerated strictly according to his own only ; in these respects, as compared with the other system, the employer is not so much, and the employed is more, benefited.

A manufacturer, employer of a thousand men, in various parts of England, thus testifies regarding his experience of piece-work :—' I have never known a change from day-work to piece-work where the workman has not done 50 per cent. more work in the same time, and increased his wages in the same proportion. In the great majority of cases, the skilful and industrious workman has doubled his wages.' [1] In some trades, indeed, such as that of jewellers for instance, the adoption of this system seems indispensable.

[1] See *Times*, January 16, 1876.

Sundry objections to the system of piece-work, however, have been frequently raised. It is said, for instance, that men are apt to overtask themselves, and to ruin their constitutions when working for themselves. But that objection may be as well made to the manner in which all men work when they have a great object in view, whether it be to benefit themselves or others; but what does it amount to? It says that when men in their eagerness are foolish enough to forget the fact that they possess only a limited strength, they will cause damage to that strength of a temporary or permanent kind. But men in general will not act thus foolishly, and some experience of the effects of overwork will soon produce a sufficient carefulness in the future. Men do not, as a matter of fact, unless exceptionally, act so as to break down their strength at piece-work; and, as a rule, they are very much more likely gradually to fortify that strength. It is also said that men will give way to intemperance when they receive high wages as the payment of piece-work. Probably this objection is a more valid one than the other; but it presupposes that men as a rule will betake themselves to gross and immoral enjoyments, instead of refined ones, whenever their material condition rapidly improves. That, however, depends upon the natural inclinations of the individuals concerned; if the men, to start with, have been totally untutored, no doubt the possibility of indulgence may verge into a probability. The very reason, however, that they have been so totally untutored lies in the fact that their parents have, mayhap, lived in hovels, sent their children to no school, and brought them up in an atmosphere of improvidence and recklessness. But these conditions are the result of poverty-stricken and depressing circumstances, out of which probably their children may enjoy the best opportunities of rising, by obtaining the remuneration of piece-

Y

work, and they would otherwise presumably perpetuate
their untutored condition.   Mr. Brassey says, in his
' Work and Wages,' that ' these objections of over-exertion
and drunkenness have not, at any rate, been felt on railways ; ' and, so far as my own experience goes, the most
self-respecting, energetic, and powerful navvies are those
who generally combine to work together in piece-work
gangs successfully.

Then, again, it is objected that those who labour by
the piece perform so much more work than they would
do otherwise, that there must consequently be so much
less work left for others to do, and that, therefore, these
others will be in a measure deprived of employment.   But
when such an objection is made, it is forgotten that the
effect of doing more work is to multiply or improve the
articles on which the work is bestowed, so that they
become cheaper.   The community is, therefore, able to
purchase more of them than formerly, and thus a greater
demand arises for the articles made by piece-work.   If
this system were then to become universal, or even very
general, no one would be a greater gainer than the workman himself ; for, first, he would receive the enhanced
wages due to piece-work, and, second, he would receive
for the same sum of money a greater value of commodities (being the production of piece-work) than before.
There can be no objection to piece-work on the ground
that the remuneration due to it cannot be easily determined, and that therefore the workman is likely to suffer
from the payment of too low a rate ; for there must be
less difficulty in determining a standard of payment for a
piece of work at which generally many men of varying
abilities will be engaged, than in determining the day
wages of such differently qualified labourers.   A council
of conciliation would therefore find its business simplified
by the general adoption of the system of piece-work, as

there would not then exist the same difficulty in arranging
a fixed scale of payment for different individuals, who
have such varied capacities.

It should, for these reasons, be the policy of trades
unions to encourage piece-work, wherever it is found to
be practicable. But, as Mr. William Thomas Thornton
remarks, ' with regard to both overtime and piece-work,
the great unionist error consists in interfering paternally
with individual liberty in matters which chiefly concern
individual interests, and in insisting on things being done
which, unless done cheerfully, had better not be done at
all. The error is one of a sort to which leading unionists,
and working class leaders generally, are peculiarly prone.
A favourite notion of theirs is that whatever seems to
them right to be done people ought to be made to do ;
and a most pestilent notion it is to be entertained by the
foremost men of a class who have just been formally invested with the power of making people do whatever
they please.' [1]

We have thus very cursorily reviewed the chief means
by which the working classes may escape from the very
unsettled and unsatisfactory conditions that exist in consequence of the antagonistic relations of capital and labour,
and we have endeavoured to estimate these means fairly,
with the view of ascertaining which of them should afford
the most permanent and important benefits. We have
come to the conclusion that courts of conciliation of a
permanent character are most likely, of all means, to
reduce the present disagreements between capitalist and
labourer to a minimum ; and, on the other hand, that of all
forms of remuneration, first, that by piece-work, and,
second, that by payment of part profits in supplement of
wages, should be the most advantageous to everyone, but
to the workman in particular. The various systems of

[1] *On Labour*, p. 338.

co-operation we have shown to arise from exceptional circumstances, and to be to some extent indications of abnormal conditions.

Although, however, the most approved systems were to be fully adopted immediately, the condition of the workman everywhere would be, on account of the constantly alternating extension and depression of trade, still liable to considerable vicissitudes. At one period there is an immense demand for all sorts of commodities, and, therefore, for all kinds of labour to produce them ; again, a few years thereafter, the demand appears to be paralysed, stocks accumulate, and workmen are paid off. Such alternations, doubtless, proceed, as before stated, from two causes principally—first, unhealthy trading; and, second, too lavish spending. The first proceeds from the doing business, more or less, upon the principle of staking little of one's own, and a good deal of other people's, capital on the chances of good fortune. As this sort of trading grows, which in good times it has a tendency to do, credit takes the place of capital, a large castle of business is built up upon a small foundation, and the least adverse wind may overthrow the whole fabric, and not only the one man's fortune, but that of all who had been leaning upon each other for mutual support. This condition of unstable equilibrium ought not to be permitted ; for these castles of business, in tumbling, cannot but seriously injure large numbers of innocent individuals. He who speculates and risks all—it may be sometimes very little—and fails, should be, in the general interest, more summarily dealt with than he is at present. No action surely can be more reprehensible than that of deliberately risking the capital and prospects of others in the pursuit of one's own profit. It may be objected that everyone is competent to take charge of his own interests, and if he does not, that he may fairly suffer for the neglect of them. But this is not a full statement of the case. Hundreds of honest traders may be brought down by the collapse of the resources of one or two dishonest ones ; a panic spreads the disaster far and wide, everyone looks on every other with suspicion, no one knows the moment in which his own doom may be sealed ; and from a condition of exuberant commercial prosperity and complete confidence, a few days may produce general collapse, distrust, and stagnation. The workman then feels the pinch, and he knows not from whence the ill-fortune comes, nor if anyone is to blame for it.

In the second case referred to, capital is expended too rapidly and indiscreetly upon, it may be, the execution of public works—such as railways—that perhaps for years cannot yield an adequate return. While the capital thus being sunk is so rapidly expended, a great demand for the necessary materials and labour is created. Men's wages rise rapidly everywhere, and a great prosperity appears. When, however, it has been discovered by the investors that their capital will yield little or no return, a panic arises, all further expenditure is as far as possible stopped, and the labourers who are employed in the various departments of the work, are thrown out of employment. In consequence of such unproductive expenditure of capital, trade will decline and wages should generally fall. But should wages be artificially maintained, as they frequently are at such times, by the concerted action and the pardonable expectations of the workmen, bad trade must continue, and the suffering caused by it also.

These fluctuations, then, that thus take place periodically produce the most serious effect upon those who are paid by wages ; and it ought therefore to be one of the first concerns of such, if possible, to discover their causes, so as to ascertain and apply the appropriate remedies. In

the first case, then, those who have become bankrupt as
a result of illegitimate trading, or overtrading, should be
held liable to a criminal indictment, and the duty and
cost of the necessary investigation and prosecution ought
not to be left with the particular creditors—who very
generally find it advantageous to compound with their
debtor, however he may have become bankrupt—but
with the State, in name of the community. If it be
objected that the cost would form too heavy a tax, let it
be considered what enormous losses—which ultimately
fall on the community—result by the present condition
of things, and also how the commercial atmosphere
would be thus purified.

In the second case, investors err and suffer first and
most severely. The exportation of such a large proportion of capital from this country to others is unquestionably greatly due to the influence of the present
land laws, whereby capital is not applied to the soil, and
to the conservation and improvement of landed estates, as
it ought to be. Little capital relatively is expended on
the land, because the people generally—the commercial
middle classes, and the working classes particularly—are
dissociated from it. Had the expenditure of wealth on
the landed property of Great Britain been comparable to
that which has taken place, for instance, in the islands of
Jersey and Guernsey, where the soil belongs generally to
middle class and peasant farmers, it is certain that less
would have been sent abroad, to be expended often profit-
lessly on works of which the investors frequently know
little or nothing. In many parts of this island, particularly in the Highlands of Scotland, one great want is the
want of capital; and many who are well acquainted with
their condition assert confidently that the population which
now diminishes, is already too sparsely spread to execute
the work that would be necessary, were the resources of

the country to be duly developed. The landlords are generally too indifferent or too burdened to develop the country they possess; although it must be said that where exceptionally the landlords do exert themselves in this direction, they do it often right royally.

It thus results that an excessive amount of capital flows out of this country to others, the effects both directly and indirectly being disadvantageous to the wage earners here.

We have thus endeavoured to indicate some of the sources of the fluctuations which so seriously affect the position and advancement of the working classes, and it may be said that until these alternating elevations and depressions are considerably reduced in intensity, a great amount of suffering must always follow. The hopes of continued and uninterrupted prosperity which fill the mind of the workman in periods of elevation lead him to regard his comfortable wages and shortened hours of work as his for ever, and nothing is fitted to produce more discontent and irritation than the dispersion of such hopes, and the sad realisation of the inevitable retrogression that must be made. The object of all his struggles and privations, it may be, that have been endured during a strike in which his family have suffered, is seen to have been comparatively valueless, but the prize that has been won is really threatened by every storm of commercial depression. Probably there is no problem more worthy of the earnest consideration and the enlightened action of the trades unionist, than this one, because, without a solution of it the most part of his other efforts will be increased, and at the same time rendered comparatively fruitless. The sudden disappearance of realised wealth even for a time, to whomsoever it may belong, is undoubtedly the immediate cause of the most serious evils which can afflict the working classes.

CHAPTER IX.

WHAT ARE THE BEST COMMERCIAL CONDITIONS OF SOCIAL WELL-BEING ?

THERE is an order that induces stagnation, and there is another order that induces progress. The first order is that wherein a privileged few dominate over the masses ; the second is that wherein the masses are interested by their own welfare to maintain it, and thereby to progress. The first induces stagnation till the masses become so slavish that the domination of the few appears to be necessary, and as likely to be perpetual, or contrariwise, till some portion of them, who have found out what is the condition of progress, become dissatisfied, and endeavour by themselves, or by acting upon the masses, to overturn that order which induces stagnation. The one is political death ; the other is political, social, moral, and intellectual life, and nascent progress. These are the two opposite poles of human experience ; the one perpetuates savagery, the other produces civilization. It therefore essentially concerns the people which of these gains the predominance in the government of their State.

Commerce is discouraged by the prevalence of privilege ; labour is regarded as degrading, and its fruits are uncertain. The consequence is that the upper classes betake themselves to the army for exercise, companionship, and enjoyment. War is the occupation of the nobility and gentry ; the destruction of those they are pleased to reckon their foes, the object of their most

earnest exertions, in which, should they distinguish themselves, they win 'glory.'

The natural sentiments of humanity are shocked by
such abuses of privilege as occasionally occur, and
these sentiments find utterance when an unsuccessful
war brings disaster on the nation. Such a period is that
wherein the privileged classes are most likely to give way
to an extension of freedom, and a corresponding curtail-
ment of privilege.

The interests of commerce will always tend to increase,
and where the dominating classes yield, they yield because
the growing power threatens them, and because a compromise is prudent. When such compromises become
the rule, then the State grows naturally, the old power
yielding to the new, as the latter is able to take the
position of the former. When, however, the course of
this development is suddenly checked, and the repressive rule of a Louis XIV., a Nicholas, or a Philip II.,
should stay all progress, and endeavour to extinguish the
existing liberty, the restrained impulses of freedom will,
as history testifies, burst out in the subsequent reigns,
and compel by one means or other a new instalment of
liberty.

Commerce, and what leads up to it, is the resource of
the masses of society who have attained social freedom,
and are in a suitable position to maintain and guard it,
and after the masses it becomes in time at least in some
measure the resource also of the upper classes. Freedom,
as we have seen, is not granted as a boon from above, for
in the act of granting it the privileged classes would destroy
themselves; it must be wrenched, as it has been both in
French and in English history, from them by force, or by
the apprehension of it. An act of freedom, therefore, if
it were not to proceed from the instinct of self-preservation, is one which must benefit the privileged classes quite

as much as it can be supposed it will benefit the masses. The intention may be humane enough, but it must not raise the latter at the expense of the former, who, by the interest of their privileges, assiduously support the throne.

The gradual enlargement of the interests of commerce is the only means by which human liberties can ever be built up upon a secure foundation. We have here the unrivalled strength of interests which are universal in their range and magnitude, and of a kind that appeals powerfully to the most untutored sense. Upon this adamantine and widespread foundation, therefore, must the progress of humanity be built up in the future, and in the degree in which this doctrine is recognised and practised will the desired progress be realised.

When freedom, therefore, has been attained, the first consideration becomes how it is to be completely consolidated. It has been created by the aggregation of individual interests, and can only be continued and strengthened by an extension of them. The great object, then, is to know by what means these interests can be most rapidly extended.

It may be at once said that no policy can be so successful as that of free trade, and the abolition of all restriction. When individual energy possesses the most unlimited field for its exercise, and when there is nothing to hamper that exercise, there will be the greatest exertion, and that exertion will be most productive. What is called for is that the energy of one shall not spoil the labours of another. No one must be allowed to obtain privileges that are inimical to the general welfare ; there must be perfect freedom, and an entire absence of artificial restriction or 'protection.' It is necessary to define how 'protection' acts.

The feeling of patriotism must cling to the word 'protection,' and to the thing supposed to be represented by that word; and therefore it becomes all the more necessary to describe what it really is, and what are its influences.

It is, then, so far different from free trade, that it is trade restricted and guided along artificial channels with the view of producing certain effects different from those that would otherwise result.   It is supposed, for instance, when a country is mostly agricultural, or when its natural advantages are acknowledged to lie in this direction, that there is a deficiency of manufacturing industry that ought to be promoted, and the Government, therefore, steps in to present certain obstacles to the free flow of the imports from foreign countries of the articles forming the subject of manufactures.   A high degree of protective, or a still higher degree of prohibitory duties, checks or stops the flow of the said articles.   But the articles—it may be, for instance, indispensable clothing—must be obtained, and they must be had from some other source. One current—the natural one—has been virtually annihilated, and an artificial one has to be created, and it must be created by a diversion of capital and labour from other occupations that had been carried on with the greatest practicable amount of success.   It may be pleaded, however, that as regards the capital, the advantages which protection affords will induce it to come from other countries, and that therefore more capital will be employed in the State that adopts this system, to the benefit of all classes.   It is forgotten, however, that capital will not flow freely to the industry protected, because the success of the industry is known to depend upon artificial restriction, which may at any time be removed.   But even should capital to an appreciable extent be introduced from abroad, it can never represent so much benefit to the community as that which was employed abroad in the manufacture of the goods whose import has been prohibited, and the resources of the country wherein industries are protected will suffer more or less   The whole labouring population who are paid by wages will feel the effect most severely, for they are deprived of those articles which would have been imported from abroad, of good quality and at a low price, and they have substitutes offered that necessarily in these respects are less advantageous to them.

But if the working classes are compelled to purchase dearer and worse goods, then their wages must be raised to enable them to do so, for, presumably, they cannot live and labour on much less than they did before the restriction was imposed. But if wages advance, profits must fall in every business except those protected. But if profits fall, less capital will be employed, and it will either be exported to other countries, or it will not come into existence. Then, as capital is reduced, business will be contracted, and the employed labourers will be discharged; and however rich the country, although awaiting the development of extensive resources, every step in the direction of protection must, *cæteris paribus*, infallibly cause a reduction in the capital of the country, and of the labourers employed. Of course it may be that in a very large country almost every article can be produced which the community can require, and it might, therefore, be supposed, that that country is self-dependent. In fact, however, no country does occupy that position, and for this reason, it will possess some advantage peculiar to it the utilisation of which will enable the energies of the citizens to be expended with the maximum amount of profit. Thus, it may possess an immense breadth of virgin soil which is ready to yield up the accumulated resources of ages in

the form of cheap food—food so cheap, perhaps, that after
it has been transported around half the globe, a peculiar
profit is left to the producer upon its sale.

The country which receives the food cannot, it may
be, pay for it more advantageously than by the exportation of a corresponding value of manufactured articles,
which the abundance of her capital and the rapid development of her mineral resources, as well as the skill of
her people, enable her again perhaps to do with a peculiar
profit. These manufactured articles, then, go to pay for
the food imported. The food growers in the first country
receive such articles at a cheaper rate than if they had
been produced in their own country, for in that case
some proportion of the farmers must have left the
cultivation of their fields to commence the manufacture
of them, having none of those advantages possessed by
the other country, and with the disadvantage of requiring
to leave their virgin soil, which demands the application
of the least labour and the least capital, to produce year
after year abundance of the cheapest food.

But instead of the natural flow of commerce being
allowed to continue unrestricted, State policy says without adequate reason, for there can be none, that there
must be 'protection' for national industries; and what
follows?

The manufactures of the second country must pay,
say, 50 per cent. on their value before they can enter
the first. The farmers of the first country, then, cannot
produce the same amount of food at the same rate
of expenditure; and if we suppose that such rate is
increased in consequence of the change of system by
one-eighth, from the necessary outlay by the farmers of
one-quarter their income on foreign manufactured articles
that have been taxed 50 per cent., their produce must—
that is to say, if we meantime leave out of account the

necessities of fiscal taxation—become dear nearly in the same ratio.

But there will be no demand for such high-priced food in foreign countries at all comparable to what it would be were the trade quite free. There will, therefore, be less land cultivated, and the capital employed will not derive that striking advantage over that employed on soils in other countries which should be derivable from the superiority of the one over the other. The natural advantage will be generally, according to the proportion in which 'protective' duties are levied, thrown away in order to encourage the growth of industries which do not possess the same natural advantages, and which, therefore, cannot grow without this hot-house system of protection being kept over them. Such a policy, therefore, is opposed to the best interests of both countries, even though the pernicious effects went no further. But they do not stop here. The manufactures that are thus protected demand for their production some part of the population and some part of the capital that would naturally have been directed to the cultivation of the fields.

If we suppose for a moment that the protection is such that capitalists may depend upon it continuing for an indefinite period, then the profits on the capital of the businesses protected will, though large at first, gradually fall to the general rate of profit, until there is no difference between the profits of the businesses protected and those not so privileged.

Should, on the other hand, the protection be deemed insecure, then the profits will stand at a rate so much above those of other businesses as to represent the risk which the capital runs, for should the policy of free trade supervene, then serious loss to the capitalist must follow. Class privileges are, therefore, established by the adoption of the system of protection, and they must be kept up, and the capitalists in the businesses protected must necessarily do everything in their power to influence the Government in continuing and intensifying their special advantages.

But what is the effect of protection on the general community? Probably a mere fraction only of the goods that had been introduced under free trade are now introduced under restriction. The balance must be manufactured at home, and at a serious disadvantage. But the disadvantage means high prices or inferior quality, or both. When the people come to buy, they cannot buy so much as before, and, therefore, there is a reduced consumption; in fact, the people are artificially impoverished. But when placed in this condition, they cannot live so comfortably, nor labour so effectively as otherwise, and, therefore, the general work of the country will be less, and the produce of it will be less, and the division of it to each inhabitant also less.

Such a result will produce occasionally dearth of employment and consequent suffering, that under a policy of freedom would have been avoided. The misery and discontent that must be engendered thereby will tend to produce social disturbances and destruction of capital, which, again, will react perniciously on the general welfare.

Such a sketch in some measure describes the economical conditions existing at the present time in the United States, and with reference to their commerce with Great Britain. The States still cling to protection, although the present unfortunate condition of the industrial population will, it is to be hoped, be sufficient to open the eyes of many to the causes of the evils which have appeared in such magnitude. Of these no doubt one of the most potent is the system of protection, although the whole evil may not proceed from this source.

The rapid course of prosperity which was due to the tremendous energy displayed in the construction of railroads, was the result of an undue expenditure of capital on fixed works, many of which have not been justified by the financial success of the outlay upon them. The relapse in the business of the country which has taken place is attributable, then, in some measure to the loss of capital consequent on such undue expenditure.

The principles of free trade appear to have been misunderstood by the statesmen of many countries; and since Mr. Cobden met Napoleon III. in Paris, on the subject of the first French treaty, a suspicion has been entertained that Great Britain is only greedy to obtain from other nations free access for her manufactures, and that suspicion has probably increased the difficulties which are now being experienced in the renewal of the various European treaties of commerce. If it were understood that the greatest interest of a nation consists in opening her doors as wide as fiscal necessities will allow to the articles that are made most advantageously and, therefore, most economically, wheresoever it be, treaties would be at once abandoned. It would be found that huckstering for favours was unnecessary, since the greatest advantages would be possessed by adopting, without reference to the actions of other States, a defined policy of one's own.

When one country excludes the produce of another that is made more advantageously and economically in that other, it voluntarily denies itself a benefit—it voluntarily handicaps itself. If we suppose, now, that semi-barbaric countries require and must be supplied with produce they cannot themselves supply—whether it be beads, cotton, rum, or any one of those numerous articles which they may be able to purchase—the handicapped country cannot engage profitably, if at all, in such trade; it is virtually fettered. The same thing happens with its trade to every other country, more or less; for, unless it possess an advantage in the production of some articles so considerable as to more than compensate the evils of restriction, it will be unable to export at all. The first requisite of a profitable export trade consists in a free import trade; for, unless the workmen are supported at the lowest possible rate, their work will be relatively dear, and the articles they produce will be too costly for exportation. If the embargo upon foreign products goes so far as to deny free entry to the great bulk of articles, then those articles must be produced within the country itself, and capital and labour must be taken away from those occupations which are naturally very productive to be employed upon those which are less productive, and this signifies more or less of loss on both. This we may illustrate in the following way. Should Great Britain determine to adopt the system of protection, and forthwith proceed to tax the import of foreign grain, so that the tax will act prohibitively, then capital and labour must be taken from the cotton, woollen, and linen manufactures, the engineering shops and the coal mines, to produce more corn and cattle. The justification for the adoption of such a course would probably be as apparent in this as in any other case, for are not the inhabitants of the country dependent for life's subsistence upon continual importations from foreign countries? Many eventualities may interpose to prevent the continuance of such: the countries exporting may, in case of war, have their ports blockaded, or the transportation across the ocean may be interrupted by naval attack.

If any country is vulnerable in these respects, Great Britain may be regarded as thus vulnerable, but yet there could be no adequate justification for such a course. It is the interest of the whole corn-producing countries of

z

the world to sell their produce to Great Britain. The interests of sellers and buyers become identical, and are the best and most permanent guarantee of peace. If, however, it could be supposed for a moment that such a policy of protection were adopted, it would produce at one blow an immense impoverishment of the inhabitants of this country, for the production of the necessary amount of food would occupy disadvantageously the energies of the greater part of the country.

But it will be instructive to treat of the actual facts of protection, and let us select the United States as an example. We find that the States tax the products of British manufacture as follows :—

On cotton thread or yarn, the tax is about one-half its value; on flax, linen, or jute yarns, the tax is from one-fourth to two-fifths ; on silk thread, it is from one-third to two-fifths ; on woollen and worsted yarns, it is about five-sixths of their value. Again, the duty levied on cotton manufactures ranges from 3d. to 4d. per square yard for one class of woven goods, and amounts to more than one-third of the value on another class ; that on linen, hempen, and jute woven manufactures amounts to an average of full one-third of the value ; on silk fabrics generally, it is from one-half to three-fifths of their value ; on woollen and worsted carpets, druggets, &c., it is about one-half their value.

Then again, with regard to metals, the United States impose a duty of 25s. per ton on pig iron ; of 5l. 4s. 2d. per ton on boiler plates less than three-sixteenths inch in thickness; of 9s. 4d. to 18s. 8d. per cwt. plus 15 per cent. *ad valorem* on iron wire, and generally from 6s. to 12s. per cwt. on the great variety of iron and steel productions; from one-third to one-half on the value of cutlery, the same on firearms and swords, and 140 per cent. on gunpowder.

The rates imposed on carriages, carts, and waggons, is

35 per cent. ; on clocks and watches, 25 to 35 per cent. ; on hats, from 30 to 60 per cent. ; on prepared woods and furniture, 30 to 35 per cent. ; on lucifer matches, 35 per cent. ; on pianos, 30 per cent. ; on pictures, 10 per cent. ; on toys, 50 per cent. ; on umbrellas and parasols, 45 to 60 per cent. ; on gloves, 35 to 50 per cent. ; on earthenware and porcelain goods, 20 to 50 per cent. ; on glasswares, 35 to 40 per cent. ; and finally, ships and boats are altogether prohibited.[1]

Such is an illustration of the kind of rates of taxation which the United States impose upon some of those articles in the production of which they are placed at a serious disadvantage when compared with other countries. Capital and labour must be abstracted from the employments in which the country does possess an advantage over others to produce these articles, which can be produced so much more economically elsewhere.

A very able and intelligent writer[2] on 'British Trade' in 'Fraser's Magazine,' thus writes upon this subject :— 'The policy of the country (the United States) is to develop, first of all, her crude resources, so to say, to make the land, which is the cheapest commodity it possesses, and the most easily worked, yield its utmost. The United States could distance almost all the world in providing endless varieties of raw produce and food grains, if the people were so inclined ; and that they have continued producing as they have done, in the face of a prohibitory customs tariff, is proof of this. But I do not think if the tariff continues in force on its present footing that this predominance can go on. Nay, I do not think it

---

[1] See *Return of the Rates of Import Duty levied in European Countries and the United States upon the Produce and Manufactures of the United Kingdom, October,* 1876.

[2] Mr. Alexander Johnstone Wilson. The article referred to is one of several which have since been republished under the title, *The Resources of Modern Countries.*

could have lasted so markedly up to now, had other
countries not been in their several ways tied up against
more effectual competition, and any material lowering of
the price of corn in Europe would produce serious results
in the States, even under present conditions. . . . .
Throughout the whole of it (the tariff) the idea runs of
making anything manufactured pay severely ; and to such
an outrageous and unreasoning extent has the theory been
carried, that, after a rather minute study of the tariff, I
should say that I am within the mark in estimating that
there must be about 1,000 articles at least on which the
duty cannot, on the average, pay for collection and trouble.
. . . . The hindrances to trade with the United States are
artificial altogether, and not natural.   Left to itself, the reciprocal business between England and the American Union
would grow beyond anything that it has ever reached.
The two countries could be the means of giving innumerable benefits to each other—we with our old deep-rooted
manufacturing capabilities, and the New World with its
boundless resources for the furnishing of raw materials.'

Now the diversion of the labour of the States population
does not proceed from, or cannot be excused by, any inability of the people to pursue agricultural avocations ; for
it is unfortunately true that the great proportion of the agricultural emigrants from other countries settle down in the
towns, chiefly in the eastern States of the Union, and to
speak particularly, almost one-half of the Irish, and more
than one-third of the German emigrants, who are chiefly
agriculturalists, settle down in the fifty chief towns of the
Union.   The knowledge which these emigrants possess of
rural affairs is, therefore, when their energies are expended
in industrial employments, lost.

The permanent or lasting result of this system of protection has been that the railways which have been constructed to develop the country have been constructed at

a needless cost, and all other permanent works likewise.
But so long as foreign capital flowed into the States freely
this evil was not regarded. When, however, this capital
began to be withheld, a crisis came, which has not yet,
after four years' duration, passed away. From 1866 to
1875 inclusive, railways of the aggregate length of 37,000
miles were constructed, which drew their supplies of
capital largely from the resources of Great Britain and
the Continent. This expenditure maintained a factitious
condition of things while it went on, and native as well
as foreign manufacturing industries appeared to flourish
and increase rapidly. The collapse came in the end of
1873, and, capital since that time being mainly withheld,
bad trade had supervened, without much hope of immediate
improvement. No departments of industry in the United
States can be said now to exist satisfactorily and securely,
except those for which the country possesses permanent
advantages—those indeed which natural conditions especially favour.

These departments are more particularly those connected with the cultivation of the land, and the more
easily acquired mineral resources, such as gold and silver,
and perhaps iron and coal, upon which a minimum of
labour is required. These, however, are now more
heavily weighted than they ought to be, and do not
possess such superlative advantages as they might have
possessed, had not artificial restriction caused an increase
in the price of nearly every article required in connection
with their working. Thus, the cultivator of cotton now
must pay more for its carriage to market than he should
have done, on account of the iron of which the railways
and their plant are constructed having been made unnecessarily dear; and he must also pay even now, while
the prohibitory tariff exists, an inordinately high price
for the implements with which he works, and for the
clothes which cover him.

The same remarks are equally applicable to the cultivation and production of the land generally. A tax must be paid by the farmer now which is not felt to be grievous, because it is an indirect one; but even though the present tariff were to be immediately abolished—a thing that could not be done without causing great suffering to multitudes—he would still be taxed on account of the heavy and disproportionate expenditure laid out on these public works that are indispensable to him.

But the Union must pay, in gold or in commodities of one kind or other, interest upon her debts to the foreign creditor; and in proportion as her debt is great so will the exports necessarily exceed the imports; and, when difficulties are raised against the importation of foreign goods, the total sum of imports and exports together will be reduced, till the relation between the exports and imports will become very disproportionate. But so little is the true significance of this disproportion understood, that we find distinguished American statesmen, and even the President himself, congratulating the country on the fact of what is called the 'balance of trade' being in its favour. No delusion can be more complete, and none can well produce more serious consequences to the well-being of a whole nation. The case of Great Britain is exactly the reverse of that of the States; her imports greatly exceed her exports, and, as trade declines, that disproportion must become more striking. Yet, though the 'balance of trade' is so much against this country, there exists a tolerable degree of comfort and prosperity amongst the population, which strikingly contrasts with the opposite condition that exists in the States.

What are the facts with reference to these exports and imports? The exports of the United States of America to Great Britain increased from 54,663,000*l.* in 1872 to 75,899,000*l.* in 1876, while the imports diminished in the same years from 45,907,000*l.* to 20,226,000*l.* If we compare these figures with those of the exports and imports of Great Britain to and from all countries, we shall find a marked contrast. These exports in 1872 amounted to the value of 256,000,000*l.*, and in 1876 to 201,000,000*l.*, whereas the imports in the same two years were respectively 354,000,000*l.* and 375,000,000*l.* Thus, while the exports from the States increased in these four years at the rate of about 40 per cent., those of Great Britain decreased at half that rate ; and while the imports of the States decreased about 60 per cent., those of Great Britain increased about 6 per cent. If we regard the total exports and imports of the States, we shall find that the latter are three-fourths lower, and the former unchanged. It is, therefore, perfectly apparent that while Great Britain is able to draw continuously from foreign countries a larger and larger value of imports in payment of the interest of her capital invested—for it increases while the value of the exports greatly diminishes—it is equally apparent that the States must, notwithstanding the uniformity of her exports, curtail greatly the value of her imports, the balance generally representing roughly what she owes to the capitalists of Europe. And, notwithstanding all the boundless and easily acquired natural resources of America, the policy of the government has been successful in restricting the foreign business of a country, twenty-five times larger than Great Britain, to less than one-half its amount.

The theory of the ' balance of trade ' might then, with immense advantage to everyone, have long since been forgotten ; and so long as it is regarded as a criterion upon which to judge of the progress of a nation, so long will it perniciously restrict trade and sever the interests of populations that are fitted mutually to confer the most valuable benefits. An excess of imports, then, is not a sign of adversity, but of prosperity. Scarcely any other nation than Britain can point to such a balance; and scarcely any other nation, while drawing wealth from every point of the compass, is so little dependent on any one country in particular.

But the whole system of international commerce seeks still to be regulated upon this exploded principle; and even within Great Britain, whose wealth and influence has been so splendidly promoted by adherence to free trade, we hear a voice occasionally, such as that of Lord Bateman, with a singular hardihood, argue for the imposition of unaccustomed restrictions. It happens at the present time that in the re-opening of negotiations in connection with the renewal of the various treaties of commerce existing between the different European States, which are now expiring, Germany finds Austria resolved to discontinue the treaty. The reason of this unfortunate determination is alleged to be the inequality of advantage derived by Austria; that is to say, while the exports of German produce to Austria have increased in the ten years by 94 per cent., those of Austrian produce to Germany have increased only 6½ per cent. Austria now proposes to raise the duties upon corn, cattle, cotton, silk, leather, glass, porcelain, and iron goods, to a height that will effectually 'protect' home industry. The German negotiators have entered into long and weary debates with the Austrian protectionists, but to little purpose, and it now appears that Austria intends to isolate herself more than before from the inestimable advantages of free commerce with the rest of the world. To damage German manufactures, she closes her doors against those numerous articles for which she has no facility or special advantage of manufacture; for, if she had, they must naturally arise of themselves. But she is now seriously intent also upon damaging her own interests. As the Prussian correspon-

dent of the 'Times' remarks :—' It is difficult to imagine
closer relations than those which have so long existed
between the two neighbouring and cognate States ; and
it is unfortunately too easy to calculate the loss to both,
should a commerce so flourishing, so necessary and profitable, be suddenly interrupted, and free trade be replaced
by the grim exclusiveness of protectionist principles.'

The result of such a course must inevitably be to
deprive the masses of the Austrian people of the relatively economical productions of Germany, and to favour
manufacturing interests, which, when so bolstered, become
in themselves unhealthy, and, in the interests of the
country, destructive.   But the evil proceeds further ; for
the German trader now demands protection against
Austria, and a policy of reciprocal damage is proposed
for adoption, with the view of reducing Austria to a
sense of the benefits of free trade and a re-continuance
of the treaty.   As we have already shown, that country
which adopts protective principles can never contend
successfully against another that follows those of free
trade, and in every respect the evil of retaliatory action
is only equalled by its folly.

It is indeed sad to reflect that, notwithstanding all
that has been said and written upon this subject since
Adam Smith, who one hundred years ago exposed the
fallacies of the 'Mercantile System,' such an overwhelming amount of ignorance yet exists upon the subject, for
even selfishness should understand that in the direction
of 'protection' there could be nothing advantageous
for it.

What is the fact with regard to German imports into
Austria?   It is that Germany, being a country that in
course of time has become more [highly developed than
Austria in the direction of manufactures as well as otherwise,
the latter being almost wholly agricultural, it is necessarily

more capable of producing a large class of articles requiring organisation, skill, and capital for their manufacture than Austria can be; but then the people of the latter find their advantage in possessing such, and in doing so are rendered more able to labour economically at their own particular work. But when restriction is put on the trade, the people are no longer able to avail themselves of the use of such articles, and they must therefore labour more painfully and less efficiently at their occupations than before. Voluntarily, therefore, to cut off this source of improvement must appear to any mind not imbued with the pernicious theory of the balance of trade to be little short of madness; and, indeed, were it not for the supreme ignorance which exists so generally upon the subject, the system of protection could not exist many days.

What Adam Smith wrote a century since cannot well be too often recalled to mind. He says:—' Consumption is the sole end and purpose of all production, and the interest of the producer ought to be attended to only so far as it may be necessary for promoting that of the consumer.

' The maxim is so self-evident that it would be absurd to attempt to prove it. But in the mercantile system the interest of the consumer is almost constantly sacrificed to that of the producer, and it seems to consider production, and not consumption, as the ultimate end and object of all industry and commerce.'

What prospects, then, present themselves to the manufacturers of a country whose government fails in obtaining reciprocal advantages (under the present system) of commerce with other countries? What, in fact, is the prospect of the British manufacturer in the event of a general resumption of the system of protection, if that should ever unfortunately occur? The British manufac-

turer would then be able to introduce fewer of his productions into those countries which set aside a moderate
fiscal tariff in favour of a protective one; but then, upon
the other hand, he would suffer from no competition
(sufficiently valid) with the manufacturers of such
countries in the introduction of his goods into countries
where they could still enter, and in this class we may
generally reckon the colonies, and semi-barbarous States
that do not attempt to improve upon nature.

The States which adopt the system of protection most
surely shut themselves out from the possibility of foreign
commerce, for if they do not freely buy they cannot
freely sell; and, besides, those articles which they do not
freely buy must be manufactured by them at such a disadvantage behind a high wall of protection that they
can never overpass it, nor extend their energies beyond
it, at least with adequate success.

From what has been said it must be apparent that the
more States refuse by the adoption of protective tariffs to
buy from other countries the more they shut themselves
out from the immense advantages, material and moral,
of foreign commerce, and the more their populations
are likely to remain poor, discontented, and ignorant. It
is as if an agricultural labourer refused to purchase
his articles of clothing, his house, and its furniture,
from the respective tradesmen who make them, and
left the labours of the fields, with which he was
thoroughly acquainted, and for which he possessed a
special aptitude, to divide his time amongst twenty other
employments which he could perform only at an extreme
disadvantage.

In attempting to do so he fails; and if he still perse-
veres under the crazy impression that that is the way to
wealth, he must sooner or later, by hard and bitter
experience, find out his error.

That is, and must be, the case equally with aggregations of men, namely, with nations; but unfortunately in the latter case there does not exist the same ready means, by comparison with other nations which act on natural principles, of discovering the source of poverty and stagnation.

When pernicious results follow, they are too often attributed to a neglect of national interests, as it is said, which means to an insufficiency of protection, instead of to the true and proper causes, and thus every period of decline in trade is seized upon by many as an occasion in which to demand a further and still more fatal amount of restriction.

Until such errors become eradicated from the minds of men, such ruinous attempts at improving upon natural freedom must always produce the same unfortunate results.

CHAPTER X.

In all the complex relations of human existence there can
be nothing more valuable than that order which is the
basis of freedom, for freedom affords the opportunity for
unlimited development.

We have endeavoured in the foregoing chapters of
this work to describe historically the cause of the origin
of such order. We have referred it to the development
of individual self-interest, and we have stated it to be
established through the co-operation of many individuals
in the pursuit of their respective material advantages.
Without a measure of order commerce could not exist,
but commerce produces at every step a fuller measure of
order; it creates its own condition as it proceeds, and with
its fullest extension there must be the securest and the
most permanent order, and there must be the utmost
development of freedom.

In the Old World the masses of the people were
generally slaves, and the order established was in a
measure maintained by force and repression; in the
Modern World, while individual freedom is recognised
as a necessity, the freedom of the efforts of individuals
generally is not yet fully established. The reason of
this lies in the fact that not a few individuals, who
may be regarded in classes, possess and desire to maintain some special privileges, and so far freedom is cur-

tailed, and the well-being of the community is disregarded. The people generally are often indifferent to these evils, not because they do not suffer from them, but because they have become accustomed to their effects, and they are ignorant of their causes.

Such an amount of freedom has now been attained for the most part by the people of Europe and America, that it but requires a greater knowledge to establish it more securely. The steps hitherto have been fitful and laborious, because unintelligent; they may be in the future easy and systematic, if they become guided by knowledge.

Nothing, then, appears to be at the present time more necessary than that the people shall be taught in what direction their interests lie, and what are those actions which attack them. The development of an enlightened self-interest at every point must ultimately eradicate the selfishness of individuals who desire to have or maintain for themselves special privileges, for then these will be regarded in their true light as abuses which can in the face of an enlightened public opinion continue to exist no longer.

The instincts of humanity in a condition of freedom and progress are good and honest, but should oppression exhibit itself, the resentment that arises against it is the fiercer in proportion to the general existing freedom. Uniform progress can, indeed, only be attained by the action of intelligence; and, where the masses are sufficiently intelligent, the vanity and selfishness of a few, however powerful, may well be regarded with unconcern.

But all knowledge must be attained by exertion, and that exertion will not be expended unless there is some palpable object to be gained thereby. He who believes he can benefit himself and others by the attainment of knowledge will attain it, but multitudes have not the opportunity. He who is weary with perpetual bodily labour will not attain it. He who thinks how he may benefit himself and his fellows by a change in the conditions of his labour will more or less, as opportunity offers, attain knowledge on the subject. But men in general, and labourers in particular, often know not where to seek the knowledge they desire. They are therefore easily led by those who put themselves forward as leaders, if those leaders be but bold enough.

There is a field vacant which is easily filled up, but as yet there has been little systematic attempt by the intelligent to fill it up. The masses do not know because they are not taught, they are suspicious because they are ignorant, and they are sometimes dangerous because they are frequently misled.

Without an intelligent view of the position which is occupied there can be no discernment of how to improve or even maintain it. If we suppose that the great majority of the political electors within a State are entirely ignorant of the principles which govern human society, we can only expect that there will be sent to the councils of the State representatives who are not distinguished for intellect or culture, but rather whose ideas and sympathies are characterised by mediocrity. Such electors will reject those who are most qualified, because they are not themselves sufficiently educated to be able to appreciate their qualifications, in favour of those whose character and position, being little elevated above those of the average voter, are more readily understood.

The result of such preference must more or less tend toward the decision of questions according to the wishes of the ignorant majority of voters, who are guided by prejudice rather than reason. And when large numbers of men are swayed by prejudice they are swayed

impulsively in masses, so that whatever plausible cry may
be got up they are liable, without much consideration of
any kind, to be at once carried away by it. It therefore appears that should the educated few possess politically only the same weight as individual electors as is possessed by the ignorant many, the direct influence of their
intelligence will inevitably be lost to the community.

We may well question, therefore, whether the interests of the lower classes themselves can be benefited by
an extension of the franchise to such as are not even
able to judge of those who are best qualified to instruct
them. In such a case, he who prophesies fair things
will undoubtedly possess the greatest influence, and
crude social remedies that appear to promise much will
be more readily accepted than more candid and less
partial appeals. 'None are so illiberal, none so bigoted
in their hostility to improvement, none so superstitiously
attached to the stupidest and worst of old forms and
usages, as the uneducated. None are so unscrupulous,
none so eager to clutch at whatever they have not and
others have, as the uneducated in possession of power.'[1]

No ignorant man can have any natural right to assist
in the government of his country, even indirectly, for
this position would enable him to influence legislation
that affects not only himself but others; he would then
be placed in a situation where he is invited to employ
his vacant mind on questions of which he knows nothing,
deciding thereon in the interests of the whole country,
not in his own interests merely. 'The power which the
suffrage gives is not over himself alone, it is power over
others also; whatever control the voter is enabled to
exercise over his own concerns, he exercises the same
degree of it over those of everyone else.'[2]

[1] *Dissertations and Discussions*, by John Stuart Mill, vol. iii. p. 26.
[2] *Ibid.* p. 18.

However much we may compassionate the condition of those who are materially and morally miserable, there can surely be no advantage to anyone in conferring upon them a political and social power which does not naturally belong to them. The adoption of such a system would undoubtedly, as we find it has done in America, bestow a preponderance of power where it cannot be wisely exercised, with the result that those who are most able to judge of the best political and social measures have in reality no weight or influence, and, feeling their powerlessness, withdraw altogether from what they find to be a vain and fruitless contest.

The spirit of enlightenment and of free and intelligent action must permeate slowly downwards to the lowest strata of human society, as it will do where the conditions of social well-being are healthy, and admit of a progressive improvement throughout all parts of the social structure. To endeavour to anticipate the action that proceeds naturally by the artificial elevation of ignorant men to positions of influence, even though the individual weight of each of them should be small, is surely an action that cannot be justified upon any rational principle. At the present day, false theories of liberalism are too apt to carry away even men of intellect and distinction; but it is of the utmost importance to guard against such dangerous tendencies, which are all the more insidious, that they bear an aspect of generosity.

The structure of society is of such a kind that no injury can occur to one part of it without the other parts being in some degree affected. If the lower orders be poor, miserable, and ignorant, then that portion of society next above them must, though comparatively well-doing and intelligent, be most seriously affected by the evils that afflict their poorer neighbours. It must, then, be the interest of this section in particular, and of all the other

sections above it, to rectify those errors whereby the
lower classes suffer.   But there is, undoubtedly, in ordinary times an abundance of sympathy ever ready to be
manifested by those who are happily situated, for those
beneath them.   The predominant evil appears to be the
absence of that knowledge by which that sympathy
may be brought into active exercise without running
counter to natural principles.   The exercise of charity,
as it is universally manifested in this country, proves
the unwillingness, perhaps the impossibility, of society
neglecting the care of its more unfortunate members.   It is to be regretted, however, that the effect of
such charity is not uncommonly towards reducing that
self-reliance and relaxing that industry which lie at the
root of virtue.   There can be no reason, therefore, to
suppose that the bulk of those who, from their position
and intelligence, are competent to exercise the franchise,
will neglect the interests of those beneath them ; indeed,
there can be no doubt that they are much more competent to judge of their political and social needs, and the
means of satisfying them, than they themselves are.

The true course of action should therefore be to
reserve political power carefully to those only who are
competent to exercise it wisely, and to bestow the chief
influence, by a superior educational qualification, upon
those who possess the largest share of knowledge and
intelligence.   Should we depart from a natural principle
of such undoubted simplicity and justice, who is there
that will prognosticate the future?   Can there, then, be
any assured expectation of uniform progress?   How
shall we be able to guard against the adoption of
measures that will irreparably damage the structure of
society?   Can the exercise of passion and prejudice fail
to produce internal discontent and external war?

There can be no guarantee against such results.   These

effects, indeed, must even be more disastrous than if they proceeded from the selfishness of a privileged but educated minority in possession of the government.

If we must distrust, on the one hand, the results of selfishness in the government of the few, we may well dread, on the other, the results of ignorance in the government of the many.

But toward lighting up the highway along which humanity is to advance, by which the obstacles to progress will be removed without impeding it, there can be nothing more valuable than the instruction of the masses. The present obstructions, and the miseries caused by them, are not always discerned as effects of ignorance, but 'the *soufflets* administered by Nature in punishment of economic ignorance are by no means trifling penalties. They are known by the names of bankruptcies, commercial crises, conflicts of capital and labour, Sheffield outrages, excess of population, pauperism, internal insurrections, international jealousies, often issuing in foreign wars;'[1] and such are the usual effects of ignorance of all kinds. Those who perceive the value of instruction, then, must co-operate to establish a machinery by which adequate means of instruction shall be continually in operation.

But it may be said that these functions are already performed daily by the newspaper press. It is true that the press where it is unfettered is the most valuable preserver of liberty, and an apt instructor on many questions, and in this country its services cannot be esteemed too highly. Yet the function of the daily press is that of reflecting public opinion, not of creating it, except so far as the knowledge of striking every-day facts may be said to guide it. Large problems remain by it almost untouched; they are conceived to be questions of the future for which the present

[1] Professor Cairnes's *Essays in Political Economy*, p. 263.

is unripe, though, when we examine into such a belief, we find them to be questions really demanding immediate attention.   How, then, is their consideration postponed? Because they do not presently fill or attract the public mind, and they are not present to it, because the facts involved are not of striking general interest.

What, then, is necessary?   That associations of individuals, having a cognisance of the importance of such questions, shall place these subjects before the public mind in such a way as to interest it.   It is satisfactory to reflect that where freedom of speech and action exists, such an important duty can scarcely be overlooked.

The public spirit which animated the late Richard Cobden and Mr. John Bright in their crusade against the Corn Laws is, we may be assured, not likely to perish, and we have satisfactory assurance now that the Liberal Associations of the country are alive to the importance of spreading correct views of liberal questions amongst the people.   It has been announced that men of intellect have been appointed by the committee of the National Federation of Liberal Associations to write upon such questions as ' Primogeniture and Entail,' ' County Reform,' ' The Relations of Landlord and Tenant,' ' Electoral Reform,' ' Free Schools,' and ' Church and State.'

But it may not be enough to promulgate liberal views in the form of pamphlets, for many are averse to study these subjects; they feel that such questions are too heavy for them, and they suppose often that they do not affect them.   Nothing surely can occupy the place which belongs to living word-of-mouth representation.

It is, then, apparent that the institution of lectureships for the promulgation of economical and liberal ideas is what is required, for by such means the results of scientific thought would be most readily disseminated among the masses.   Public opinion would thus be roused to a lively interest in questions that are presently relegated to an indefinite future, and the formation and extension of intelligent views would necessarily be the immediate prelude to political action.

Unjust privilege would then be readily recognised and removed, an entire freedom would be successfully established and maintained, and the development of new relations would proceed upon a healthy basis. Human society would be more uniformly progressive whenever full knowledge became the constant attendant of human action.

It is to the future, then, that we must look for the complete realisation of those conditions of social well-being, the nature of which we have endeavoured to describe. We may hope that, as time rolls on, peoples will be more and more united together by an increasing perception of the harmoniousness and indivisibility of their several interests, and that their efforts will be conjoined and guided uninterruptedly along the irradiated path of illimitable improvement.

THE END.

LONDON : PRINTED BY
SPOTTISWOODE AND CO., NEW-STREET SQUARE
AND PARLIAMENT STREET

NOTICES BY THE PRESS.

MECHANICS' MAGAZINE.

'The want of a complete set of Earthwork Tables has long been felt. From the over-condensed character of Mr. Bidder's Tables, they are, to a certain extent, useless. But the fault of Mr. Bidder's Tables is absent from Sir John MacNeill's, yet here the other extreme is met with, and from their unwieldy expansion Sir John's Tables are somewhat unsatisfactory. Now, to hit the happy medium between these two extremes is to meet all views, and we think this has been effected in a highly satisfactory manner by Mr. DAVID CUNNINGHAM in his 'Earthwork Tables.' He felt the want of a set of Tables possessing compactness without too great compression of matter, and completeness without unwieldy expansion. Setting himself to work, he has succeeded in producing this desideratum, and a most creditable production it is. The Tables start with a base 6 feet wide. . . . A Table is also appended which the Author has designed for a rough and ready method of measuring earthwork by means of transparent paper or horn. This will prove very useful to resident engineers and contractors in the cursory measurement of works. Various other Tables are added—those for gradients and resistances on roads amongst others. The whole appears to have been carefully checked, and the volume is one which may safely be left to work its own way amongst those for whose assistance it has been prepared.'

RAILWAY NEWS.

'A complete set of Earthwork Tables has been hitherto wanted among engineering works. This desideratum has just been supplied by Mr. CUNNINGHAM. . . . Of all the Tables extant, those of Mr. Bidder and Sir John MacNeill are deservedly most in favour with their fellow-engineers. But each of these has a fault. That of the former is that it is too condensed, and that of the latter engineer arises from its unwieldy expansion. The happy medium has, we believe, been obtained in the present work. . . . Ample instructions are given for the use of every part of the book, which is certainly a most compact and useful work.'

PRACTICAL MECHANICS' JOURNAL.

'There are two great Earthwork Tables hitherto in use among British engineers—those of Mr. Bidder and Sir John MacNeill. . . . There is no doubt but that a set of Tables workable with facility was a professional want, which has thus been supplied. . . . The work commences, as all such should, by developing the formulæ upon which the Tables are constructed, and in showing certain contrivances for rapidly and approximately ascertaining and checking quantities, &c.'

ARTISAN.

'A complete set of Earthwork Tables, supplying all that is required in the way of data, and being at the same time sufficiently condensed to be handy for reference, has long been a desideratum, for until the publication of this work we have seen none possessing those combined qualifications.'

ENGLISH MECHANIC.

'Respecting the treatment of the subject by Mr. CUNNINGHAM we have nothing to say but what is commendatory.'

SEPTEMBER 1877

CLASSIFIED LISTS OF BOOKS

(NEW WORKS AND NEW EDITIONS)

IN

MISCELLANEOUS

AND

GENERAL LITERATURE

FOLLOWED BY

AN ALPHABETICAL INDEX UNDER AUTHORS' NAMES

London

Longmans, Green & Co.

Paternoster Row

1877.

39 PATERNOSTER ROW, E.C.

LONDON, *September* 1877.

GENERAL LIST OF WORKS

PUBLISHED BY

MESSRS. LONGMANS, GREEN, & CO.

———◆———

——◆◆◆◆◆——

HISTORY, POLITICS, HISTORICAL MEMOIRS, &c.

A History of England

from the Conclusion of the Great War in 1815. By SPENCER WALPOLE, Author of the 'Right Hon. Spencer Perceval.' Vols. I. & II. 8vo.
. [*In preparation.*]

The History of England

from the Accession of James II. By the Right Hon. Lord MACAULAY.

STUDENT'S EDITION, 2 vols. cr. 8vo. 12s.
PEOPLE'S EDITION, 4 vols. cr. 8vo. 16s.
CABINET EDITION, 8 vols. post 8vo. 48s.
LIBRARY EDITION, 5 vols. 8vo. £4.

Critical and Historical

Essays contributed to the Edinburgh Review. By the Right Hon. Lord MACAULAY.

CHEAP EDITION, crown 8vo. 3s. 6d.
STUDENT'S EDITION, crown 8vo. 6s.
PEOPLE'S EDITION, 2 vols. crown 8vo. 8s.
CABINET EDITION, 4 vols. 24s.
LIBRARY EDITION, 3 vols. 8vo. 36s.

Lord Macaulay's Works.

Complete and uniform Library Edition. Edited by his Sister, Lady TREVELYAN. 8 vols. 8vo. with Portrait, £5. 5s.

The History of England
from the Fall of Wolsey to the Defeat of the Spanish Armada. By J. A. FROUDE, M.A.
CABINET EDITION, 12 vols. cr. 8vo. £3. 12s.
LIBRARY EDITION, 12 vols. 8vo. £8. 18s.

The English in Ireland
in the Eighteenth Century. By J. A. FROUDE, M.A.   3 vols. 8vo. £2. 8s.

Journal of the Reigns of
King George IV. and King William IV. By the late C. C. F. GREVILLE, Esq.   Edited by H. REEVE, Esq. Fifth Edition.   3 vols. 8vo. price 36s.

The Life of Napoleon III.
derived from State Records, Unpublished Family Correspondence, and Personal Testimony. By BLANCHARD JERROLD. In Four Volumes, 8vo. with numerous Portraits and Facsimiles. VOLS. I. to III. price 18s. each.
⁎ The Fourth Volume is in the press.

Introductory Lectures on
Modern History delivered in Lent Term 1842 ; with the Inaugural Lecture delivered in December 1841. By the late Rev. T. ARNOLD, D.D.   8vo. price 7s. 6d.

On Parliamentary Go-
vernment in England ; its Origin, Development, and Practical Operation. By ALPHEUS TODD.   2 vols. 8vo. price £1. 17s.

The Constitutional His-
tory of England since the Accession of George III. 1760-1870. By Sir THOMAS ERSKINE MAY, K.C.B. D.C.L. Fifth Edition.   3 vols. crown 8vo. 18s.

Democracy in Europe ;
a History. By Sir THOMAS ERSKINE MAY, K.C.B. D.C.L.   2 vols. 8vo.
[In the press.

History of Civilisation in
England and France, Spain and Scotland. By HENRY THOMAS BUCKLE.   3 vols. crown 8vo. 24s.

Lectures on the History
of England from the Earliest Times to the Death of King Edward II. By W. LONGMAN, F.S.A.   Maps and Illustrations.   8vo. 15s.

History of the Life &
Times of Edward III. By W. LONGMAN, F.S.A.   With 9 Maps, 8 Plates, and 16 Woodcuts.   2 vols. 8vo. 28s.

The Life of Simon de
Montfort, Earl of Leicester, with special reference to the Parliamentary History of his time. By GEORGE WALTER PROTHERO, Fellow and Lecturer in History, King's College, Cambridge. With 2 Maps, Crown 8vo. 9s.

History of England un-
der the Duke of Buckingham and Charles the First, 1624-1628. By S. R. GARDINER, late Student of Ch. Ch.   2 vols. 8vo. with 2 Maps, 24s.

The Personal Govern-
ment of Charles I. from the Death of Buckingham to the Declaration of the Judges in favour of Ship Money, 1628-1637. By S. R. GARDINER, late Student of Ch. Ch.   2 vols. 8vo. 24s.

Popular History of
France, from the Earliest Times to the Death of Louis XIV. By ELIZABETH M. SEWELL.   With 8 Maps. Crown 8vo. 7s. 6d.

History of Prussia, from
the Earliest Times to the Present Day ; tracing the Origin and Development of her Military Organisation. By Capt. W. J. WYATT.   VOLS. I. & II. A.D. 700 to A.D. 1525.   8vo. 36s.

A Student's Manual of
the History of India from the Earliest Period to the Present. By Col. MEADOWS TAYLOR, M.R.A.S. Second Thousand.   Crown 8vo. Maps, 7s. 6d.

Indian Polity ; a View of
the System of Administration in India. By Lieut.-Col. G. CHESNEY.   2nd Edition, revised, with Map. 8vo. 21s.

Essays in Modern Mili-
tary Biography. By Col. C. C. CHESNEY, R.E.   8vo. 12s. 6d.

Waterloo Lectures ; a
Study of the Campaign of 1815. By Col. C. C. CHESNEY, R.E. Third Edition. 8vo. Map, 10s. 6d.

The Oxford Reformers—
John Colet, Erasmus, and Thomas More ; being a History of their Fellow-Work. By F. SEEBOHM. Second Edition. 8vo. 14s.

The Mythology of the
Aryan Nations. By the Rev. G. W. Cox, M.A. late Scholar of Trinity College, Oxford. 2 vols. 8vo. 28s.

A History of Greece. By
the Rev. G. W. Cox, M.A. VOLS. I. & II. 8vo. Maps, 36s.

General History of Greece
to the Death of Alexander the Great ; with a Sketch of the Subsequent History to the Present Time. By the Rev. G. W. Cox, M.A. Crown 8vo. with Maps, 7s. 6d.

General History of Rome
from the Foundation of the City to the Fall of Augustulus, B.C. 753–A.D. 476. By Dean MERIVALE, D.D. Crown 8vo. Maps, 7s. 6d.

History of the Romans
under the Empire. By Dean MERIVALE, D.D. 8 vols. post 8vo. 48s.

The Fall of the Roman
Republic ; a Short History of the Last Century of the Commonwealth. By Dean MERIVALE, D.D. 12mo. 7s. 6d.

The History of Rome.
By WILHELM IHNE. VOLS. I. to III. 8vo. price 45s.

The Sixth Oriental Mo-
narchy ; or, the Geography, History, and Antiquities of Parthia. By G. RAWLINSON, M.A. With Maps and Illustrations. 8vo. 16s.

The Seventh Great Ori-
ental Monarchy ; or, a History of the Sassanians. By G. RAWLINSON, M.A. With Map and 95 Illustrations. 8vo. 28s.

Encyclopædia of Chro-
nology, Historical and Biographical ; comprising the Dates of all the Great Events of History, including Treaties, Alliances, Wars, Battles, &c. By B. B. WOODWARD, B.A. and W. L. R. CATES. 8vo. 42s.

The History of European
Morals from Augustus to Charlemagne. By W. E. H. LECKY, M.A. 2 vols. crown 8vo. 16s.

History of the Rise and
Influence of the Spirit of Rationalism in Europe. By W. E. H. LECKY, M.A. 2 vols. crown 8vo. 16s.

History of the Mongols
from the Ninth to the Nineteenth Century. By HENRY H. HOWORTH, F.S.A. VOL. I. the Mongols Proper and the Kalmuks ; with Two Coloured Maps. Royal 8vo. 28s.

Islam under the Arabs.
By ROBERT DURIE OSBORN, Major in the Bengal Staff Corps. 8vo. 12s.

Introduction to the Sci-
ence of Religion, Four Lectures delivered at the Royal Institution ; with Two Essays on False Analogies and the Philosophy of Mythology. By MAX MÜLLER, M.A. Crown 8vo. 10s. 6d.

Zeller's Stoics, Epicu-
reans, and Sceptics. Translated by the Rev. O. J. REICHEL, M.A. Cr. 8vo. 14s.

Zeller's Socrates & the
Socratic Schools. Translated by the Rev. O. J. REICHEL, M.A. Second Edition, enlarged from the Author's Materials. Crown 8vo. 10s. 6d.

Zeller's Plato & the Older
Academy. Translated by S. FRANCES ALLEYNE and ALFRED GOODWIN, B.A. Crown 8vo. 18s.

Sketch of the History or
the Church of England to the Revolution of 1688. By T. V. SHORT, D.D. sometime Bishop of St. Asaph. Crown 8vo. 7s. 6d.

The History of Philo-
sophy, from Thales to Comte. By GEORGE HENRY LEWES. Fourth Edition. 2 vols. 8vo. 32s.

The Childhood of the

English Nation; or, the Beginnings of English History. By ELLA S. ARMITAGE. Fcp. 8vo. 2s. 6d.

Epochs of Modern History.

Edited by E. E. MORRIS, M.A. J. S. PHILLPOTTS, B.C.L. and C. COLBECK, M.A. Eleven volumes now published, each complete in itself, in fcp. 8vo. with Maps & Index :—

Cordery's French Revolution to the Battle of Waterloo, 1789—1815. [*In the press.*

Cox's Crusades, 2s. 6d.

Creighton's Age of Elizabeth, 2s. 6d.

Gairdner's Houses of Lancaster and York, 2s. 6d.

Gardiner's Puritan Revolution, 2s. 6d.
———— Thirty Years' War, 2s. 6d.

Hale's Fall of the Stuarts, 2s. 6d.

Lawrence's Early Hanoverians. [*In the press.*

Longman's Frederick the Great and the Seven Years' War. [*In the press.*

Ludlow's War of American Independence, 2s. 6d.

Morris's Age of Anne, 2s. 6d.

Seebohm's Protestant Revolution, price 2s. 6d.

Stubbs's Early Plantagenets, 2s. 6d.
———— Empire under the House of Hohenstaufen. [*In preparation.*

Warburton's Edward III. 2s. 6d.

The Student's Manual of

Modern History; containing the Rise and Progress of the Principal European Nations. By W. COOKE TAYLOR, LL.D. Crown 8vo. 7s. 6d.

The Student's Manual of

Ancient History; containing the Political History, Geographical Position, and Social State of the Principal Nations of Antiquity. By W. COOKE TAYLOR, LL.D. Crown 8vo. 7s. 6d.

Epochs of Ancient History.

Edited by the Rev. G. W. COX, M.A. and by C. SANKEY, M.A. Ten volumes, each complete in itself, in fcp. 8vo. with Maps & Index :—

Beesly's Gracchi, Marius & Sulla, 2s.6d.

Capes's Age of the Antonines, 2s. 6d.
———— Early Roman Empire, 2s. 6d.

Cox's Athenian Empire, 2s. 6d.
—— Greeks & Persians, 2s. 6d.

Curteis's Macedonian Empire, 2s. 6d.

Ihne's Rome to its Capture by the Gauls, 2s. 6d.

Merivale's Roman Triumvirates, 2s. 6d.

Sankey's Spartan & Theban Supremacies, 2s. 6d.

Smith's Rome & Carthage, the Punic Wars. [*In the press.*

BIOGRAPHICAL WORKS.

Memorials of Charlotte

Williams-Wynn. Edited by her Sister. Crown 8vo. with Portrait, price 10s. 6d.

The Life and Letters of

Lord Macaulay. By his Nephew, G. OTTO TREVELYAN, M.P. Second Edition, with Additions and Corrections. 2 vols. 8vo. Portrait, 36s.

The Life of Sir William

Fairbairn, Bart. F.R.S. Partly written by himself; edited and completed by W. POLE, F.R.S. 8vo. Portrait, 18s.

Arthur Schopenhauer, his

Life and his Philosophy. By HELEN ZIMMERN. Post 8vo. Portrait, 7s. 6d.

Gotthold Ephraim Lessing,

his Life and Works. By HELEN ZIMMERN. Crown 8vo. [*In the press.*

The Life, Works, and

Opinions of Heinrich Heine. By WILLIAM STIGAND. 2 vols. 8vo. Portrait, 28s.

The Life of Mozart.

Translated from the German Work of Dr. LUDWIG NOHL by Lady WALLACE. With Portraits of Mozart and his Sister. 2 vols. crown 8vo. 21s.

Felix Mendelssohn's Letters
from Italy and Switzerland, and Letters from 1833 to 1847. Translated by Lady WALLACE. With Portrait. 2 vols. crown 8vo. 5s. each.

Life of Robert Frampton,
D.D. Bishop of Gloucester, deprived as a Non-Juror in 1689. Edited by T. S. EVANS, M.A. Crown 8vo. Portrait, price, 10s. 6d.

Autobiography. By JOHN
STUART MILL. 8vo. 7s. 6d.

Isaac Casaubon, 1559-
1614. By MARK PATTISON, Rector of Lincoln College, Oxford. 8vo. 18s.

Biographical and Critical
Essays. By A. HAYWARD, Q.C. Second Series, 2 vols. 8vo. 28s. Third Series, 1 vol. 8vo. 14s.

Leaders of Public Opi-
nion in Ireland; Swift, Flood, Grattan, O'Connell. By W. E. H. LECKY, M.A. Crown 8vo. 7s. 6d.

The Memoirs of Sir John
Reresby, of Thrybergh, Bart. M.P. 1634-1689. Edited from the Original Manuscript by J. J. CARTWRIGHT, M.A. 8vo. 21s.

Essays in Ecclesiastical
Biography. By the Right Hon. Sir J. STEPHEN, LL.D. Crown 8vo. 7s. 6d.

Dictionary of General
Biography; containing Concise Memoirs and Notices of the most Eminent Persons of all Ages and Countries. By W. L. R. CATES. 8vo. 25s.

Life of the Duke of Wel-
lington. By the Rev. G. R. GLEIG, M.A. Crown 8vo. Portrait, 5s.

Memoirs of Sir Henry
Havelock, K.C.B. By JOHN CLARK MARSHMAN. Crown 8vo. 3s. 6d.

Vicissitudes of Families.
By Sir BERNARD BURKE, C.B. Two vols. crown 8vo. 21s.

MENTAL and POLITICAL PHILOSOPHY.

Comte's System of Posi-
tive Polity, or Treatise upon Sociology. Translated from the Paris Edition of 1851–1854, and furnished with Analytical Tables of Contents :—

VOL. I. General View of Positivism and Introductory Principles. Translated by J. H. BRIDGES, M.B. 8vo. price 21s.

VOL. II. The Social Statics, or the Abstract Laws of Human Order. Translated by F. HARRISON, M.A. 8vo. 14s.

VOL. III. The Social Dynamics, or the General Laws of Human Progress (the Philosophy of History). Translated by E. S. BEESLY, M.A. 8vo. 21s.

VOL. IV. The Theory of the Future of Man ; together with COMTE'S Early Essays on Social Philosophy. Translated by R. CONGREVE, M.D. and H. D. HUTTON, B.A. 8vo. 24s.

Democracy in America.
By ALEXIS DE TOCQUEVILLE. Translated by HENRY REEVE, Esq. Two vols. crown 8vo. 16s.

Essays, Critical and Bio-
graphical. By HENRY ROGERS. 2 vols. crown 8vo. 12s.

Essays on some Theolo-
gical Controversies of the Time. By HENRY ROGERS. Crown 8vo. 6s.

On Representative Go-
vernment. By JOHN STUART MILL. Crown 8vo. 2s.

On Liberty. By JOHN
STUART MILL. Post 8vo. 7s. 6d. crown 8vo. 1s. 4d.

Principles of Political
Economy. By JOHN STUART MILL. 2 vols. 8vo. 30s. or 1 vol. crown 8vo. 5s.

Essays on some Unset-
tled Questions of Political Economy. By JOHN STUART MILL. 8vo. 6s. 6d.

Utilitarianism. By JOHN
STUART MILL. 8vo. 5s.

A System of Logic, Ratiocinative and Inductive. By JOHN STUART MILL. 2 vols. 8vo. 25s.

Examination of Sir William Hamilton's Philosophy, and of the principal Philosophical Questions discussed in his Writings. By JOHN STUART MILL. 8vo. 16s.

Dissertations and Discussions. By JOHN STUART MILL. 4 vols. 8vo. price £2. 6s. 6d.

Analysis of the Phenomena of the Human Mind. By JAMES MILL. With Notes, Illustrative and Critical. 2 vols. 8vo. 28s.

The Law of Nations considered as Independent Political Communities; the Rights and Duties of Nations in Time of War. By Sir TRAVERS TWISS, D.C.L. 8vo. 21s.

Church and State; their Relations Historically Developed. By H. GEFFCKEN, Prof. of International Law in the Univ. of Strasburg. Translated, with the Author's assistance, by E. F. TAYLOR. 2 vols. 8vo. 42s.

A Systematic View of the Science of Jurisprudence. By SHELDON AMOS, M.A. 8vo. 18s.

A Primer of the English Constitution and Government. By S. AMOS, M.A. Crown 8vo. 6s.

Outlines of Civil Procedure; a General View of the Supreme Court of Judicature and of the whole Practice in the Common Law and Chancery Divisions. By E. S. ROSCOE, Barrister-at-Law. 12mo. 3s. 6d.

A Sketch of the History of Taxes in England from the Earliest Times to the Present Day. By STEPHEN DOWELL. VOL. I. to the Civil War 1642. 8vo. 10s. 6d.

Principles of Economical Philosophy. By H. D. MACLEOD, M.A. Barrister-at-Law. Second Edition in Two Volumes. VOL. I. 8vo. 15s. VOL. II. PART I. price 12s.

The Institutes of Justinian; with English Introduction, Translation, and Notes. By T. C. SANDARS, M.A. 8vo. 18s.

Lord Bacon's Works, collected & edited by R. L. ELLIS, M.A. J. SPEDDING, M.A. and D. D. HEATH. 7 vols. 8vo. £3. 13s. 6d.

Letters and Life of Francis Bacon, including all his Occasional Works. Collected and edited, with a Commentary, by J. SPEDDING. 7 vols. 8vo. £4. 4s.

The Nicomachean Ethics of Aristotle, newly translated into English by R. WILLIAMS, B.A. Second Edition. Crown 8vo. 7s. 6d.

Aristotle's Politics, Books I. III. IV. (VII.) the Greek Text of Bekker, with an English Translation by W. E. BOLLAND, M.A. and Short Introductory Essays by A. LANG, M.A. Crown 8vo. 7s. 6d.

The Politics of Aristotle; Greek Text, with English Notes. By RICHARD CONGREVE, M.A. 8vo. 18s.

The Ethics of Aristotle; with Essays and Notes. By Sir A. GRANT, Bart. LL.D. 2 vols. 8vo. 32s.

Bacon's Essays, with Annotations. By R. WHATELY, D.D. 8vo. 10s. 6d.

Picture Logic; an Attempt to Popularise the Science of Reasoning. By A. SWINBOURNE, B.A. Fcp. 8vo. 5s.

Elements of Logic. By R. WHATELY, D.D. 8vo. 10s. 6d. Crown 8vo. 4s. 6d.

Elements of Rhetoric. By R. WHATELY, D.D. 8vo. 10s. 6d. Crown 8vo. 4s. 6d.

An Introduction to Mental Philosophy, on the Inductive Method. By J. D. MORELL, LL.D. 8vo. 12s.

Philosophy without Assumptions. By the Rev. T. P. KIRKMAN, F.R.S. 8vo. 10s. 6d.

The Senses and the Intellect. By A. BAIN, LL.D. 8vo. 15s.

The Emotions and the Will. By A. BAIN, LL.D. 8vo. 15s.

Mental and Moral Science; a Compendium of Psychology and Ethics. By A. BAIN, LL.D. Crown 8vo. 10s. 6d. Or separately, PART I. Mental Science, 6s. 6d. PART II. Moral Science, 4s. 6d.

An Outline of the Necessary Laws of Thought: a Treatise on Pure and Applied Logic. By W. THOMPSON, D.D. Archbishop of York. Crown 8vo. 6s.

On the Influence of Authority in Matters of Opinion. By the late Sir. G. C. LEWIS, Bart. 8vo. 14s.

Hume's Treatise on Human Nature. Edited, with Notes, &c. by T. H. GREEN, M.A. and the Rev. T. H. GROSE, M.A. 2 vols. 8vo. 28s.

Hume's Essays, Moral, Political, and Literary. By the same Editors. 2 vols. 8vo. 28s.

*** The above form a complete and uniform Edition of HUME's Philosophical Works.

MISCELLANEOUS & CRITICAL WORKS.

The London Series of English Classics. Edited by JOHN W. Hales, M.A. and by CHARLES S. JERRAM, M.A. Fcp. 8vo. in course of publication :—
Bacon's Essays, annotated by E. A. ABBOT, D.D. 2 vols. 6s.
Macaulay's Clive, by H. C. BOWEN, M.A. 2s. 6d.
Marlowe's Doctor Faustus, by W. WAGNER, Ph.D. 2s.
Milton's Paradise Regained, by C. S. JERRAM, M.A. 2s. 6d.
Pope's Select Poems, by T. ARNOLD, M.A. 2s. 6d.
Ben Jonson's Every Man in his Humour, by H. B. WHEATLEY, F.S.A. 2s. 6d.

Mesmerism, Spiritualism &c. Historically and Scientifically Considered.. By W. B. CARPENTER, C.B. M.D. LL.D. F.R.S. &c. Second Edition. Crown 8vo. 5s.

Evenings with the Skeptics ; or, Free Discussion on Free Thinkers. By JOHN OWEN, Rector of East Anstey, Devon. Crown 8vo. [*Just ready.*

Selections from the Writings of Lord Macaulay. Edited, with Occasional Explanatory Notes, by G. O. TREVELYAN, M.P. Cr. 8vo. 6s.

Lord Macaulay's Miscellaneous Writings.
LIBRARY EDITION, 2 vols. 8vo. 21s.
PEOPLE'S EDITION, 1 vol. cr. 8vo. 4s. 6d.

Lord Macaulay's Miscellaneous Writings and Speeches. Student's Edition. Crown 8vo. 6s.

Speeches of the Right Hon. Lord Macaulay, corrected by Himself. Crown 8vo. 3s. 6d.

The Rev. Sydney Smith's Essays contributed to the Edinburgh Review. Crown 8vo. 2s. 6d. sewed, 3s. 6d. cloth.

The Wit and Wisdom of the Rev. Sydney Smith. Crown 8vo. 3s. 6d.

Miscellaneous and Posthumous Works of the late Henry Thomas Buckle. Edited, with a Biographical Notice, by HELEN TAYLOR. 3 vols. 8vo. £2. 12s. 6d.

Short Studies on Great Subjects. By J. A. FROUDE, M.A. 3 vols. crown 8vo. 18s.

B

Manual of English Literature, Historical and Critical. By T. ARNOLD, M.A. Crown 8vo. 7s. 6d.

German Home Life; a Series of Essays on the Domestic Life of Germany. Crown 8vo. 6s.

Miscellaneous Works of Thomas Arnold, D.D. late Head Master of Rugby School. 8vo. 7s. 6d.

Realities of Irish Life. By W. STEUART TRENCH. Crown 8vo. 2s. 6d. sewed, or 3s. 6d. cloth.

Lectures on the Science of Language. By F. MAX MÜLLER, M.A. 2 vols. crown 8vo. 16s.

Chips from a German Workshop; Essays on the Science of Religion, and on Mythology, Traditions & Customs. By F. MAX MÜLLER, M.A. 4 vols. 8vo. £2. 18s.

Chapters on Language. By F. W. FARRAR, D.D. Crown 8vo. price 5s.

Families of Speech. Four Lectures delivered at the Royal Institution. By F. W. FARRAR, D.D. Crown 8vo. 3s. 6d.

Apparitions; a Narrative of Facts. By the Rev. B. W. SAVILE, M.A. Crown 8vo. 4s. 6d.

Miscellaneous Writings of John Conington, M.A. Edited by J. A. SYMONDS, M.A. With a Memoir by H. J. S. SMITH, M.A. 2 vols. 8vo. 28s.

The Essays and Contributions of A. K. H. B. Uniform Cabinet Editions in crown 8vo.

Recreations of a Country Parson, Two Series, 3s. 6d. each.

Landscapes, Churches, and Moralities, price 3s. 6d.

Seaside Musings, 3s. 6d.

Changed Aspects of Unchanged Truths, 3s. 6d.

Counsel and Comfort from a City Pulpit, 3s. 6d.

Lessons of Middle Age, 3s. 6a.

Leisure Hours in Town, 3s. 6d.

Autumn Holidays of a Country Parson, price 3s. 6d.

Sunday Afternoons at the Parish Church of a University City, 3s. 6d.

The Commonplace Philosopher in Town and Country, 3s. 6d.

Present-Day Thoughts, 3s. 6d.

Critical Essays of a Country Parson, price 3s. 6d.

The Graver Thoughts of a Country Parson, Three Series, 3s. 6d. each.

DICTIONARIES and OTHER BOOKS of REFERENCE.

Dictionary of the English Language. By R. G. LATHAM, M.A. M.D. Abridged from Dr. Latham's Edition of Johnson's English Dictionary. Medium 8vo. 24s.

A Dictionary of the English Language. By R. G. LATHAM, M.A. M.D. Founded on the Dictionary of Dr. S. Johnson, as edited by the Rev. H. J. TODD, with numerous Emendations and Additions. 4 vols. 4to. £7.

Thesaurus of English Words and Phrases, classified and arranged so as to facilitate the expression of Ideas, and assist in Literary Composition. By P. M. ROGET, M.D. Crown 8vo. 10s. 6d.

Handbook of the English Language. For the Use of Students of the Universities and the Higher Classes in Schools. By R. G. LATHAM, M.A. M.D. Crown 8vo. 6s.

A Practical Dictionary of

the French and English Languages. By Léon Contanseau, many years French Examiner for Military and Civil Appointments, &c. Post 8vo. price 7s. 6d.

Contanseau's Pocket

Dictionary, French and English, abridged from the Practical Dictionary by the Author. Square 18mo. 3s. 6d.

A New Pocket Diction-

ary of the German and English Languages. By F. W. Longman, Balliol College, Oxford. Square 18mo. price 5s.

A Practical Dictionary

of the German Language; German-English and English-German. By Rev. W. L. Blackley, M.A. and Dr. C. M. Friedländer. Post 8vo. 7s. 6d.

A Dictionary of Roman

and Greek Antiquities. With 2,000 Woodcuts illustrative of the Arts and Life of the Greeks and Romans. By A. Rich, B.A. Crown 8vo. 7s. 6d.

The Critical Lexicon and

Concordance to the English and Greek New Testament; together with an Index of Greek Words and several Appendices. By the Rev. E. W. Bullinger, St. Stephen's, Walthamstow. Medium 8vo. 30s.

A Greek-English Lexi-

con. By H. G. Liddell, D.D. Dean of Christchurch, and R. Scott, D.D. Dean of Rochester. Crown 4to. 36s.

A Lexicon, Greek and

English, abridged for Schools from Liddell and Scott's Greek-English Lexicon. Square 12mo. 7s. 6d.

An English-Greek Lexi-

con, containing all the Greek Words used by Writers of good authority. By C. D. Yonge, M.A. 4to. 21s.

Mr. Yonge's Lexicon,

English and Greek, abridged from his larger Lexicon. Square 12mo. 8s. 6d.

English Synonymes. By

E. J. Whately. Edited by R. Whately, D.D. Fcp. 8vo. 3s.

A Latin-English Diction-

ary. By John T. White, D.D. Oxon. and J. E. Riddle, M.A. Oxon. Sixth Edition, revised. 1 vol. 4to. 28s.

White's College Latin-

English Dictionary; abridged from the Parent Work for the use of University Students. Medium 8vo. 15s.

A Latin-English Diction-

ary adapted for the use of Middle-Class Schools. By John T. White, D.D. Oxon. Square fcp. 8vo. 3s.

White's Junior Student's

Complete Latin-English and English-Latin Dictionary. Square 12mo. price 12s.

Separately { English-Latin, 5s. 6d.
            { Latin-English, 7s. 6d.

M'Culloch's Dictionary,

Practical, Theoretical, and Historical, of Commerce and Commercial Navigation. Re-edited and corrected to 1876 by, Hugh G. Reid, Assistant-Comptroller II.H. Stationery Office. With 11 Maps and 30 Charts. 8vo. price 63s.

A General Dictionary of

Geography, Descriptive, Physical, Statistical, and Historical; forming a complete Gazetteer of the World. By A. Keith Johnston. New Edition (1877). Medium 8vo. 42s.

The Public Schools Atlas

of Ancient Geography, in 28 entirely new Coloured Maps. Edited with an Introduction by the Rev. G. Butler, M.A. In imperial 8vo. or imperial 4to. price 7s. 6d. cloth.

The Public Schools Atlas

of Modern Geography, in 31 entirely new Coloured Maps. Edited with an Introduction by Rev. G. Butler, M.A. Imperial 8vo. or imperial 4to. 5s.

ASTRONOMY and METEOROLOGY.

The Universe and the Coming Transits; Researches into and New Views respecting the Constitution of the Heavens. By R. A. PROCTOR, B.A. With 22 Charts and 22 Diagrams. 8vo. 16s.

Saturn and its System. By R. A. PROCTOR, B.A. 8vo. with 14 Plates, 14s.

The Transits of Venus; A Popular Account of Past and Coming Transits. By R. A. PROCTOR, B.A. 20 Plates (12 Coloured) and 27 Woodcuts. Crown 8vo. 8s. 6d.

Essays on Astronomy. A Series of Papers on Planets and Meteors, the Sun and Sun-surrounding Space, Star and Star Cloudlets. By R. A. PROCTOR, B.A. With 10 Plates and 24 Woodcuts. 8vo. 12s.

The Moon; her Motions, Aspects, Scenery, and Physical Condition. By R. A. PROCTOR, B.A. With Plates, Charts, Woodcuts, and Lunar Photographs. Crown 8vo. 15s.

The Sun; Ruler, Light, Fire, and Life of the Planetary System. By R. A. PROCTOR, B.A. With Plates & Woodcuts. Crown 8vo. 14s.

The Orbs Around Us; a Series of Essays on the Moon & Planets, Meteors & Comets, the Sun & Coloured Pairs of Suns. By R. A. PROCTOR, B.A. With Chart and Diagrams. Crown 8vo. 7s. 6d.

Other Worlds than Ours; The Plurality of Worlds Studied under the Light of Recent Scientific Researches. By R. A. PROCTOR, B.A. With 14 Illustrations. Cr. 8vo. 10s. 6d.

Outlines of Astronomy. By Sir J. F. W. HERSCHEL, Bart. M.A. Latest Edition, with Plates and Diagrams. Square crown 8vo. 12s.

The Moon, and the Condition and Configurations of its Surface. By E. NEISON, F.R.A.S. With 26 Maps & 5 Plates. Medium 8vo. 31s. 6d.

Celestial Objects for Common Telescopes. By T. W. WEBB, M.A. With Map of the Moon and Woodcuts. Crown 8vo. 7s. 6d.

A New Star Atlas, for the Library, the School, and the Observatory, in 12 Circular Maps (with 2 Index Plates). By R. A. PROCTOR, B. A. Crown 8vo. 5s.

Larger Star Atlas, for the Library, in Twelve Circular Maps, photolithographed by A. Brothers, F.R.A.S. With Introduction and 2 Index Plates, By R. A. PROCTOR, B.A. Folio, 25s.

Dove's Law of Storms, considered in connexion with the Ordinary Movements of the Atmosphere. Translated by R. H. SCOTT, M.A. 8vo. 10s. 6d.

Air and Rain; the Beginnings of a Chemical Climatology. By R. A. SMITH, F.R.S. 8vo. 24s.

Air and its Relations to Life, 1774-1874; a Course of Lectures delivered at the Royal Institution. By W. N. HARTLEY, F.C.S. With 66 Woodcuts. Small 8vo. 6s.

Schellen's Spectrum Analysis, in its Application to Terrestrial Substances and the Physical Constitution of the Heavenly Bodies. Translated by JANE and C. LASSELL, with Notes by W. HUGGINS, LL.D. F.R.S. 8vo. Plates and Woodcuts, 28s.

NATURAL HISTORY and PHYSICAL SCIENCE.

Professor Helmholtz'
Popular Lectures on Scientific Subjects. Translated by E. ATKINSON, F.C.S. With numerous Wood Engravings. 8vo. 12s. 6d.

On the Sensations of
Tone, as a Physiological Basis for the Theory of Music. By H. HELMHOLTZ, Professor of Physiology in the University of Berlin. Translated by A. J. ELLIS, F.R.S. 8vo. 36s.

Ganot's Natural Philosophy
for General Readers and Young Persons ; a Course of Physics divested of Mathematical Formulæ and expressed in the language of daily life. Translated by E. ATKINSON, F.C.S. Second Edition, with 2 Plates and 429 Woodcuts. Crown 8vo. 7s. 6d.

Ganot's Elementary
Treatise on Physics, Experimental and Applied, for the use of Colleges and Schools. Translated and edited by E. ATKINSON, F.C.S. Seventh Edition, with 4 Coloured Plates and 758 Woodcuts. Post 8vo. 15s.

Arnott's Elements of Physics
or Natural Philosophy. Seventh Edition, edited by A. BAIN, LL.D. and A. S. TAYLOR, M.D. F.R.S. Crown 8vo. Woodcuts, 12s. 6d.

The Correlation of Physical Forces.
By the Hon. Sir W. R. GROVE, F.R.S. &c. Sixth Edition, revised and augmented. 8vo. 15s.

Weinhold's Introduction
to Experimental Physics ; including Directions for Constructing Physical Apparatus and for Making Experiments. Translated by B. LOEWY, F.R.A.S. With a Preface by G. C. FOSTER, F.R.S. 8vo. Plates & Woodcuts 31s. 6d.

Principles of Animal Mechanics.
By the Rev. S. HAUGHTON, F.R.S. Second Edition. 8vo. 21s.

Fragments of Science.
By JOHN TYNDALL, F.R.S. Fifth Edition, with a New Introduction. Crown 8vo. 10s. 6d.

Heat a Mode of Motion.
By JOHN TYNDALL, F.R.S. Fifth Edition, Plate and Woodcuts. Crown 8vo. 10s. 6d.

Sound.
By JOHN TYNDALL, F.R.S. Third Edition, including Recent Researches on Fog-Signalling ; Portrait and Woodcuts. Crown 8vo. price 10s. 6d.

Researches on Diamagnetism and Magne-Crystallic Action;
including Diamagnetic Polarity. By JOHN TYNDALL, F.R.S. With 6 Plates and many Woodcuts. 8vo. 14s.

Contributions to Molecular Physics in the domain of Radiant Heat.
By JOHN TYNDALL, F.R.S. With 2 Plates and 31 Woodcuts. 8vo. 16s.

Six Lectures on Light,
delivered in America in 1872 and 1873. By JOHN TYNDALL, F.R.S. Second Edition, with Portrait, Plate, and 59 Diagrams. Crown 8vo. 7s. 6d.

Lessons in Electricity at
the Royal Institution, 1875-6. By JOHN TYNDALL, D.C.L. LL.D. F.R.S. Professor of Natural Philosophy in the Royal Institution of Great Britain. With 58 Woodcuts. Cr. 8vo. 2s. 6d.

Notes of a Course of
Seven Lectures on Electrical Phenomena and Theories, delivered at the Royal Institution. By JOHN TYNDALL, F.R.S. Crown 8vo. 1s. sewed, or 1s. 6d. cloth.

Notes of a Course of Nine
Lectures on Light, delivered at the Royal Institution. By JOHN TYNDALL, F.R.S. Crown 8vo. 1s. sewed, or 1s. 6d. cloth.

A Treatise on Magnetism, General and Terrestrial.
By H. LLOYD, D.D. D.C.L. 8vo. 10s. 6d.

Elementary Treatise on
the Wave-Theory of Light. By H. LLOYD, D.D. D.C.L. 8vo. 10s. 6d.

Text-Books of Science,

Mechanical and Physical, adapted for the use of Artisans and of Students in Public and Science Schools.   Small 8vo. with Woodcuts, &c.

Anderson's Strength of Materials, 3s. 6d.

Armstrong's Organic Chemistry, 3s. 6d.

Barry's Railway Appliances, 3s. 6d.

Bloxam's Metals, 3s. 6d.

Goodeve's Mechanics, 3s. 6d.

———— **Mechanism,** 3s. 6d.

Gore's Electro-Metallurgy, 6s.

Griffin's Algebra & Trigonometry, 3/6.

Jenkin's Electricity & Magnetism, 3/6.

Maxwell's Theory of Heat, 3s. 6d.

Merrifield's Technical Arithmetic, 3s. 6d.

Miller's Inorganic Chemistry, 3s. 6d.

Preece & Sivewright's Telegraphy, 3/6.

Shelley's Workshop Appliances, 3s 6d.

Thomé's Structural and Physiological Botany, 6s.

Thorpe's Quantitative Analysis, 4s. 6d.

Thorpe & Muir's Qualitative Analysis, price 3s. 6d.

Tilden's Systematic Chemistry, 3s. 6d.

Unwin's Machine Design, 3s. 6d.

Watson's Plane & Solid Geometry, 3/6.

The Comparative Anatomy and Physiology of the Vertebrate Animals.

By RICHARD OWEN, F.R.S. With 1,472 Woodcuts. 3 vols. 8vo. £3. 13s. 6d.

Kirby and Spence's Introduction to Entomology,

or Elements of the Natural History of Insects. Crown 8vo. 5s.

Light Science for Leisure Hours;

Familiar Essays on Scientific Subjects, Natural Phenomena, &c. By R. A. PROCTOR, B.A. 2 vols. crown 8vo. 7s. 6d. each.

Homes without Hands;

a Description of the Habitations of Animals, classed according to their Principle of Construction. By the Rev. J. G. WOOD, M.A. With about 140 Vignettes on Wood. 8vo. 14s.

Strange Dwellings;

a Description of the Habitations of Animals, abridged from 'Homes without Hands.' By the Rev. J. G. WOOD, M.A. With Frontispiece and 60 Woodcuts. Crown 8vo. 7s. 6d

Insects at Home;

a Popular Account of British Insects, their Structure, Habits, and Transformations. By the Rev. J. G. WOOD, M.A. With upwards of 700 Woodcuts. 8vo. price 14s.

Insects Abroad;

being a Popular Account of Foreign Insects, their Structure, Habits, and Transformations. By the Rev. J. G. WOOD, M.A. With upwards of 700 Woodcuts. 8vo. 14s.

Out of Doors;

a Selection of Original Articles on Practical Natural History. By the Rev. J. G. WOOD, M.A. With 6 Illustrations. Crown 8vo. 7s. 6d.

Bible Animals;

a Description of every Living Creature mentioned in the Scriptures, from the Ape to the Coral. By the Rev. J. G. WOOD, M.A. With 112 Vignettes. 8vo. 14s.

The Polar World:

a Popular Description of Man and Nature in the Arctic and Antarctic Regions of the Globe. By Dr. G. HARTWIG. With Chromoxylographs, Maps, and Woodcuts. 8vo. 10s. 6d.

The Sea and its Living Wonders.

By Dr. G. HARTWIG. Fourth Edition, enlarged. 8vo. with numerous Illustrations, 10s. 6d.

The Tropical World.

By Dr. G. HARTWIG. With about 200 Illustrations. 8vo. 10s. 6d.

The Subterranean World.

By Dr. G. HARTWIG. With Maps and Woodcuts. 8vo. 10s. 6d.

The Aerial World;

a Popular Account of the Phenomena and Life of the Atmosphere. By Dr. G. HARTWIG. With Map, 8 Chromoxylographs & 60 Woodcuts. 8vo. 10s. 6d.

A Familiar History of Birds.

By E. STANLEY, D.D. late Bishop of Norwich. Fcp. 8vo. with Woodcuts, 3s. 6d.

The Geology of England and Wales;

a Concise Account of the Lithological Characters, Leading Fossils, and Economic Products of the Rocks. By H. B. WOODWARD, F.G.S. Crown 8vo. Map & Woodcuts, 14s.

The Primæval World of Switzerland.

By Professor OSWAL IIEER, of the University of Zurich. Edited by JAMES HEYWOOD, M.A. F.R.S. President of the Statistical Society. With Map, 19 Plates, & 372 Woodcuts. 2 vols. 8vo. 28s.

The Puzzle of Life and How it Has Been Put Together :

a Short History of Vegetable and Animal Life upon the Earth from the Earliest Times; including an Account of Pre-Historic Man, his Weapons, Tools. and Works. By A. NICOLS, F.R.G S. With 12 Illustrations. Crown 8vo. 3s. 6d.

The Origin of Civilisation,

and the Primitive Condition of Man ; Mental and Social Condition of Savages. By Sir J. LUBBOCK, Bart. M.P. F.R.S. Third Edition, with 25 Woodcuts. 8vo. 18s.

The Ancient Stone Implements, Weapons, and Ornaments of Great Britain.

By JOHN EVANS, F.R.S. With 2 Plates and 476 Woodcuts. 8vo. 28s.

The Elements of Botany for Families and Schools.

Eleventh Edition, revised by THOMAS MOORE, F.L.S. Fcp. 8vo. Woodcuts, 2s. 6d.

The Rose Amateur's Guide.

By THOMAS RIVERS. Latest Edition. Fcp. 8vo. 4s.

A Dictionary of Science, Literature, and Art.

Re-edited by the late W. T. BRANDE (the Author) and the Rev. G. W. COX, M.A. 3 vols. medium 8vo. 63s.

The History of Modern Music,

a Course of Lectures delivered at the Royal Institution of Great Britain. By JOHN HULLAH, LL.D. 8vo. price 8s. 6d.

Dr. Hullah's 2nd Course of Lectures

on the Transition Period of Musical History, from the Beginning of the 17th to the Middle of the 18th Century. 8vo. 10s. 6d.

Loudon's Encyclopædia of Plants ;

comprising the Specific Character, Description, Culture, History, &c. of all the Plants found in Great Britain. With upwards of 12,000 Woodcuts. 8vo. 42s.

De Caisne & Le Maout's System of Descriptive and Analytical Botany.

Translated by Mrs. HOOKER ; edited and arranged according to the English Botanical System, by J. D. HOOKER, M.D. With 5,500 Woodcuts. Imperial 8vo. 31s. 6d.

Hand-Book of Hardy Trees, Shrubs, and Herbaceous Plants ;

containing Descriptions &c. of the Best Species in Cultivation. With 720 Original Woodcut Illustrations. By W. B. HEMSLEY. Medium 8vo. 12s.

CHEMISTRY and PHYSIOLOGY.

Miller's Elements of Chemistry, Theoretical and Practical. Re-edited, with Additions, by H. MACLEOD, F.C.S. 3 vols. 8vo.

PART I. CHEMICAL PHYSICS, New Edition in October.

PART II. INORGANIC CHEMISTRY, 21s.

PART III. ORGANIC CHEMISTRY, New Edition in the press.

Animal Chemistry: or, the Relations of Chemistry to Physiology and Pathology : including the Results of the most recent Scientific Researches and Experiments. By CHARLES T. KINGZETT, F.C.S. Lond. & Berlin. Consulting Chemist. 8vo. [*In the press.*

Health in the House : Twenty-five Lectures on Elementary Physiology in its Application to the Daily Wants of Man and Animals. By CATHERINE MARIA BUCKTON. New and Cheaper Edition. Crown 8vo. Woodcuts, 2s.

A Dictionary of Chemistry and the Allied Branches of other Sciences. By HENRY WATTS, F.C.S. assisted by eminent Scientific and Practical Chemists. 7 vols. medium 8vo. £10. 16s. 6d.

Supplementary Volume, completing the Record of Chemical Discovery to the year 1876. [*In preparation.*

Select Methods in Chemical Analysis, chiefly Inorganic. By WM. CROOKES, F.R.S. With 22 Woodcuts. Crown 8vo. 12s. 6d.

The History, Products, and Processes of the Alkali Trade, including the most recent Improvements. By CHARLES T. KINGZETT, F.C.S. Lond. and Berlin, Consulting Chemist. With 32 Woodcuts. 8vo. 12s.

Outlines of Physiology, Human and Comparative. By J. MARSHALL, F.R.C.S. Surgeon to the University College Hospital. 2 vols. crown 8vo. with 122 Woodcuts, 32s.

The FINE ARTS and ILLUSTRATED EDITIONS.

Poems. By W. B. SCOTT. Illustrated by Seventeen Etchings by L. A. TADEMA and W. B. SCOTT. Crown 8vo. 15s.

Half-hour Lectures on the History and Practice of the Fine and Ornamental Arts. By W. B. SCOTT. Cr. 8vo. Woodcuts, 8s. 6d.

A Dictionary of Artists of the English School : Painters, Sculptors, Architects, Engravers, and Ornamentists. By S. REDGRAVE. 8vo. 16s.

In Fairyland ; Pictures from the Elf-World. By RICHARD DOYLE. With a Poem by W. ALLINGHAM. With 16 coloured Plates, containing 36 Designs. Folio, 15s.

Lord Macaulay's Lays of Ancient Rome. With Ninety Illustrations on Wood from Drawings by G. SCHARF. Fcp. 4to. 21s.

Miniature Edition of Lord Macaulay's Lays of Ancient Rome. With G. Scharf's Ninety Illustrations reduced in Lithography. Imp. 16mo. 10s. 6d.

Moore's Lalla Rookh, an Oriental Romance. TENNIEL'S Edition, with 68 Wood Engravings from Original Drawings. Fcp. 4to. 21s.

Moore's Irish Melodies, MACLISE'S Edition, with 161 Steel Plates. Super royal 8vo. 21s.

The New Testament,
Illustrated with Wood Engravings after the Early Masters, chiefly of the Italian School. Crown 4to. 63s.

Sacred and Legendary
Art. By Mrs. JAMESON. 6 vols. square crown 8vo. price £5. 15s. 6d.

Legends of the Saints
and Martyrs. With 19 Etchings and 187 Woodcuts. 2 vols. 31s. 6d.

Legends of the Monastic
Orders. With 11 Etchings and 88 Woodcuts. 1 vol. 21s.

Legends of the Madonna.
With 27 Etchings and 165 Woodcuts. 1 vol. 21s.

The History of our Lord,
with that of his Types and Precursors. Completed by Lady EASTLAKE. With 13 Etchings and 281 Woodcuts. 2 vols. 42s.

The Three Cathedrals
dedicated to St. Paul in London; their History from the Foundation of the First Building in the Sixth Century to the Proposals for the Adornment of the Present Cathedral. By W. LONGMAN, F.S.A. With numerous Illustrations. Square crown 8vo. 21s.

Lectures on Harmony,
delivered at the Royal Institution. By G. A. MACFARREN. Second Edition, with numerous Engraved Musical Examples and Specimens. 8vo. 12s.

The USEFUL ARTS, MANUFACTURES, &c.

The Amateur Mechanics'
Practical Handbook; describing the different Tools required in the Workshop, the uses of them, and how to use them. By A. H. G. HOBSON. With 33 Woodcuts. Crown 8vo. 2s. 6d.

The Engineer's Valuing
Assistant. By H. D. HOSKOLD, Civil and Mining Engineer, 16 years Mining Engineer to the Dean Forest Iron Company. 8vo. 31s. 6d.

The Whitworth Measuring Machine; including Descriptions of the Surface Plates, Gauges, and other Measuring Instruments made by Sir J. WHITWORTH, Bart. By T. M. GOODEVE, M.A. and C. P. B. SHELLEY, C.E. With 4 Plates and 44 Woodcuts. Fcp. 4to. 21s.

Industrial Chemistry; a
Manual for Manufacturers and for Colleges or Technical Schools; a Translation of Stohmann and Engler's German Edition of PAYEN's 'Précis de Chimie Industrielle,' by Dr. J. D. BARRY. With Chapters on the Chemistry of the Metals, by B. H. PAUL, Ph.D. 8vo. Plates & Woodcuts. [In the press.

Gwilt's Encyclopædia of
Architecture, with above 1,600 Woodcuts. Revised and extended by W. PAPWORTH. 8vo. 52s. 6d.

Lathes and Turning, Simple, Mechanical, and Ornamental. By W. H. NORTHCOTT. Second Edition, with 338 Illustrations. 8vo. 18s.

Hints on Household
Taste in Furniture, Upholstery, and other Details. By C. L. EASTLAKE. With about 90 Illustrations. Square crown 8vo. 14s.

Handbook of Practical
Telegraphy. By R. S. CULLEY, Memb. Inst. C.E. Engineer-in-Chief of Telegraphs to the Post-Office. 8vo. Plates & Woodcuts, 16s.

A Treatise on the Steam
Engine, in its various applications to Mines, Mills, Steam Navigation, Railways and Agriculture. By J. BOURNE, C.E. With Portrait, 37 Plates, and 546 Woodcuts. 4to. 42s.

Recent Improvements in
the Steam Engine. By J. BOURNE, C.E. Fcp. 8vo. Woodcuts, 6s.

C

Catechism of the Steam
Engine, in its various Applications. By JOHN BOURNE, C.E. Fcp. 8vo. Woodcuts, 6s.

Handbook of the Steam
Engine By J. BOURNE, C.E. forming a Key to the Author's Catechism of the Steam Engine. Fcp. 8vo. Woodcuts, 9s.

Encyclopædia of Civil
Engineering, Historical, Theoretical, and Practical. By E. CRESY, C.E. With above 3,000 Woodcuts. 8vo. 42s.

Ure's Dictionary of Arts,
Manufactures, and Mines. Seventh Edition, re-written and enlarged by R. HUNT, F.R.S. assisted by numerous contributors. With 2,100 Woodcuts. 3 vols. medium 8vo. £5. 5s.

VOL. IV. Supplementary, completing all the Departments of the Dictionary to the beginning of the year 1877, is preparing for publication.

Practical Treatise on Me-
tallurgy. Adapted from the last German Edition of Professor KERL'S Metallurgy by W. CROOKES, F.R.S. &c. and E. RÖHRIG, Ph.D. 3 vols. 8vo. with 625 Woodcuts. £4. 19s.

The Theory of Strains in
Girders and similar Structures, with Observations on the application of Theory to Practice, and Tables of the Strength and other Properties of Materials. By B. B. STONEY, M.A. M. Inst. C.E. Royal 8vo. with 5 Plates and 123 Woodcuts, 36s.

Railways and Locomo-
tives ; a Series of Lectures delivered at the School of Military Engineering, Chatham, in the year 1877. *Railways*, by JOHN WOLFE BARRY, M. Inst. C.E. *Locomotives*, by F. J. BRAMWELL, F.R.S. M. Inst. C.E. [*In the press.*

Useful Information for
Engineers. By Sir W. FAIRBAIRN, Bart. With many Plates and Woodcuts. 3 vols. crown 8vo. 31s. 6d.

The Application of Cast
and Wrought Iron to Building Purposes. By Sir W. FAIRBAIRN, Bart. With 6 Plates and 118 Woodcuts. 8vo. 16s.

Practical Handbook of
Dyeing and Calico-Printing. By W. CROOKES, F.R.S. &c. With numerous Illustrations and specimens of Dyed Textile Fabrics. 8vo. 42s.

Anthracen; its Constitution,
Properties, Manufacture, and Derivatives, including Artificial Alizarin, Anthrapurpurin, &c. with their Applications in Dyeing and Printing. By G. AUERBACH. Translated by W. CROOKES, F.R.S. 8vo. 12s.

Mitchell's Manual of
Practical Assaying. Fourth Edition, revised, with the Recent Discoveries incorporated, by W. CROOKES, F.R.S. Crown 8vo. Woodcuts, 31s. 6d.

Loudon's Encyclopædia
of Gardening ; comprising the Theory and Practice of Horticulture, Floriculture, Arboriculture, and Landscape Gardening. With 1,000 Woodcuts. 8vo. 21s.

Loudon's Encyclopædia
of Agriculture ; comprising the Laying-out, Improvement, and Management of Landed Property, and the Cultivation and Economy of the Productions of Agriculture. With 1,100 Woodcuts. 8vo. 21s.

RELIGIOUS and MORAL WORKS.

An Exposition of the 39
Articles, Historical and Doctrinal. By E. H. BROWNE, D.D. Bishop of Winchester. Latest Edition. 8vo. 16s.

A Commentary on the
39 Articles, forming an Introduction to the Theology of the Church of England. By the Rev. T. P. BOULTBEE, LL.D. New Edition. Crown 8vo. 6s.

Historical Lectures on

the **Life of Our Lord Jesus Christ.**
By C. J. ELLICOTT, D.D. 8vo. 12s.

Sermons Chiefly on the

Interpretation of Scripture. By the late Rev. T. ARNOLD, D.D. 8vo. 7s. 6d.

Sermons preached in the

Chapel of **Rugby School;** with an Address before Confirmation. By T. ARNOLD, D.D. Fcp. 8vo. 3s. 6d.

Christian Life, its Course,

its Hindrances, its Helps; Sermons preached in the Chapel of Rugby School. By T. ARNOLD, D.D. 8vo. 7s. 6d.

Christian Life, its Hopes,

its Fears, and its Close; Sermons preached in the Chapel of Rugby School. By T. ARNOLD, D.D. 8vo. 7s. 6d.

Synonyms of the Old Tes-

tament, their Bearing on Christian Faith and Practice. By the Rev. R. B. GIRDLESTONE. 8vo. 15s.

The Primitive and Ca-

tholic Faith in Relation to the Church of England. By the Rev. B. W. SAVILE, M.A. 8vo. 7s.

The Eclipse of Faith ; or

a Visit to a Religious Sceptic. By HENRY ROGERS. Fcp. 8vo. 5s.

Defence of the Eclipse of

Faith. By H. ROGERS. Fcp. 8vo. 3s. 6d.

Three Essays on Reli-

gion: Nature ; the Utility of Religion ; Theism. By JOHN STUART MILL. 8vo. 10s. 6d.

A Critical and Gram-

matical Commentary on St. Paul's Epistles. By C. J. ELLICOTT, D.D. 8vo. Galatians, 8s. 6d. Ephesians, 8s. 6d. Pastoral Epistles, 10s. 6d. Philippians, Colossians, & Philemon, 10s. 6d. Thessalonians, 7s. 6d.

The Life and Epistles of

St. Paul. By Rev. W. J. CONYBEARE, M.A. and Very Rev. JOHN SAUL HOWSON, D.D. Dean of Chester. Three Editions, copiously illustrated.

Library Edition, with all the Original Illustrations, Maps, Landscapes on Steel, Woodcuts, &c. 2 vols. 4to. 42s.

Intermediate Edition, with a Selection of Maps, Plates, and Woodcuts. 2 vols. square crown 8vo. 21s.

Student's Edition, revised and condensed, with 46 Illustrations and Maps. 1 vol. crown 8vo. 9s.

The Jewish Messiah ; a

Critical History of the Messianic Idea among the Jews, from the Rise of the Maccabees to the Closing of the Talmud. By JAMES DRUMMOND, B.A. Professor of Theology in Manchester New College, London. 8vo.
[*In the press.*

Evidence of the Truth of

the Christian Religion derived from the Literal Fulfilment of Prophecy. By A. KEITH, D.D. 40th Edition, with numerous Plates. Square 8vo. 12s. 6d. or post 8vo. with 5 Plates, 6s.

The Prophets and Pro-

phecy in Israel; an Historical and Critical Inquiry. By Prof. A. KUENEN, Translated from the Dutch by the Rev. A. MILROY, M.A. with an Introduction by J. MUIR, D.C.L. 8vo. 21s.

Mythology among the

Hebrews and its Historical Development. By IGNAZ GOLDZIHER, Ph.D. Translated by RUSSELL MARTINEAU, M.A. 8vo. 16s.

Historical and Critica'

Commentary on the Old Testament; with a New Translation. By M. M. KALISCH, Ph.D. Vol. I. Genesis, 8vo. 18s. or adapted for the General Reader, 12s. Vol. II. Exodus, 15s. or adapted for the General Reader, 12s. Vol. III. Leviticus, Part I. 15s. or adapted for the General Reader, 8s. Vol. IV. Leviticus, Part II. 15s. or adapted for the General Reader, 8s.

The History and Literature of the Israelites, according to the Old Testament and the Apocrypha. By C. DE ROTHSCHILD & A. DE ROTHSCHILD. 2 vols. crown 8vo. 12s. 6d. 1 vol. fcp. 8vo. 3s. 6d.

Ewald's History of Israel.
Translated from the German by J. E. CARPENTER, M.A. with Preface by R. MARTINEAU, M.A. 5 vols. 8vo. 63s.

Ewald's Antiquities of Israel.
Translated from the German by H. S. SOLLY, M.A. 8vo. 12s. 6d.

Behind the Veil; an Outline of Bible Metaphysics compared with Ancient and Modern Thought. By the Rev. T. GRIFFITH, M.A. Prebendary of St. Paul's. 8vo. 10s. 6d.

The Trident, the Crescent & the Cross; a View of the Religious History of India during the Hindu, Buddhist, Mohammedan, and Christian Periods. By the Rev. J. VAUGHAN. 8vo. 9s. 6d.

The Types of Genesis,
briefly considered as revealing the Development of Human Nature. By ANDREW JUKES. Crown 8vo. 7s. 6d.

The Second Death and the Restitution of all Things; with some Preliminary Remarks on the Nature and Inspiration of Holy Scripture. By A. JUKES. Crown 8vo. 3s. 6d.

History of the Reformation in Europe in the time of Calvin. By the Rev. J. H. MERLE D'AUBIGNÉ, D.D. Translated by W. L. R. CATES. 7 vols. 8vo. price £5. 11s.

VOL. VIII. completing the English Edition is nearly ready.

Commentaries, by the Rev. W. A. O'CONOR, B.A. Rector of St. Simon and St. Jude, Manchester.

Epistle to the Romans, crown 8vo. 3s. 6d.
Epistle to the Hebrews, 4s. 6d.
St. John's Gospel, 10s. 6d.

Supernatural Religion; an Inquiry into the Reality of Divine Revelaton. 3 vols. 8vo. 38s.

The Four Gospels in Greek, with Greek-English Lexicon. By JOHN T. WHITE, D.D. Oxon. Rector of St. Martin Ludgate. Square 32mo. price 5s.

Passing Thoughts on Religion. By ELIZABETH M. SEWELL. Fcp. 8vo. 3s. 6d.

Thoughts for the Age.
by ELIZABETH M. SEWELL. New Edition. Fcp. 8vo. 3s. 6d.

Some Questions of the Day. By ELIZABETH M. SEWELL. Crown 8vo. 2s. 6d.

Self-Examination before Confirmation. By ELIZABETH M. SEWELL. 32mo. 1s. 6d.

Preparation for the Holy Communion; the Devotions chiefly from the works of Jeremy Taylor. By ELIZABETH M. SEWELL. 32mo. 3s.

Bishop Jeremy Taylor's Entire Works; with Life by Bishop Heber. Revised and corrected by the Rev. C. P. EDEN. 10 vols. £5. 5s.

Hymns of Praise and Prayer. Corrected and edited by Rev. JOHN MARTINEAU, LL.D. Crown 8vo. 4s. 6d. 32mo. 1s. 6d.

Spiritual Songs for the Sundays and Holidays throughout the Year. By J. S. B. MONSELL, LL.D. Fcp. 8vo. 5s. 18mo. 2s.

Lyra Germanica; Hymns translated from the German by Miss C. WINKWORTH. Fcp. 8vo. 5s.

The Temporal Mission of the Holy Ghost; or, Reason and Revelation. By HENRY EDWARD MANNING, D.D. Cardinal-Archbishop. Third Edition. Crown 8vo. 8s. 6d.

Hours of Thought on
Sacred Things; a Volume of Sermons. By JAMES MARTINEAU, D.D. LL.D. Crown 8vo. Price 7s. 6d.

Endeavours after the
Christian Life; Discourses. By JAMES MARTINEAU, D.D. LL.D. Fifth Edition. Crown 8vo. 7s. 6d.

The Pentateuch & Book
of Joshua Critically Examined. By J. W. COLENSO, D.D. Bishop of Natal. Crown 8vo. 6s.

Lectures on the Penta-
teuch and the Moabite Stone; with Appendices. By J. W. COLENSO, D.D. Bishop of Natal. 8vo. 12s.

TRAVELS, VOYAGES, &c.

A Voyage Round the
World in the Yacht 'Sunbeam.' By Mrs. BRASSEY. With a Map, Eight Full-page Illustrations engraved on Wood, and nearly a Hundred Woodcuts in the text. 8vo. price 21s.

A Year in Western
France. By M. BETHAM-EDWARDS. Crown 8vo. Frontispiece, 10s. 6d.

Journal of a Residence in
Vienna and Berlin during the eventful Winter 1805-6. By the late HENRY REEVE, M.D. Crown 8vo. 8s. 6d.

One Thousand Miles up
the Nile; a Journey through Egypt and Nubia to the Second Cataract. By AMELIA B. EDWARDS. With Facsimiles, Plans, Maps, and 80 Illustrations engraved on Wood from Drawings by the Author. Imperial 8vo. 42s.

The Indian Alps, and How
we Crossed them; Two Years' Residence in the Eastern Himalayas, and Two Months' Tour into the Interior. By a LADY PIONEER. With Illustrations from Drawings by the Author. Imperial 8vo. 42s.

Discoveries at Ephesus,
Including the Site and Remains of the Great Temple of Diana. By J. T. WOOD, F.S.A. With 27 Lithographic Plates and 42 Wood Engravings. Medium 8vo. 63s.

Through Bosnia and the
Herzegovina on Foot during the Insurrection, August and September 1875. By ARTHUR J. EVANS, B.A. F.S.A. Second Edition. Map & Illustrations. 8vo. 18s.

Italian Alps; Sketches in
the Mountains of Ticino, Lombardy, the Trentino, and Venetia. By DOUGLAS W. FRESHFIELD. Square crown 8vo. Illustrations, 15s.

Over the Sea and Far
Away; a Narrative of a Ramble round the World. By T. W. HINCHLIFF, M.A. F.R.G.S. President of the Alpine Club. With 14 full-page Illustrations. Medium 8vo. 21s.

The Frosty Caucasus; an
Account of a Walk through Part of the Range, and of an Ascent of Elbruz in the Summer of 1874. By F. C. GROVE. Map and Illustrations. Crown 8vo. 15s.

Tyrol and the Tyrolese;
an Account of the People and the Land, in their Social, Sporting, and Mountaineering Aspects. By W. A. BAILLIE GROHMAN. Second Edition. Crown 8vo. with Illustrations, 6s.

Two Years in Fiji, a De-
scriptive Narrative of a Residence in the Fijian Group of Islands. By LITTON FORBES, M.D. Crown 8vo. 8s. 6d.

Memorials of the Dis-
covery and Early Settlement of the Bermudas or Somers Islands, from 1615 to 1685. By Major-General Sir J. H. LEFROY, R.A. C.B. K.C.M.G. F.R.S. &c. (In 2 vols.) VOL. I. imp. 8vo. with 2 Maps, 30s.

Eight Years in Ceylon.
By Sir SAMUEL W. BAKER, M.A. Crown 8vo. Woodcuts, 7s. 6d.

The Rifle and the Hound
in Ceylon. By Sir SAMUEL W. BAKER, M.A. Crown 8vo. Woodcuts, 7s. 6d.

The Dolomite Mountains.
Excursions through Tyrol, Carinthia, Carniola, and Friuli. By J. GILBERT and G. C. CHURCHILL, F.R.G.S. Square crown 8vo. Illustrations, 21s.

The Alpine Club Map of
the Chain of Mont Blanc, from an actual Survey in 1863-1864. By A. ADAMS-REILLY, F.R.G.S. In Chromolithography, on extra stout drawing paper 10s. or mounted on canvas in a folding case 12s. 6d.

The Alpine Club Map of
the Valpelline, the Val Tournanche, and the Southern Valleys of the Chain of Monte Rosa, from actual Survey. By A. ADAMS-REILLY, F.R.G.S. Price 6s. on extra stout drawing paper, or 7s. 6d. mounted in a folding case.

Untrodden Peaks and
Unfrequented Valleys ; a Midsummer Ramble among the Dolomites. By AMELIA B. EDWARDS. With numerous Illustrations. 8vo. 21s.

Guide to the Pyrenees,
for the use of Mountaineers. By CHARLES PACKE. Crown 8vo. 7s. 6d.

The Alpine Club Map of
Switzerland, with parts of the Neighbouring Countries, on the scale of Four Miles to an Inch. Edited by R. C. NICHOLS, F.R.G.S. In Four Sheets in Portfolio, price 42s. coloured, or 34s. uncoloured.

The Alpine Guide. By
JOHN BALL, M.R.I.A. late President of the Alpine Club. Post 8vo. with Maps and other Illustrations.

The Eastern Alps, 10s. 6d.

Central Alps, including all
the Oberland District, 7s. 6d.

Western Alps, including
Mont Blanc, Monte Rosa, Zermatt, &c. Price 6s. 6d.

Introduction on Alpine
Travelling in general, and on the Geology of the Alps. Price 1s. Either of the Three Volumes or Parts of the 'Alpine Guide' may be had with this Introduction prefixed, 1s. extra. The 'Alpine Guide' may also be had in Ten separate Parts, or districts, price 2s. 6d. each.

How to see Norway. By
J. R. CAMPBELL. Fcp. 8vo. Map & Woodcuts, 5s.

WORKS of FICTION.

The Atelier du Lys; or an
Art-Student in the Reign of Terror. By the author of ' Mademoiselle Mori.' Third Edition. Crown 8vo. 6s.

Novels and Tales. By the
Right Hon. the EARL of BEACONSFIELD. Cabinet Editions, complete in Ten Volumes, crown 8vo. 6s. each.

Lothair, 6s.	Venetia, 6s.
Coningsby, 6s.	Alroy, Ixion, &c. 6s.
Sybil, 6s.	Young Duke &c. 6s.
Tancred, 6s.	Vivian Grey, 6s.
Henrietta Temple, 6s.	
Contarini Fleming, &c. 6s.	

Whispers from Fairyland.
By the Right Hon. E. H. KNATCHBULL-HUGESSEN, M.P. With 9 Illustrations. Crown 8vo. 3s. 6d.

Higgledy-Piggledy ; or,
Stories for Everybody and Everybody's Children. By the Right Hon. E. H. KNATCHBULL-HUGESSEN, M.P. With 9 Illustrations. Cr. 8vo. 3s. 6d.

Becker's Gallus; or Roman
Scenes of the Time of Augustus. Post 8vo. 7s. 6d.

Becker's Charicles: Illustrative of Private Life of the Ancient Greeks. Post 8vo. 7s. 6d.

The Modern Novelist's Library.

Atherstone Priory, 2s. boards; 2s.6d. cloth.

BRAMLEY-MOORE's Six Sisters of the Valleys, 2s. boards; 2s. 6d. cloth.

Burgomaster's Family, 2s. and 2s. 6d.

Coningsby. By the Rt. Hon. the EARL of BEACONSFIELD. 2s. boards; 2s. 6d. cloth.

Elsa, a Tale of the Tyrolean Alps. Price 2s. boards; 2s. 6d. cloth.

Lothair. By the Rt. Hon. the EARL of BEACONSFIELD. 2s. boards; 2s. 6d. cloth.

Mlle. Mori, 2s. boards; 2s. 6d. cloth.

MELVILLE'S Digby Grand, 2s. and 2s. 6d.

——— General Bounce, 2s. & 2s. 6d.

——— Gladiators, 2s. and 2s. 6d.

——— Good for Nothing, 2s. & 2s. 6d.

——— Holmby House, 2s. & 2s. 6d.

——— Interpreter, 2s. and 2s. 6d.

——— Kate Coventry, 2s. and 2s. 6d.

——— Queen's Maries, 2s. & 2s. 6d.

Sybil. By the Rt. Hon. the EARL of BEACONSFIELD. 2s. boards; 2s. 6d. cloth.

Tancred. By the Rt. Hon. the EARL of BEACONSFIELD. 2s. boards; 2s. 6d. cloth.

TROLLOPE'S Warden, 2s. and 2s. 6d.

——— Barchester Towers, 2s. & 2s. 6d.

Unawares, a Story of an old French Town. Price 2s. boards; 2s. 6d. cloth.

Stories and Tales. By

ELIZABETH M. SEWELL. Cabinet Edition, in Ten Volumes, each containing a complete Tale or Story :—

Amy Herbert, 2s. 6d.

Gertrude, 2s. 6d.

The Earl's Daughter, 2s. 6d.

Experience of Life, 2s. 6d.

Cleve Hall, 2s. 6d.

Ivors, 2s. 6d.

Katharine Ashton, 2s. 6d.

Margaret Percival, 3s. 6d.

Laneton Parsonage, 3s. 6d.

Ursula, 3s. 6d.

Tales of Ancient Greece.

By the Rev. G. W. COX, M.A. late Scholar of Trinity College, Oxford. Third Edition. Crown 8vo. 6s.

Parry's Origines Romanæ;

Tales of Early Rome from Livy, Latin Text with English Notes. Revised Edition. Crown 8vo. 4s.

Parry's Reges et Heroes;

a Collection of Tales from Herodotus, Greek Text with English Notes. Revised Edition. Crown 8vo. 3s. 6d.

POETRY and THE DRAMA.

Milton's Lycidas. Edited,

with Notes and Introduction, by C. S. JERRAM, M.A. Crown 8vo. 2s. 6d.

Lays of Ancient Rome;

with Ivry and the Armada. By LORD MACAULAY. 16mo. 3s. 6d.

Horatii Opera. Library

Edition, with English Notes, Marginal References & various Readings. Edited by the Rev. J. E. YONGE, M.A. 8vo. price 21s.

Southey's Poetical

Works, with the Author's last Corrections and Additions. Medium 8vo. with Portrait, 14s.

Beowulf, a Heroic Poem

of the Eighth Century (Anglo-Saxon Text and English Translation), with Introduction, Notes, and Appendix. By THOMAS ARNOLD, M.A. 8vo. 12s.

Poems by Jean Ingelow.

2 vols. fcp. 8vo. 10s.

FIRST SERIES, containing 'Divided,' 'The Star's Monument,' &c. Fcp. 8vo. 5s.

SECOND SERIES, 'A Story of Doom,' 'Gladys and her Island,' &c. 5s.

Poems by Jean Ingelow.

First Series, with nearly 100 Woodcut Illustrations. Fcp. 4to. 21s.

Festus, a Poem. By

PHILIP JAMES BAILEY. The Tenth Edition, enlarged and revised. Crown 8vo. price 12s. 6d.

The Iliad of Homer, Ho-

mometrically translated by C. B. CAYLEY, Translator of Dante's Comedy, &c. 8vo. 12s. 6d.

The Æneid of Virgil.

Translated into English Verse. By J. CONINGTON, M.A. Crown 8vo. 9s.

Bowdler's Family Shak-

speare. Cheaper Genuine Edition, complete in 1 vol. medium 8vo. large type, with 36 Woodcut Illustrations, 14s. or in 6 vols. fcp. 8vo. 21s.

RURAL SPORTS, HORSE and CATTLE MANAGEMENT, &c.

Annals of the Road; or,

Notes on Mail and Stage-Coaching in Great Britain. By Captain MALET, 18th Hussars. To which are added Essays on the Road, by NIMROD. With 3 Woodcuts and 10 Coloured Illustrations. Medium 8vo. 21s.

Down the Road; or, Re-

miniscences of a Gentleman Coachman. By C. T. S. BIRCH REYNARDSON. Second Edition, with 12 Coloured Illustrations. Medium 8vo. 21s.

Blaine's Encyclopædia of

Rural Sports; Complete Accounts, Historical, Practical, and Descriptive, of Hunting, Shooting, Fishing, Racing, &c. With above 600 Woodcuts (20 from Designs by J. LEECH). 8vo. 21s.

A Book on Angling ; or,

Treatise on the Art of Fishing in every branch ; including full Illustrated Lists of Salmon Flies. By FRANCIS FRANCIS. Post 8vo. Portrait and Plates, 15s.

Wilcocks's Sea-Fisher-

man : comprising the Chief Methods of Hook and Line Fishing, a glance at Nets, and remarks on Boats and Boating. Post 8vo. Woodcuts, 12s. 6d.

The Fly-Fisher's Ento-

mology. By ALFRED RONALDS. With 20 Coloured Plates. 8vo. 14s.

Horses and Riding. By

GEORGE NEVILE, M.A. With numerous Illustrations engraved on Wood. Crown 8vo.   [Just ready.

On Horse-breaking, shew-

ing the defects of the system of horse-breaking at present in use, and how to remedy the same : teaching the breaking of horses to saddle and harness, with instructions how to teach horses their different paces ; describing also the different classes of horses required for the different kinds of . work, &c. Founded on experience obtained in England, Australia, and America. By ROBERT MORETON, M.R.C.V.S. Cr. 8vo. price 5s.

Horses and Stables. By

Colonel F. FITZWYGRAM, XV. the King's Hussars. With 24 Plates of Illustrations. 8vo. 10s. 6d.

Youatt on the Horse.

Revised and enlarged by W. WATSON, M.R.C.V.S. 8vo. Woodcuts, 12s. 6d.

Youatt's Work on the

Dog. Revised and enlarged.   8vo. Woodcuts, 6s.

The Dog in Health and

Disease. By STONEHENGE. With 73 Wood Engravings. Square crown 8vo. 7s. 6d.

The Greyhound. By

STONEHENGE. Revised Edition, with 25 Portraits of Greyhounds, &c. Square crown 8vo. 15s.

Stables and Stable Fittings. By W. MILES. Imp. 8vo. with 13 Plates, 15s.

The Horse's Foot, and

How to keep it Sound. By W. MILES. Imp. 8vo. Woodcuts, 12s. 6d.

A Plain Treatise on

Horse-shoeing. By W. MILES. Post 8vo. Woodcuts, 2s. 6d.

Remarks on Horses'

Teeth, addressed to Purchasers. By W. MILES. Post 8vo. 1s. 6d.

The Ox, his Diseases and

their Treatment; with an Essay on Parturition in the Cow. By J. R. DOBSON, M.R.C.V.S. Crown 8vo. Illustrations, 7s. 6d.

WORKS of UTILITY and GENERAL INFORMATION.

Maunder's Treasury of

Knowledge and Library of Reference ; comprising an English Dictionary and Grammar, Universal Gazetteer, Classical Dictionary, Chronology, Law Dictionary, Synopsis of the Peerage, Useful Tables, &c. Fcp. 8vo. 6s.

Maunder's Biographical

Treasury. Latest Edition, reconstructed and partly re-written, with above 1,600 additional Memoirs, by W. L. R. CATES. Fcp. 8vo. 6s.

Maunder's Scientific and

Literary Treasury ; a Popular Encyclopædia of Science, Literature, and Art. Latest Edition, in part rewritten, with above 1,000 new articles, by J. Y. JOHNSON. Fcp. 8vo. 6s.

Maunder's Treasury of

Geography, Physical, Historical, Descriptive, and Political. Edited by W. HUGHES, F.R.G.S. With 7 Maps and 16 Plates. Fcp. 8vo. 6s.

Maunder's Historical

Treasury ; General Introductory Outlines of Universal History, and a Series of Separate Histories. Revised by the Rev. G. W. COX, M.A. Fcp. 8vo. 6s.

Maunder's Treasury of

Natural History ; or, Popular Dictionary of Zoology. Revised and corrected Edition. Fcp. 8vo. with 900 Woodcuts, 6s.

The Treasury of Botany,

or Popular Dictionary of the Vegetable Kingdom ; with which is incorporated a Glossary of Botanical Terms. Edited by J. LINDLEY, F.R.S. and T. MOORE, F.L.S. With 274 Woodcuts and 20 Steel Plates. Two Parts, fcp. 8vo. 12s.

The Treasury of Bible

Knowledge ; being a Dictionary of the Books, Persons, Places, Events, and other Matters of which mention is made in Holy Scripture. By the Rev. J. AYRE, M.A. With Maps, Plates, and many Woodcuts. Fcp. 8vo. 6s.

A Practical Treatise on

Brewing ; with Formulæ for Public Brewers & Instructions for Private Families. By W. BLACK. 8vo. 10s. 6d.

The Theory of the Modern Scientific Game of Whist.

By W. POLE, F.R.S. Eighth Edition. Fcp. 8vo. 2s. 6d.

The Correct Card ; or,

How to Play at Whist ; a Whist Catechism. By Captain A. CAMPBELL-WALKER, F.R.G.S. New Edition. Fcp. 8vo. 2s. 6d.

The Cabinet Lawyer ; a

Popular Digest of the Laws of England, Civil, Criminal, and Constitutional. Twenty-Fourth Edition, corrected and extended. Fcp. 8vo. 9s.

D

Chess Openings. By F.W.
LONGMAN, Balliol College, Oxford.
Second Edition. Fcp. 8vo. 2s. 6d.

English Chess Problems.
Edited by J. PIERCE, M.A. and W.
T. PIERCE. With 608 Diagrams.
Crown 8vo. 12s. 6d.

Pewtner's Comprehensive Specifier;
a Guide to the Practical Specification of every kind of Building-Artificer's Work. Edited by W. YOUNG. Crown 8vo. 6s.

Hints to Mothers on the
Management of their Health during the Period of Pregnancy and in the Lying-in Room. By THOMAS BULL, M.D. Fcp. 8vo, 2s. 6d.

The Maternal Management
of Children in Health and Disease. By THOMAS BULL, M.D. Fcp. 8vo. 2s. 6d.

The Elements of Banking.
By H. D. MACLEOD, M.A. Third Edition. Crown 8vo. 7s. 6d.

The Theory and Practice
of Banking. By H. D. MACLEOD, M.A. 2 vols. 8vo. 26s.

Modern Cookery for Private Families,
reduced to a System of Easy Practice in a Series of carefully-tested Receipts. By ELIZA ACTON. With 8 Plates and 150 Woodcuts. Fcp. 8vo. 6s.

Our New Judicial System
and Civil Procedure as Reconstructed under the Judicature Acts, including the Act of 1876; with Comments on their Effect and Operation. By W. F. FINLASON, Barrister-at-Law. Crown 8vo. 10s. 6d.

Willich's Popular Tables
for ascertaining, according to the Carlisle Table of Mortality, the value of Life-hold, Leasehold, and Church Property, Renewal Fines, Reversions, &c. Also Interest, Legacy, Succession Duty, and various other useful tables. Eighth Edition. Post 8vo. 10s.

HISTORICAL KNOWLEDGE for the YOUNG.

Epochs of English History.
Edited by the Rev. MANDELL CREIGHTON, M.A. late Fellow and Tutor of Merton College, Oxford. 8 vols. fcp. 8vo.

Early England, up to the
Norman Conquest. By FREDERICK YORK POWELL, M.A. With 4 Maps, price 1s.

England a Continental
Power, from the Conquest to Magna Charta, 1066 – 1216. By LOUISE CREIGHTON. With Map, 9d.

The Rise of the People,
and Growth of Parliament, from the Great Charter to the Accession of Henry VII., 1215-1485. By JAMES ROWLEY, M.A. With 4 Maps, price 9d.

The Tudors and the Reformation,
1485-1603. By the Rev. MANDELL CREIGHTON, M.A. With 3 Maps, price 9d.

The Struggle Against
Absolute Monarchy, from 1603-1688. By BERTHA MERITON CORDERY. With Two Maps, price 9d.

The Settlement of the
Constitution, from 1688 to 1778. By JAMES ROWLEY, M.A. With Four Maps, price 9d.

England during the
American and European Wars, from 1778 – 1820. By O. W. TANCOCK, M.A. [In the press.

Modern England, from
1820-1875. By OSCAR BROWNING, M.A. [In preparation.

INDEX.

INDEX.

MODERN HISTORICAL EPOCHS.

In course of publication, each volume in fcp. 8vo. complete in itself,

EPOCHS OF MODERN HISTORY:

A SERIES OF BOOKS NARRATING THE

HISTORY of ENGLAND and EUROPE

At SUCCESSIVE EPOCHS SUBSEQUENT to the CHRISTIAN ERA.

EDITED BY

E. E. MORRIS, M.A. Lincoln Coll. Oxford;

J. S. PHILLPOTTS, B.C.L. New Coll. Oxford; and

C. COLBECK, M.A. Fellow of Trin. Coll. Cambridge.

'This striking collection of little volumes is a valuable contribution to the literature of the day, whether for youthful or more mature readers. As an abridgment of several important phases of modern history it has great merit, and some of its parts display powers and qualities of a high order. Such writers, indeed, as Professor STUBBS, Messrs. WARBURTON, GAIRDNER, CREIGHTON, and others, could not fail to give us excellent work. . . . The style of the series is, as a general rule, correct and pure; in the case of Mr. STUBBS it more than once rises into genuine, simple, and manly eloquence; and the composition of some of the volumes displays no ordinary historical skill. . . . The Series is and deserves to be popular.' THE TIMES.

The BEGINNING of the MIDDLE AGES; Charles the Great and Alfred; the History of England in connexion with that of Europe in the Ninth Century. By the Very Rev. R. W. CHURCH, M.A. &c. Dean of St. Paul's. With 3 Coloured Maps. Price 2s. 6d.

The CRUSADES. By the Rev. G. W. Cox, M.A. late Scholar of Trinity College, Oxford; Author of the 'Aryan Mythology' &c. With a Coloured Map. Price 2s. 6d.

The AGE of ELIZABETH. By the Rev. M. CREIGHTON, M.A. late Fellow and Tutor of Merton College, Oxford. With 5 Maps and 4 Genealogical Tables. 2s. 6d.

'Notwithstanding the severe compression required, Mr. CREIGHTON has succeeded in presenting a far from unreadable book, which will be of great assistance to the student. Although prominence is given to the history of England, the contemporaneous history of Europe has not been neglected, and the Author has shewn, wherever it was possible, the connexion of events passing in different countries. An impartial view is taken of the causes which led to the rise and progress of the Reformation in Europe, due weight being given to the political and social, as well as to the religious element, shewing how by the course of events that great inevitable change was led to adopt the character which it eventually assumed....After all that has been written about the reign of ELIZABETH, Mr. CREIGHTON may be congratulated in having produced an epitome which is valuable, not only to the student, but to all who are in any degree interested in the history of that period.' ACADEMY.

The HOUSES of LANCASTER and YORK; with the CONQUEST and LOSS of FRANCE. By JAMES GAIRDNER, of the Public Record Office; Editor of 'The Paston Letters' &c. With 5 Coloured Maps. Price 2s. 6d.

'This series of Epochs of History is one of the most useful contributions to school literature within our knowledge. The division of our national history into portions is an assistance to its acquisition as a whole; and each portion forms a definite amount of work adapted to a definite portion of the school year. The chief merit of these little volumes, however, is to be found in their authorship. It is—to borrow their title—an epoch in the history of school histories, when, as in this series, we find amongst their Authors a few eminent historians. The writer of the volume on the Wars of the Roses is distinguished by his researches into the close of the period of which it treats, and by his publication of Papers illustrative of the reigns of Richard III. and Henry VII. The treatment which the whole of this period receives in this short volume is very admirable. What is chiefly required in compiling such a book is the art of leaving out. Selections must be made of the persons to be described and of the events to be narrated, and this involves a large knowledge besides a discriminating judgment. Mr. GAIRDNER says the age of the Wars of the Roses is towards its close one of the most obscure in English history. But it is one that a schoolboy thinks he knows best. The invasion of France by HENRY V. and the struggles of two Kings with WARWICK, have such a dramatic interest, and stand out so prominently, that the social condition of the people is lost sight of. This Epoch is published opportunely, as the subject is, in part at least, prescribed for the next middle-class examination. It will be found well adapted to class work, and useful for its preparation. NONCONFORMIST.

London, LONGMANS & CO. [*Continued.*

EPOCHS OF MODERN HISTORY—*continued.*

The THIRTY YEARS' WAR, 1618–1648. By SAMUEL RAWSON
GARDINER, late Student of Ch. Ch.; Author of 'History of England from the Accession of
James I. to the Disgrace of Chief Justice Coke' &c. With a Coloured Map. Price 2s. 6d.

The FIRST TWO STUARTS and the PURITAN REVOLUTION,
1603–1660. By SAMUEL RAWSON GARDINER, Author of 'The Thirty Years' War, 1618–1648.'
With 4 Coloured Maps. Price 2s. 6d.

The FALL of the STUARTS; and WESTERN EUROPE from 1678
to 1697. By the Rev. EDWARD HALE, M.A. Assistant-Master at Eton. With Eleven Maps and
Plans. Price 2s. 6d.

The NORMANS in EUROPE. By Rev. A. H. JOHNSON, M.A. late
Fellow of All Souls College, Oxford; Historical Lecturer to Trinity, St. John's, Pembroke, and
Wadham Colleges. With 3 Maps. Price 2s. 6d.

The WAR of AMERICAN INDEPENDENCE, 1775–1783. By JOHN
MALCOLM LUDLOW, Barrister-at-Law. With 4 Coloured Maps. Price 2s. 6d.

The AGE of ANNE. By E. E. MORRIS, M.A. Lincoln College, Oxford;
Head Master of the Melbourne Grammar School, Australia; Original Editor of the Series.
With 7 Maps and Plans. Price 2s. 6d.

'Mr. MORRIS shines in biography. His miniature portraits of QUEEN ANNE, the Duke of MARL-
BOROUGH, and Lord PETERBOROUGH are especially
good; not professing anything original, but presenting the popular conception of their respective
characters in a few well-chosen words calculated
to make a permanent impression.
PALL MALL GAZETTE.
'The period selected is a good one for the purpose, and it has fallen into able hands. The
Author disclaims originality of research, but he
has chosen his authorities with great judgment,
and the result of his labours is very satisfactory.
The causes which led to the great War of the
Spanish Succession are very clearly explained, and
the campaigns of MARLBOROUGH are admirably
related. The literature of this reign is very important, and one of the best chapters is that
devoted to this interesting subject. The social

life of the nation is not forgotten, and the whole
reign is illustrated by seven excellent maps.'
SCHOOLMASTER.
'The plan of the series of Epochs of Modern
History has been in no former volume more
faithfully carried out than in the Age of
Anne. In not one of the new set have the advantages of this mode of presenting history for
study been more happily demonstrated. This is
a good opportunity for explaining, by means of
the example before us, for the benefit of those
who are not familiar with the Epochs, how these
miniature histories are constructed....A little
time spent over this volume is sufficient to satisfy
any teacher of history that the way in which to
convey an adequate picture of the reign of ANNE
is to combine it with the story of Europe during
the time that the Queen occupied the throne.
SCHOOL BOARD CHRONICLE.

The ERA of the PROTESTANT REVOLUTION. By F. SEEBOHM.
Author of 'The Oxford Reformers—Colet, Erasmus, More.' With 4 Coloured Maps and 12
Diagrams on Wood. Price 2s. 6d.

The EARLY PLANTAGENETS. By the Rev. W. STUBBS, M.A.
Regius Professor of Modern History in the University of Oxford. With 2 coloured Maps.
Price 2s. 6d.

EDWARD the THIRD. By the Rev. W. WARBURTON, M.A. late
Fellow of All Souls College, Oxford; Her Majesty's Senior Inspector of Schools. With 3
Coloured Maps and 3 Genealogical Tables. Price 2s. 6d.

Volumes in preparation, in continuation of the Series :—

FREDERICK the GREAT and the SEVEN YEARS' WAR. By F. W.
LONGMAN, of Balliol College, Oxford.

The EARLY HANOVERIANS. By the Rev. T. J. LAWRENCE, B.A.
late Fellow and Tutor of Downing College, Cambridge.

The FRENCH REVOLUTION to the BATTLE of WATERLOO, 1789–
1815. By BERTHA M. CORDERY, Author of 'The Struggle Against Absolute Monarchy.'

The EMPIRE under the HOUSE of HOHENSTAUFEN. By the Rev.
W. STUBBS, M.A. Regius Professor of Modern History in the University of Oxford.

London, LONGMANS & CO.

Spottiswoode & Co., Printers, New-street Square, London.